INTERNATIONAL DEVELOPMENT IN FOCUS

Skills and Jobs in Brazil
An Agenda for Youth

Rita K. Almeida and Truman G. Packard

WORLD BANK GROUP

Contents

Figures

Preface

It is a truism that prospects for youth determine a country's future. On this measure, Brazil should be concerned. Despite significant social progress achieved over the past decades, many of Brazil's social and economic institutions still contribute to exclusion. Public policies and spending favor insiders and the elderly and leave many young people disconnected, disenfranchised, and economically disengaged. Unless it fully engages its young people in the economy, Brazil's productivity will continue to languish. This book argues that to navigate the country successfully to a higher-income, more equitable society, Brazil's leaders will have to place youth at the center of an ambitious skills and jobs policy reform agenda.

Moderate growth expectations in the medium term only increase the urgency to engage youth and to upgrade their skills. Although the goal of inclusion remains a priority—particularly of the young people who are the most disconnected geographically, economically, and socially—the new urgency arises from the rapid aging of Brazil's population. This means that growth going forward will benefit far less from increases in the labor force than it has over the past three decades, and will have to rely much more on the growth of worker productivity. Indeed, the last wave of Brazil's demographic transition is starting to crest. With the right skills and jobs policies, Brazil could ride this wave out of middle-income status. However, unless much more is done to prepare youth for and integrate them better into the labor market, Brazil may not only face the prospect of ever greater youth disengagement, but also of stagnant productivity and living standards for all Brazilians, young and old.

Acknowledgments

Skills and Jobs: An Agenda for Youth is focused on assessing the main skills and jobs challenges Brazilian youth face today in achieving higher employability and productivity in the labor market. The book was prepared by a team led by Rita K. Almeida (Senior Economist, co-Task Team Leader) and Truman G. Packard (Lead Economist, co-Task Team Leader).

The team is indebted to Ricardo Paes de Barros, the Ayrton Senna Institute Chair, Insper, for the suggestion to focus this second phase of the Brazil Skills and Jobs Analytical Services and Advisory Program on the prospects for young people and their full engagement in meeting Brazil's productivity challenge. The book benefited from background analyses led by Diego Angel-Urdinola (Senior Economist, Education Global Practice - Latin America and the Caribbean Region), Marcelo Barbosa (Universidade Federal Ceara), Luis Caseiro (Instituto Nacional de Estudos e Pesquisas Educacionais Anisio Teixeira, INEP), Joana Costa (Instituto de Pesquisa Econômica Aplicada, IPEA, Brazil), Leandro Costa (Senior Economist, GED04), Vanessa Moreira da Silva (Consultant, Social Protection and Labor Global Practice - Latin America and the Caribbean Region), Miguel Foguel (IPEA, Brazil), Maira Franca (IPEA, Brazil), Renata Mayer Gukovas (Research Analyst, Social Protection and Labor Global Practice - Europe and Central Asia Region), Uriel Kejsefman (Analyst, GED04), Andre Loureiro (Senior Economist, GED04), Ana Luiza Machado (Consultant, Transport and Digital Development Global Practice - Latin America and the Caribbean Region), Aguinaldo Maciente (IPEA), Miriam Muller (Social Scientist, Poverty and Equity Global Practice - Latin America and the Caribbean Region), Paulo Meyer Nascimento (IPEA), Eduardo Rios-Neto (Lemann Professor, University of Illinois Urbana-Champaign), Robert Verhine (Universidade Bahia, Brazil), and Pui Shen Yoong (Economist, Macroeconomics, Trade, and Investment Global Practice - East Asia and Pacific Region).

The book benefited from a close collaboration with other Brazilian researchers at IPEA and INEP, and with multiple Brazilian universities and think tanks, including the International Finance Corporation (IFC; Washington, DC, and São Paulo), Universidade Bahia, Insper, Fundação Getúlio Vargas (FGV), and Universidade de São Paulo (USP), Department of Economics. In addition to the Brazilian experts mentioned above, the team is deeply grateful for the valuable insights provided by Carlos Henrique Corseuil (IPEA),

Naercio Menezes Filho (Insper, São Paulo), Andre Portela (FGV, São Paulo), Renata Narita (USP), Margaret Grosh (Senior Advisor, Social Protection and Labor Global Practice), Matteo Morgandi (Senior Economist, GSP04), and Rafael de Hoyos (Lead Economist, GED04). Alonso Sanchez (Economist, GED04), and Joana Silva (Senior Economist, Social Protection and Jobs Global Practice - Latin America and the Caribbean Region) also provided comments on the background papers and/or participated and led inputs in two of the authors' workshops hosted in São Paulo, Brazil, and Washington, DC. The team is also grateful to the peer reviewers at the different stages of the project, including Roberta Gatti (Chief Economist, Human Development Vice-Presidency), Deon Filmer (Lead Economist, Development and Economics Research Group, Human Development), Reynaldo Fernandes (USP), and Naercio Menezes-Filho (Insper), and to Halsey Rogers (Lead Economist, Education Global Practice).

The team is grateful for the management guidance and support provided by the World Bank's Brazil Country Management Unit team, including Martin Raiser (Country Director, Brazil), Pedro Olinto (Program Leader, LCC5C), Reema Nayar (Practice Manager, GED04), and Pablo Gottret (Practice Manager, GSP04). The book also benefited from a collaboration with the IFC team based in Washington, DC, and São Paulo, especially the collaboration of Carmen De Paula (Principal Investment Officer, IFC, Health and Education), Juliana Guaqueta Ospina (Industry Specialist, CMGCS), and the Brazil IFC's country manager, Hector Gomez Ang. Vanessa M. Silva and Jonathan P. Mallek provided outstanding empirical analysis and policy research support for the overview report. Peter Ballou, Federico Antonio Beckley, and Angela Maria Rubio provided outstanding administrative and logistical support throughout the course of this programmatic task.

About the Authors

Rita K. Almeida is Senior Economist in the World Bank's Education Global Practice. In 2002, she joined the Bank as a Research Economist in the Development Economics Department, and later became a Senior Economist in the Global Knowledge Team of the Social Protection and Jobs practice. Her areas of expertise include education and skills development policies, labor market analysis, activation and graduation policies for the most vulnerable, labor market regulations, social protection for workers, firm productivity and innovation policies, public expenditure reviews, and the evaluation of social programs. Almeida has led several World Bank publications, including *The Right Skills for the Job? Rethinking Training Policies for Workers*, and *Toward More Efficient and Effective Public Social Spending in Central America*. Her work has been featured in the news media and leading world economic reports, and has been published in top general-interest and specialized journals, including *The Economic Journal, American Economic Journal: Applied Economics, Journal of International Economics,* and *Journal of Development Economics and Labour Economics*. Almeida holds a doctorate in economics from Universitat Pompeu Fabra, and a Licenciatura in economics from Universidade Católica Portuguesa.

Truman G. Packard is a Lead Economist in the World Bank's Social Protection and Jobs Global Practice. He has worked at the World Bank since 1997, providing advisory assistance to governments in emerging markets on how to improve labor regulation and social security to create jobs. Packard has worked with countries in Latin America, Central Europe, and East Asia; currently, he focuses on Brazil and Indonesia. Trained as a labor economist, he holds a doctorate from the University of Oxford in the United Kingdom. His published work focuses on how labor law and social insurance programs—retirement benefits, unemployment insurance, and health coverage—affect peoples' incentives to work and save.

Abbreviations

AA	Australian Apprenticeships
ALMP	active labor market program
BAM	Becoming a Man
BNCC	Base Nacional Comum Curricular
BRICS	Brazil, Russia, India, China, and South Africa
BSM	Brazil Sem Miseria
CBI	cognitive behavioral intervention
CONAES	Comissão Nacional de Avaliação do Ensino Superior
CONSED	Committee of State and Municipal Secretary of Education
CPI	consumer price index
CV	curriculum vitae
DF	Distrito Federal
EJA	Educação de Jovens e Adultos
ENADE	Exame Nacional de Desempenho de Estudantes
ENEM	Exame Nacional do Ensino Médio
EPL	employment protection legislation
FAT	Fundo de Amparo ao Trabalhador
FGTS	Fundo de Guarantia por Tempo de Servico
FGV	Fundação Getúlio Vargas
FIES	Financing of Higher Education
FTS	full-time school
GDP	gross domestic product
GED	General Equivalency Diploma
GTO	group training organization
IBGE	Instituto Brasileiro de Geografia e Estatística
ICT	information and communication technology
IDEB	Index of Basic Education Development
IFC	International Finance Corporation
IGC	General Index of Courses
ILO	International Labour Organization
INEP	Instituto Nacional de Estudos e Pesquisas Educacionais Anisio Teixeira
IPEA	Instituto de Pesquisa Econômica Aplicada
ISC	Industry Skills Council

LAC	Latin America and the Caribbean
LM	labor market
M&E	monitoring and evaluation
MDIC	Ministério da Indústria, Comércio Exterior e Serviços
MEC	Ministério da Educação
MIUR	Italian Ministry of Education, University, and Research
NEET	not in education, employment, or training
NEP	National Education Plan
NGO	nongovernmental organization
NRI	Networked Readiness Index
OECD	Organisation for Economic Co-operation and Development
OLS	ordinary least squares
PDE	Plano de Desenvolvimento da Escola
PE	potential experience
PES	public employment service
PISA	Program for International Student Assessment
PLMP	passive labor market program
PME	Pesquisa Mensal de Emprego
PNAD	Pesquisa Nacional por Amostra de Domicílios
PPP	purchasing power parity
Pronatec	National Program for Access to Technical Education and Employment
RA	registered apprenticeship
RAIS	Annual Social Information Registry
RTC	randomized controlled trial
RTO	registered training organization
SAFE	sequenced, active, focused, and explicit
SEB	Secretaria de Educação Básica
SEDLAC	Socio-Economic Database for Latin America and the Caribbean
SEE	Secretaria Estadual Educação
SES	socio-emotional skills
SINAES	National System of Evaluation of Higher Education
SINE	Sistema Nacional de Emprego
SISTEC	National System of Vocational Education and Information Technology
SMW	statutory minimum wage
TAFE	Technical and further education
TERCE	Third Regional Comparative and Explanatory Survey
TFP	total factor productivity
TOP	teen outreach program
TVET	technical and vocational education and training
USP	Universidade de São Paulo
WDI	World Development Indicators
WDR	*World Development Report*
WEF	World Economic Forum

1 Overview

POPULATION AGING, TECHNOLOGICAL CHANGE, AND THE PRODUCTIVITY IMPERATIVE

An essential determinant of any country's labor productivity potential and, ultimately, of its economic development is its human capital—that is, the labor force and its skills.[1] Many economists consider human capital to be the most vital part of "the changing wealth of nations," to paraphrase the title of a recent global report on the subject from the World Bank (World Bank 2018b). Brazil is emerging from a stage in its development when labor was abundant, and years of sustained public and private investment equipped an expanding share of its labor force with basic education. The country has, moreover, benefited enormously from a "demographic dividend" paid by a long period when the share of working-age people in the population was substantially higher than that of dependent children and the elderly—a dividend it augmented by ensuring widespread and expanding access to primary and secondary education. Advances in technology also released many from subsistence toil to work in more productive forms of agriculture and the nonagricultural economy in rural areas and to move to jobs in manufacturing and services in towns and cities.

But even a country abundant in human capital requires a competitive and efficient labor market to ensure this resource is put to its best use. It is also vital that an effective set of workforce development policies is in place to ensure working people have sought-after skills. A recent, prolonged period of high growth fueled by external demand for commodity exports drew new workers into the labor market, many into regulated, "formal" (registered, regulated, and taxed) employment. These gains were also socially progressive; leading scholars in Brazil have noted that from 2001 to 2015, the average annual labor income rose twice as fast among working people in the lowest three deciles of the income distribution as for those in the top three (Paes de Barros et al. 2017). Yet, even with favorable economic tailwinds, these outcomes were neither predetermined nor inevitable. Government policy, in particular, policies that made education more accessible to the most vulnerable, helped to shape these outcomes. Brazil now needs more such policy efforts to sustain its gains, for despite the advances resulting from demographic and structural change, productivity has been disappointing in comparison to other countries in Latin America and other regions.

This book is a companion volume to *Brazil's Promise: Boosting Productivity for Shared Prosperity* (World Bank 2018a), a World Bank analysis of productivity constraints across Brazil's product and factor markets. From the perspective of human development, it examines the institutions, regulations, and interventions that create the bedrock of skills in the economy and channel people into the right jobs. The best way to raise productivity is to find better ways to combine capital, labor, and skills in core sectors of the economy. Here we scrutinize the most binding constraints on and obstacles to this process on the supply side of the labor market, particularly with regard to the structures Brazil has put in place to prepare youth to be productive participants. Although the broader *Brazil's Promise* concludes that distortions in other factor markets present more acute problems, the skills-development system and Brazil's labor markets could also function much better. As a result of their deficiencies, the productivity of labor in Brazil has been notably stagnant for many years, barely moving since 1980, while that of neighbors such as Chile and Argentina, as well as of such erstwhile peers as Japan and the Republic of Korea, has soared.

One reason increasing labor productivity in Brazil has become both imperative and urgent is the aging of its population (see figure 1.1), the rapid onset of which has augmented the challenges faced by the skills development system and the labor market in raising the country's productivity potential. Indeed, Brazil's demographic profile will soon start to resemble that of many European countries, although at a much lower level of economic development and per-capita value added. Soon the share of Brazil's population ages 15–64 years ("working age," by global statistical conventions) will peak. The population dependency rate—the sum of children ages 0 to 14 and of elderly ages 65 and over—will start rising in 2020, driven mainly by the growing share of elderly in the population. The old-age dependency ratio—that is, the ratio of the share of people in the population ages 65 and older to the share of people of working age—is already higher than the average for Latin America and the Caribbean, and among the BRICS[2] and upper-middle income countries, the pace of aging in Brazil is surpassed only in China.

To achieve high-income status, the best chance for Brazil, "the Country of the Future," is to engage its young people—those currently ages 15–29—more fully in the economy. Brazil's productivity potential will be increasingly determined by the capacity of its skills development and labor market institutions to engage its youth.

The last wave of demographic transition is cresting for Brazil, but its power can be harnessed. It is worth noting that, starting around 1990, population aging accelerated faster in Korea than in Brazil. Despite this, Korea's labor and total factor productivity, its rate of growth, and its overall development have remained consistently strong and resilient to financial and economic crises. Korea's example, along with those of China and Japan, is the best evidence that a country's demography does not have to dictate its economic destiny. Keeping the elderly economically active longer is one imperative. But ensuring that each cohort of new entrants to the labor market is equipped and fully engaged is another. This book suggests how policymakers in Brazil can respond to the imperative of engaging its youth.

FIGURE 1.1

Brazil's population is aging rapidly

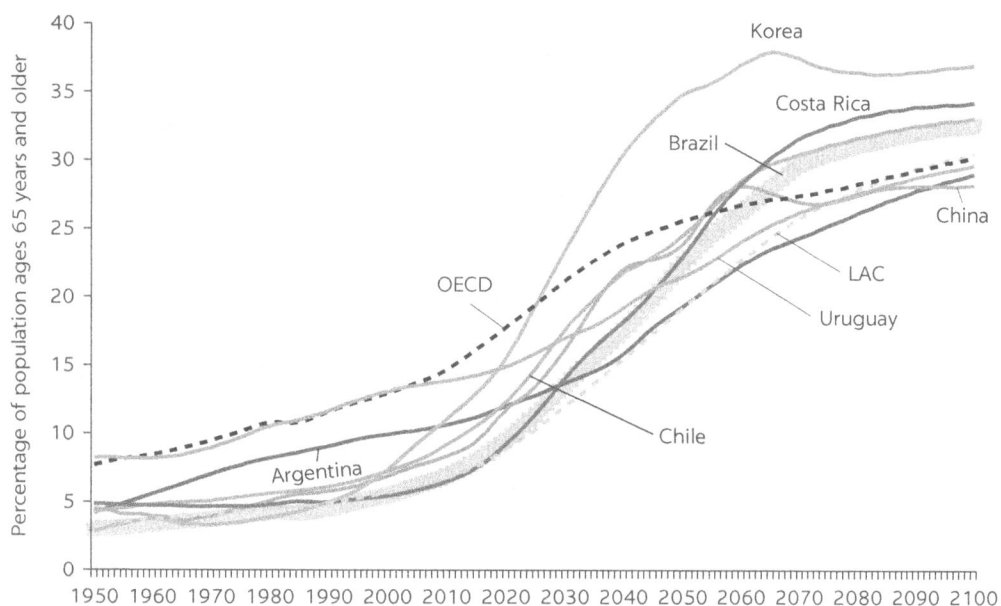

Source: *World Population Prospects: The 2017 Revision,* United Nations Department of Economic and Social Affairs.

The policy agenda outlined in this book is urgent for yet another reason: the adoption of digital technology is rapidly changing the task content of occupations and, hence, the skills demanded by Brazilian employers. Like population aging and the declining share of the working-age population, technological change puts youth at the center of any discussion of productivity. While digital technology adoption among businesses in Brazil is in line with other countries in Latin America and the Caribbean—that is, still at a relatively low level (Dutz, Almeida, and Packard, 2018)[3]—that pattern is changing, albeit slowly, which in turn is changing what is required of young people to be viable and competitive in the labor market. Recent evidence for Brazil shows businesses that rely on higher levels of digital technology adoption and were first to be exposed to the Internet are less likely to hire employees who carry out routine activities and do manual work (Almeida, Corseuil, and Poole 2017). In contrast, following adoption, firms look for workers with analytical and higher-order cognitive abilities, such as clear mathematical reasoning, that equip them to perform effectively such nonroutine activities as interacting with computers. Furthermore, following adoption of digital technology, Brazilian firms are also making greater use of socioemotional skills than in the past, including more interactive, communication-based abilities, such as oral expression and clear speech.[4]

If the basic education and skills development system is ready and responsive to meet the shifting demands of employers, young minds are more likely to keep pace with and meet changing demands. Like population aging, the transformation of the labor market by technological change increases the urgency of the youth engagement agenda. To the vital challenge of increasing social inclusion is now added the challenge of raising productivity and economic growth, which raises the importance of Brazil's education and skills development system. The added challenge sets new priorities for the system to focus on new competencies, as well as on digital skills, to support employability and labor productivity further.

Skills acquisition while in school and at work, therefore, becomes part of Brazil's human capital and an essential determinant both of productivity and inclusion prospects. While Brazil's progress in placing children in school and promoting access to upper secondary education has been significant, many concerns remain with the quality of education and the relevance of the skills students are acquiring (Corseuil and Botelho 2014). Because youth today will be the prime-age workers of tomorrow, attention should be focused not only on the foundational skills developed earlier in life but on the learning that takes place on the job and in training programs. Box 1.1 illustrates the importance of the three different types of skills—cognitive, technical, and socioemotional skills—as highlighted by the World Bank's *World Development Report 2018*

BOX 1.1

Placing the focus on cognitive, socioemotional, and technical skills

Knowing how to do something and carrying out a task can be quite different things. One might think of knowledge, for instance, as being mainly acquired in the classroom and skills through on-the-job training. Even the concept of "skills" can be very diverse, with cognitive, socioemotional, and technical skills all quite unique in their own respect. An efficient and well-trained person in a certain trade will have all three types of skills, in addition to knowledge. Promoting such a range of skills means "educating for a mastery of a wide range of competencies that will help mitigate the challenges posed by our changing world context" (World Bank 2018c).

Briefly put, cognitive skills form the foundation of learning for most students. They are typically learned in elementary school and built upon throughout life. Cognitive skills allow students to think critically and are generally academic, including basics such as reading, counting, and telling time. They are the core skills used by the brain to think, reason, and pay attention, and they will be used every day.

Socioemotional skills are learned as part of navigating social and interpersonal interactions, as well as social structures. They are the behaviors, attitudes, and values a person may express at any given time, and they determine how that person may react in various situations. Socioemotional skills can include self-awareness, relationship skills, and conversational skills, and they make up the "life skills" necessary to succeed in life beyond the carefully structured confines of school and family life in youth. They are applicable to a wide range of disciplines and can be learned in many facets of life, including at home, at school, or in the workplace.

Technical skills comprise the acquired knowledge and experience needed to carry out tasks. They can be quite specific and include the mastery of topics and the use of certain materials or technologies. Technical skills are often learned after cognitive and socioemotional skills in later years of schooling, such as secondary school, technical school, or tertiary education.

Cognitive, socioemotional, and technical skills interact to form a well-rounded person and allow him or her to handle a variety of challenges and situations. They all reinforce each other, with cognitive as the foremost skill needed to form the start of learning. Acquiring a solid base of cognitive and socioemotional skills can set the course for a lifetime trajectory of success, allowing the easier acquisition of technical skills later in life.

continued

Box 1.1, *continued*

FIGURE B1.1.1

The multidimensionality of skills

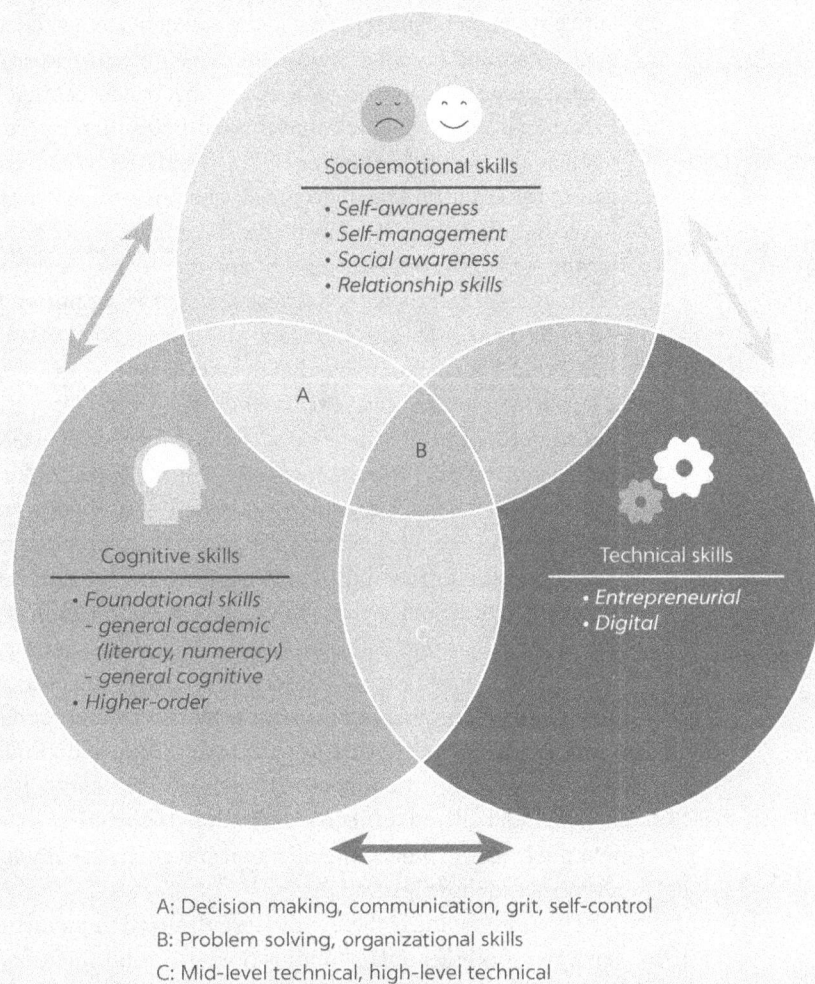

A: Decision making, communication, grit, self-control
B: Problem solving, organizational skills
C: Mid-level technical, high-level technical

Source: World Bank 2018c, figure S3.1, 103.

(2018c). All three types of skills can be acquired throughout life, but early childhood is the optimal time at which to learn the most in these areas, as they can quickly build upon one another and give youth a head start.

In addition to the two "megatrends" of population aging and technology adoption, at least three contextual factors distinguish the discussion about skills and jobs policies for youth in Brazil from that in other countries in Latin America and the Caribbean. While not discussed at length in this book, they are important for readers to keep in mind when considering the challenge Brazil faces to building, sustaining, and deploying its human capital to raise productivity.

The first contextual factor is Brazil's size, the relative dispersion of its population, and its geographically uneven development and growth. As the fifth largest country on Earth, both in land area and population, Brazil is often referred to as a continent unto itself. Only slightly smaller in land mass than Canada, China, and the United States, it is three times as large as Argentina, the next biggest country in Latin America. Its size makes Brazil more diverse, in terms of both environment and terrain and the extent of connectedness of its population settlements and agglomeration centers. This matters, as economic dynamism is often accompanied and propelled by centripetal forces that concentrate growth in certain places. It should come as no surprise, therefore, that economic development and growth are uneven in Brazil and heavily concentrated in the southeast of the country. The unevenness, of course, in part determines the options for economic engagement available to young people. The tax base of a given locality will determine the extent and quality of the services it can afford to offer, unless the provision of these services is supported by an effective and equitable system of fiscal transfers.

Second, the economy, like that of many large countries, has historically been autarkic and insular and is still relatively so, even after a long period of slow integration. For years, it developed behind a formidable wall of tariff and nontariff barriers to trade. Despite focused efforts at liberalization and more regional and global economic integration since the 1990s, exports and imports remain a small share of economic activity relative to their importance in many of Brazil's neighboring countries and among its peers. The limited links to global markets has blunted the spurs to performance that come from foreign competition, while the relative isolation and protection from competitive pressures has allowed product and factor markets to remain relatively uncontestable.[5] Low levels of competition have created an environment that can succor businesses that would otherwise be uncompetitive or that can be viable at unproductively small sizes. The extent of isolation from regional and international markets affects the demand for skills that Brazil's institutions were designed and evolved to build and the extent to which liberalization and greater technology adoption will be disruptive to those institutions.

The third factor is the highly decentralized implementation of policies in social sectors essential to building human capital, including health, education, labor, and social protection. State and municipal authorities and local agencies in Brazil play a greater role in delivering health and education services than in other countries in Latin America and the Caribbean. On the one hand, this can make service providers more accountable to households seeking high-quality health care and education and support when they suffer a shock to their livelihoods, such as the loss of a job. In this regard, decentralization of decision making and administration might, arguably, increase not only the responsiveness but the local relevance of human capital–building services. On the other hand, differing capacities across subnational administrative units to deliver services are reflected in substantial variations in quality throughout the country. Again, this variation in services can play a vital part in determining opportunities for economic engagement. The resulting variation in the quality of human capital can also tie people down or keep them disconnected from where work is being created, adding to the costs of mobility and adjustment (Dix-Carneiro and Kovak 2017).

In addition to being a companion volume to *Brazil's Promise* (World Bank 2018a), this book is the second installment of a World Bank analytical services and advisory program for the government of Brazil focused on skills and jobs policies. The first installment, *Sustaining Employment and Wage Gains in Brazil: A Skills and Jobs Agenda* (Silva, Almeida, and Strokova 2015) highlighted the policies Brazil needs to safeguard the economic and social advances made during the long period of economic growth that ended so dramatically in 2014. Its main emphasis was on social inclusion policies. This installment gives new urgency to the skills and jobs policy agenda against the backdrop of rapid population aging. It considers the economic contraction the country has suffered but with an emphasis on future productivity, and it sharpens the focus on engaging young people in school and in work. The foundational premise of this focus is that a country that fails to provide opportunities for young people to engage, build, and apply their talent and abilities is at an acute disadvantage as it attempts to develop to high income in the last stage of its demographic transition.

In short, Brazil simply cannot afford to grow old before it grows to high-income status, and the pace of population aging implies it can no longer rely on a growing labor force. Where *Brazil's Promise* (World Bank 2018a) examined constraints on productivity that lie in the regulation and institutions of other product and factor markets, this book dives deeper into the remaining constraints: those in the education and training system and the labor market that prevent Brazil from reaching its productivity potential. The key to increasing that potential lies in augmenting its human capital and combining it more effectively with other productive factors.

Can Brazil more effectively fully engage its young people in school and work, to raise their productivity? This core question has several component queries that this book seeks to answer: Is Brazil equipping its youth with the necessary skills and competencies for the future workplace? Can youth have high levels of employability and labor productivity, and can they play a critical role in the final wave of its demographic transformation? How many young Brazilians are disengaged from the formal schooling system and in the labor market? How different are these patterns for young men and young women? Is the ongoing *ensino médio* (upper secondary school) reform doing all that is needed to reduce grade repetition and, ultimately, to support the acquisition of the right skills for the future of work? Is the ongoing reform to de jure job protection regulations de facto strengthening youth's labor market outcomes, or are more reforms needed?

This book is organized as follows. Chapter 2 provides a conceptual framework, developed by Angel-Urdinola and Gukovas (2018) and Rios-Neto (2017) for this volume, which we use to grapple analytically with the concept of youth economic engagement. Chapter 3 presents key facts descriptive of the education and labor market participation patterns of young people since the early 2000s. Chapter 4 covers policies and programs in the formal schooling system at the upper secondary level and the significant efforts of the government of Brazil to improve learning and retention at this level of schooling. Chapter 5 discusses the labor market institutions, regulations, and interventions that shape incentives for young people to work and for employers to hire them and that help determine the quality of job matches between firms and young workers, whether they are first-time jobseekers or workers making transitions across sectors and market engagements. Finally, chapter 6 examines training and other active labor market measures, focusing especially on youth policies that foster the development of skills employers seek and that lead to more productive work. The analysis, findings, and conclusions presented in these chapters are summarized in the remainder of this opening chapter.

YOUTH ECONOMIC ENGAGEMENT: NEW CONCEPTUAL INSIGHTS AND THE EXTENT OF YOUTH DISENGAGEMENT IN BRAZIL

Chapter 2 of this book provides a conceptual framework, grounded in human capital theory, within which to grapple analytically with the concept of economic engagement among young people. The model is based on seminal human capital formation models charting pathways of skills development that lead from the home and community through study and continue as youth take up employment full time (see figure 1.2). The conceptual framework emphasizes the importance not only of attending school but of the quality of education and of learning opportunities at work, yielding the novel insight that "economic disengagement" can take several forms and vary in intensity, even when young people are in school or working (see figure 1.3). The framework thus extends the definition of disengagement beyond just the small segment of young people who are neither studying nor working to the larger population of young people who appear to be on a risky path: students who are suffering from grade–age distortions (that is, they are older than they should be had they been in the appropriate grade) or who repeat grades at high rates, or youth who are already working but in low-productivity and informal and/or poorly paid jobs, with few protections from shocks and scant opportunities to build their skills further.

According to the concepts developed in chapter 2, today more than 50 percent of youth in Brazil can be considered "at-risk" of disengagement, as they are either out of school and out of work, or in school or working, but failing to acquire relevant human capital. Chapter 3 shows that, according to the most recent available survey data, approximately 23 percent of youth (in Brazil, those 15–29 years of age) are "not in education, employment,

FIGURE 1.2

"Disengagement" happens when youth are no longer accumulating human capital

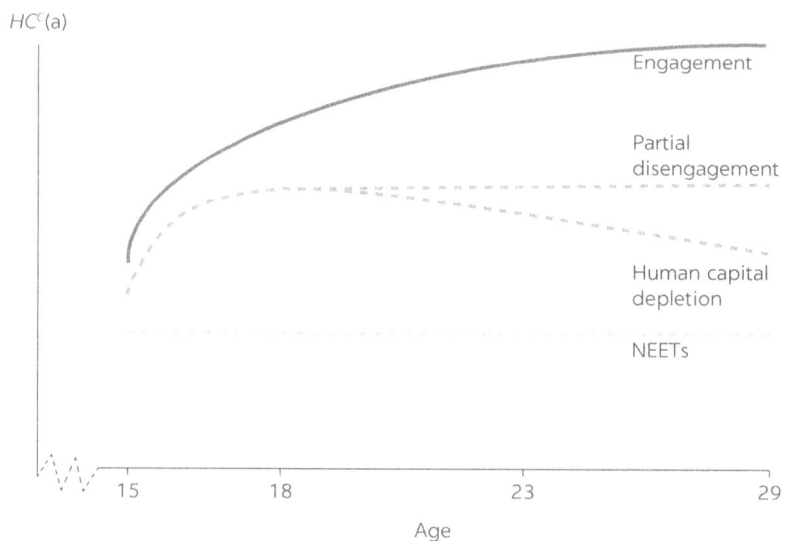

Note: Figure reports a heuristic illustration of alternative pathways of youth economic engagement throughout life. It considers a pattern of full engagement and of partial disengagement, one of human capital depletion, and the NEETs (defined as youth who are not in education, employment, or training). Youth are individuals ages 15–29.

FIGURE 1.3

Portraits of youth disengagement from a skills and jobs perspective

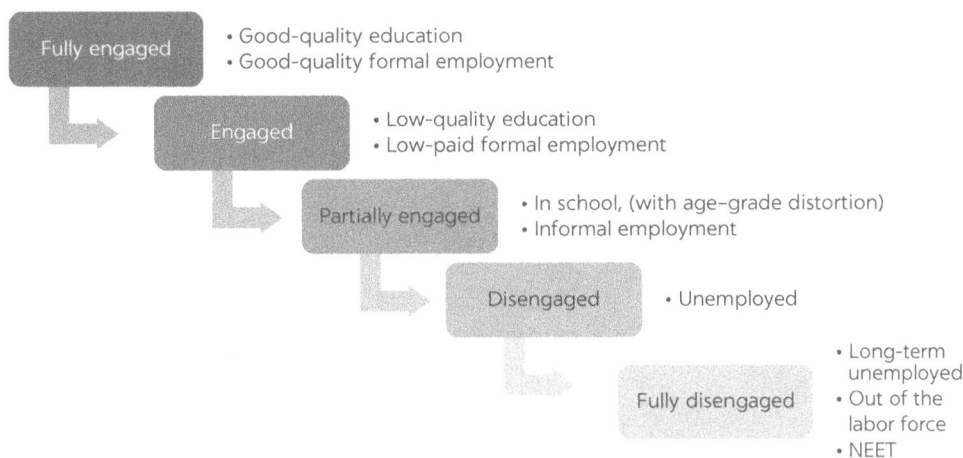

Fully engaged
- Good-quality education
- Good-quality formal employment

Engaged
- Low-quality education
- Low-paid formal employment

Partially engaged
- In school, (with age–grade distortion)
- Informal employment

Disengaged
- Unemployed

Fully disengaged
- Long-term unemployed
- Out of the labor force
- NEET

Source: Angel-Urdinola and Gukovas 2018, and Rios-Neto 2017.

or training" (from which is derived the label NEETs, or *nem-nems*) and are thus facing the most extreme form of disengagement. The application of the new conceptual framework outlined in chapter 2, however, shows that the share of youth who are less than fully engaged can rise as high as 50 percent. This fact need be neither alarming nor paralyzing. Rather, the book proposes this measure of disengagement as a motivation for taking earlier and bolder policy action to keep young people engaged.

With this broader concept of economic disengagement, chapter 3 charts recent trends in education and market participation to distill key facts describing the education and labor market participation patterns of young people since the early 2000s. Descriptive statistics compare the choices young people make in how to use their time with those of youth in other countries, as well as with older members of Brazil's labor force. Education outcomes are presented and, when possible, benchmarked internationally, including students' grade trajectories and completion and dropout rates; the transition from study to work; patterns of labor market insertion; and the quality of jobs held by young people.

Although youth disengagement is less, on average, than in previous years, its extent still varies highly across Brazilian states. Map 1.1 shows the rate of disengagement by state, with higher levels appearing darker. On a positive note, across the country, youth economic disengagement fell from 61.7 percent in 2004 to 52.2 percent in 2015—this despite the increase in the share of *nem-nems* over the same period. The drop was mainly driven by falling age–grade distortion rates for those in school and falling labor informality for those already in the labor market. More critically, the figure illustrates how the rates of youth economic disengagement still varied substantially by 2015, being highest for the northeastern states and lowest in the southern region of the country.

Despite the comforting decline since 2004 in average youth disengagement and its within-country dispersion, this trend has recently, and worrisomely, reverted (see figure 1.4), with rising numbers of *nem-nems* and increases in youth informality and unemployment. Evidence in chapter 3 shows that during Brazil's recent economic crisis (2015–16), transitions from out of school and out of work became more difficult. The recently increasing trend in youth unemployment

MAP 1.1

Youth economic engagement varied widely across Brazil in 2015

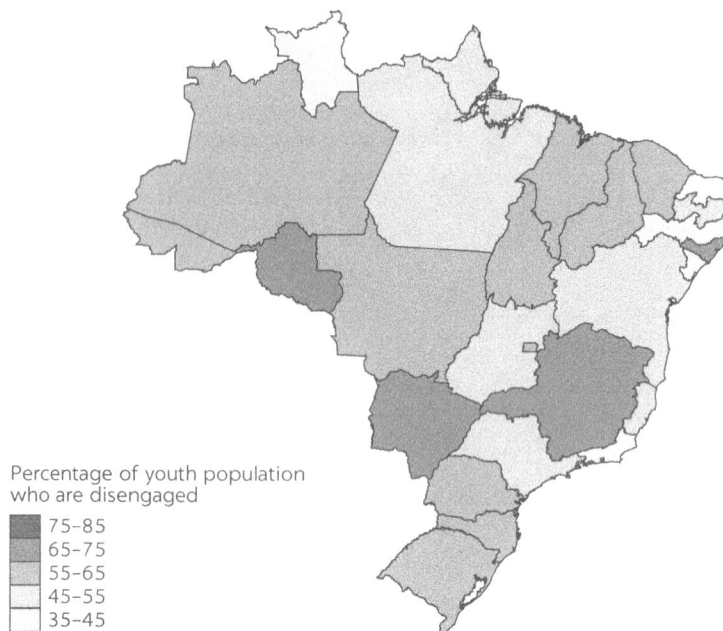

Percentage of youth population
who are disengaged

- 75–85
- 65–75
- 55–65
- 45–55
- 35–45

Source: Estimates based on data from the Pesquisa Nacional por Amostra de Domicílios (PNAD), 2015.
Note: The map shows the shares of disengaged youth in each state relative to the state's youth population. Disengaged youth are those 15–29 years old who (1) work in the informal sector (including those only working and those also studying); (2) only attend school, but are lagging in learning (with a grade–age gap); or (3) do not work or attend school (that is, are out of school and out of work, regardless of being active or inactive).

and informality is also cause for concern. The key for policymakers is whether past achievements in engaging young people can be sustained in less buoyant economic conditions. This is a worry for a country whose productivity potential now depends so heavily on engaging its young people.

EDUCATION OUTCOMES AND THE MOTIVATIONS TO INVEST IN HUMAN CAPITAL

Brazilian youth today complete more years of education than previous generations, especially those at the bottom of the income distribution, yet labor productivity in the country continues to languish behind most of the comparator economies of the Organisation for Economic Co-operation and Development (OECD). Since the first decade of the 2000s, access to education for Brazilian youth, including higher education, has gone through a massive expansion. The most vulnerable youth have especially benefited (Costa et al. 2017). But, puzzlingly, although wages have been growing, growth in aggregate labor productivity has been both low (below both the Latin America and the Caribbean regional average and the average for OECD-member countries) and stagnant (with an average annual growth since 1995 of 1 percent) over the past 15 years (Paes de Barros et al. 2017).

FIGURE 1.4

Youth disengagement fell during the period of rapid economic growth, but is now rising: Trends by region and nationally, 2004–15

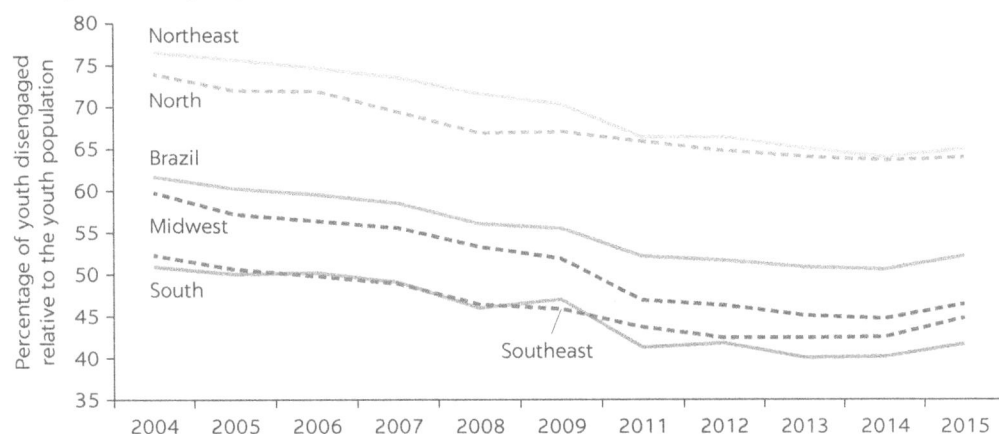

Source: Estimates based on data from the Pesquisa Nacional por Amostra de Domicílios (PNAD), 2004–15.
Note: PNAD was not conducted in 2010. The graph reports the trends for the shares of disengaged youth in each state relative to the state's youth population at the state level and nationwide. Disengaged youth are those 15–29 years old who (1) work in the informal sector (including those only working and those also studying); (2) only attend school but are lagging in learning (with a grade-age gap); or (3) do not work or attend school (that is, are out of school and out of work, regardless of being active or inactive).

This book argues that this education/growth "puzzle" is likely driven by three factors. First, labor demand has been heavily constrained by shifts in the aggregate domestic demand and an economy still characterized by low-productivity activities and distorted product, labor, and capital markets, which has generated a labor demand oriented disproportionately toward less skilled workers. Some of these patterns are discussed in depth by Dutz (2018) and Messina and Silva (2018). Second, Brazil has a low-quality education system whose reputation among youth, especially girls, is rarely able to overcome "heavy" and outdated gender-biased social norms. The latter tend to be especially harmful for women. And, third, evidence is presented here of misinformation regarding the returns on education, shedding additional light on the increasing youth disengagement.

Brazil is facing a severe learning crisis. Despite generous education spending and high enrollment levels, young people are not learning the skills that will make them competitive workers. This learning crisis is not specific to Brazil but is, rather, a global crisis, as spotlighted by the *World Development Report* (WDR) *2018* (World Bank 2018c). While greater access to education through expanded enrollment, including in Brazil, is a proud achievement, improvements in learning have been far more limited (see figure 1.5). As of 2015, Brazil still ranked very low on international learning achievement tests relative to neighbors and peer countries, and progress in learning performance has been slow. The WDR 2018 estimates that, based on current trends, Brazil would take over 260 years to reach the OECD-member average scores for reading performance (World Bank 2018c). Learning shortfalls during the school years show up as weak skills in the workforce.

FIGURE 1.5

Learning still lags

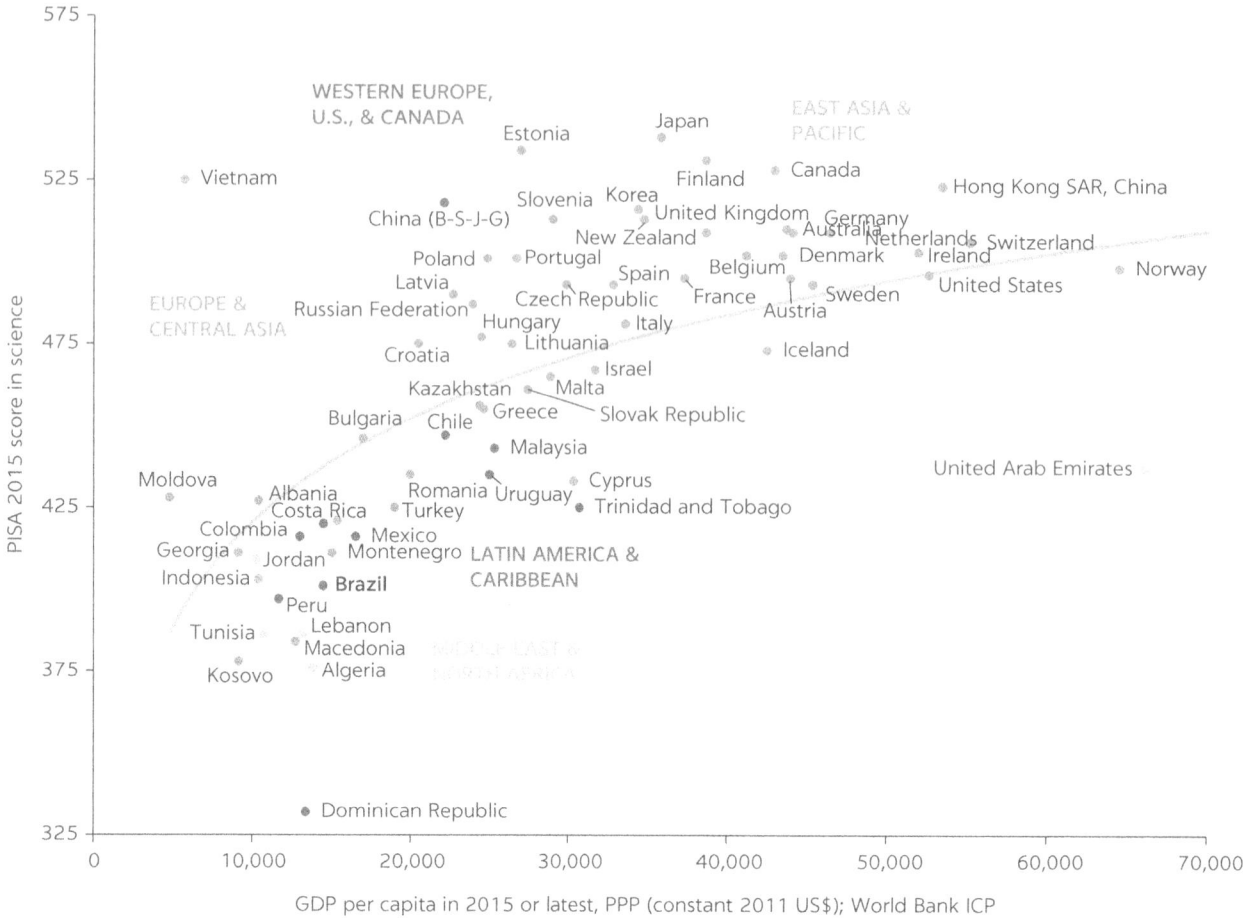

Source: World Bank. LAC PISA 2016.
Notes: Figure shows the relationship between GDP per capita and performance on PISA Science in 2015.

As of 2015, only 38 percent of Brazilian teenagers (ages 15 and 16 years old) were in the right grade in school according to their ages, and more than 13 percent were already out of school. Most 15- and 16-year-olds complete *ensino fundamental* (fundamental education, grades one through nine), but many have important deficiencies in learning. Figure 1.6 shows that by this age, when students should be attending their first year of *ensino médio* (upper secondary education) if they have not had any type of age–grade distortion, approximately one out of every eight has already dropped out of the formal schooling system. For those who remain in school, only 37.9 percent are in the right grade for their age, while most of the remaining are already lagging by at least two full years of education (that is, are attending eighth grade or lower). This implies that youth start *ensino médio* with highly deficient learning trajectories on core foundational skills, including academic, cognitive, and behavioral skills, from their years of *ensino fundamental*.

Learning deficiencies are cumulative and start early in students' school careers. They lead to a lack of interest in building human capital and motivate many adolescents to drop out of school. The main reason students

FIGURE 1.6

Youth ages 15–16 enrolled in school and youth who are out of school, 2015

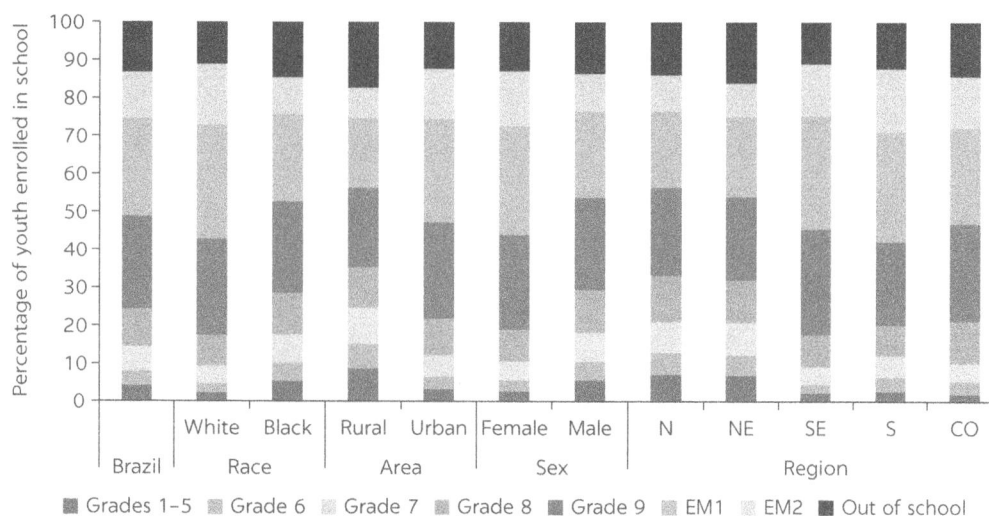

Source: Calculations based on Pesquisa Nacional por Amostra de Domicílios (PNAD), 2015.
Note: Ensino fundamental comprises grades 1–9 years and *ensino médio* grades 10–12. Youth ages 15–16 with no age-grade distortion should be attending grade 10. The age-grade distortion indicator is positive when students are older than what they should be had they not repeated any grade in the schooling system. Age is measured as of March 31 of the reference year. Under race, "black" includes self-reported races "*preta*" and "*parda*." A category for "other races" (including indigenous and East-Asian origin) is not reported due to very low frequencies (less than 1 percent of the sample).

report for dropping out of upper secondary education in Brazil is lack of interest. An overloaded curriculum and time perceived as wasted are likely important drivers. The curriculum used today in *ensino fundamental* and *ensino médio* is geared heavily toward memorization rather than critical thinking and rarely goes into depth on specific topics. If youth find additional education to be ill suited to jobs within their desired labor markets, and/or if they value current events much more than future events (that is, have high "discount rates"), they are more likely to drop out of the formal schooling system and attempt to join the labor market with the education they have rather than flounder in school, where they lack both opportunity and income.

Qualitative work prepared as background to this book also shows that the reputation of the schooling system is rarely strong enough to overcome deeply rooted and stringent social norms which, coupled with reduced aspirations, lead many girls to drop out of school. Machado and Muller (2018) gathered evidence from interviews with young women and men revealing that the motivations for and process of dropping out are quite different across genders. For all students, however, the lack of support systems and incentives to continue investing in human capital are important determining factors.

The earnings premium for education and labor market experience in Brazil has been steadily falling (see figure 1.7), reducing the incentives for young people to invest in education; but it is still, by and large, considerable. Broken down by type of institution, the net return on university degrees is higher in almost all fields compared to professional institutes and technical trainings. A main question the book attempts to answer is whether selection can explain part of this

FIGURE 1.7

Education earnings premiums have been falling across levels of completed education

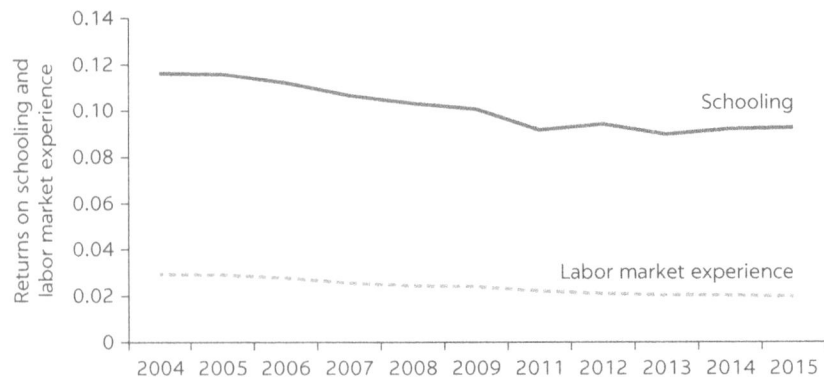

Source: Estimates based on Pesquisa Nacional por Amostra de Domicílios (PNAD), 2004–15.
Note: PNAD was not conducted in 2010. This figure presents the ordinary least squares (OLS) estimates of the continuous variable for years of schooling and the returns on experience evaluated at the average years of potential experience, as defined by Montenegro and Patrinos (2014). The sample includes only wage earners (employees, military, and civil servants) ages 15–64.

result, or whether it reflects real labor market gains for similar individuals. New evidence collected for this book (Almeida et al. 2018) shows high individual wage rate returns on the investment in higher education and large heterogeneity across different providers, even after accounting for differences across students in many observable and frequently unobservable characteristics (such as differences in ability at entry). There are also significant and heterogeneous wage premiums for secondary-level technical and vocational education and training (TVET) in Brazil (see Neri 2010 and Almeida et al. 2015). Since only 12 percent of Brazilians have completed some form of higher education, considerable room remains for gains in employment and earnings.

Despite these large earnings premiums, misinformation about (and wide diversity in) the perceived returns on education by students and their families likely contributes to rising youth disengagement. Coupled with the poor quality of education provided in schools, this misinformation likely reduces the individual incentives for investing in human capital, both at school and at work. New evidence collected for this book (Gukovas and Kejsefman 2017), based on a new youth survey, suggests Brazil's youth are uncertain as well as misinformed about the benefits of human capital investment when it comes to schooling. When provided with the average income of a worker with a certain level of education and asked what someone with additional years of education might make on the job, the vast majority of survey respondents in Brazil underestimated the true value of additional years of school. Among the respondents of the youth survey, over 40 percent thought a worker with just fundamental education who makes R$1,226, on average, would fetch the same salary as a worker who had completed secondary education; only 14 percent overestimated the value of the same investment (see figure 1.8). And the reality is quite different. A worker with secondary education earns a premium of more than 50 percent over the base rate for a worker with completed fundamental education (R$1,900 to R$2,100, on average).

FIGURE 1.8

Most Brazilians substantially underestimate the value of education in the labor market

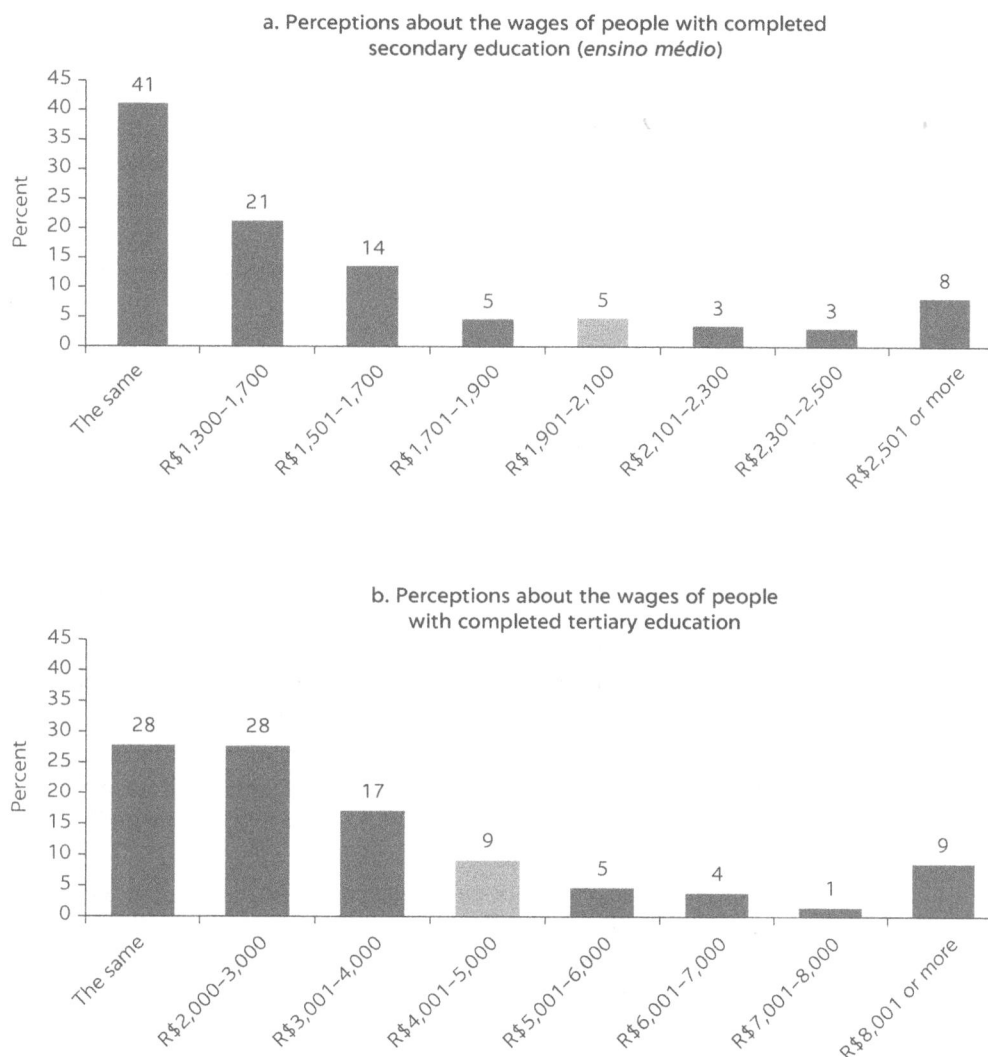

a. Perceptions about the wages of people with completed
secondary education (*ensino médio*)

b. Perceptions about the wages of people
with completed tertiary education

Source: Gukovas and Kejsefman 2017, using a new youth survey conducted by RIWI 2016.
Notes: Figures refer to the Brazilian youth's perceptions regarding investments in human capital. Respondents were provided with the average monthly wage of a worker with completed *ensino fundamental* and completed *ensino médio*, respectively. Then they were asked to estimate the wages of people who complete the following level of education by choosing one alternative out of different wage ranges. The vertical bars show the percentage of youth in the sample stating that wages are "the same"; between "Reais 1,300- Reais 1,700"; and so on. The light blue bar indicates the actual *average* monthly wage in the labor market, for that same educational level, in the PNAD household survey (2016). The two questions were asked in sequence; after the respondent had answered the first, he or she would learn the average wage of a worker who had completed secondary education.

The good news is that government and stakeholders are engaged in enacting solutions to these performance problems in the education system. Chapter 4 covers policies and programs in the formal schooling system at the upper secondary level and the significant efforts being made by the government of Brazil to improve learning and reduce grade repetition at this level of schooling. While recognizing that learning pathways among teenagers also reflect life-long choices since early child education (and even before that), as well as opportunities, the chapter focuses on policies anchored in *ensino médio*. In 2017, authorities were very active in enacting an important reform in *ensino médio* designed to modernize the curriculum and extend the school day, to keep adolescents in school through completion, and to create life-long learners who would be more resilient to changing technology and demands in the labor market. The chapter reviews international evidence and proposes concrete policies to help maximize the educational impacts of this reform.

Yet these efforts are not enough. Brazil can, and should, do more, especially if the country aims soon to have a workforce fully equipped with 21st century skills. Chapter 4 discusses important human resource reforms for teachers and school principals in support of increased quality and motivation among these staff members. It also reviews complementary policies needed to tackle more aggressively the challenges of noncompletion of and dropouts from *ensino médio*.

YOUTH LABOR MARKET OUTCOMES

Unemployment in Brazil is particularly high among its youth. It has risen fast since 2013, and it threatens to undo some of the social achievements of the previous decade. The unemployment rate for younger members of the workforce is higher in most countries for several reasons. Younger people have limited job search experience; they present riskier prospects to employers than older workers; and many need to "shop around," experimenting with different sectors or jobs before committing to one. These reasons explain not only a higher unemployment rate among youth, but also higher levels of turnover, or churn, and shorter spells of employment. In times of financial and economic crisis, younger members of the labor force also usually comprise the segment hit first by layoffs, and during a protracted economic contraction, they have the greatest difficulty finding new employment. Through much of Brazil's high-growth period, from 2003 to 2014, the youth unemployment rate followed the overall rate, but the difference between the two started to widen significantly from 2012, with the job prospects among people of prime working age (30–54) becoming far more robust (see figure 1.9).

The changing job status of working youth presents a nuanced picture. The youth segment (those ages 15–29) has shown higher rates of formal labor insertion than the working-age population. This could reflect an advantageous position of the current cohort of 25–29 years, which has higher levels of completed education than this age group had in the past and was successfully inserted into formal employment during the high-growth years. But among the "youngest youth"—working people ages 15–24—the rate of informal employment is higher than for the overall employed labor force (see figure 1.10). This pattern of market activity is similar to the observed patterns of the "youngest youth" in other countries. To the extent that spells of informal employment provide platforms on which young people can gain work experience and technical skills and act as "stepping stones" to later, higher-paying jobs offering more opportunities, this pattern gives little cause for worry. A mounting body of evidence from several high- and middle-income countries indicates this might not be the case, however.

Spells of unemployment or long periods of informal employment can have lasting, adverse impacts on the human capital of young people and their future job prospects. The motivations and circumstances that lead a person into informal work (such as tax avoidance or evasion, preferences for flexibility, and exclusion from formal employment), are as numerous as forms of informal work

FIGURE 1.9

The rise in unemployment in Brazil has been steepest among youth

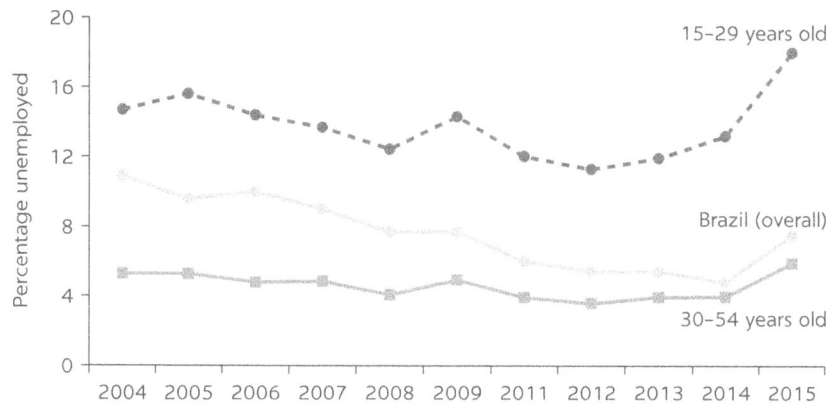

Source: Estimates based on Pesquisa Nacional por Amostra de Domicílios (PNAD), 2004–15, and IPEA data, based on Instituto Brasileiro de Geografia e Estatística, Pesquisa Mensal de Emprego (IBGE/PME).
Note: PNAD was not conducted in 2010. Unemployment rate is the number of unemployed over the economically active population (occupied + unemployed). Until March 2016, unemployment rates in Brazil were reported monthly based on Pesquisa Mensal de Emprego (PME). Since Pesquisa Nacional por Amostra de Domicílios (PNAD) occurs annually in September, national data are shown as rates for the month of September. Ages were considered as of March 31, of the year of the survey.

FIGURE 1.10

Informal employment is highest among the youngest cohorts of the workforce

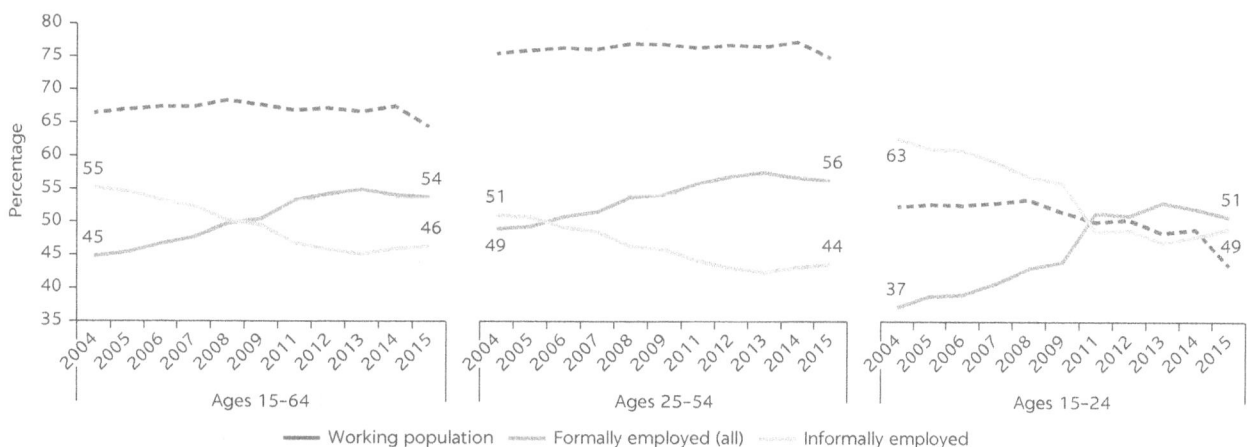

Source: Estimates based on Pesquisa Nacional por Amostra de Domicílios (PNAD).
Note: PNAD was not conducted in 2010. The charted indicator is the share of the population that worked during the reference period as a proportion of the total. Formal with a signed employment contract (*carteira assinada*) is the share of the working population who mainly work in jobs with a *carteira assinada* (employee or domestic worker). Informal jobs are those employees: without *carteira assinada*; employees without *carteira assinada*; domestic workers without *carteira assinada*; self-employed; self-employed in production for own consumption; construction workers for own use; unpaid workers; and workers who did not declare the type of occupation. Wage < minimum wage is the proportion of people that works (either works only or works and attends school) with wages below the minimum wage for the year of reference. Contributing to social security is the share of the working population that contributes to any kind of social security, for any of the jobs. Self-employed or employers is the share of the working population who were declared as such in the reference week. others contributing to social security is the share of self-employed or employers that made contribution to social security.

(unpaid family worker, uncontracted wage employee, day laborer, small business owner, or sole trader). All forms of informal work entail a higher element of risk, however, especially when a person's options are heavily constrained and the only jobs on offer are dependent employment without a signed contract. An early and protracted spell in informal jobs can put young people on a path of less-than-full engagement. Higher rates of informal work among youth raise the risk of unemployment and informality later in working life, as well as lower hourly wages in adulthood (Cruces, Ham, and Viollaz 2012; Gukovas and Moreira 2017). These adverse impacts dissipate over time if youth have the chance to acquire more education and job-relevant capabilities.[6] The "scarring" will, however, be substantial for those who are out of school and out of work, relative to those in formal jobs. Young men who experience long spells out of school and out of work are particularly affected and face a statistically significantly higher likelihood of future unemployment and informal employment and lower pay later in life. The effects on wages do not seem to dissipate as the individuals age. Their higher rates of unemployment can last until approximately age 35, while the higher likelihood of informality persists until age 45 (Gukovas and Moreira 2017).

LABOR POLICIES AND JOB PROSPECTS FOR YOUTH

Human capital is the most important asset in which households can invest, and the labor market is where people go to seek a return on that investment. Like many markets, the labor market has imperfections and failures that motivate actions by government to help improve people's prospects. These policies vary widely across countries in their character, the combination in which they are deployed, and the extent to which the authorities have implementation, monitoring, and enforcement capacity to make the measures amount to more than just pages in the labor code (World Bank 2012). The objectives of most governments in deploying labor market policies are similar, however—that is, to ensure the labor market is safe, fair, and a place where people's skills and enterprise are rewarded. Having these assurances is particularly important for the newest entrants to the labor market, who may be fresh from full-time education but lacking in real-world experience.

Concern is growing, however, that the current set of policy interventions has aggravated the impact on the labor market of Brazil's contraction, particularly for youth. Chapter 5 covers labor market institutions, regulations, and interventions that shape incentives to work and to hire youth and that help determine the quality of matches between firms and young workers (either first-time jobseekers or others). The chapter shows how Brazil's labor market policies have long privileged (mainly older) "insiders" at the expense of opportunities for younger people. Although the employment impact of labor policies on the workforce as a whole is actively debated in many countries, a growing consensus is that restrictive labor regulations are particularly prejudicial to the job prospects of young people. In Brazil, a large body of empirical evidence supports the notion that the enforcement of a restrictive labor code can lead to more underemployment and unemployment, especially among young workers (Almeida and Carneiro 2009, 2012). The adverse impact is particularly notable with respect to the statutory minimum wage.

Analyzing the impact of minimum wage increases in Brazil has been tricky, given the unification of regional minimum wages in 1984, as well as the linkage of minimum wages to inflation and the growth in gross domestic product (GDP) since 2005 (Jales 2017). In 2002, the World Bank and IPEA's *Brazil Jobs Report* found little evidence of the labor market segmentation usually attributable to statutory minimum wages that is sometimes found in other countries.

The report cited an "*efeito farol*" (the so-called "lighthouse" effect), in which informal employment agreements appeared to be informed by the level of the statutory minimum wage (Neri, Gonzaga, and Camargo 2001; Fajnzylber 2001). Indeed, analysis of the earnings distribution of formal and informal workers in Brazil over the period 2001–15 shows that, while the share of informally employed people earning less than the minimum wage has always been substantial, the statutory minimum continues to shape the earnings of people working informally.

More recently, the introduction of valuation policies and the specific parameters of an adjustment formula have caused the statutory minimum wage to rise steadily. Since 2003, Brazil has followed a "minimum wage valuation policy" that entails annual adjustments of the national minimum wage based on predetermined rules, including an explicit formula. Brazil's statutory minimum wage is adjusted by the inflation rate in the previous year, plus the real rate of GDP growth two years previously. The adjustment rule was extended in 2015 for the period 2016–19. The valuation policy and adjustment rule have delivered a real rise in the minimum wage of more than 77 percent over the period 2003–16 (see figure 1.11). Even in the midst of a deep recession, its nominal value increased from R$678 per month in 2013 to R$937 in 2017.

At 70 percent of the median wage, Brazil's minimum wage also appears high by international benchmark levels (see figure 1.12). The average statutory minimum wage among OECD-member countries has remained stable, at between 45 percent and 50 percent of median wages. Some other countries in Latin America (Colombia, Chile, and Cosa Rica) have higher minimum wages than Brazil by this metric. When demand for labor slackens, real labor costs adjust downward to contain unemployment. The new adjustment policies prevent that from happening in Brazil. Unfortunately, after a long period of decline, the share of working people earning less than the minimum wage in the country is rising again, along with unemployment. The rise has been steepest for Brazilian youth (see figure 1.13).

FIGURE 1.11

Brazil's federal statutory minimum wage has been rising steadily since 2003

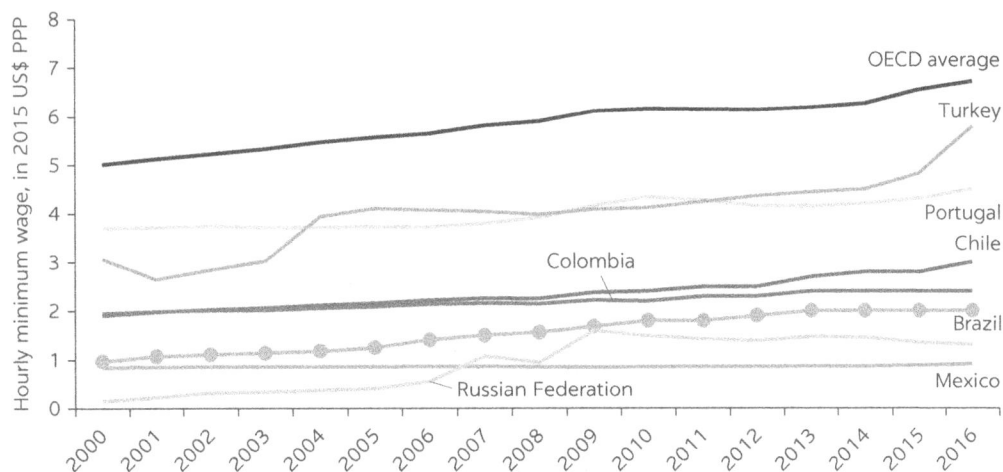

Source: Estimates based on data from OECD Stata (https://data.oecd.org).
Notes: Real hourly minimum wage in 2015 constant prices in 2015 US$ PPPs.

FIGURE 1.12

Relative to median earnings, Brazil's federal statutory minimum wage is higher than the average of OECD member countries and BRICs

Minimum wage, as a percentage of median wage, 2008–13, and for Brazil, 2014 and 2015

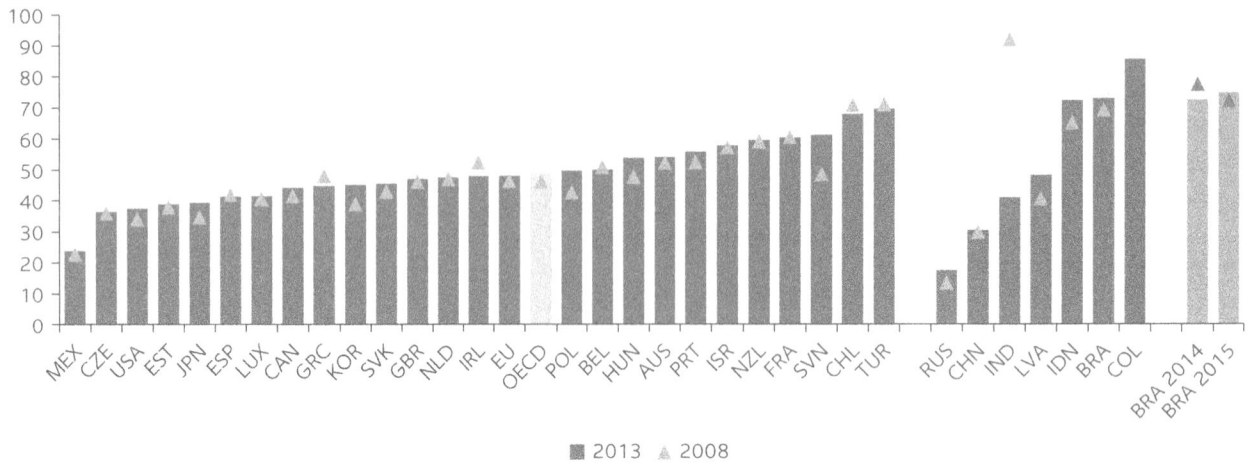

■ 2013 ▲ 2008

Source: Estimates based on data from OECD Employment Outlook database, Going for Growth 2016 and 2017 Interim Reports.
Notes: Figure reports minimum wage as a percentage of the median wage in each country. Missing countries do not have a national statutory minimum wage, except for Mexico. Data for Brazil are from 2014 and 2015. Data for India are from 2004–5 and 2009–10, and for Chile from 2009 (instead of 2008). For China, Indonesia, the Russian Federation, and India, the indicator shows the level of the statutory minimum wage as a percentage of the average wage. For OECD countries, exactly half of all workers have wages either below or above the median wage.

FIGURE 1.13

After a long period of decline, the share of workers earning less than the minimum wage is rising with unemployment, particularly for youth

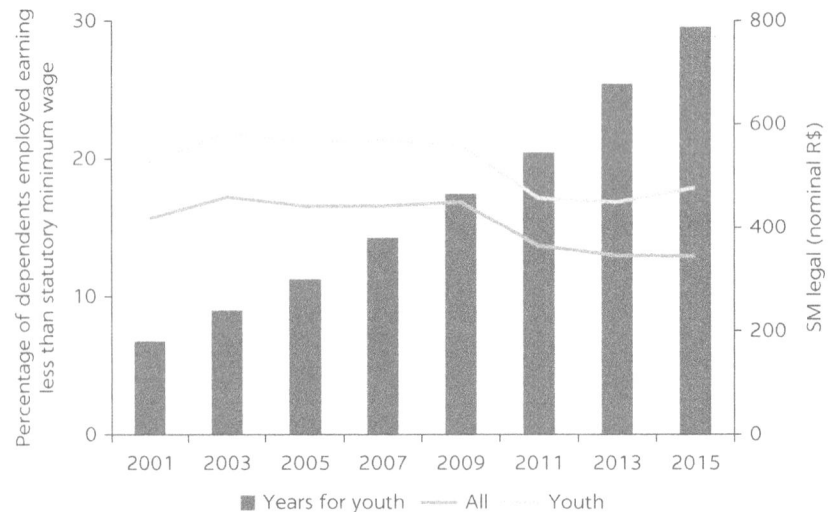

■ Years for youth —— All   Youth

Source: Estimates based on PNAD.

For Brazil's labor force overall, empirical evidence of the impact of minimum wages on employment outcomes has been ambiguous. While some researchers have found negative employment effects from minimum wage increases (Foguel 1998; Neumark, Salas, and Wascher 2014; Ulyssea and Foguel 2006; Foguel, Ramos, and Carneiro 2015; Jales 2015), others have found no such significant effects (Lemos 2004, 2009; Broecke, Forti, and

Vandeweyer 2015). The evidence of consistent, negative impacts on the job prospects of young people in particular, however, is clearer. Fajnzylber (2001) found an increase of 10 percent in the minimum wage to be associated with a decrease in employment of 3.8 percent. Komatsu and Menezes-Filho, (2016) found that minimum wage increases reduced the likelihood of teenagers' working by 3 percent (although they attributed the reduction to an intrahousehold reallocation of labor). Broecke and Vandeweyer (2015) found a larger effect of 7.8 percent. They also found an increase of 10 percent in the minimum wage as a share of the average wage to be associated with a decline in formality by 3–4 percent, on average. Similarly, Foguel et al. (2015) found that minimum wage hikes increase young people's transitions from employment into inactivity and into unemployment. These transitions and the negative effects of minimum wages are amplified during economic downturns.

Evidence from many countries shows that employment protection regulations also have a stronger negative impact on the job prospects of youth than on those of older workers. As new entrants to the labor market, youth are less skilled and less productive than more experienced, prime-age workers. All else being equal, younger workers can be riskier for employers to take on. More stringent employment protection regulations can make firms reluctant to hire young people if they remain unproductive and are difficult to dismiss, for example. Tenure-based restrictions on dismissal can also make firms reluctant to fire existing, older workers in response to an economic contraction, even if they are less productive, and instead to let younger workers go. The empirical literature shows that more restrictive regulations adversely affect those for whom labor demand is more elastic (that is, less-skilled groups), including young people (Bassanini and Duvall 2006). The effect is substantial: Bassanini and Duvall (2006) found a decline in the OECD's employment protection legislation (EPL) indicator by two standard deviations to be associated with an increase of four percentage points in youth employment. For Chile, Montenegro and Pagés (2004; 2007) found job security provisions lowered the probability for youth (as well as less-skilled workers and women) to be employed. As a result of high levels of employment protection for workers with indefinite contracts, youth are more likely to be offered informal jobs or only temporary employment (Kahn 2012). In OECD countries in 2012, nearly a quarter of workers 15–24 years of age were employed in temporary jobs.

Although its statutory requirements for dismissing formal workers on indefinite contracts are lighter than those of OECD member countries and its neighbors, Brazil has had very stringent restrictions on firms' use of flexible forms of hiring. True, measures of de jure employment protection applied to people with "regular" (that is, indefinite) labor contracts suggest Brazil has few restrictions on dismissals (even if the direct costs paid by employer in fines, or *multas*, for nondisciplinary, involuntary separations can be high). But comparisons of measures of regulation on employers' decisions to use outsourcing and fixed term and temporary forms of employment show firms to have been far more restricted. This extreme regulatory stance can be particularly damaging to the prospects of young people, who are more likely to prefer or need part-time and flexible employment than people of prime working age. These restrictions are also severely constraining to productivity, as they make it difficult for firms to innovate, experiment with new technology and business processes, or adjust their labor and skills inputs to rapidly shifting market demands.

Furthermore, restrictions on the use of part-time and flexible hiring increase the likelihood of informal employment. The tight restrictions on when firms can use outsourced labor, as well as the limitations on the use of fixed-term and less than full-time employment, have forced most firms to engage these human resources informally. This has been bad for firms, which have had to spend time and resources avoiding detection and enforcement; it has been bad for working people who have a preference for flexibility, including not only young people who might want to combine work with study and training, but also young parents who need to balance market and household responsibilities; and it has ultimately been bad for society, in that it has forced firms and households reasonably pursuing economic opportunities into evasion of laws and regulations. A culture of broadly accepted noncompliance and evasion as a social norm is arguably the most challenging obstacle to bringing more market activity in from the shadows of the informal economy (Packard, Koettl, and Montenegro 2012).

Finally, Brazil's labor market programs have long privileged (mainly older) "insiders" at the expense of opportunities for younger people. Drawing on analysis for the recently released World Bank *Brazil Expenditure Review* (2017), chapter 6 documents the country's underinvestment in programs that help people—particularly young people with the least experience—navigate the labor market. The deployment of labor market interventions in Brazil is weighted heavily toward "passive" income support programs for people who lose formal jobs, which account for 83 percent of total labor program expenditure, and away from "active" intermediation and job search assistance programs (see figure 1.14). Most labor market interventions are financed from the federal budget or dedicated levies and funds (specifically, *Fundo de Amparo ao Trabalhador*, or FAT, a fund financed from statutory payroll contributions that finances unemployment insurance and other labor programs). The bulk of public spending on labor market programs goes to people who already have formal jobs rather than to jobseekers. The policies and programs Brazil puts in place to help correct failures of the labor market are skewed away from the intermediation services that could improve the quality of matches between firms and jobseekers.

Although still modest relative to public spending on pensions for the elderly and people living with disabilities, public spending on labor market programs has been rising in recent years. Drawing on the World Bank's recent review of Brazil's federal budget (World Bank 2017), while public spending on labor programs in 2000 was historically low, at 0.4 percent of GDP, this category of social expenditure grew hand in hand with the relatively high levels of employment creation until 2014, reaching 0.85 percent of GDP in 2011 and 0.99 percent in 2014. In 2015, expenditure accelerated to 1.1 percent of GDP as the country slipped into economic crisis and unemployment began to surge. This figure was dwarfed by public spending from the federal budget on old-age, survivor, and disability pensions, which rose to 11.1 percent of GDP in 2015, and was less than spending on social assistance targeted to the poorest (1.5 percent of GDP in 2015). Nonetheless, spending on labor programs intended to assist people who have lost and are looking for new jobs represents a substantial segment of Brazil's budget. Spending on labor market interventions finances mainly the "passive" labor market programs (that is, income support for people who have lost jobs), which constitute 83 percent of total labor program expenditure. This means the system benefits almost exclusively relatively well-off, formally employed workers; only 1.8 percent of labor program expenditure is accessible

FIGURE 1.14

Public spending on labor market programs is weighted heavily to "passive" income support, over the "active" services that help people find jobs

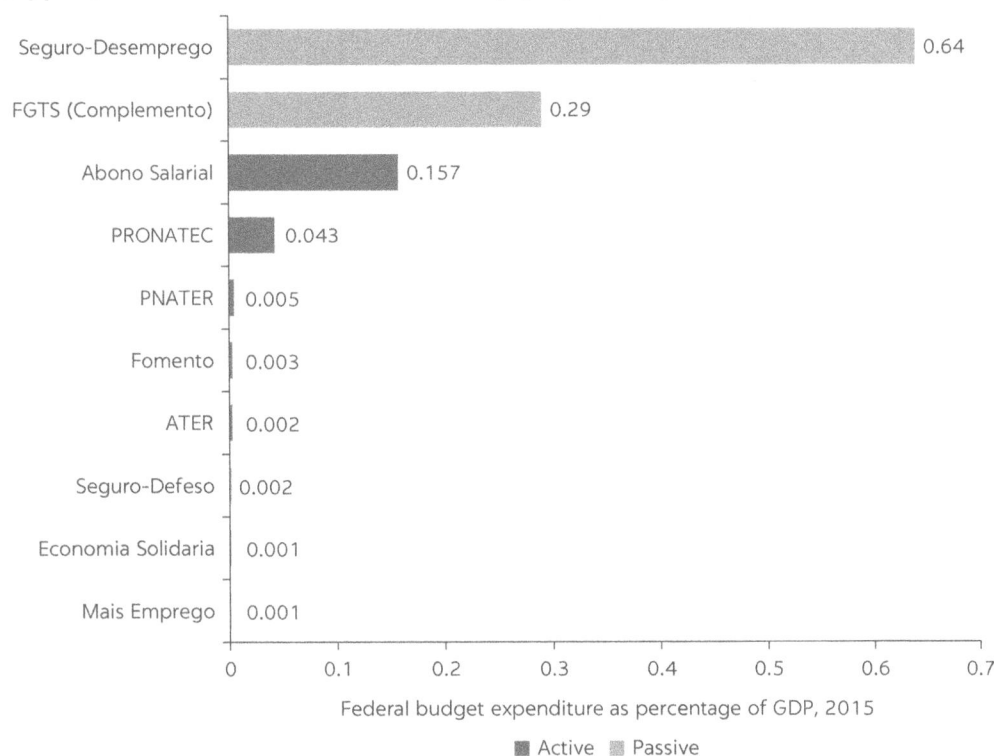

Source: World Bank, *Brazil Expenditure Review* 2017, Labor Programs. Figures derived from analysis of BOOST database, federal-level, based on data from SIOP *Sistema Integrado de Planejamento e Orçamento* for Social Protection and Labor Program Inventory.

to workers who are not necessarily formalized—that is, workers without signed contracts, referred to in Brazil as *"sem carteira assinada."*

Public spending on programs that actively promote labor market insertion of the unemployed and economically inactive remains very small, even after taking into account the recent increased spending on skills training (see figure 1.15). A wage top-up program, Abono Salarial, is meant to provide incentive for formal employment. By design, however, it does not play an explicit role in activating the out-of-work, since it requires a five-year history of employment for eligibility. Other Brazilian programs that fall squarely under the internationally used definition of "active labor market programs" are training for vulnerable groups and the unemployed (Pronatec-BSM and Pronatec-Seguro Desemprego, Projovem), public employment services (Mais Emprego), and entrepreneurship programs (Programa de Fomento de Atividades Produtivas Rurais, Asistência Técnica e Extensão Rural). Although it has received significant attention because of its rapid growth since 2011, PRONATEC was only a modest driver of expenditure on labor programs, and it continues to represent a small share of the total (3.8 percent in 2015).[7] Federal spending on labor market intermediation services represented by the Sistema Nacional de Emprego (SINE) has remained persistently low, and it is probably the least adequately financed labor function in the Brazilian social protection and labor policy architecture. Chapter 6 points to policy solutions

FIGURE 1.15

Spending on "active" labor programs in Brazil is allocated mainly to wage top-up subsidies, leaving little for intermediation services and training

Share of expenditures on ALMPs in Brazil, OECD, and Latin American countries by functional category

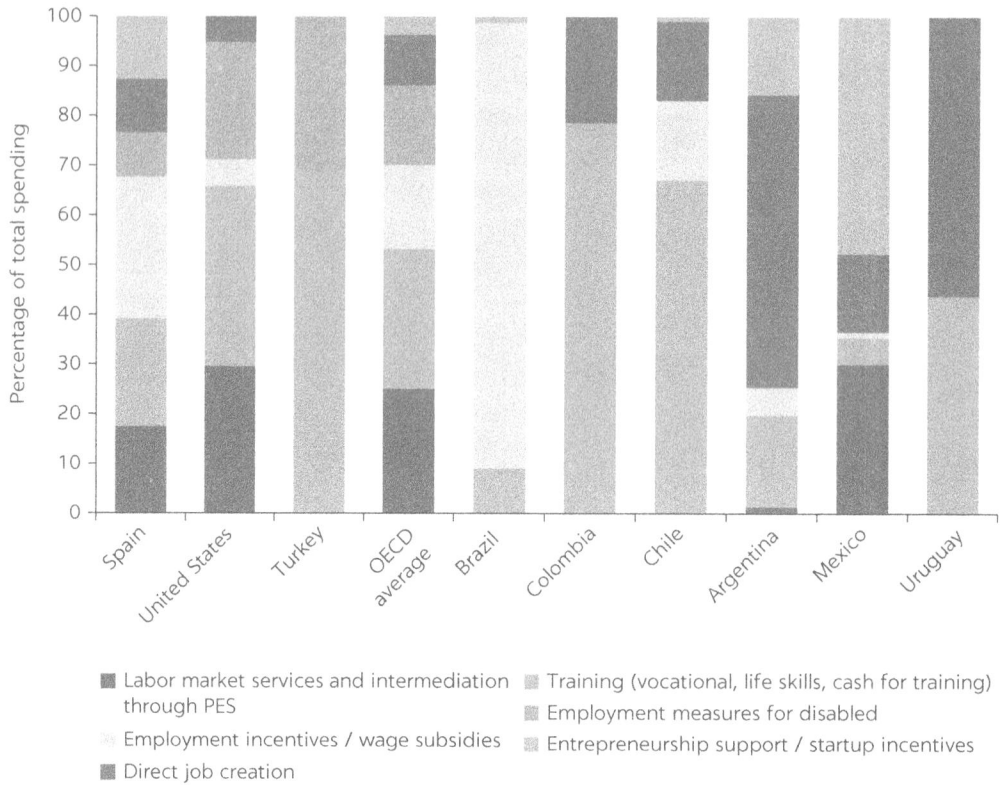

Labor market services and intermediation through PES

Employment incentives / wage subsidies

Direct job creation

Training (vocational, life skills, cash for training)

Employment measures for disabled

Entrepreneurship support / startup incentives

Source: World Bank *Brazil Expenditure Review* 2017, Labor Programs chapter, using data from OECD SOCx data set and analysis of BOOST database, federal level, based on data from SIOP *Sistema Integrado de Planejamento e Orçamento*, for SPL Program Inventory.

to each of these problems and recommends structural changes to improve the efficiency of the labor market.

In this context, the chapter also discusses reforms to the labor code that were legislated in 2017 and postulates what their impact will be on the prospects of working youth. These reforms constitute an ambitious step in the right direction that could reduce insider advantages, increase the share of formally employed young people, and improve the quality of matches between firms and young workers. Despite these advances, however, policies and programs left unchanged by the reforms create perverse incentives that constrain the creation of human capital and could, in aggregate, lower the speed limit on economic growth already imposed by an aging population.

MESSAGES FOR POLICYMAKERS: SHAPING A SKILLS AND JOBS AGENDA TO ENGAGE YOUTH

This book suggests new policy changes and measures that Brazil should prioritize to catch the last wave of its demographic transition. The government of Brazil has been very active in the arena of skills and labor policy. The year 2017 was one of ambitious policy change, both to *ensino médio* and to the labor code. Chapters 4 and 5 use these two education and labor reforms as a solid starting point for the discussion. They are important steps in the right direction but will take time to deliver the expected positive results. The *ensino médio* reform efforts, in particular, are as deep as they are broad. Yet chapters 4, 5, and 6 go on to discuss a formidable agenda of complementary policy changes to the skills development system and labor market programs that could be pursued to raise Brazil's productivity potential by facilitating labor market transitions across employment states.

This is an agenda in three parts. First, to improve learning trajectories for youth, incentives must be provided for completion of upper secondary education (chapter 4), and the workforce development system must be modernized to produce workers with the skills firms are seeking and are likely to seek in the future and enable them to keep pace with the shifting demands of firms in a globally competitive economy (chapter 6). Second, to lengthen spells of employment, labor market incentives created by worker protection structures—such as the statutory minimum wage (*seguro desemprego*) and the unemployment savings accounts (*fundo de garantia por tempo de servico*)—must be improved (chapter 5). Third, to support jobseekers and improve the matches between firms and workers, modern intermediation services must be provided (chapter 6).

While the creation of a new competency-based curriculum and adoption of the full-time school model are important steps, reform efforts must focus on tracking the quality of subnational implementation. Considering courses that foster socioemotional skills among teenagers will pay off with improved skills (such as resilience, empathy, and grit), ensuring a more relevant technical education, through closer partnerships with the private sector, will develop technical skills that are aligned with business needs and ensuring that the full-time school model delivers an extended and high-quality model will pay off with improved learning and reduced school dropouts. These discussions will build on and complement previous analytical mapping of institutional policies in the Brazilian technical education system (Almeida, Amaral, and Felicio 2016). Furthermore, at the federal level, the risk of increased inequities in access to high-quality education posed by the 2017 reform in *ensino médio* creates an opportunity for a new role for the Ministry of Education (MEC) in promoting innovative and cost-effective subnational implementation models that could then be provided with incentives and adopted at scale.

Yet these reform efforts are not enough. Brazil can—and should—do more to take advantage of these reforms to improve learning trajectories among adolescents. At the center of the recommendations offered in chapter 4 are vital reforms of human resources practices for teachers, such as the nationwide creation of a teacher entrance exam, selection of the "best and brightest" for the profession, development of accreditation standards for preservice teacher training programs, and support for a more holistic teacher evaluation system. Such an evaluation system would consider not only proficiency in subject knowledge but also effectiveness in the development of socioemotional skills among students and the use of effective pedagogical practices in the classroom. In addition, there is tremendous scope to rethink the careers of school principals, who are not yet systematically selected based on merit and often lack management and pedagogical preparedness to take up this important leadership position. Chapter 4 also points to the opportunity that is missed by using a world-class system for assessing learning comprehensively but failing to use it systematically to place learning at the center of education policy, as is already common in several OECD countries.

Chapter 4 further recommends the use of complementary interventions to the existing reforms to support completion of *ensino médio*. These policies are designed to increase further the perceived benefits of attending school and/or reduce the direct—and more immediate—costs of attending. Given the large share of GDP already spent on education, the chapter gives special attention to low-cost measures, including school-based interventions to reduce teen pregnancy, the introduction of merit-based scholarships, and the creation of more information campaigns targeted to youth and their families on the returns on education and TVET. Experiences from elsewhere in Latin America and other regions of the world suggest that, if well designed and implemented, such interventions can be cost-effective ways to reduce high school dropout rates.

Chapter 5 argues that the distortions created by a statutory minimum wage can be minimized if future adjustments to its level are made with greater reference to changes in workers' productivity. Although the current adjustment formula is simple and clear, the years of economic contraction showed it to be inflexible and unresponsive to changes in the economy; despite a deep recession and an unemployment rate in the double digits, the federal statutory minimum wage surged upward. This book argues that the formula should be scrutinized and changed to reduce this problem. Chapter 5 also suggests modification of the adjustment policy to encourage more continuous and systematic engagement of stakeholders, with the results of the formula used as the starting point in negotiations to set the minimum wage, rather than being a predetermined, and unquestionable outcome. Additionally, Brazil could consider introducing an age-varying statutory minimum wage for young people 15–24 years of age to lower the distortions to their employment prospects, although similar benefits may eventually be delivered by changes made to the regulation in 2017 that make it easier for employers to hire workers at less than full time and require pro-rata, proportional hourly payment of the minimum wage. An age-differentiated schedule of statutory minimum wage levels has become a feature of leading practice among countries, such as the United Kingdom, that have introduced national statutory minimum wages relatively recently. While the experience of countries with lower–statutory wage floors for younger people has been mixed, the evidence is, on balance, mainly positive.

Brazil should also build on the labor reforms it passed in 2017 by making supportive changes to unemployment protection programs. In the first half of 2017, Brazil legislated changes to its labor market policies[8] designed to give firms greater freedom in how they employ people and organize their workforces, to improve collective bargaining institutions, and to lower the uncertain costs of resolving labor disputes. The government's objective was to increase flexibility, reduce the costs and uncertainty of labor disputes, extend access to worker protection, and, specifically, to make it easier for firms to bring more working women and young people into formal employment.

The 2017 reforms are controversial. Because they make no direct changes to the main policy drivers of labor costs, it is difficult to predict what their impact will be on labor demand and job creation in the short term, given what is still a fragile recovery from the 2015–16 recession. That said, it is reasonable to expect efficiency savings in the medium and long terms. The reform package offers firms and individuals more options to enter regulated and protected work arrangements; provides greater flexibility by shifting weight away from legislation and toward the bargaining table; creates incentives for unions to be more responsive and accountable to members; and lowers the legal uncertainty and other costs of resolving labor disputes.

Reforms should help the labor market create better matches between workers and companies, fewer matches outside the legal framework, and less adversarial workplace relations, and they should help reduce deterrents to investment. While reversal of some measures is always a risk, and an awkward period of adjustment by firms and people to the new rules is to be expected, changes could be made to the parameters of Brazil's "passive" unemployment income support programs—Fundo de Guarantia por Tempo de Servico (FGTS), and Seguro Desemprego—to lower perverse incentives and improve their effectiveness. Chapter 5 of the book presents a specific reform proposal for how Seguro Desemprego could underpin the FGTS and, in doing so, improve incentives and provide fiscal space for more support to lower earners and those who have difficulty finding new jobs. Many of the latter are likely to be younger people with less marketable experience and savvy at navigating transitions from job to job. Policy reform simulations presented in chapter 5 show that the changes we propose could shorten the duration of unemployment, lengthen employment spells, and reduce separations from formal jobs.

Finally, chapter 6 recognizes that more can be done for youth who have either dropped out of the formal schooling system or need to improve their skills by strengthening the delivery of skills development programs. The diagnostic and discussion included in the book show that policy needs to consider targeting groups of adolescents and youth who are already out of the formal schooling system; who have completed degrees but need additional support to quickly find high-productivity jobs; and who are in low-productivity jobs and in need of modern skills-upgrading programs. Taking into account that profiling of these groups is critical for the design and implementation of these policies, chapter 6 makes concrete recommendations for the reform of second-chance programs, orienting them more toward the development of foundational skills and strengthening certification mechanisms to signal to prospective employers that they have relevant skills. In addition, the chapter cites an urgent need to offer employers a more prominent role in the skills development system by strengthening opportunities for on-the-job learning, influencing contents of the curricula, or strengthening teacher training.

Chapter 6 also highlights the potential for making reforms to income support more effective with strengthened active intermediation assistance and targeted demand-side incentives to support better matches between firms and jobseekers. Brazil, like many of its neighbors in Latin America, needs to shift greater public support to labor market intermediation and job search assistance. The lack of emphasis on active labor market support—particularly in these areas—is a weakness of Brazil's approach to labor programs that contributes to youth disengagement. The bias against more active labor measures and job search assistance will need to be corrected to serve better the labor market of a globally integrated economy supportive of innovation. As a start, current spending on wage top ups for people already in formal employment could be shifted to provide incentive for job offers to first-time jobseekers or people who have struggled over a longer than average period of time to find employment.

Labor intermediation services in Brazil require both more resources and modernization. Reforming SINE, the main public provider of these services, is essential to support youth, who rarely have the job search skills or experience necessary to navigate the labor market. OECD countries spend, on average, 10 percent of their active labor market program budgets on placement and related services, resulting in much higher spending as a share of gross national product. Brazil's spending on public employment services barely registers, at .01 percent of GDP (Silva, Almeida, and Strokova 2015). SINE can be strengthened to facilitate job searches and matches by adopting a management approach that is more focused on actual job placements than on simple registrations and search matches.

Fortunately, policymakers in Brazil have a solid base on which to build efficient and effective labor market training programs for market participants. Investing in improving the existing structure of active interventions and bolstering them to focus more on youth will accomplish much in closing the gap for the young. If the new and improved programs are to be successful, however, it will be essential, first, that policies invest more in labor intermediation and job search services as effective, low-cost tools; second, that new emphasis be placed, not just on technical skills, but on building personal skills and hands-on learning; and third, that greater attention be paid to complementary policies for entrepreneurship, in both training and financing aspects.

NOTES

1. World Bank (2018a) analyzes in detail the challenges of low-productivity growth in Brazil and the concepts of labor productivity and total factor productivity (TFP). While related, this book focuses on the challenges to labor productivity growth from the perspective of youth.
2. Brazil, Russia, India, China, and South Africa.
3. Dutz, Almeida, and Packard (2018) point out that, while Chile ranks reasonably well, Brazil ranks 14th in the business environment subindex of the World Economic Forum (WEF) Networked Readiness Index (NRI), which shows enormous potential for reforms to encourage greater adoption of digital technologies. The business environment subindex is constructed using 18 indicators that cover product market policies; skills and labor market policies (including tertiary education and quality of management schools); and technology generation and diffusion support policies.
4. Around the world, concern is growing that technology adoption will have adverse impacts on the labor market—especially on the prospects of the less-skilled workers who may be especially affected—unless the productivity gains from technology adoption generate significant increases in output and employment (Acemoglu and Restrepo 2017 and forthcoming). Some fear the new technologies will reduce manufacturing jobs, especially in emerging economies, thus undermining their main vehicle of economic integration and economic growth (Hallward-Driemeier and Nayyar 2017). Dutz, Almeida, and Packard (2018), however, argue that the potential for technology adoption to generate increases in productivity, output, and employment overall in Latin America more than compensates for employment losses in certain geographical areas, industries, or firms.
5. A country with uncontestable markets is less open to trade and provides greater shelter from competitive forces to its workers and firms. This can allow inefficient, overly costly production to continue and, over time, cause stagnation.
6. Cruces, Ham, and Viollaz (2012) show that for Brazil, spells of unemployment among youth increase the probability of being informally employed and unemployed in early adulthood, but, again, these effects dissipate after the age of 35.

7. Part of the reason is that Sistema S, which offers many of the training courses that are now financed by PRONATEC, also now has to provide courses to the same type of beneficiaries with its own (levy-financed) revenues.

8. Law No. 13.429 on outsourcing (*"Lei da terceirização"*) in March 2017; Law No. 13.446 (*"Rentabilidade de contas FGTS"*) in May 2017; Law No. 13.456 (*"Programa Seguro-Emprego prazo de vigência"*) in June 2017; and Law No. 13.467 on the labor code (*"Reforma trabalhista"*) in July 2017.

REFERENCES

Acemoglu, Daron, and Pascual Restrepo. 2017. "Robots and Jobs: Evidence from US Labor Markets." Working paper 23285, National Bureau of Economic Research, Cambridge, MA.

——. Forthcoming. "Artificial Intelligence, Automation and Work." In *Economics of Artificial Intelligence*, ed. Ajay Agarwal, Avi Godfarb, and Joshua Gans.

Almeida, R., N. Amaral, and F. de Felicio. 2016. "Assessing Advances and Challenges in Technical Education in Brazil." Publication 22726, World Bank, January. https://openknowledge .worldbank.org/handle/10986/22726.

Almeida, R., L. Anazawa, N. Menezes Filho, and L. Vasconcellos. 2015. "Investing in Technical and Vocational Education and Training: Does It Yield Large Economic Returns in Brazil?" Policy Research Working Paper Series 7246. World Bank, Washington, DC.

Almeida, R., and P. Carneiro. 2009. "Enforcement of Labor Regulation and Firm Size." *Journal of Comparative Economics* 37 (1): 28–46.

——. 2012. "Enforcement of Labor Regulation and Informality." *American Economic Journal: Applied Economics* 4 (3): 64–89.Almeida, R., L. Caseiro, A. Maciente, and P. Nascimento. 2018. "Wages and Employability of Higher Education Graduates in Brazil: Evidence from matched employer employee data." Mimeo. IPEA/World Bank.

Almeida, R.K., C. Corseuil, and Jennifer Pamela Poole. 2017. "The Impact of Digital Technologies on Routine Tasks: Do Labor Policies Matter?" Policy Research Working Paper 8187. World Bank, Washington, DC.

Angel-Urdinola, D., and R. Gukovas. 2018. "A Skills-Based Human Capital Framework to Understand the Phenomenon of Youth Economic Disengagement." World Bank Policy Research Paper 8348, Washington, DC: World Bank.

Bassanini, A., and R. Duval. 2006. "The Determinants of Unemployment across OECD Countries: Reassessing the Role of Policies and Institutions." *OECD Economic Studies* 42 (1): 7.

Broecke, Stijn, Alessia Forti, and Marieke Vandeweyer. 2017. "The Effects of Minimum Wages on Employment in Emerging Economies: A Literature Review." *Oxford Development Studies*, 45 (3): 366–91.

Corseuil, C., and R. Botelho. 2014. *Desafios à trajetória profissional dos jovens Brasileiros*. Rio de Janeiro: IPEA. http://www.ipea.gov.br/portal/index.php?option=com_content&view=article &id=23414.

Costa, J., M. Foguel, M. França, and R. Almeida. 2017. "Brazilian Youth Choices: Categorizing and Evaluating the Time Allocation Decisions: Cohort Evidence between 1995 and 2014." Unpublished presentation, World Bank, Washington, DC.

Cruces, G., A. Ham, and M. Viollaz. 2012. "Scarring Effects of Youth Unemployment and Informality: Evidence from Brazil." Mercados laborales el crecimiento inclusivo en América Latina. http://conference.iza.org/conference_files/worldb2012/viollaz_m8017.pdf.

Dix-Carneiro, R., and B. Kovak. 2017. "Trade Liberalization and Regional Dynamics." *American Economic Review* 107 (10): 2908–46.

Dutz, M., R. Almeida, and T. Packard. 2018. "Technology Adoption and Inclusive Growth: Impacts of Digital Technologies on Productivity, Jobs and Skills in Latin America." Mimeo. World Bank.

Fajnzylber, P. 2001. "Minimum Wage Effects throughout the Wage Distribution: Evidence from Brazil's Formal and Informal Sectors." No. 151. Cedeplar, Universidade Federal de Minas Gerais.

Foguel, Miguel, Lauro Ramos, and Francisco Carneiro. 2015. "The Impacts of the Minimum Wage on the Labor Market, Poverty and Fiscal Budget in Brazil" IPEA Discussion Paper No. 108, IPEA: Brasilia and Rio de Janeiro.

Gukovas, R., and U. Kejsefman. 2017. "Pieces of the Disengagement Puzzle." Unpublished presentation and paper, World Bank, Washington, DC.

Gukovas, R., and V. Moreira. 2017. "Scarring Effects of a Poor Early Labor Market Experience: Evidence from Brazil." Unpublished mimeo. World Bank

Kahn, L. M. 2012. "Labor Market Policy: A Comparative View on the Costs and Benefits of Labor Market Flexibility." *Journal of Policy Analysis and Management* 31 (1): 94–110.

Hallward-Driemeier, Mary, and Gaurav Nayyar. 2017. *Trouble in the Making? The Future of Manufacturing-Led Development.* Washington, DC: World Bank.

Jales, H. 2017. "Estimating the Effects of the Minimum Wage in a Developing Country: A Density Discontinuity Design Approach." *Journal of Applied Econometrics* 33 (1): 29–51.

Komatsu, Bruno, and Naercio Menezes-Filho, 2016. "Does the Rise of the Minimum Wage Explain the Fall of Wage Inequality in Brazil?" Policy Paper No. 16, June. INSPER Centro de Politicas Publicas: São Paulo.

Lemos, S. 2009. "Minimum Wage Effects in a Developing Country." *Labour Economics* 16 (2): 224–37.

Machado, Ana Luiza, and Miriam Muller. 2018. "'If It's Already Tough, Imagine for Me…:' A Qualitative Perspective on Youth Out of School and Out of Work in Brazil." Policy Research Working Paper; No. 8358. Washington, DC: World Bank. https://openknowledge.worldbank.org/handle/10986/29424

Messina, Julian, and Joana Silva. 2018. "Wage Inequality in Latin America: Understanding the Past to Prepare for the Future." Latin American Development Forum, World Bank, Washington, DC. https://openknowledge.worldbank.org/handle/10986/28682.

Montenegro, C., and C. Pagés. 2004. "Who Benefits from Labor Market Regulations? Chile, 1960–1998," NBER chapters, in: Law and Employment: Lessons from Latin America and the Caribbean, 401–34. National Bureau of Economic Research, Inc.

——. (2007). "Job Security and the Age-Composition of Employment: Evidence from Chile," Estudios de Economia, University of Chile, Department of Economics, vol. 34 (2 Year 20), December, 109–39.

Montenegro, Claudio E., and Harry Anthony Patrinos. 2014. "Comparable Estimates of Returns to Schooling around the World (English)." Policy Research Working Paper WPS 7020. World Bank, Washington, DC.

Neri, M. C. 2010. *A Educação profissional e você no mercado de trabalho* [Professional Education and You in the Labor Market]. Rio de Janeiro: Instituto Votorantim FGV/CPS.

Neri, Marcelo, Gustavo Gonzaga, and José Márcio Camargo. 2001. "Salário mínimo, 'efeito farol' e pobreza" [Minimum Wage, Lighthouse Effect and Poverty]. *Revista de Economia Politica* 21 (2): 82.

Neumark, D., J. I. Salas, and W. Wascher. 2014. "Revisiting the Minimum Wage—Employment Debate: Throwing Out the Baby with the Bathwater?" *Industrial & Labor Relations Review* 67 (3 suppl): 608–48

OECD (Organisation for Economic Co-operation and Development). 2014. "Investing in Youth in Brazil." http://www.oecd.org/publications/investing-in-youth-brazil-9789264208988-en.htm.

Paes de Barros, R., D. Coutinho, M. de Cuffa, S. Franco, B. Garcia, R. Mendonça, L. Machado, and C. Soares. 2017. "Sustainable Inclusive Growth in Brazil: Past Achievements and Challenges Ahead." Presentation for End of Poverty Day, World Bank Office, Brasilia, October 17.

Packard, T., J. Koettl, and C. Montenegro. 2012. "In from the Shadow: Integrating Europe's Informal Labor." Directions in Development: Human Development. Washington, DC: World Bank.

Rios-Neto, E. 2017. "A Framework for Youth Disengagement in Brazil." Unpublished paper. Washington, DC: World Bank.

Silva, J., R. Almeida, and V. Strokova. 2015. "Sustaining Employment and Wage Gains in Brazil: A Skills and Jobs Agenda." Directions in Development: Human Development. Washington, DC: World Bank. https://openknowledge.worldbank.org/handle/10986/22545.

Ulyssea, Gabriel, and Miguel N. Foguel. 2006. Efeitos do Salário Mínimo Sobre o Mercado de Trabalho Brasileiro. Rio de Janeiro, fevereiro 2006. Texto para discussão 1168, Instituto de Pesquisa Econômica Aplicada (IPEA).

World Bank (2002). *Brazil: Jobs Report*. Social Protection and Labor, Regional Office for Latin America and Caribbean. Washington, DC: World Bank.

——. 2012. *World Development Report 2013: Jobs*. Washington, DC: World Bank

——. 2016. *Brazil: Systematic Country Diagnostic: Retaking the Path to Inclusion, Growth and Sustainability*. Washington, DC: World Bank Group.

——. 2017. *Brazil Expenditure Review*. Washington, DC: World Bank Group.

World Bank. 2018a. *Brazil's Promise: Boosting Productivity for Shared Prosperity*. Washington, DC: World Bank.

——. 2018b. *The Changing Wealth of Nations 2018: Building a Sustainable Future*, ed. Glenn-Marie Lange, Quentin Wodon, and Kevin Carey. Washington, DC: World Bank Group.

——. 2018c. *World Development Report 2018: Learning to Realize Education's Promise*. Washington, DC: World Bank.

.

2 A Skills-Based Framework for Youth Economic Disengagement

ABSTRACT Chapter 1 revisits traditional human capital models and proposes a new conceptual framework of human capital accumulation, anchored in skills development. This framework helps us gain an understanding of youth economic disengagement and its implications for individuals and for the economy in the aggregate. It defines youth economic disengagement as a temporary or permanent state in which individuals, ages 15–29 years old, stop accumulating human capital because of inadequate access to and poor quality of opportunities for skills development in education and work. Complete economic disengagement is a rational choice youth can make when the formal education system and/or work do not contribute to building skills valued by the market and when the costs of economic engagement (that is, of studying and/or working) surpass its benefits. Economic disengagement has lifelong implications that not only constrain future earnings but also undermine prospects for improving productivity and growth.

MORE THAN MINCER AND NOT JUST *NEM-NEMS*

The process of human capital accumulation is a central determinant of economic growth (Acemoglu and Autor 2012; Acemoglu 2009; Goldin and Katz 2007).[1] Traditional human capital models are built on the assumption that an individual's decision to invest in human capital is based on an assessment of the net present value of the costs and benefits of making the investment (Becker 1964; Mincer 1974). In other words, individuals invest in developing their skills—that is, they pay to acquire skills and/or forego earnings—with the expectation of receiving returns on their investments (Veum 1995). People make most skills investments when they are young. This is rational, as foregone earnings are relatively low in early years; also, the earlier the skills investments are made, the longer they can render returns (Ben-Porath 1967; Cunha and Heckman 2007).

Hence, investment decisions made in childhood and youth have long-lasting consequences.

The framework proposes that individual's abilities—innate or acquired—are the result of a series of inputs: the "human capital" production function (Acemoglu and Autor 2012; Acemoglu and Autor 2010; Ben-Porath 1967). Human capital forms in three main arenas. The first is the home, especially for children below school age; the second is school, for school-aged children; and the third is the labor market, where individuals who make partial or complete transitions from education into employment learn through work or on-the-job training (Behrman, De Hoyos, and Székely 2014; Acemoglu and Autor 2012; Hanushek and Woessman 2008; Veum 1995). Taking these channels into account, the number of years of schooling and/or employment experience is considered a standard predictor of individuals' human capital endowments (Krueger and Lindahl 2001; Barro 2001; Barro and Sala-i-Martin 1995).[2]

In the literature, youth economic disengagement is presented as youth who are not in education, employment, or training (NEET) and so are not accumulating human capital. The "NEETs" (or "*nem-nems*") comprise a—perhaps simplistically defined—group of disengaged youth who have long been a concern of policymakers; from a schooling and labor market perspective, they represent both a potentially underutilized human resource and a condition many young people find difficult to overcome, contributing to inequality and social exclusion (De Hoyos, Rogers, and Popova 2013; Bynner and Parsons 2002; Croxford and Raffe 2000).

But emerging evidence indicates that simply capturing access to education and employment, while necessary, is not sufficient to measure adequately human capital accumulation, especially among youth. It is not only the years of schooling or work experience that matters to building human capital. Hanushek and Woesman (2008) and Hanuschek and Zhang (2009), for instance, argue that years of schooling is a poor proxy for human capital, since it undermines both the quality of schooling received and the quality of the skills acquired, whether cognitive, technical, or socioemotional (Cunningham and Villaseñor 2016; Heckman and Rubenstain 2001). Also, while the conventional "Mincerian" wisdom postulates that wages are an increasing and concave function of work experience, recent evidence shows some workers experience wage stagnation or even deteriorating earnings prospects with increasing work experience. This is often explained by the "churning" in modern labor markets (Burdett, Carrillo-Tudela, and Coles 2011).

Based on this more nuanced view of time spent in education and work, the conceptual framework presented in this chapter considers a concept of youth economic disengagement that is a continuum and allows for less extreme stages of disengagement than youth who are out of school and out of work. Here economic disengagement is any state (temporary or permanent) during which individuals stop accumulating human capital. This state can arise from inadequate access to and/or low-quality opportunities for skills development at school and learning through work. Hence, youth who are out of school and out of work comprise just one segment of a larger population of economically disengaged young people—the segment whose disengagement is the most extreme. This larger population of disengaged youth is mostly ignored in the computation of youth disengagement national statistics around the world, and in Brazil. Furthermore, it is often overlooked in policy discussions on how to boost a country's productivity and growth potential.

A SKILLS-BASED HUMAN CAPITAL FRAMEWORK

Building on seminal models of human capital formation and assuming the presence of competitive markets (Becker 1964; Mincer 1974), the optimal choice of human capital accumulation in our conceptual framework is achieved when the marginal benefits of investments in human capital equal their marginal costs. As markets are competitive, an increasing supply of human capital will increase in turn the relative output of skills-intensive activities and, thus, reduce the skills premium enjoyed by educated workers (Goldin and Katz 2007).

Human capital augments effective units of labor and makes workers more productive. At the macro level, the aggregate production of the economy (Y) depends on physical capital (K), human capital (HK) measured as efficiency units of labor, and technology (A) (Goldin and Katz 2007). The production function is assumed to have constant returns to scale on K and HK:

$$Y = f(K, HK, A) \qquad (1)$$

At the micro level, $HK^c(a)$ denotes the human capital accumulated by an individual at age a. The model assumes human capital accumulation occurs throughout life (Behrman, de Hoyos, and Székely 2014; Cunha and Heckman 2007). The stock of human capital accumulated at any given age a, denoted here by $HK^c(a)$, depends on the human capital accumulated until age $a-1$ and on the marginal human capital acquired at age a. In other words, investments made in previous years influence the decisions individuals make concerning human capital investments today. Additionally, the framework allows for the possibility that human capital can deplete at an exogenous rate, ρ_a, which can vary with time.

$$HK_a^C = \rho_a HK_{a-1}^c + HK_a \qquad (2)$$

where $0 < \rho_a < 1$ if $HK_a = 0$ and $\rho_a = 1$ if $HK_a > 0$.

Youth economic disengagement, defined by $dHK_a^C/d_a \leq 0$, reflects a partial or permanent stop in human capital accumulation, during which the stock of human capital remains unchanged and/or depletes. Using the definition of "youth" that is widely used in Brazil, figure 2.1 shows different illustrations of alternative paths for the accumulation of human capital, across ages 15 to 29 years old.

In figure 2.1, a fully engaged individual follows the trajectory of the upper (blue) curve in the figure, accumulating human capital throughout his or her life cycle. This curve represents the "aspirational" norm for youth engagement. The level and shape of this trajectory may, of course, vary across different contexts and individual characteristics, but, in general, it represents a top-performing student who receives a high-quality education before joining the labor market in a rewarding and constructive job that offers opportunities for learning. At the other end of the engagement spectrum is the lower (dotted red) line in the figure, representing an individual who is out of school and out of the labor market, and whose human capital is stagnant throughout his or her life.

While these two extreme cases are a simplistic representation of the reality, they are needed to keep the model tractable.[3] In between these two extreme disengagement states are intermediate stages encompassing youth who are in the formal school system but enrolled in low-quality education or training institutions, youth who are out of school and holding first-time jobs in the informal

FIGURE 2.1

Heuristic illustration of youth economic engagement and disengagement paths

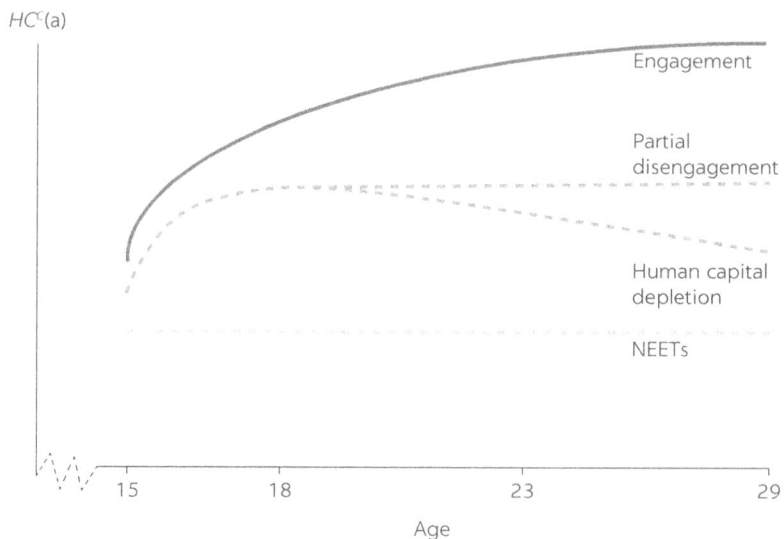

Sources: Angel-Urdinola and Gukovas 2018, and Rios-Neto 2017.

FIGURE 2.2

Portraits of youth disengagement from a skills and jobs perspective

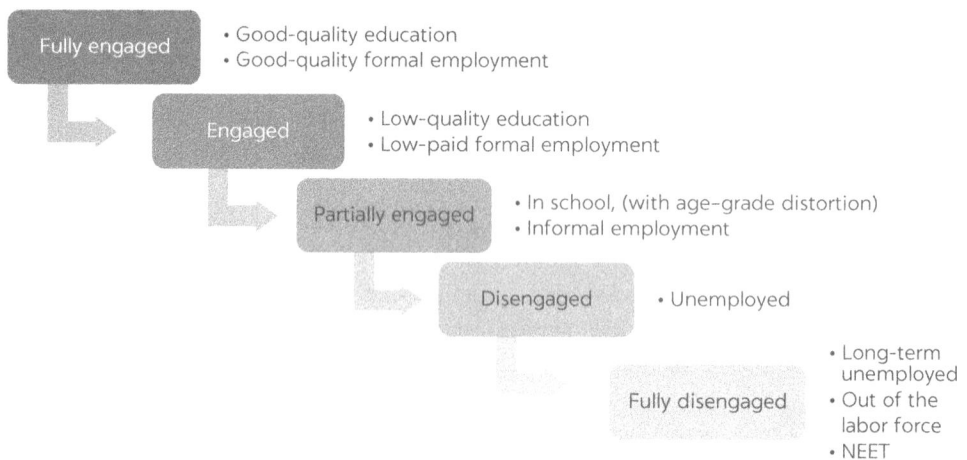

Sources: Angel-Urdinola and Gukovas 2018, and Rios-Neto 2017.

sector and/or with temporary contracts, and youth who are holding jobs for which they are not qualified. The two black dotted lines in figure 2.2 document this range of possibilities. Understanding these different states and the factors that generate them is essential to determining the education and labor market policies that might bring individuals closer to the aspirational norm of full economic engagement.

Table 2.1 offers some examples of different stages of youth disengagement, at school and/or in the labor market, across different age ranges. Across columns it reports different "stages" of engagement, from full school and labor engagement to full disengagement, and including intermediate stages. Going beyond school

TABLE 2.1 **Alternative types of youth engagement, by age**

AGE RANGE	FULLY ENGAGED	PARTIAL ENGAGEMENT I	PARTIAL ENGAGEMENT II	DISENGAGED
15–17 years	Attending high school without age–grade distortion; learning at proficiency levels for all types of skills	Attending high school without age–grade distortion; starting an apprenticeship program	Attending lower secondary school with some age–grade distortion and learning trajectories with cumulative deficiencies	Out of school with incomplete secondary school; either out of work or in a low-quality job
18–23 years	High school graduate attending a high-quality higher education course; doing an internship program	High school graduate attending a low-quality (likely private) university; working at a full-time job	Attending high school with age–grade distortion or attending a second-chance program; having a first labor market experience in a temporary/low-quality job	School dropout with incomplete secondary; either out of work or in a low-quality job
24–29 years	Tertiary graduate in a full-time job (white-collar) in the private sector (large firm) or as public servant	Tertiary degree; full-time worker, potentially white collar in any private sector firm; working less than full time	High school graduate (low-quality public school or second-chance program); in temporary or low-paid job (even if formal)	Incomplete secondary school; either out of work or in a low-quality job

Notes: In Brazil, apprenticeship programs are regulated by the Apprenticeship Law ("*Lei do Aprendiz*"). An apprentice has a paid formal labor contract and pays lower taxes than a full-time worker; the apprenticeship must, however, be tied to a registered technical course and aim to provide on-the-job experience. Individuals should have a maximum daily commitment of six hours of work and time in the technical course combined, and apprentices who have not yet completed upper secondary school must be enrolled in school. An internship, which can be paid or unpaid, is regulated by the Internship Law and is arranged by a formal contract associated with a tertiary-level degree. An intern must be enrolled in a tertiary institution and should not have more than six hours of work per day. For a discussion, see Marra et al. 2015.

attendance and labor market participation, it proposes some of the actual school and labor market characteristics influencing learning (in school or at work) that influence the extent of human capital accumulation throughout life. For teenagers between the ages of 15 and 17, for example, the degree of age–grade distortion (that is, students are older than they should be for the grades they are in) signals learning challenges in school, while for young adults ages 18–23, attendance at a high-quality university will potentially provide skills that are of value to the labor market. In the work arena, an internship that complements what the student is learning in the forma classroom is potentially better than being unemployed or an holding an informal, low productivity job, where the opportunities for on the job training are reduced.

Maximizing the utility function

Individual wages, w_a, are determined by the market price and the individual's human capital at any given age a, denoted by a_a. Individuals need to be employed to render wages:[4]

$$w_a = \alpha_a HK_{a-1}^C \qquad (3)$$

In every period, individuals can choose to study, work, or stay idle. The number of hours spent in formal education and working, denoted by h_a^e and h_a^l, respectively, are bound by a time constraint H. Domestic activities and house care have an hourly cost, denoted by P_a. Individuals who study or work need to bear this cost. With a discount rate, δ_a, in every period, individuals maximize their utility function, determined by a vector of consumption items, C_a, over their life cycles, subject to their maximum disposable income, E_a:

$$Max \sum_{a_{min}}^{a_{max}} \delta_a U\left(C_a, h_a^l\right) \ s.t. \begin{cases} C_a \leq E_a \\ h_a^e + h_a^l \leq H \end{cases} \text{for every } a, \qquad (4)$$

where

$$E_a = y_a - p_d \left(h_a^e + h_a^l \right) \qquad (5)$$

Individual income, y_a, consists of the individual's wages, if employed, plus other income, denoted by y_o, from such external sources as family allocations and government transfers:

$$y_a = w_a h_a^l + y_o \qquad (6)$$

Solving the previous maximization model, we find that

$$\delta_a \frac{\partial U}{\partial C_a} w_a + \delta_a \frac{\partial U}{\partial h_a^l} = \sum_{t>a}^{a_{max}} \delta^t \frac{\partial U}{\partial C_t} h_t^l \left(\frac{\partial w_t}{\partial h_a^e} - \frac{\partial w_t}{\partial h_a^l} \right) \text{ for every } a. \qquad (7)$$

Equation (7) indicates individuals' optimal allocation of time between study and work. The left side of the equation denotes the marginal utility gain the person obtains when working. For every additional hour worked, the individual gets paid more, consumes more, and, ultimately, gains utility from such consumption. The right side indicates an individual's optimal choice will be to work one extra hour if the expected increase in future wages from doing so is larger than the expected increase in future wages for an extra hour of education.

To understand individuals' decisions better, one can use equation (3) to express changes in their marginal wages as a function of their human capital and its labor market value:

$$\frac{\partial w_t}{\partial h_a^j} = \alpha \frac{\partial HK_t^C}{\partial h_a^j} = \alpha \prod_{i=a}^{t} \rho_i \frac{\partial HK_t}{\partial h_a^j}, \text{ where } j = \{e, l\}. \qquad (8)$$

Substituting (8) into (7), we have that

$$\frac{\partial HK_a}{\partial h_a^e} B = \delta_a \frac{\partial U}{\partial C_a} w_a + \delta_a \frac{\partial U}{\partial h_a^l} + \frac{\partial HK_a}{\partial h_a^l} B, \qquad (9)$$

where $B = \sum_{t>a}^{a_{max}} \left(\delta^t \frac{\partial U}{\partial C_t} w_t \alpha \prod_{i=a}^{t} \rho_i \right)$ epresents the discounted present value of future consumption purchased through future wages. The left-hand side of equation (9) represents the marginal lifelong benefits from studying an extra hour.

The decision only to study

Looking at equation (9), an individual will choose to study only if the following are true:

a) The marginal return on human capital from studying is greater than that from working.
b) The individual expects to be rewarded for this investment in the future, when the skills acquired in education will render higher wages when the individual chooses to work (so that $B > 0$).
c) The individual can afford to forego wages today while paying the price of domestic care and consuming (y_0 is large enough).

When individuals are young and have not yet learned the basic skills that are acquired though education, the decision only to study is clearly their best option.

If the quality of education is good enough for individuals to increase their human capital, which will be rewarded in the future, and if the transfers are enough to provide for consumption and bear their costs of care, they will remain only in school.

The decision to start working

Equation (9) provides some intuitive information about when individuals choose to join the labor market:

a) When the potential gains from working an extra hour become larger than the gains from studying an extra hour

b) If w_a becomes attractive enough so that the utility brought by the consumption is larger than the disutility of an extra hour of work

c) When the present restrictions require the individual to enter the labor market— that is, if y_0 becomes insufficient to pay for the minimum consumption and care

The decision to quit school

Still regarding equation (9), individuals will choose to leave school if the following are true:

a) The marginal gain in human capital from an extra hour of work is greater than that from an extra hour of study.

b) The marginal gain in human capital from an extra hour of study is greater than that from an extra hour of work, but y_0 is small, and w_a and p_d are large.[5]

c) The individual does not receive enough returns in the future on the accumulation of human capital through education to compensate for foregone consumption today—that is, B is close to zero.

The decision to become a nem-nem

After individuals drop out of school, they will choose to work if one or more of the following are true:

a) The discounted expected wages are more than enough to pay the expected value of domestic care.

b) The individual expects to receive enough returns on the accumulation of human capital through employment in the future to compensate for the foregone consumption today.

c) Transfers are large enough that individuals can afford to work with wages that are lower than the cost of domestic care while still accumulating human capital.

If at least one of these three conditions is not satisfied, individuals are better off being NEETs.

Disengaged employment

Individuals may choose to work even if they do not gain any human capital from doing so. This will occur if, in any period a, given the individuals' human capital, the wages obtained would allow them to consume more than if they stay idle. A final implication of the framework is that, even if conditions are completely adverse, individuals may be forced to work to be able to afford some minimum level of consumption.

The human capital production function

The production function individuals face when making human capital investment decisions is a complex system of technical, institutional, and price factors that determine what inputs contribute to skills development. This framework assumes human capital is mainly formed through education and acquisition of skills on the job and the ways in which these combine and augment a person's intrinsic ability. The returns on these inputs (that is, their marginal products) depend on several exogenous factors at the individual/family level (such as health and nutrition), community level (such as quality of available infrastructure), and macro level (such as government policies, technology, and public spending; Behrman, Hoyos, and Székely 2014; Ben-Porath 1967). In such a context, the human capital production function can be described as follows:

$$HK(a) = f\left(E\left(h_a^e, \gamma_a\right), L\left(h_a^l, \gamma_a\right), U(\gamma_a)\right),$$ (11)

where $E\left(h_a^e, \gamma_a\right)$ denotes the skills acquired through formal education, $L\left(h_a^l, \gamma_a\right)$ denotes the skills acquired through employment experience, and γ_a is a set of exogenous factors at the individual, family, community, and macro levels that influence the skills development process. The model assumes education and employment are imperfect substitute-factor inputs in the production function. In other words, formal education cannot fully develop the skills individuals can acquire while in the labor market, and vice versa. Finally, U denotes the individual's intrinsic ability, which is assumed to be age invariant.

Human capital accumulation through formal education

The framework here assumes being in school is a necessary but not sufficient condition for human capital accumulation through formal education. As expressed by equation (3), human capital accumulation contributes to increasing the individual's earnings only if education attainment contributes to the improvement of the individual's skills set. In other words, human capital accumulation through formal education occurs only if the system has the capacity to promote additional cognitive, technical, and socioemotional skills, denoted respectively by s_c^e, s_t^e, s_s^e:

$$E\left(h_a^e, \gamma_a\right) = f\left(s_j^e\left(h_a^e, \gamma_a\right)\right); j = \{c, t, s\},$$ (12)

as formalized by Glewwe and Kremer (2006); in the context of formal education, skills development follows a production function that depends on an individual's completed years of education, the quality of school inputs, and schooling prices. Hence,

$$s_j^e\left(h_a^e, \gamma_a\right) = f\left[YS(a), Q(\gamma_a, EP), I(\gamma_a), H(\gamma_a), P(\gamma_a, EP)\right]; j = \{c, t, s\},$$ (13)

where YS denotes the years of completed education, Q represents education quality, I and H represent student and household characteristics, respectively, and *P* represents the price of schooling. The quality of school inputs is influenced by exogenous factors (γ_a). Additionally, school inputs *Q* and schooling price *P* are also influenced by education-specific policies, denoted by *EP*.

Human capital accumulation through work experience

Standard models assume every year of work experience increases human capital (Becker 1964; Mincer 1974). Such increases, however, slow down with age, following a concave pattern throughout the worker's employment cycle (Rubinstein and Weiss 2007). The classical approach assumes labor market experience (*l*) could help workers develop firm-specific skills, s^l_f, as well as other cognitive, technical, and socioemotional skills, denoted respectively by s^l_c, s^l_t, s^l_s:

$$L\left(h^l_a, \gamma_a\right) = f\left(s^l_j\left(h^l_a, \gamma_a\right)\right); j = \{f, c, t, s\}. \tag{14}$$

A worker's decision to change jobs will occur when, for a similar level of human capital, the new job offers a higher human capital rental value. Workers who enter unemployment and become economically disengaged experience human capital decumulation (deterioration). Employed and unemployed workers receive job offers per a Poisson process with parameter $\tau_E > 0$. Job destruction shocks bring individuals into unemployment according to a Poisson process with parameter $\tau_U > 0$. A job offer with a higher rental value will contribute to increasing the worker's wage.

While jobs provide workers with wages, having a job may not be a sufficient condition for human capital development if the job does not contribute, over time, to building the worker's skills set. In this context, a worker's capacity to build skills through employment experience can be formalized as follows:

$$\begin{aligned} s^e_j\left(h^l_a, \gamma_a\right) = f\Big[&YOE(a), T(a, LP, EP), \tau^a_E\left(\gamma_a, LP\right), \\ &\tau^a_U\left(\gamma_a, LP, K\right), IT\left(\gamma_a, P_{IT}\right)\Big] \text{ for } j = \{f, c, t, s\}, \end{aligned} \tag{15}$$

where *YOE* denotes the worker's years of experience, *T* denotes the quality and relevance of training provided to the worker by the firm, *IT* denotes the firm's investments in technology, P_{IT} denotes the price of technology, and *K* denotes a worker's contract security (for example, no contract versus fixed term versus open ended). *LP* and *EP* denote labor and education policies, respectively. Implicitly, equation (15) suggests workers' skills development through employment experience occurs when jobs provide adequate training opportunities along the course of their careers; if workers move up into better jobs; and if they are less exposed to job destruction shocks.

Equation (15) contains other important messages. First, job creation and job destruction shocks can vary over time and depend on exogenous factors at the individual, family, community/sector, and macro levels. Second, the quality of training provided by the firms, as well as job creation and destruction shocks, are influenced by the worker's contract type as well as by labor and training policies, such as labor regulation, minimum wage policy, and regulation of technical and vocational education and planning (TVET) and apprenticeships.

HOW THE ANALYTICAL FRAMEWORK INFORMS POLICYMAKING

Several features of this conceptual framework are pertinent to rethinking the design of education and labor policies in Brazil for youth to encourage a more relevant skills development process.

First, the risk of youth economic disengagement can arise even when individuals are studying or working if they are not building skills that are valued in the workplace. Indeed, individuals can study and work for long periods of time and face a complete stagnation in their human capital development. This occurs primarily if the formal education system and labor market do not contribute to building skills and competencies that are valued in the labor market. Therefore, simply observing only individuals' time allocation is insufficient to determine their potential level of engagement. A population with a low proportion of NEETs may still have a high likelihood of engagement, and ultimately face stagnant productivity, if workers and students do not have opportunities to continue acquiring skills.

Second, policies and programs that support higher levels of economic engagement, in school and work, are best implemented as early in the life of beneficiaries as possible, and even before adolescence years. On the one hand, early investments in human capital formation have the potential to bring returns for a longer time horizon, throughout the individuals' productive lives (added output effect). On the other, the increased marginal return of an additional hour invested may change individuals' time allocation, increasing even more their human capital (substitution effect). This book focuses mainly on the process of human capital accumulation, and the decisions involved in this process, for teenagers and young adults. Describing it as a dynamic model, however, also acknowledges that the process begins much earlier. Cunha and Heckman (2007) and Heckman (2011) have already shown the importance of early childhood development throughout the entire process of human capital formation.

Third, even if study and work are contributing to the development of individual's human capital, they may choose to drop out of school or quit work if the costs of engagement are higher than the benefits. Individuals may drop out of school, for instance, if their income is insufficient to meet their consumption needs. In such cases, they choose to forego future utility to consume today. The framework also suggests entering the NEET state is a rational decision made by some individuals. This happens when, for given human capital endowments, the returns on employment are low, and the income available to them allows them more utility than if they were employed. Those individuals who are employed can have their utility reduced (compared to those out of work) because of the hours actually worked, and they may also bear a cost of home care. This case is particularly relevant for women with low levels of human capital, who often account for the largest segment of the youth NEET population. It is also relevant for teenagers and young adults who have ceased to accumulate human capital in school and face a labor market that offers low wages and no learning opportunities, while still counting on transfers from parents or the government.

In addition, the framework shows that the returns on investments in human capital diminish when the individual does not anticipate working in the future. Moreover, it shows individuals choose not to work when wages are low, the cost of home care is high, and they have enough income transfers to cover the costs of their consumption and domestic care duties. Considering these two facts, policies that improve labor market conditions, raise earnings, and reduce the cost of home care will have a direct impact on the incentives to engage the current adult population. They will also indirectly increase the investment in human capital of the younger generation by offering them incentives to invest.

A last implication is that policies can make a critical difference to whether time allocated to education or work directly contributes to the actual development of human capital. In the case of education, policymakers should look beyond school enrollment to focus as well on ensuring the quality of learning is adequate, that what is taught in schools and universities is valued by the market, and that access to education remains affordable. In the case of work, policies that encourage firms to contract with workers formally, deliver relevant on-the-job training, and support the use of new technologies that increase workers' productivity will affect the individual investments. In addition, policies that ensure faster transitions across jobs and are supported by incentive-compatible and financially sustainable consumption-smoothing (insurance or savings) instruments, job intermediation, and job search support services are also important.

NOTES

1. This chapter of the book draws heavily on Angel-Urdinola and Gukovas (2018), and Rios-Neto (2017).
2. The literature has often measured human capital as the present value of the labor incomes that could be expected to be generated over the lifetimes of the people currently living, given their levels of education and experience (Jorgenson and Fraumeni 1989, 1992a, 1992b).
3. The new qualitative work developed for this book by Machado and Muller (2018) documents wide diversity in these categories. Not all "nem-nem" youth, for instance, are necessarily in extreme forms of idleness.
4. The value of the parameter α_a depends on contextual variables affecting labor productivity and price, such as labor market regulation, sector of specialization, factor technology, and other macroeconomic conditions.
5. Recall that $h_a^e \leq H - h_a^l$, and $C_a \leq w_a h_a^l + y_0 - p_d\left(h_a^e + h_a^l\right)$ for every a. They are equal when the restrictions are binding.

REFERENCES

Acemoglu, D. 2009. *Introduction to Modern Economic Growth*. Princeton and New York: Princeton University Press.

Acemoglu, D., and D. Autor. 2010. "Skills, Tasks and Technologies: Implications for Employment and Earnings." In *Handbook of Labor Economics* 4B, edited by David Card and Orley Ashenfelter, 1043–71. San Diego and Amsterdam, North-Holland: Elsevier.

———. 2012. "What Does Human Capital Do? A Review of Goldin and Katz's *The Race between Education and Technology*." *Journal of Economic Literature* 50 (2): 426–63.

Angel-Urdinola, D., and R. Gukovas. 2018. "A Skills-Based Human Capital Framework to Understand the Phenomenon of Youth Economic Disengagement." World Bank Policy Research Paper 8348, Washington, DC: World Bank.

Barro, R. J. 2001. "Human Capital and Growth." *American Economic Review* 91 (2): 12–17.

Barro, R. J., and X. Sala-i-Martin. 1995. *Economic Growth*. New York: McGraw-Hill.

Becker, G. 1964. *Human Capital: A Theoretical and Empirical Analysis with Special Reference to Education*. Chicago, IL: University of Chicago Press.

Behrman, J., R. de Hoyos, and M. Székely. 2014. "Out of School and Out of Work: A Conceptual Framework for Investigating 'Ninis' in Latin America and the Caribbean." Background paper for the regional study, "Out of School and Out of Work: Challenges and Solutions around the Ninis in Latin America." World Bank, Washington, DC.

Ben-Porath, Y. 1967. "The Production of Human Capital and the Life Cycle of Earnings." *Journal of Political Economy* 75 (4, part 1): 352–65.

Burdett, K., C. Carrillo-Tudela, and M. G. Coles. 2011. "Human Capital Accumulation and Labor Market Equilibrium." *International Economic Review* 52 (3): 657–77.

Bynner, J., and S. Parsons. 2002. "Social Exclusion and the Transition from School to Work: The Case of Young People Not in Education, Employment or Training." *Journal of Vocational Behavior* 60: 289–309.

Croxford, L., and D. Raffe. 2000. "Young People Not in Education, Employment or Training: An Analysis of the Scottish School Leavers Survey." Report to Scottish Executive, Edinburgh: CES, University of Edinburgh.

Cunha, F., and J. Heckman. 2007. "The Technology of Skill Formation." *American Economic Review* 97 (2): 31–47

Cunningham, W., and P. Villaseñor. 2016. "Employer Voices, Employer Demands, and Implications for Public Skills Development Policy Connecting the Labor and Education Sectors." *World Bank Research Observer* 31 (1): 102–34.

De Hoyos, R., H. Rogers, and A. Popova. 2013 "Out of School and Out of Work: A Diagnostic of Ninis in Latin America." Background paper for the regional study, "Out of School and Out of Work: Challenges and Solutions around the Ninis in Latin America." World Bank, Washington, DC.

Glewwe, P., and M. Kremer. 2006. "Schools, Teachers, and Education Outcomes in Developing Countries." In *Handbook of the Economics of Education* 1, edited by E. Hanushek and F. Welch. Amsterdam, North-Holland: Elsevier.

Goldin, C., and L. F. Katz. 2007. "Long Run Changes in the Wage Structure: Narrowing, Widening, Polarizing." *Brookings Papers on Economic Activity* 2: 135–65.

Hanushek, E., and L. Zhang. 2009. "Quality-Consistent Estimates of International Schooling and Skill Gradients." *Journal of Human Capital* 3 (2): 107–43.

Hanushek, E. A., and L. Woessmann. 2008. "The Role of Cognitive Skills in Economic Development." *Journal of Economic Literature* 46 (3): 607–68.

Heckman, J., and Y. Rubenstein. 2001. "The Importance of Noncognitive Skills: Lessons from the GED Testing Program." *American Economic Review* 91 (2): 145–9.

Heckman, J. J. 2011. "The Economics of Inequality: The Value of Early Childhood Education." *American Educator* 35 (1): 31.

Jorgenson, D. W., and B. M. Fraumeni. 1989. "The Accumulation of Human and Non-Human Capital, 1948–1984." In *The Measurement of Savings, Investment, and Wealth*, edited by R. E. Lipsey and H. S. Tice. Chicago: University of Chicago Press.

——. 1992a. "Investment in Education and U.S. Economic Growth." *Scandinavian Journal of Economics* 94 (suppl.): 51–70.

——. 1992b. "The Output of the Education Sector." In *Output Measurement in the Service Sectors*, ed. Z. Griliches. Chicago: University of Chicago Press.

Krueger, A. B., and M. Lindahl. 2001. "Education for Growth: Why and for Whom?" *Journal of Economic Literature* 39 (4): 1101–36.

Machado, Ana Luiza, and Miriam Muller. 2018. "'If It's Already Tough, Imagine for Me...:' A Qualitative Perspective on Youth Out of School and Out of Work in Brazil." Policy Research Working Paper 8358, World Bank, Washington, DC. https://openknowledge.worldbank.org/handle/10986/29424.

Marra, K., J. Luz, J. Silva, and R. Gukovas. 2015. "Mapping of the Current Network of Active Labor Market Programs (ALMPs)." Policy report. World Bank, Washington, DC.

Mincer, J. 1974. "Schooling, Experience and Earnings." New York: National Bureau of Economic Research.

Rios-Neto, E. 2017. "A Framework for Youth Disengagement in Brazil." Unpublished paper. World Bank, Washington, DC.

Rubinstein, Y., and Y. Weiss. 2007. "Post Schooling Wage Growth: Investment, Search and Learning." In *Handbook of the Economics of Education* 1, edited by Eric A. Hanushek and Finis Welch. Amsterdam, North-Holland: Elsevier.

Veum, J. 1995. "Training, Wages, and the Human Capital Model." Bureau of Labor Statistics Working Paper 262. U.S. Department of Labor, Washington DC, https://www.bls.gov/ore/pdf/ec950160.pdf.

3 The Youth School-to-Work Transitions, and Challenges Ahead

ABSTRACT The risk of youth disengagement in Brazil goes well beyond the large—and recently increasing—numbers who are out of school and out of work. Today, more than 60 percent of Brazilian youth 15 years of age start *ensino médio* with significant learning gaps and high age–grade distortion rates. These deficient learning trajectories across a range of competencies often start during *ensino fundamental*, or even earlier in the life cycle, and are never reversed by a low quality public education system. In addition, the risk of school and work disengagement continues throughout life, with high rates of informal employment among the younger segment of the youth population. Furthermore, youth in the labor market are subject to important "scarring effects," sustained over time, from early periods of inactivity. The present holds reasons to be concerned about the future. The patterns of falling youth informality and the lessening likelihood of being both out of school and out of work began reversing with the financial crisis of 2015–16. Furthermore, the trend of falling returns to education and the misperceptions among youth of the actual returns to education likely reduce further the incentives of youth to undertake further investments in education.

THE RISK OF YOUTH DISENGAGEMENT: BEYOND THE STATUS OF OUT OF SCHOOL AND OUT OF WORK

The concept of youth disengagement proposed in the previous chapter goes beyond the status of being out of school and out of work to capture the lack of human capital accumulation even while in school and/or working.[1] This broader concept of being at risk of disengagement includes youth who are in school but already have delays in learning and some level of age–grade distortion and, thus, are unlikely to be acquiring the right competencies for an increasingly competitive labor market. These youth do not necessarily end up both out of school and out of work, but they are still settling for less than their optimal potential; they are forced to accept lower-paying jobs or join the informal labor market, or they actively look for jobs but are unable to find them. Broadening the focus of education and labor market reforms to include the less-than-fully-engaged segments of society beyond those within the out-of-school and out-of-work category is crucial to achieving real advances in Brazilian youth engagement.

Table 3.1 reports several trends in basic statistics on youth disengagement between 2004 and 2015, using the Brazilian national household survey, *Pesquisa Nacional por Amostra de Domicílios* (PNAD).[2] The table shows that, as of 2015, 52.2 percent of youth could be considered at risk of disengagement, as

TABLE 3.1 School and labor market engagement of Brazilian youth, 2004–15

Percent

	2004 (1)	2015 (2)
Share of population 15–29 years old in total population that are:	27.2	23.5
Studying only	19.0	22.0
School–age gap (*)	36.5	21.3
Studying and working	15.4	11.5
Informal (*)	64.9	51.7
Wage < minimum wage	43.4	37.6
Out of school and out of work (*)	20.2	23.2
Active	32.1	36.3
Inactive	67.9	63.7
Working only	45.4	43.3
Informal (*)	54.1	42.3
Wage < minimum wage	28.6	20.1
Disengaged youth, of which:	61.7	52.2
Males	46.5	48.2
Females	53.5	51.8
Teen moms, disengaged	80.6	73.5

Sources: Based on *Pesquisa Nacional por Amostra de Domicílios* (PNAD); IBGE 2004–15.
Notes: "Working only" refers to the share of youth who only worked during the reference period. "Informal without *carteira assinada*" is the share of youth who only worked in jobs without *carteira assinada* (employees without *carteira assinada*, domestic workers without *carteira assinada*, self-employed, self-employed in production for their own consumption, construction workers for their own use, unpaid workers, and workers who did not declare the type of occupation). "Wage < minimum wage" is the share of youth working (only) with monthly wages below the minimum wage. "Studying only" is the share of youth who only attended school. Age–grade distortion is defined for students ages 15–29 years as the difference between current age (measured as of March 31, of the reference year) and the appropriate age for the grade in which he or she was enrolled. "Studying and working" is the share of youth who worked and attended school. "Out of school and out of work" are the share of youth that does not work or attend school. "Active out of school and out of work" are those out of school and out of work that searched for jobs in the reference period. "Inactive out of school and out of work" did not search for jobs. "Disengaged youth" are the youth 15 to 29 years old that (1) work in the informal sector (regardless of only working or also studying), (2) only attends school, but are lagging in learning (with a school-age gap) and, (3) do not work or attend school (are out of school and out of work, regardless of being active or inactive). These statistics are denoted with (*). "Teen-moms, disengaged" is the proportion of teenage mothers that are disengaged. Teenage mothers are those less than 18 years old by the time of birth of the last child born alive.

they were out of school and out of work or in school or working but failing to acquire relevant human capital for high-productivity jobs. It also reports the breakdown of disengaged youth across different groups for 2004 and 2015, respectively. Drawing on the conceptual framework in chapter 2, we define disengaged youth as those 15–29 years old who are out of school and out of work or are working in the informal sector (either only working and not attending school or doing both) and those who attend school but have some age–grade distortion (all denoted by (*) in the table). We consider out of school and out of work those who are not working and not attending school, whether or not they are searching for a job.

The overall risk of becoming disengaged from school or work fell by almost 10 percentage points in the decade between 2004 and 2015. Table 3.1 shows that this fall in the likelihood of being disengaged is driven by two factors. First, Brazilian youth today are more likely to be only studying than ever before. The share of those only studying increased from 19 percent to 22 percent from 2004 to 2015. Furthermore, the age–grade distortion rate has also improved. In 2004, 36.5 percent of youth had some age–grade distortion; by 2015, this had dropped to 21.3 percent.

This progress, however, hides some heterogeneity across education levels. While the average age–grade distortion rate for those students still attending *ensino fundamental* (until grade 9) decreased (from 59 percent in 2004 to 56.4 percent in 2015), for those in *ensino médio*, it rose slightly, by 3 percentage points. This change was likely driven by the increased access to *ensino médio* and the likely lower ability of the (new) entering students, leading to an increase in the average age–grade distortion rate. Second, when working, Brazilian youth are now significantly less likely to be informal workers (or to hold low-paid jobs, defined as jobs paying monthly wages below the minimum).

The increased access to school has benefited most the youngest and the most vulnerable youth. Costa et al. (2017a) have documented patterns in how youth in Brazil have allocated their time since 1995. They found a substantial change, with an overall increase in time spent attaining education. Figure 3.1 shows the changes in time allocation nationwide for youth of different ages. Among the youngest subset, ages 15 to 17, the likelihood of "studying only" increased by

FIGURE 3.1

Time allocation of Brazilian youth, 1995 and 2015

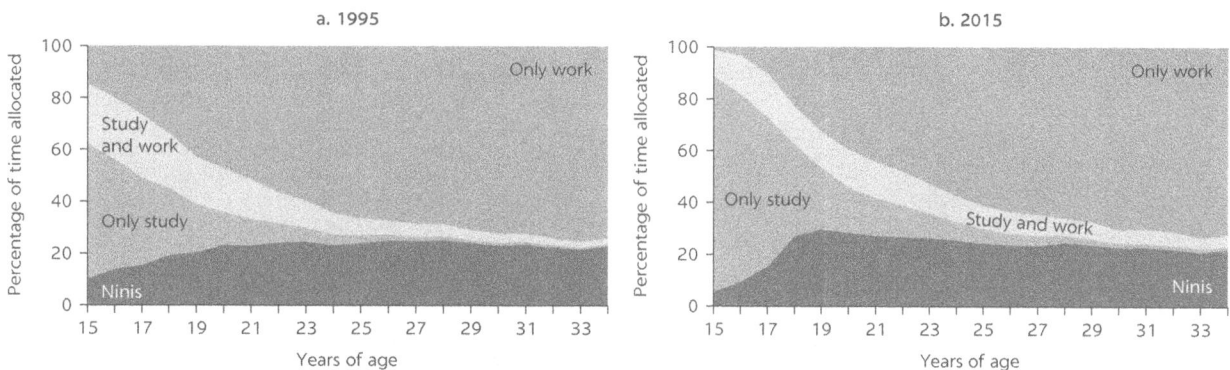

Source: Costa et al. 2017a, based on *Pesquisa Nacional por Amostra de Domicílios* (PNAD), 1995 and 2015.
Notes: For comparability, data do not include households in rural areas of the northern region. "Only study" represents students who do not hold formal or informal jobs; "Only work" represents youth who are not enrolled in school but hold formal or informal employment.

24 to 31 percentage points in the two decades leading up to 2015. The share of this youngest group who "only work[ed]" decreased by 14 to 17 percentage points. This important progress was especially pronounced among the most vulnerable of the youngest group, defined as black women between the ages of 15 and 17 with age–grade distortion, in the first income quintile, living in the rural area of Brazil's northeast region. As shown in figure 3.2, these young people became significantly more likely to be only studying, with that percentage more than doubling, from 21 percent in 1995 to 55 percent in 2015.

The risk of disengagement among youth also fell because of the decreasing likelihood of their holding informal contracts, and, until around 2008, the decreasing probability of their being both out of school and out of work, as shown in figure 3.3, panel a. This decline was mainly driven by the performance of women, whose share of idle youth fell from 31 percent in 1995 to 27 percent in 2008, as seen in figure 3.3, panel c. In contrast, for men, the out-of-school and out-of-work rate remained constant over this same period (figure 3.3, panel b). Table 3.1 reports that, of all youth ages 15–29 who only worked in 2015 (20.8 million), 42.3 percent (8.8 million) did so informally and 20.1 percent (4.2 million) for less than the minimum wage. This is an improvement from 2004, when the rates of youth informality and below–minimum wage work with respect to the working-only youth population were 54.1 percent and 28.6 percent, respectively. This progress is important, as these jobs, while not paying well, also very rarely provide the opportunity for youth to build necessary skills for better jobs later in life, leaving a substantial number of those who only work lacking the human and financial capital they so badly need.

FIGURE 3.2

Change in time allocation for youth ages 15–17, by vulnerability group

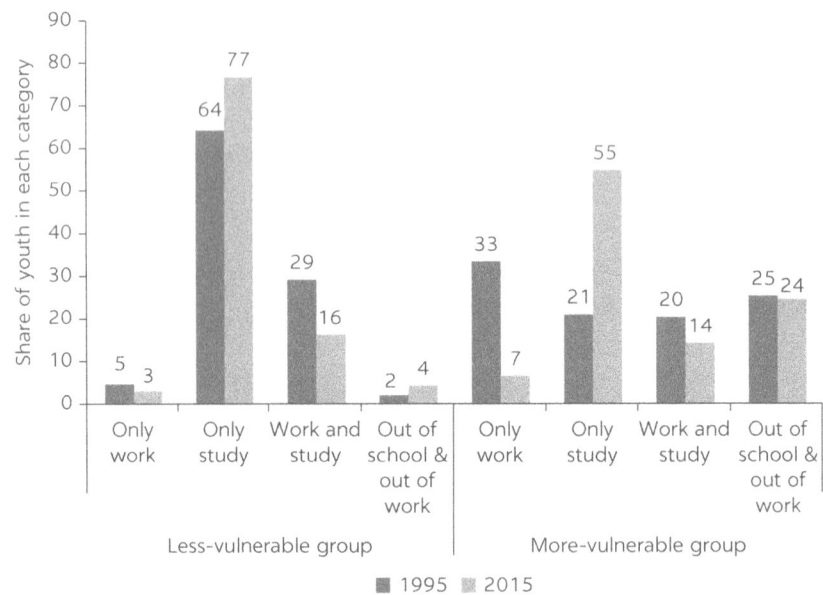

Source: Costa et al. 2017a.
Notes: For comparability, data do not include households in rural areas of the northern region. The "Out of school & out of work" category represents youth who are not engaged in education, employment, or training. The less-vulnerable group comprises men who are white, without age-grade-distortion, in the fifth income quintile, urban, and from the southeast region. The more-vulnerable group comprises women who are black, with age-grade distortion, in the first income quintile, rural, and from the northeast region.

FIGURE 3.3

Brazilian youth out of school and out of work by age and gender, 1995-2015

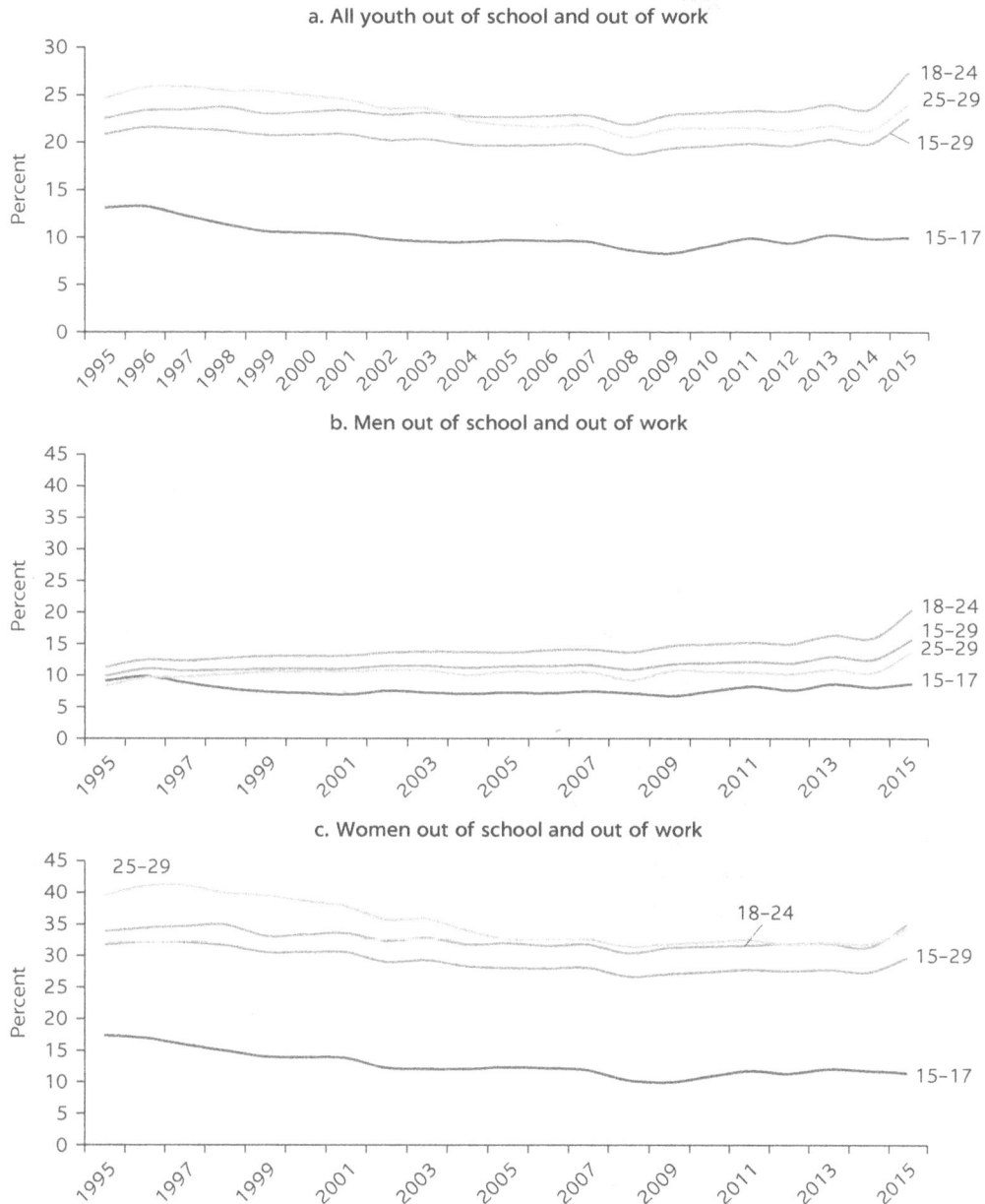

a. All youth out of school and out of work

b. Men out of school and out of work

c. Women out of school and out of work

Source: Costa et al. 2017a.
Notes: For comparability, data do not include households in rural areas of the northern region.

OVERALL, LEVELS OF YOUTH DISENGAGEMENT ARE HIGH AND UNEQUAL WITHIN THE COUNTRY

Most teenagers in Brazil (15–16 years of age) complete *ensino fundamental* (grades 1 through 9) but already have important deficiencies in learning. The first column in figure 3.4 reports the share of this group who are either in school or have dropped out. Two facts are worth noting. First, by age 15–16—when students should be attending the first year of *ensino médio,* had they not had any

FIGURE 3.4

Youth ages 15–16 enrolled in school and youth who are out of school, 2015

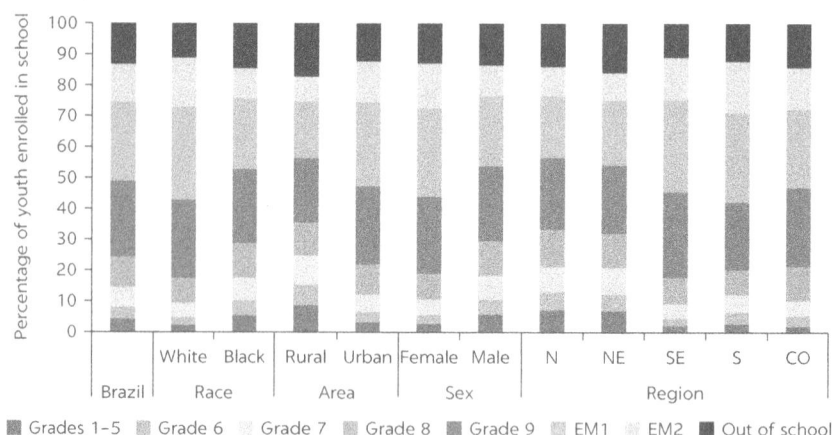

Source: *Pesquisa Nacional por Amostra de Domicílios* (PNAD); IBGE 2015.
Note: *Ensino fundamental* comprises grades 1–9 and *ensino médio* grades 10–12. Youth ages 15–16 with no age–grade distortion should be attending grade 10. Age–grade distortion is defined for students ages 15–29 years in the education system as the difference between their current age (measured as of March 31, of the reference year) and the appropriate age for the grade they are enrolled in. In the race category, "black" includes self-reported races *"preta"* and *"parda."* Other races (indigenous and East-Asian origin) are not reported due to very low frequencies (less than 1 percent of the sample combined).

type of age–grade distortion—13.2 percent (approximately one of eight) are already out of school and have dropped out of the formal schooling system. Second, among those remaining in school, only 37.9 percent are in the appropriate grades for their current ages, while most of the students (24.4 percent) are lagging by at least two full years of education (that is, they are attending eighth grade or less). This implies that youth start *ensino médio* with highly deficient learning trajectories on core foundational skills—academic, cognitive, and behavioral skills—from their years of *ensino fundamental*.

Although Brazil has made some advances in improving learning since 2000, it is still among the countries in Latin America and the Caribbean (LAC) with the lowest proficiency levels among 15-year-olds. The country has stagnated and perhaps even regressed since 2012 as measured by the international assessments of student learning across most subject areas. Brazil's Program for International Student Assessment (PISA) score for math, for instance, which was 334 in 2000, peaked at 391 in 2012, but fell to 377 in 2015 (not reported). This placed it well behind neighbors such as Argentina and Chile and well below the OECD average. Furthermore, over half of 15-year-olds in Brazil scored below the basic level of proficiency in both reading and science (World Bank 2017; see figure 3.5). These have tremendously negative consequences for future learning, leading to stunted achievement trajectories.

These learning deficiencies certainly contribute to Brazil's having among the highest grade repetition and dropout rates and the lowest completion rates for upper secondary education in the Latin American region (see figure 3.6). Despite improvements in access to *ensino médio* achieved since 2004, most Brazilian students today still do not complete it, and many drop out of the formal schooling system without the relevant skills to be productive in the workplace. Chronic overage, deficient learning, and large dropout rates among *ensino médio*

FIGURE 3.5

GDP per capita and PISA 2015 performance, international comparison

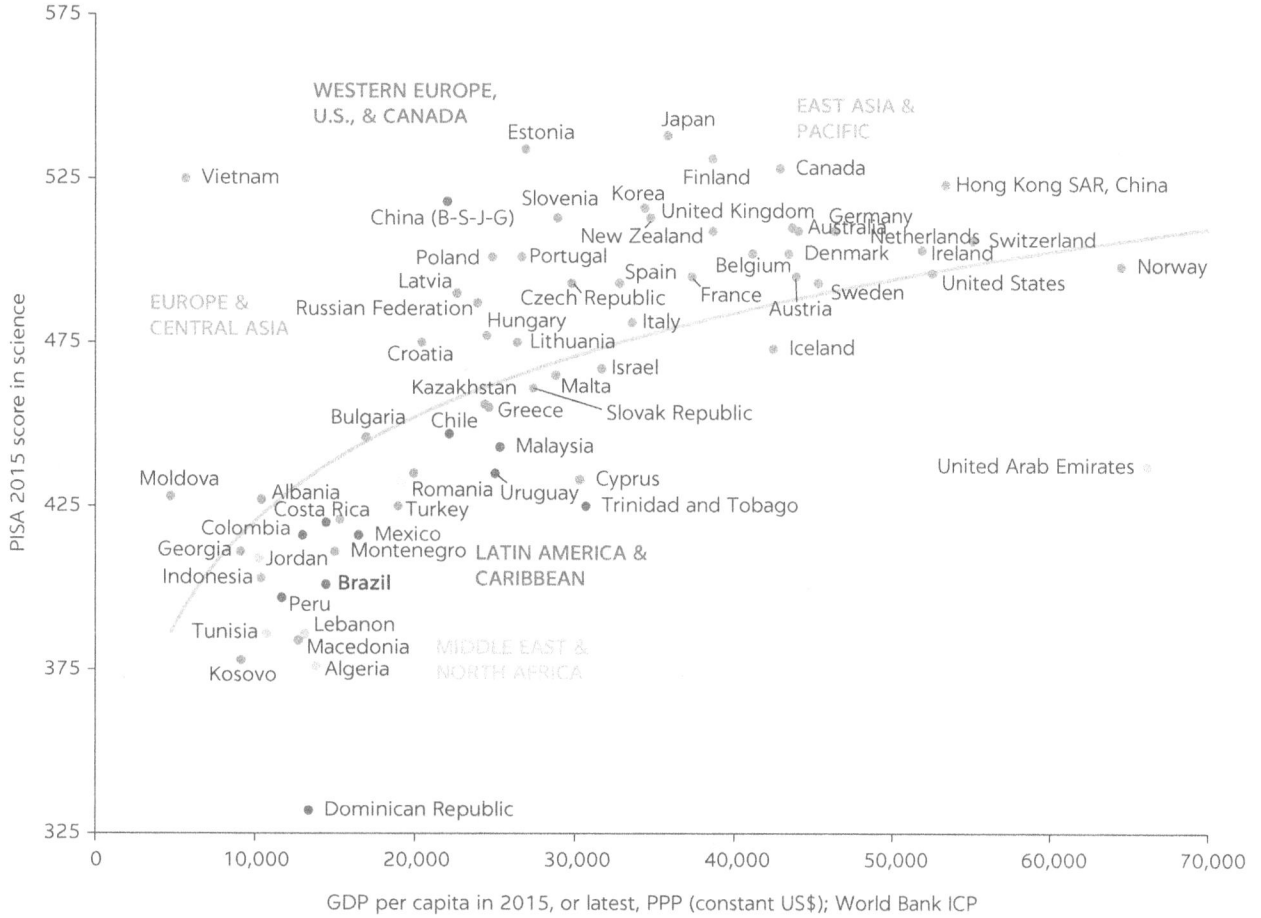

Source: World Bank 2017.

Notes: GDP = gross domestic product. Figure shows the relationship between GDP per capita and performance on PISA Science in 2015.

FIGURE 3.6

Enrollment by age in selected Latin American countries, urban, 2015

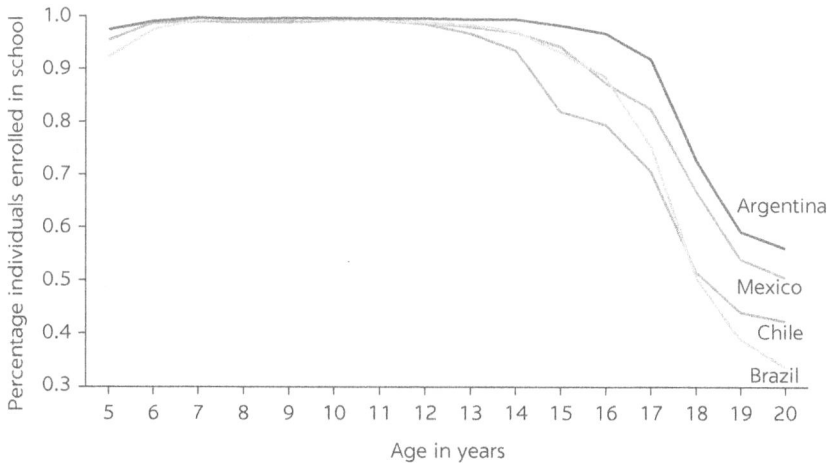

Source: Based on SEDLAC 2011.

Notes: Data for Brazil and Chile are for 2015, and Argentina and Mexico for 2014.

FIGURE 3.7

Brazilians ages 25 and older, with completed secondary education or more

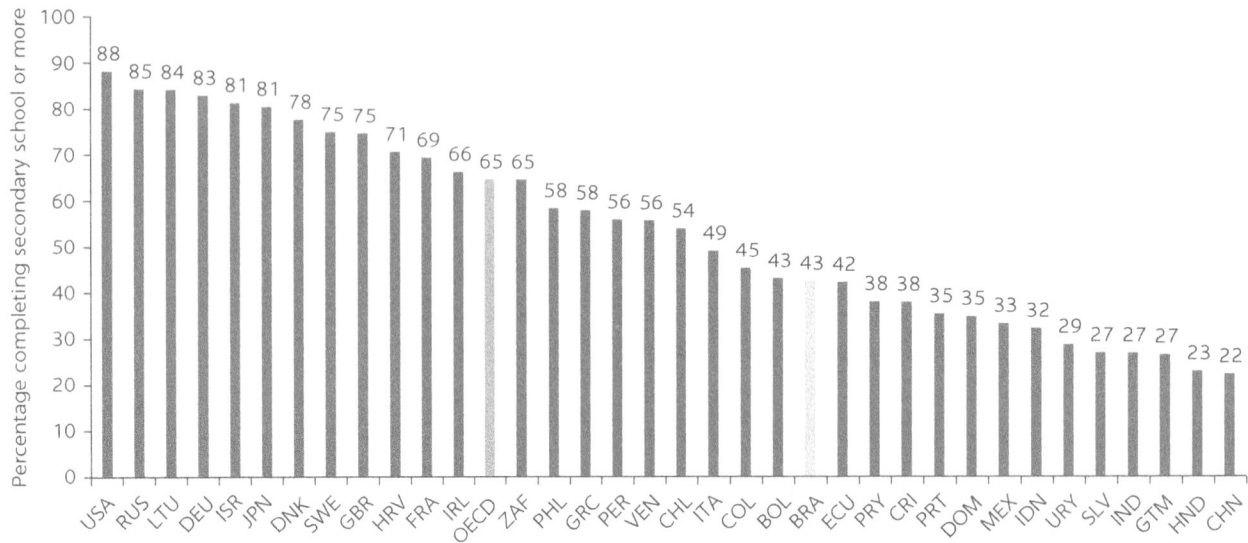

Source: Based on the World Development Indicators (WDI), World Bank.
Note: Years vary by country: China, Japan, and Russia 2010; Croatia, India, and Ireland 2011; Bolivia 2012; Chile, El Salvador, and the Philippines 2013; Brazil, Guatemala, Honduras, and UK 2014; all other countries 2015.

students—large even from an international perspective—lead to secondary completion rates well below those of other LAC countries. The green curve in figure 3.6 represents Brazil's school enrollment by age. Notable is that Brazil has the steepest drop of all countries represented, indicating that dropouts become quite common at that stage of education.[3] Figure 3.7 shows that only 43 percent of the Brazilian population age 25 or over had completed secondary education, in contrast to 54 percent in Chile and 65 percent for the OECD.

Brazil's low school completion rates are of concern and have important implications. First, in a country with increased access to and use of digital technologies (Almeida, Corseuil, and Poole 2017) and shifting demands for skills, holding an upper secondary degree is a minimum prerequisite for access to higher-quality jobs. Second, these low completion rates are also keeping youth from enrolling in tertiary education, with the greater access it provides to higher-quality jobs in the formal sector.

By the time youth reach 18 years of age in Brazil, more than half are out of school and without the solid set of skills they need to achieve high employability and attain productive jobs; hence, they are more likely to be unemployed. Figure 3.8 shows time allocation for youth ages 15–29 for Brazil and Chile in 2015 and Argentina and Mexico in 2014, comparing urban areas in the four countries. Beyond reporting in each the shares of youth who are both out of school and out of work or working and/or studying, it also classifies the employment of those working according to type of contract in the labor market (that is, wage earners versus others). Among the half of Brazilian youth who are already out of school when they turn 18, an important share is out of work as well. Brazil stands out in LAC and around the world for the magnitude of this problem (De Hoyos, Rogers, and Székely 2016)—a performance in contrast to much longer stays in school for all the other countries. In Chile, it is only by age 21 that half of youth are out of

FIGURE 3.8

Time allocation for urban youth in selected Latin American countries

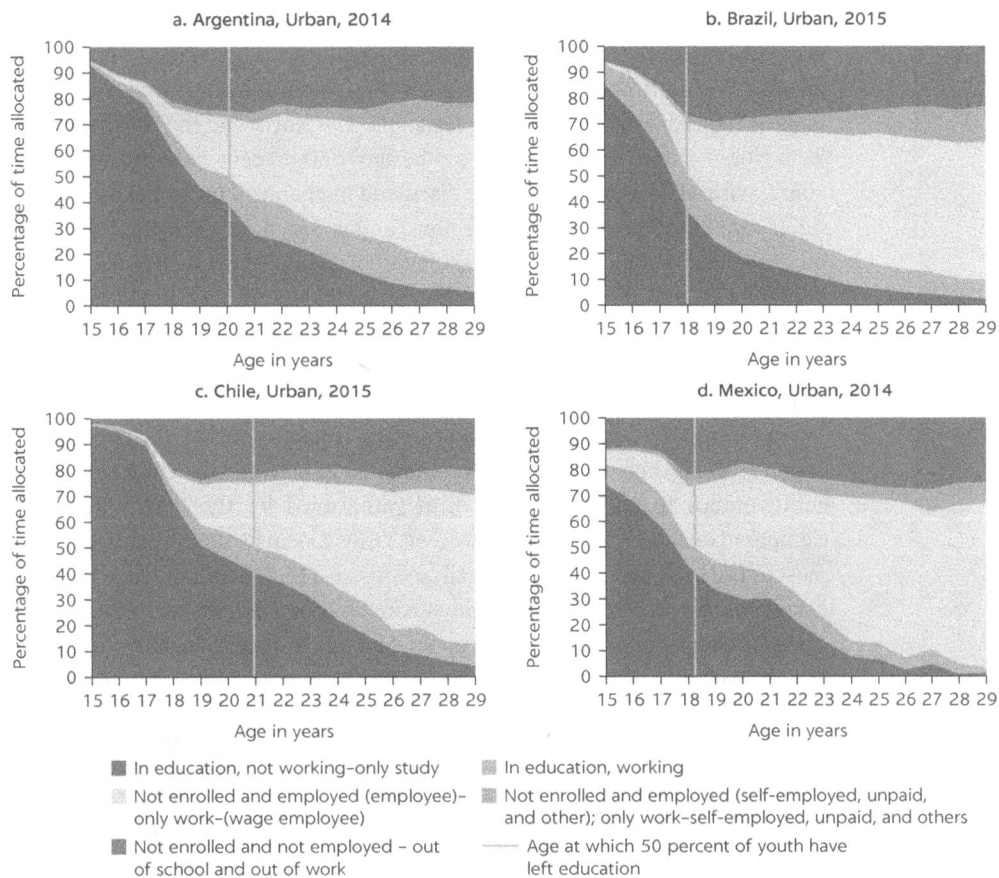

a. Argentina, Urban, 2014

b. Brazil, Urban, 2015

c. Chile, Urban, 2015

d. Mexico, Urban, 2014

- In education, not working–only study
- Not enrolled and employed (employee)- only work–(wage employee)
- Not enrolled and not employed – out of school and out of work
- In education, working
- Not enrolled and employed (self-employed, unpaid, and other); only work–self-employed, unpaid, and others
- Age at which 50 percent of youth have left education

Source: Based on SEDLAC 2011.
Notes: Data for Brazil and Chile are for 2015, and Argentina and Mexico for 2014. Sample is limited to urban areas for comparability to the sample for Argentina, which covers only urban areas.

FIGURE 3.9

Unemployment rates for urban youth in selected Latin American countries, by age

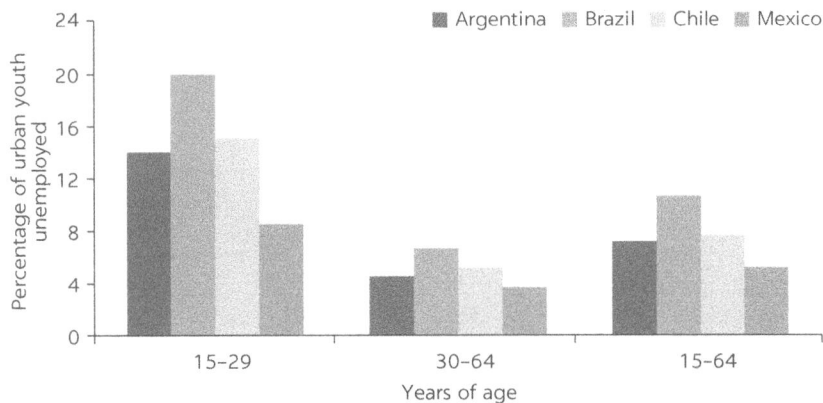

Source: Based on SEDLAC 2011.
Notes: Data for Brazil and Chile are for 2015, and Argentina and Mexico for 2014.
Unemployment rate is percentage of economically active population that is unemployed.

school; approximately 70 percent of Chileans 18 years of age are still in school, and almost 80 percent are in school and working.

Aside from low education completion and proficiency rates, other drivers of youth disengagement in Brazil include regional location, gender, and household income. Within Brazil there is a large—although diminishing—diversity in the rates of youth disengagement across regions. The North and the Northeast perform worst. There disengagement can be above 60 percent, as compared to the South, with 41.7 percent. Evidence discussed in chapter 1 (map 1.1) had shown significant heterogeneity within regions, and across the 27 Brazilian states. In the Northeast, states with the lowest levels of disengagement include Sergipe, Pernambuco, and Rio Grande do Norte. Since 2004, however, Brazil has made important progress in reducing the risk of disengagement, with the lagging states starting to catch up to the better-performing ones. Figure 3.10 shows some convergence over that period.

Another essential predictor for learning trajectories and for completing *ensino médio* is income. The positive relationship between income and student achievement in *ensino fundamental* (measured by the Third Regional Comparative and Explanatory Survey, or TERCE) can be observed throughout most of LAC and also clearly in Brazil (see figure 3.11). This shows how learning disadvantages for students from lower-income households start forming in *ensino fundamental*, continue into upper secondary education, and potentially can last well into life. In 2004, approximately 50 percent of youth in the lowest income quintile completed more than five years of education, with a dismal 12 percent or fewer continuing in school through *ensino médio*. While those numbers had improved considerably by 2015, they were still unacceptably low. Of youth in the lowest quintile, 50 percent remained through eight years of education, and nearly 20 percent completed *ensino médio*. Those among the highest quintile, on the other hand, completed *ensino médio* at rates above 60 percent in 2004 and 80 percent in 2015. The gaps between curves observed in figure 3.12

FIGURE 3.10

Youth disengagement fell during the period of rapid economic growth, but is now rising: Trends by region and nationally, 2004–15

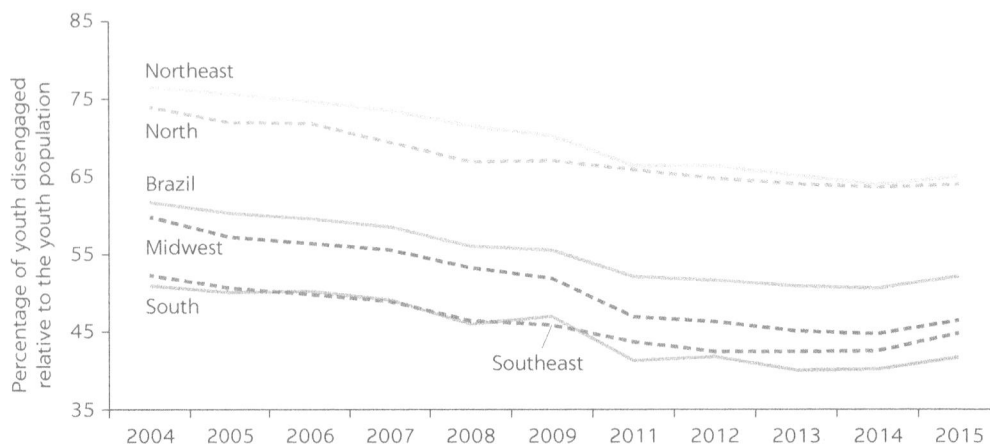

Source: Estimates based on *Pesquisa Nacional por Amostra de Domicílios* (PNAD), 2004–15.
Note: PNAD was not conducted in 2010. The graph reports the trends for the shares of disengaged youth in each state relative to the state's youth population at the state level and nationwide. Disengaged youth are those 15–29 years old who (1) work in the informal sector (including those only working and those also studying); (2) only attend school but are lagging in learning (that is, have some age–grade distortion); or (3) do not work or attend school (that is, are out of school and out of work, regardless of being active or inactive).

FIGURE 3.11

Cross-national comparison of reading scores, by income, 2013

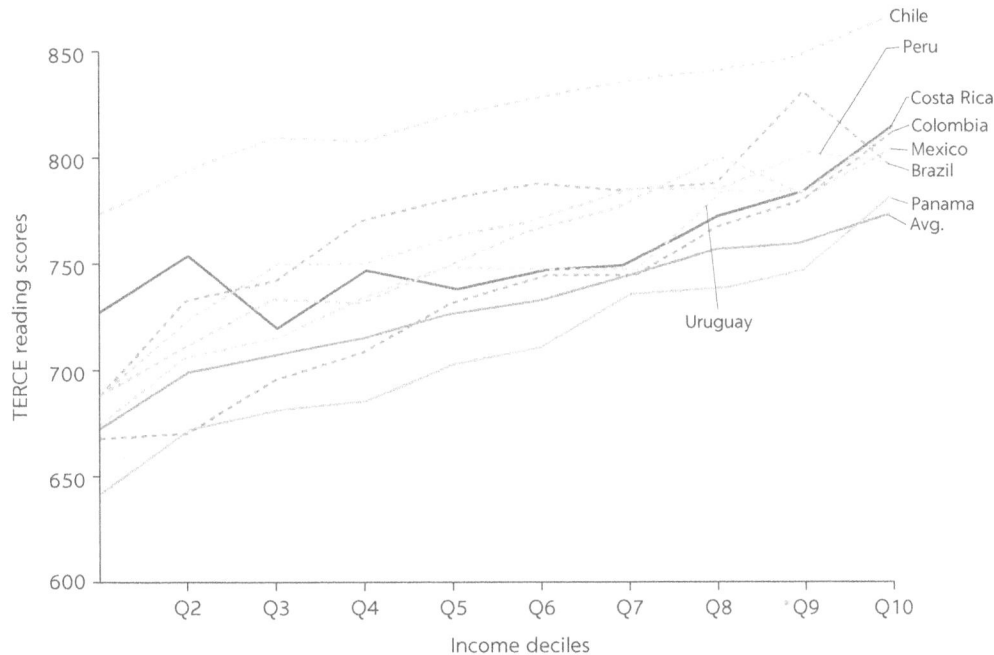

Source: Almeida and Oosterbeek 2016.
Notes: TERCE was conducted by the Latin American Laboratory for Assessment of the Quality of Education in 2013. It tests reading, writing, and mathematics for students in 3rd and 6th grades, with an additional natural sciences test for 6th graders. The average reflects the reading exam average score in the countries.

FIGURE 3.12

School completion by income quintile, 2004 and 2015

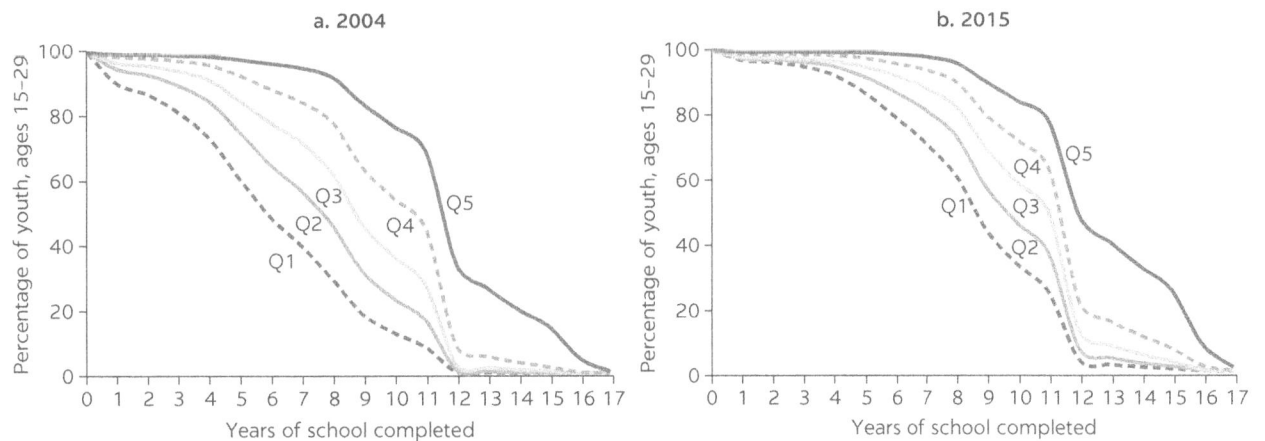

Source: Based on *Pesquisa Nacional por Amostra de Domicílios* (PNAD), 2004 and 2015.

illustrate this wide disparity in education completion for youth at different income levels.

Youth disengagement also has an important gender dimension. Table 3.1 (above) shows that, as of 2015, 51.8 percent of the disengaged youth in Brazil were females. This is largely explained by the large share of women with children who are out of school and out of work. Costa et al. (2017a) have found that, although the share of women who are out of school and out of work had fallen as of 2015, the largest share of youth neither studying nor employed could still be attributed to women with children, just as in 1995. The share of women with children among the group of "*nem-nems*" fell by over 15 percentage points, from 50.4 percent in 1995 to 35.3 percent in 2015 (figure 3.13, panel a). As of 2015, however, the share of NEET youth among young females

FIGURE 3.13

Demographic breakdown of out-of-school and out-of-work youth, 1995–2015

a. Distribution of out-of-work and out-of-school youth (15–29 years old), by gender

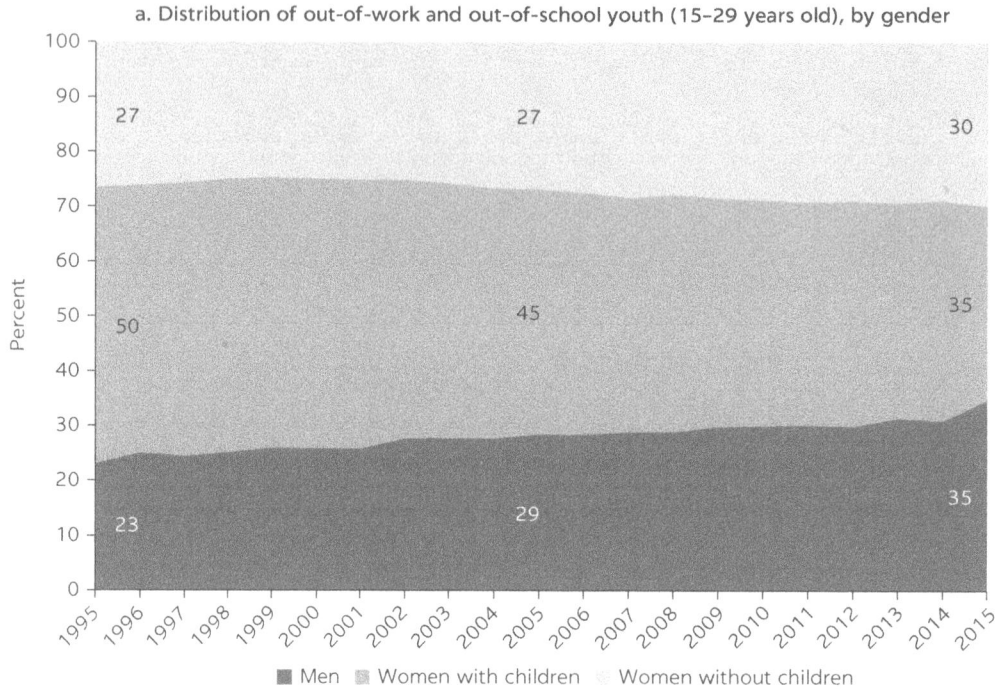

b. Share of out-of-work and out-of-school youth among women (1995 and 2015), by age groups

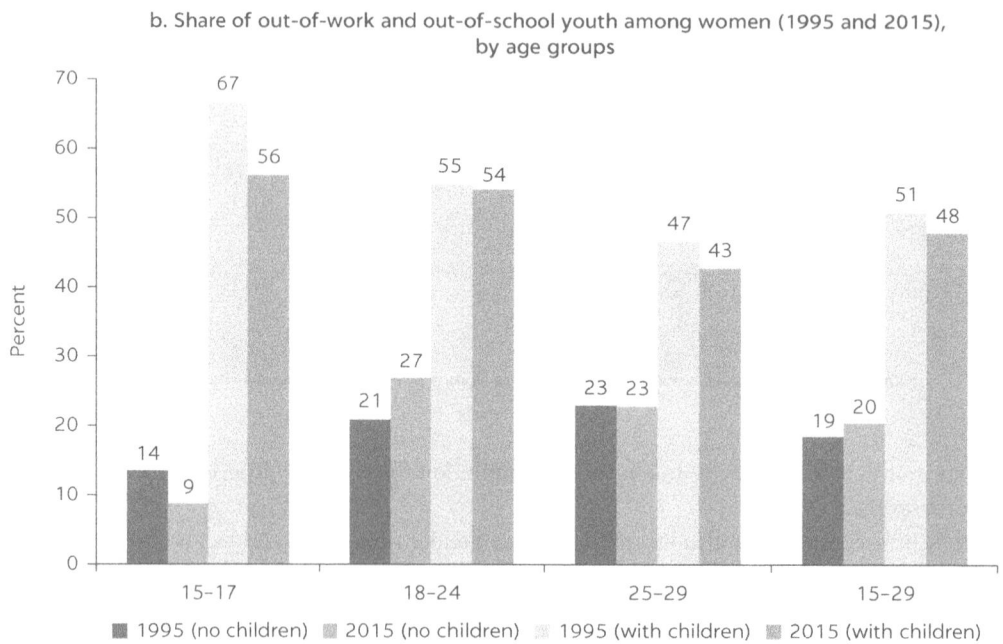

Source: Costa et al. 2017a, based on *Pesquisa Nacional pro Amostra de Domicílios* (PNAD), 1995 and 2015.

(both with and without children) was still close 50 percent (figure 3.13, panel b), despite the large progress made by this group in increasing their school attendance during the period. Box 3.1 discusses how very strong gender norms and reduced motivation and aspirations are especially binding constraints for women, ultimately determining their youth disengagement and

---

BOX 3.1

A qualitative perspective on out-of-school and out-of-work youth

In a new qualitative study, Machado and Muller (2018) examine the school and labor trajectories and the attitudes and perceptions of out-of-school and out-of-work youth in the Brazilian state of Pernambuco. The study is based on interviews with young men and women ages 18–25, and it covers a wide range of themes, including, in particular, perceived barriers to future aspirations. To benchmark this group, the researchers also collected information for a set of "positive deviance cases" of youth who had completed high school and were attending tertiary education institutions and/or were about to enter the labor market. Three different profiles of out-of-school and out-of-work youth emerged from this study, depending on the types of barriers faced:

- **Barriers to internal motivation** characterize youth lacking aspirations or an internal predisposition to return to school and/or work. This group includes mainly women living with partners and women with small children. The main constraint is their internalization of restrictive social norms that enforce their role as caregivers whose lives are focused on the domestic sphere. Such norms include the roles of "good wives and mothers" for girls and "breadwinners" for boys and partners' and communities' control over women's mobility (for instance, the negative associations imposed on "outgoing women"). In addition, women's work is considered less meaningful and important than men's. These factors, de facto, shape women's aspirations and actions in their transitions to adulthood.
- **Barriers to action** characterize youth who, unattracted by the low-skilled jobs available to them, aspire to resume formal schooling to pursue specific careers but do not act to achieve their goals. This group includes predominantly single youth without children. The absence of role models seems to be one driver of their behavior.

- **External barriers** limit even motivated youth, who aspire to return to work and/or school and continually try to do so but cannot overcome these obstacles. Examples include lack of job opportunities, lack of human capital for certain opportunities, and lack of financial resources, and/or other practical difficulties in combining work and study. Other factors are long distances, inadequate school hours, or gender discrimination by employers, constraining especially women.

Beyond profiling, the research highlights the need for more customized skills and job policies for youth that address the barriers faced by the different groups in Brazil. Machado and Muller also stress that the "capacity to aspire" is adaptive to individuals' social environment, and that it can be changed. The "positive deviance cases" of urban youth, for instance, show they are more likely to interpret difficulties as "stepping stones" to the achievement of their longer-term goals. They proactively tend to seek new opportunities to progress with their plans and build resilience strategies based on increased perseverance, self-confidence and self-reliability. This resilience is based on solid relationships with parents, peers, and/or partners. Greater exposure to role models and networks provide them—particularly young women—with a greater sense of "possibility." Second, tackling gender norms that influence youth's main references for attainable work and/or education trajectories is essential. Finally, multidimensional interventions that tackle internal and external barriers are needed everywhere, but especially in rural areas, where all these constraints seem to be more binding. There, where jobs and industries are scarcer and farming is considered a suitable profession only for males, youth perceive fewer good economic opportunities.

Source: Machado and Muller 2018.

labor trajectories. As figure 3.14 shows, half of the female respondents to a 2016 survey who were out of school and out of work agreed that "taking care of children should be the mother's responsibility even if sacrificing work and study" (Gukovas and Kejsefman 2017).

Being a male and having completed upper secondary education are important variables pushing individuals out of the out-of-school and out-of-work status. Young people making these transitions out of the out-of-school and out-of-work status differ across gender, age, educational attainment, and geographical area. From the first quarter of 2012/2013 to that of 2013/2014 (a period of one year), the exit rate into employment or employment and study was about 35 percent (see figure 3.15). Almost 50 percent of the men exited, but

FIGURE 3.14

Women's perception of their child care responsibilities, 2016

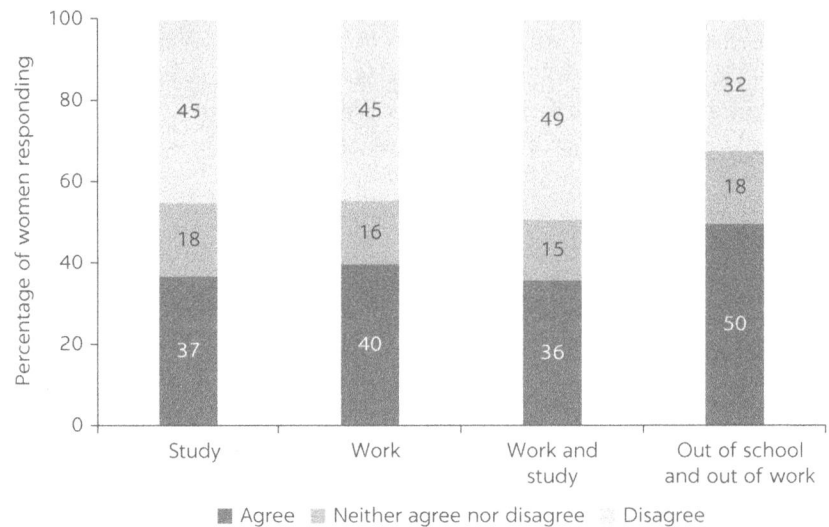

Source: Gukovas and Kejsefman 2017, using RIWI survey 2016.
Notes: Figure reports women's perception regarding the responsibilities of child care. Respondents were asked the following question: "Do you agree, neither agree nor disagree, or disagree with the following statement? "Taking care of children should be the mother's responsibility even if sacrificing work and study." The graph reports the percentage of women across occupational states who strongly agreed or disagreed with the statement in 2016.

FIGURE 3.15

Youth exiting from out of school and out of work, 2012–14

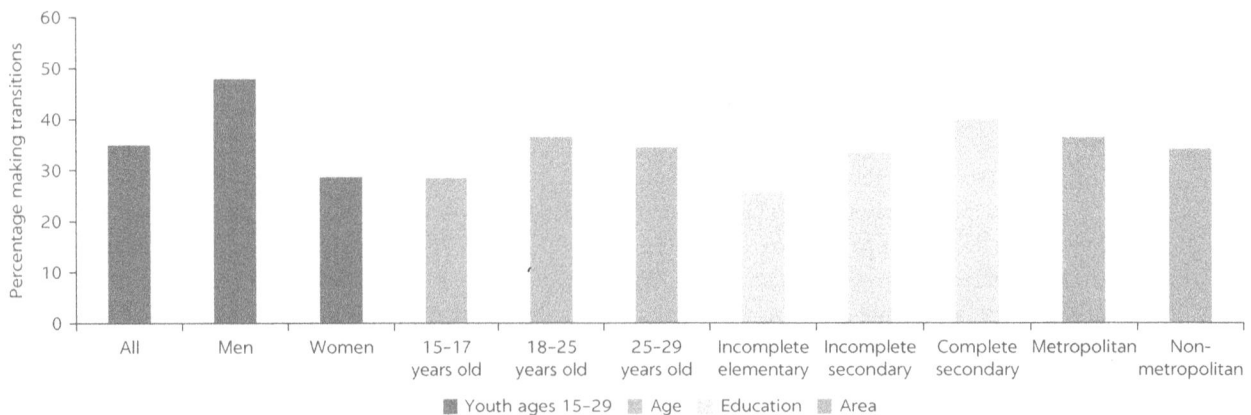

Source: Costa et al. 2017b.

only 30 percent of the women. The exit rate was higher for older youth, as well as youth who lived in metropolitan (as opposed to rural) areas and had completed more education. The substantial disparity this represents across socioeconomic backgrounds corresponds with the reasons youth fall into the out-of-school and out-of-work status in the first place.

YOUTH DISENGAGEMENT PATTERNS IN THE FUTURE

During the economic crisis of 2015–16, the transitions from the out-of-school and out-of-work status became more difficult. The overall rate of transition from the first quarter of 2015/2016 to that of 2016/2017 dropped to only 30 percent (see figure 3.16). Heterogeneity among exiting youth in gender, geographical area, age, and educational attainment remained similar to that in 2012–14. Statistically, a 15-year-old girl who had not completed *ensino fundamental* and was living in a rural area had the lowest chance of going back to school or joining the labor force; conversely, a mid-20s male with completed secondary education living in an urban setting had the highest probability of leaving the out-of-school and out-of-work category.

In other words, the NEET "trap" became even more persistent during the financial crisis. Over 60 percent of NEET youth remained in the category from the first quarter of 2015/2016 to that of 2016/2017. This means the average probability for an individual in the NEET category at the beginning of the period of being in that group at the end of the year was greater than 60 percent. This rate increased from 57.6 percent (not reported) during the pre-crisis period to 61.3 percent during the crisis (see table 3.2).

Costa et al. (2017b) also showed that the patterns of transition out of the NEET category, as in the earlier period, were quite heterogeneous across socioeconomic backgrounds. Furthermore, they found about 20 percent of youth ages 15–17 who were in "only study" at the beginning of the later period fell into the out-of-school and out-of-work group or the "only work" group one year later. This share was especially high for females. Finally, only 10 percent of youth ages 18–24 in full-time study at the beginning of the period were employed a year later.

Youth exiting from out of school and out of work, 2015–17

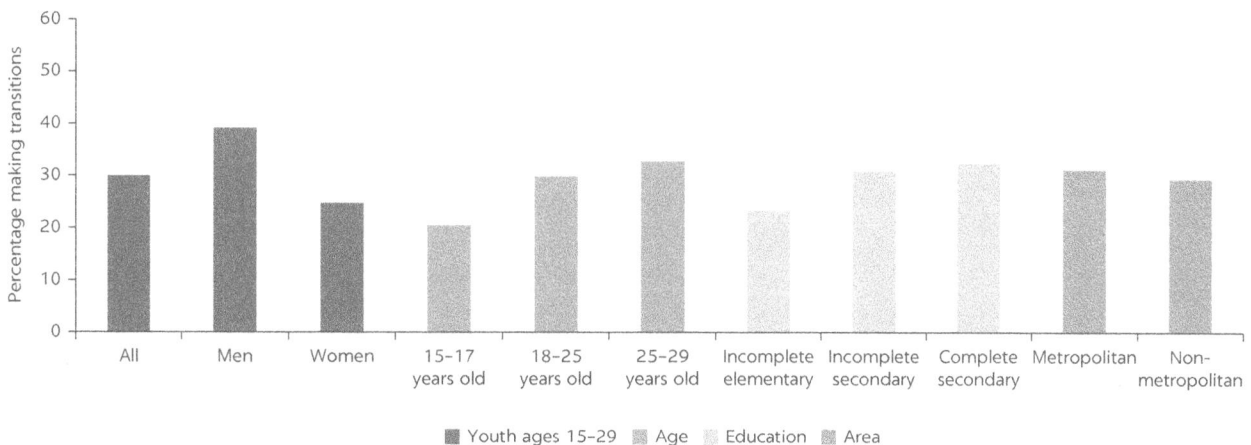

Source: Costa et al. 2017b.

TABLE 3.2 **Youth ages 15–29 remaining in NEET category during financial crisis, 2015–16**

FIRST QUARTER, YEAR t (%)	FIRST QUARTER, YEAR t + 1 (%)				
	NEET	ONLY WORK	STUDY AND WORK	ONLY STUDY	TOTAL
NEET	61.3	27.6	2.3	8.8	100
Only work	15.3	78.2	5.1	1.3	100
Study and work	10.7	27.4	43.0	19.0	100
Only study	18.0	6.2	10.7	65.2	100

Source: Costa et al. 2017b.
Notes: Table reports the transition rates across each of the states, NEET, only work, study and work, and only study, in Brazil, between quarter 1 of time t and quarter 1 of year t + 1.

FIGURE 3.17

Percentage of workers in informal jobs by age, 2004–15

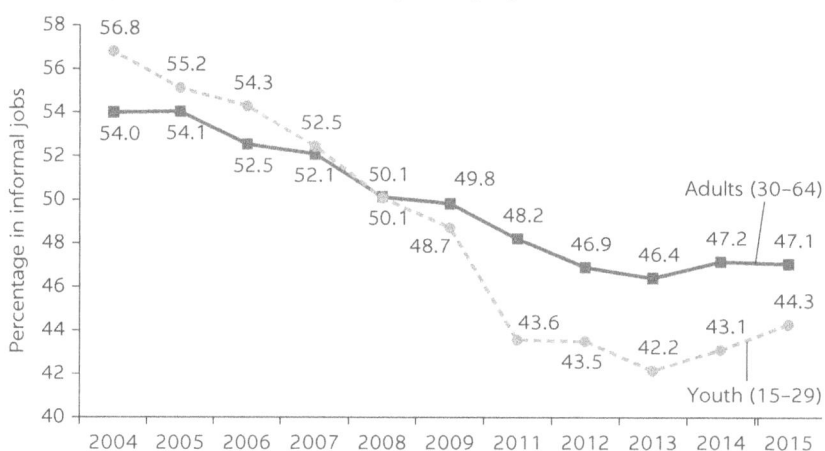

Source: Based on *Pesquisa Nacional por Amostra de Domicílios* (PNAD), 2004–15.
Notes: PNAD was not conducted in 2010. Informal jobs include the following categories: Other employees without *carteira assinada*, employees without *carteira assinada*, domestic workers without *carteira assinada*, self-employed, self-employed in production for the own consumption, construction workers for their own use, unpaid workers and workers that did not declared the type of occupation.

Of further concern have been increasing trends in youth unemployment, in the propensity of being out of school and out of work, and in informality. According to Costa et al. (2017a), the positive pattern of falling NEET rates observed since 1995 has recently reverted. As figure 3.3 (above) shows, the lowest disengagement level—captured by the NEET rate—for all youth was 13.5 percent in 2009. After that, NEET rates began to rise for all youth, back to levels seen in the early 2000s. By 2014, the rate for men, at 8 percent, was nearly the highest it had been for the previous 20 years. To Foguel et al. (2017a), this pattern suggests that NEET rates and levels of disengaged youth act countercyclically to the health of the economy.

As the fall in the returns on labor market experience seems to have stalled in Brazil at 2 percent, there are concerns about further progress in closing the youth labor earnings gap. Figure 3.19 reports estimates for the experience and education earnings premium for all wage earners ages 15–64 between 2004 and 2015.[4] Several interesting facts emerge. First, consistent with Aedo and Walker (2012), Montenegro and Patrinos (2014), and Ferreira, Firpo, and Messina (2014), the returns on education have fallen in Brazil. This is likely

FIGURE 3.18

Unemployment by age, 2004–15

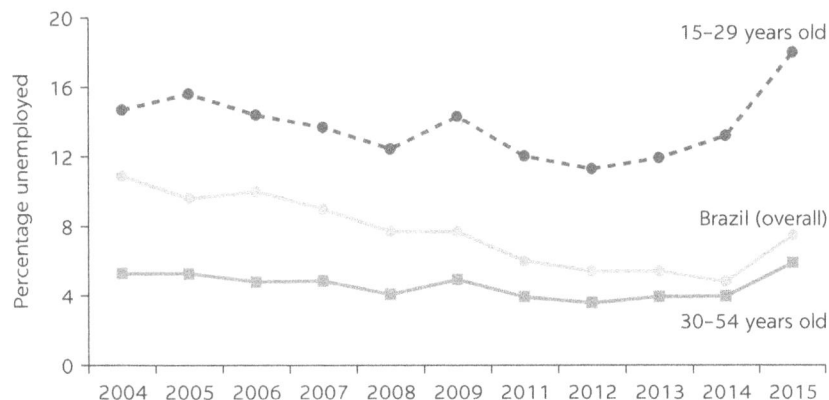

Source: Based on *Pesquisa Nacional por Amostra de Domicílios* (PNAD), 2004–15, and *IPEAdata*, based on *Pesquisa Mensal de Emprego* (IBGE/PME).
Notes: PNAD was not conducted in 2010. Unemployment rate is percentage of economically active population that is unemployed.

FIGURE 3.19

Evolution of education earning premiums in Brazil, 2004–15

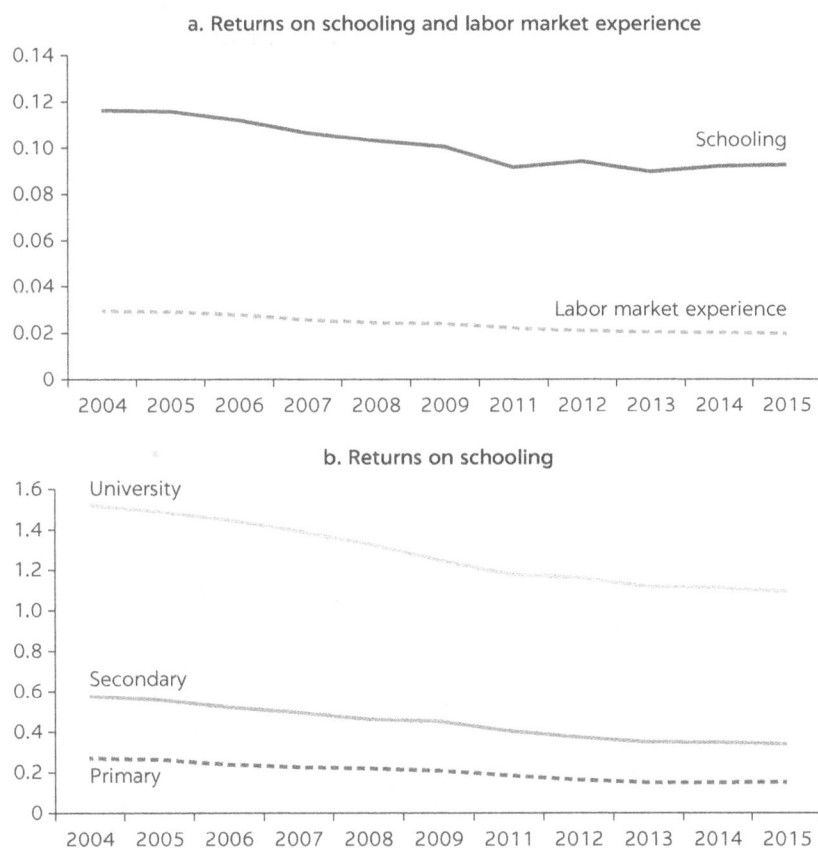

a. Returns on schooling and labor market experience

b. Returns on schooling

Source: Based on *Pesquisa Nacional por Amostra de Domicílios* (PNAD), 2004–15.
Notes: PNAD was not conducted in 2010. Panel a reports the OLS estimates of the additional years of schooling and the returns on experience, as defined in Montenegro and Patrinos (2014). Panel b reports the OLS estimates of the dummy variables to denote completed levels of schooling (primary, secondary, and tertiary). The sample only includes wage earners (employees, military, and civil servants) ages 15–64.

FIGURE 3.20

Wage returns on higher education in LAC, ca. 2010

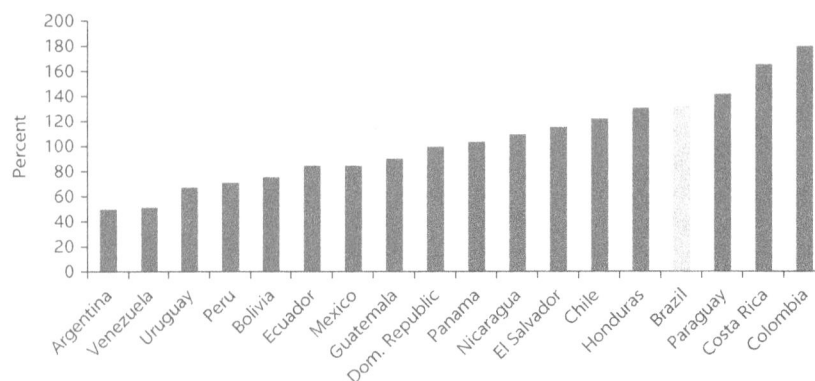

Source: Ferreyra et al. 2017.

related to the increase in the supply of education documented above running ahead of the increase in the demand for education. This trend may reduce the incentives for youth to invest in education. Second, there is a steeper fall in the returns on completed tertiary education as compared to the completion of secondary and primary education degrees. Third, the rise in the minimum wage has driven part of the fall in the returns to labor market experience.[5] Significant evidence indicates this pattern held across the formal and informal sectors, as the minimum wage is also a benchmark in the informal sector (Silva et al. 2015; Ferreira, Firpo, and Messina 2014).

After decades of expansion in access, falling and diverse wage returns have also been reducing the incentives of youth to invest in higher education. Figure 3.20 shows that holding a higher education degree in Brazil yields, on average, an earnings premium of 125 percent, which is above the Latin American average of 104 percent (Ferreyra et al. 2017). Broken down by type of institution, the net return on university degrees is higher in almost all fields compared to professional institutes and technical trainings. Since only 12 percent of Brazilians have completed some form of higher education, considerable room remains for gains in employment and earnings. One important question is whether selection can explain part of this result, or whether it reflects real labor market gains for similar individuals. Almeida et al. (2017) considered this question. They still found high individual wage rate returns on the investment in higher education and large heterogeneity across different higher education providers, even after accounting for differences across students in many observable and frequently unobservable characteristics (such as quality at entry).

Misinformation—and wide variation—in the perceived returns on education also reduce the incentives for investing in human capital, at school or at work. New evidence collected for this report through a new youth survey collected by RIWI suggests Brazil's youth are uncertain as well as misinformed about the benefits of human capital investment when it comes to schooling (Gukovas and Kejsefman 2017). When provided with the average income of a worker with a certain level of education and asked what someone with additional years of education might make on the job, the vast majority of the survey respondents underestimated the true value of additional years of school. Of respondents in a new survey, for instance, over 40 percent thought a worker with just fundamental education who makes R$1,226, on average, would fetch the same salary as a worker

FIGURE 3.21

Perceptions of benefits of human capital investment, 2016

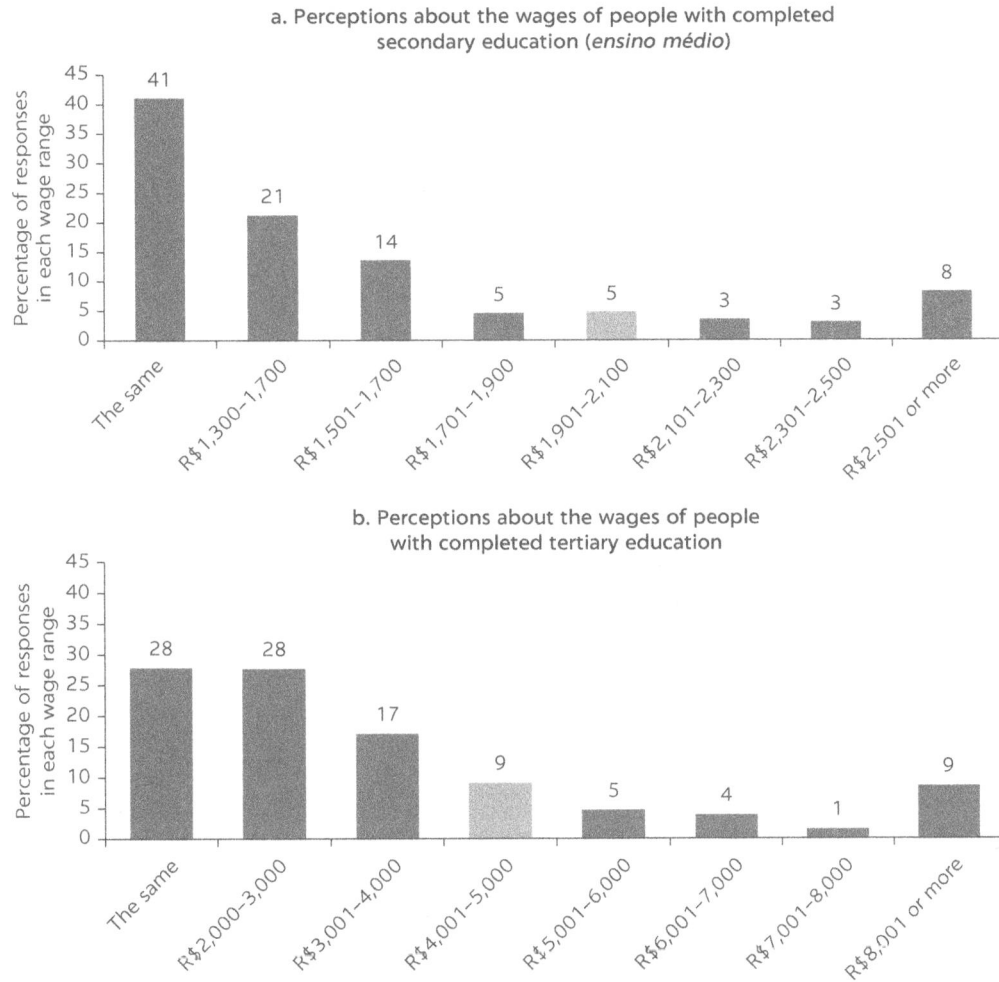

a. Perceptions about the wages of people with completed
secondary education (*ensino médio*)

b. Perceptions about the wages of people
with completed tertiary education

Source: Gukovas and Kejsefman 2017, based on a new youth survey collected by RIWI in Brazil 2016.
Notes: Figure shows people's perceptions regarding investments in human capital. Respondents were provided
with the average monthly wage of a worker with completed basic or secondary level of education and were
asked to estimate the wages of people who complete a specified level of education by choosing one alternative
out of different wage ranges. The light blue bar indicates the average monthly wage that is observed in the
labor market, for that same educational level, in the PNAD household survey (2016). The two questions were
made in sequence; after answering the first, the respondent would be told the average wage of a worker with
secondary education complete.

who had completed secondary education; only 14 percent overestimated the
value of the same investment. And the reality is quite different. A worker with
secondary education earns a premium of more than 50 percent over the base rate
for a worker with completed fundamental education (R$1,900 to R$2,100, on
average). See figure 3.21 for the complete response to the survey question.[6]

The high unemployment rates among youth are likely a reflection of
especially high turnover rates and do not necessarily represent protracted
unemployment periods (Cunningham 2009). While young adults are more
likely to become unemployed than prime-aged adults, they are also more likely
to leave unemployment, to have greater turnover in the labor market in general,
and to have periods of unemployment of similar duration to those of prime-
aged adults. Cunningham (2009) netted out young adults' higher general

turnover rates to find they were no more or less likely to be unemployed than members of other age groups. This suggests that young people's elevated unemployment rates in Brazil reflect higher rates of turnover than among other age groups, similar to findings about unemployment among European youth (Quntini et al. 2007). The turnover may reflect the "shopping around" hypothesis, where young people may be trying out different types of jobs to find those that best meet their interests and needs.

Rather than a sign of a dynamic labor market, the high rate of churn comes at a cost to total factor productivity, however. Rocha, Pero, and Corseuil (2017) found that in firms where turnover is lower and the average duration of employment is longer, total factor productivity is higher. They argued that a "learning by doing" effect obtains, allowing firms at which workers stay longer to develop firm-specific human capital. This gives those firms a significant productivity advantage that is borne out in the data and is robust to alternative specifications of total factor productivity and to analysis using control variables.[7]

High levels of churn may also reveal perverse incentives created by employment regulation and worker protection programs. A debate as to why turnover is so high has been going on among labor economists in Brazil for years. Although definitive evidence is so far lacking, a strong link between worker movements and the system of entitlements, such as access to unemployment income support, is becoming apparent. Gonzaga (2003) and Zylberstajn and Silva (2015), for example, have shown high turnover despite earnings losses in the destination workplace. Pinto (2015) has documented evidence of induced dismissals: a spike in the share of dismissals at the de jure vesting period for unemployment insurance and a finding that 6 percent of those dismissed "without just cause" returned to the same firm after a period more or less equivalent to the maximum payout period for unemployment insurance.

Exploiting evidence from variation in the enforcement of labor regulations within Brazil (captured by labor inspections), Almeida and Carneiro (2009; 2012) found that stricter enforcement of labor market regulations leads to higher unemployment, especially among youth. As enforcement becomes more stringent, workers at the top of the formal wage distribution bear the cost of the mandated benefits by receiving lower wages. Wage rigidity (due, say, to imposition of the minimum wage) prevents this downward adjustment at the bottom of the income distribution. Hence, formal sector jobs at the bottom of the distribution become more attractive, inducing the low-skilled, self-employed to search for formal jobs. Unemployment is more likely to increase among youth and females than among other groups. Almeida and Carneiro (2009) have also found that stricter enforcement of labor regulation constrains firm size and leads to higher unemployment.

Failing to accumulate high-quality human capital early in their professional careers leads youth to persistently lower labor market outcomes during adulthood. According to Cruces, Ham, and Viollaz (2012) and Gukovas and Moreira (2017), in a new background paper prepared for this report, higher informality rates among youth 16-24 lead to higher unemployment and informality rates and lower hourly wages in adulthood nationwide. Evidence also shows, however, that the negative labor market impacts of early informality spells dissipate over time if youth acquire more education and job-relevant competencies.[8] As might be expected, the "scarring impacts"[9] on the labor market are even higher when youth is out of school and out of work early in life (as opposed to being employed in informal jobs). The authors show that cohorts with a larger incidence of young people out of school and out of the labor market have significantly worse labor market outcomes, particularly for males. This negative impact of being out of school and out of work between the ages of 16 and 24 is statistically significant with regard to the probability of holding informal jobs, being unemployed, or receiving lower-paid jobs later in life. Interestingly, the scarring impacts on wages do not seem to dissipate as the individuals age, while the effects on unemployment last until approximately age 35 and on informality until age 45.

NOTES

1. The qualitative work produced as a background to this book by Machado and Muller (2018) shows the categories used to define the *nem-nem* group are a simplification. Particularly, most Brazilian women who are *nem-nems* are engaged in some form of unpaid work.

2. Unless noted, statistics in this chapter were computed based on PNAD, which is collected by the Instituto Brasileiro de Geografia e Estatística (IBGE) annually. PNAD is a nationally representative household survey, with a stratified and clustered sampling design that ensures coverage of rural and urban areas in every Brazilian state. Prior to 2004, it did not include households from the rural areas in the northern region of Brazil. "Youth" is considered the population between 15 and 29 years of age. The chapter considers that a child enters the first year of elementary school at age six. Elementary school is compulsory and comprises nine years of education (ages 6–15), while high school generally comprises three years of education (ages 16–18). The *"ninis"* or *"nem-nems"* category captures youth who are not engaged in education, employment, or training. We use the terms *"ninis"* and *"nem-nems"* interchangeably for youth who are out of school and out of work.

3. While the curves in figure 3.6 appear similarly steep for all the countries represented, Brazil still has much worse enrollment outcomes than the others. In addition, it generally spends more on education as a percentage of gross domestic product (GDP) than Argentina, Chile, and Mexico, respectively. Brazil's government expenditure per secondary student is nearly 22 percent of GDP per capita, while Chile spends 15 percent and Mexico 16 percent of GDP per student. This underscores the need for reform in Brazil's education system aimed at improving efficiency and getting more out of spending, rather than just engaging in more spending.

4. The regression includes as main dependent variable the log (monthly wages) for all wage earners. The main dependent variables are average years of schooling, a female dummy variable, years of experience, years of experience squared, region dummies, an urban dummy, and a dummy for whether the person is black (including either African American or *mestiço*) and another for indigenous. We also include a dummy variable for whether the person is in informal employment (formal is omitted). Figure 3.19, panel b, reports the same regression, but with years of education replaced by three dummy variables: completed primary, completed upper secondary (*ensino médio*), and completed tertiary school. The "education" omitted category is having zero years of education completed in the first regression and having less than primary education completed in the second. All standard errors are clustered at the region level.

5. Measured here by age minus years of schooling minus six.

6. The survey is described in detail in Gukovas and Kejsefman (2017), and information about the survey firm is available here at https://riwi.com/. In a third question, respondents were provided with the average wage of an academic secondary school graduate and asked to estimate the average wage of a technical secondary school graduate. Of the respondents, 51 percent estimated a lower wage for the technical secondary school graduate, while 26 percent overestimated it.

7. At the individual level, the international literature says it is less clear that short unemployment spells have a lasting impact on the labor market. Newmark (2002) showed that staying in the same job had positive impacts on wages for both men and women in the United States, while Gregory and Jukes (2001) showed churning itself to be a smaller issue than long unemployment spells.

8. Cruces, Ham, and Viollaz (2012) show that for Brazil, a spell of unemployment among youth increases the probability of being informal and unemployed in early adulthood, but, again, these effects dissipate after the age of 35.

9. Ruhm (1991) first defined "scarring" as the lasting effects spells of unemployment can have into adulthood, as opposed to "blemish," when the worker is affected only for a short period after the unemployment spell.

REFERENCES

Aedo, C., and I. Walker. 2012. "Skills for the 21st Century in Latin America and the Caribbean." Directions in Development Series. Washington, DC: World Bank.

Almeida, R., and Pedro Carneiro. 2009. "Enforcement of Labor Regulation and Firm Size." *Journal of Comparative Economics* 37 (1): 28–46.

———. 2012. "Enforcement of Labor Regulation and Informality." *American Economic Journal: Applied Economics* 4 (3): 64–89.

Almeida, R., L. Caseiro, A. Maciente, and P. Nascimento. "Wages and Employability of Higher Education Graduates in Brazil: Evidence from Matched Employer-Employee Data." Unpublished presentation, World Bank, Washington, DC.

Almeida, Rita Kullberg, Carlos H. L. Corseuil, and Jennifer Pamela Poole. 2017. "The Impact of Digital Technologies on Routine Tasks: Do Labor Policies Matter?" Policy Research Working Paper 8187. World Bank, Washington, DC.

Almeida, R., and O. Oosterbeek. 2016. "The Relations between Water and Sanitation and School Outcomes." Unpublished manuscript. World Bank, Washington, DC.

Costa, J., M. Foguel, M. França, and R. Almeida. 2017a. "Brazilian Youth Choices: Categorizing and Evaluating the Time Allocation Decisions: Cohort Evidence between 1995 and 2014." Unpublished presentation, World Bank, Washington, DC.

Costa, J., M. Foguel, M. França, and R. Almeida. 2017b. "Youth School Dropout and Time Allocation: Micro Determinants 2012–2016." Unpublished presentation, World Bank, Washington, DC.

Cruces, G., A. Ham, and M. Viollaz. 2012. "Scarring Effects of Youth Unemployment and Informality. Evidence from Brazil." CEDLAS working paper. http://conference.iza.org/conference_files/YULMI2012/viollaz_m8017.pdf.

Cunningham, Wendy. 2009. "Unpacking Youth Unemployment in Latin America." Policy Research Working Paper 5022. World Bank, Washington, DC.

De Hoyos, R., H. Rogers, and M. Székely. 2016. *Out of School and Out of Work: Risk and Opportunities for Latin America's Ninis*. Washington, DC: World Bank. https://openknowledge.worldbank.org/handle/10986/22349.

Da Rocha, L. , V. Pero, and C. Corseuil. 2017. "Turnover, Learning by Doing, and the Dynamics of Productivity in Brazil." IPEA (mimeo) Rio de Janeiro.

Ferreira, F., S. Firpo, and J. Messina. 2014. "A More Level Playing Field? Explaining the Decline in Earnings Inequality in Brazil, 1995–2012." IRIBA (International Research Initiative on Brazil and Africa) Working Paper 12, University of Manchester, UK.

Ferreyra, M. M., C. Avitabile, J. Botero Álvarez, F. Haimovich Paz, S. Urzúa. 2017. *At a Crossroads: Higher Education in Latin America and the Caribbean*. Directions in Development: Human Development, World Bank, Washington, DC. https://openknowledge.worldbank.org/handle/10986/26489.

Gonzaga, Gustavo. 2003. "Labor Turnover and Labor Legislation in Brazil." *Economía* 4 (1): 165–222.

Gregory, M., and R. Jukes. 2001. "Unemployment and Subsequent Earnings: Estimating Scarring among British Men 1984–1994." *Economic Journal* 111 (475): F607–25.

Gukovas, R., and U. Kejsefman. 2017. "Pieces of the Disengagement Puzzle." Unpublished presentation and paper, World Bank, Washington, DC.

Gukovas, R., and V. Moreira. 2017. "Scarring Effects of a Poor Early Labor Market Experience: Evidence from Brazil." Unpublished manuscript. Washington DC: World Bank.

IBGE (Brazilian Institute of Geography and Statistics). 2004–15. *"Pesquisa Nacional por Amostra de Domicílios* (PNAD)."

Machado, Ana Luiza, and Miriam Muller. 2018. "'If It's Already Tough, Imagine for Me…:' A Qualitative Perspective on Youth Out of School and Out of Work in Brazil." Policy Research Working Paper; No. 8358. Washington, DC: World Bank. https://openknowledge.worldbank .org/handle/10986/29424

Montenegro, C., and H. A. Patrinos. 2014. "Comparable Estimates of Returns to Schooling around the World." Policy Research Working Paper WPS 7020. Washington, DC: World Bank.

Newmark, A. J. 2002. "An Integrated Approach to Policy Transfer and Diffusion." *Review of Policy Research* 19: 151–78.

Pinto, Rafael de Carvalho Cayres. 2015. "Three Essays on Labor Market Institutions and Labor Turnover in Brazil." Pontifícia Universidade Católica do Rio de Janeiro. Departamento de Economia, Rio de Janeiro.

Quntini, Glenda and John P. Martin Sébastien Martin. 2007. "The Changing Nature of the School-to-Work Transition Process in OECD Countries." IZA, discussion paper 2582. http://www.oecd.org/employment/emp/38187773.pdf.

Rocha, L., V. Pero, and Carlos Corseuil. "Turnover, Learning by Doing, and the Dynamics of Productivity in Brazil (2017) " Mimeo IPEA. Rio de Janeiro, Brazil.

Ruhm, C. 1991. "Are Workers Permanently Scarred by Job Displacements?" *American Economic Review* 81 (1): 319–24

SEDLAC (2011). "Socio-Economic Database for Latin America and the Caribbean." CEDLAS and World Bank. http://sedlac.econo.unlp.edu.ar/eng/index.php.

World Bank. 2017. "PISA Country Briefs." Mimeo. World Bank, Washington, DC.

Zylberstajn, E., and J. Silva. 2015. "Earnings Consequences of Labor Turnover: The Case of Brazil." Institute of Economic Research Foundation, University of São Paulo (FIPE-USP) and World Bank, Washington, DC.

4 Developing School-Based Skills for Higher Productivity

ABSTRACT A low-quality education system, coupled with misinformation about the real returns on education, are key drivers of school disengagement among young people in Brazil. Deficiencies in learning trajectories start well before *ensino médio* and are not reversed by a low-quality education system. They lead to high grade repetition and age–grade distortion rates in *ensino médio* and to one of the lowest high school completion rates in Latin America and the Caribbean (LAC). Implementation of the 2017 education reform will create both challenges and opportunities to improve student engagement, but complementary interventions are needed to reduce grade repetition in and dropouts from *ensino médio*. While tackling deficiencies in learning trajectories for students before they start *ensino médio* is important, identifying and prioritizing a policy agenda for youth ages 15 and over in the formal schooling system is also essential.[1]

Chapter 3 argued that the education system in Brazil is facing a learning crisis brought about by its failure to reach all students, especially adolescents and young adults. The *World Development Report 2018* (WDR; World Bank 2018) acknowledges the recent strong expansion in access to education around the world, including in Brazil, but flags as a very worrisome trend the slow progress in improving learning levels. Figure 4.1 shows that high-performing Brazilian students in the Programme for International Student Assessment (that is, those at the 75th percentile or above in the PISA learning distribution) would rank in the bottom quarter (that is, at the 25th percentile or below) in a wealthier country, such as Korea, or when benchmarking against the average of the Organization for Economic Co-operation and Development (OECD) countries.[2]

Learning shortfalls during the school years of *ensino fundamental* eventually show up as weak skills in the workforce. Successful student trajectories in *ensino médio* are very much determined by the quality of those trajectories, including with regard to learning and grade repetition at early stages of the life cycle.

The focus of this chapter, however, is on secondary and postsecondary reforms, where learning among many adolescents and young adults in *ensino médio* has been stagnant for years (see figure 4.2, for example).[3]

Cumulative learning deficiencies, starting early in life, are not reversed by the public education system. They lead to a lack of interest and motivation in school among adolescents and, ultimately, in high dropout rates from the formal schooling system. As shown in figure 4.3, the main reason students drop out of upper

FIGURE 4.1

Cross-national comparison of PISA mathematics scores, 2015

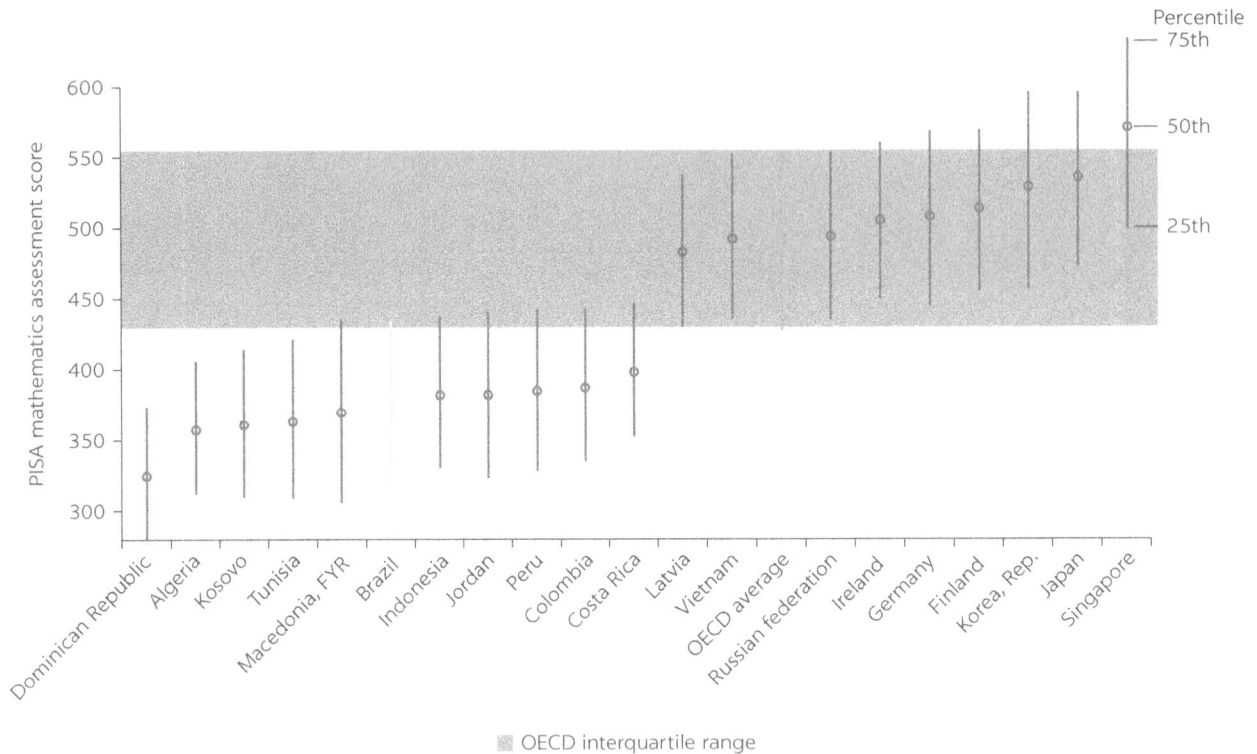

Source: World Bank 2018.

FIGURE 4.2

Proficiency trend for math learning in Brazil, 2009–15

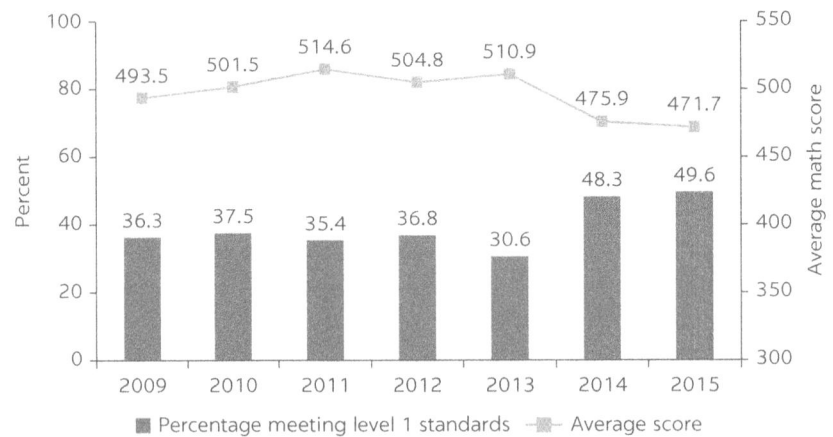

Source: Barbosa and Costa 2017.
Notes: Figure reports the average proficiency and the share of students who meet level-1 standards in math.

FIGURE 4.3

Reasons for not attending school by gender, 2006

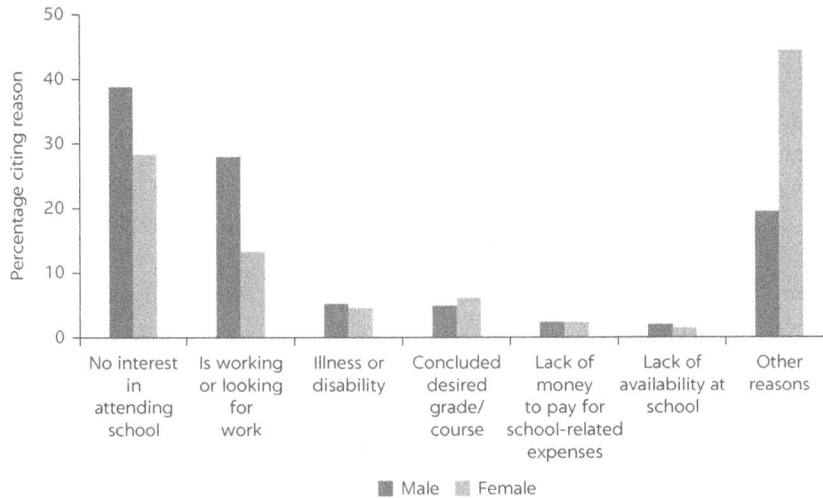

Source: Based on *Pesquisa Nacional por Amostra de Domicílios* (PNAD), 2006.
Notes: Based on the group of students ages 15–29 years old, who have dropped out of the formal schooling system.

secondary education in Brazil is lack of interest in what school offers (see also Neri 2009). An overloaded curriculum and perceived waste of time are likely important drivers. The curriculum currently used in both *ensino fundamental* and *médio* is geared heavily toward memorization rather than critical thinking and rarely goes into depth on specific topics. If youth find additional education ill-suited to jobs within the labor markets they want to enter, they are more likely to drop out and attempt to join the labor market with the education they have, rather than flounder in school where they lack both opportunity and income. As Machado and Muller (2018) also show, the process of dropping out is quite different for boys and girls. For both, however, the lack of support systems and incentives to continue investing in education are important.[4]

This chapter discusses the 2017 *ensino médio* reform and proposes complementary reforms and policies to increase the value of education as perceived by adolescents and young adults and reduce the costs of school engagement. The first section of the chapter revisits the reform, which proposes a new competence-based curriculum and the expansion of the full-time school model nationwide. This discussion is informed by relevant international experiences with the design and implementation of such reforms. Second, the chapter reviews complementary education programs and policies aimed at improving the learning trajectories of youth and reducing grade repetition and, ultimately, reducing dropout rates from *ensino médio*. Last, the chapter discusses selected interventions to help promote more transitions among adolescents to high-quality higher education opportunities and reviews the progress that has been made.

THE 2017 *ENSINO MÉDIO* REFORM: SEVERAL OPPORTUNITIES DURING IMPLEMENTATION

In 2017, the federal government of Brazil passed a reform of the upper secondary education system, including the introduction of a competence-based curriculum (the *ensino médio* reform) and the extension of the full-time school (FTS) model. The ongoing upper secondary reform aims mainly to address the overloaded curriculum—focused on memorization of academic subjects—reduced school hours and instruction time, and the perceived irrelevance of the curriculum for entry into the labor market and higher education. Until 2017, Brazilian high school students had 13 mandatory subjects during a four-hour public school day. Approximately 40 percent of young boys identified lack of interest, including in the contents of a poorly structured curriculum, as their main reason for dropping out (figure 4.3). It is, thus, reasonable to establish a link between this lack of school engagement and the general lack of skills needed for the labor market among graduates from public upper secondary schools. Moreover, public school students find it difficult to progress to tertiary education, as they must compete with better-prepared private school students, especially for admission to the tuition-free public universities.

The *ensino médio* reform supports a new competence-based curriculum, with streamlined core academic subjects and the teaching of higher-order cognitive and socioemotional skills. Adding flexibility to the curriculum is key; the old upper secondary curriculum included thirteen mandatory subjects, and students had little or no flexibility in pursuing their fields of study. The recent reform proposes, first, to reduce number of mandated subjects from thirteen to three (core) subjects: Portuguese, math, and English; second, to allow each student to select a "learning itinerary" from one of five broad knowledge areas: languages, mathematics, natural sciences, humanities, or technical education; and, third, to base the curriculum on the development of core competencies, including socioemotional skills. In addition, those who choose the technical itinerary are now offered a more balanced workload, as the hours allocated to technical courses and/or internships in firms are included in total study time—hence reducing mandatory study time in academic subjects.

The new curriculum is a long overdue and promising reform to reduce the number of dropouts while supporting learning among adolescents. Drawing from experiences in Mexico and other OECD countries, such as Poland and Portugal, the addition of flexibility to a new competence-based curriculum can be an important step in increasing student motivation and engagement in Brazil. Strengthening access to relevant technical subjects while maintaining a good balance between basic foundational and technical skills is also important to increase the attractiveness of secondary education (Almeida, Amaral, and Felicio 2015). In most OECD countries, the offering of accelerated, flexible curricular pathways instead of sequential courses is associated with greater student retention and final certification.

The 2017 reform also extends the full-time school (FTS) model, with the objective of meeting the targets defined in the National Education Plan (Plano Nacional de Educação, or NEP). The FTS program lengthens the school day at the upper secondary level,[5] where most students in public schools have, on average, four hours of daily classes. The reform provides financial support for states to increase the school day to at least five hours in all schools and to seven hours in selected targeted schools (that is, from 800 to 1,400 hours per year in the latter).[6] The extension of the FTS model is intended to accompany the new curriculum and the provision of new school facilities (such as new labs).

While these reforms are an important part of Brazil's education policy, they are not without challenges and risks. The federal government establishes the functional norms for all levels of education, including the new core secondary curriculum—Base Nacional Comum Curricular (BNCC)—but implementation is subnational, as upper secondary education is the responsibility of the states.[7] Hence, the extent to which federal law can regulate how states will ultimately implement these reforms is limited. While promoting flexibility and encouraging different modalities, curriculum reform has the potential to create and deepen educational inequities, as some states and schools will be more efficient in the redesign of their curricula to be aligned fully with the BNCC and the NEP legal framework, while others will do a better job of integrating new technologies and adapting textbooks; others will offer better teacher training programs to SEEs officials, technical staff, school principals, and pedagogical coordinators; and still others will be more effective in redeploying teachers.

At the federal level, this poses a unique opportunity for the MEC to address such inequalities by strengthening its monitoring and evaluation (M&E) system, increasing the technical capacity it provides to states, and, most importantly, encouraging and rewarding good practices in their implementation. A revamped governance structure in the education sector could support new delivery models, piloting and evaluating them rigorously before their broader scale up. Ministries of education in several countries have innovated by implementing such "labs" as they seek more cost-effective solutions than their existing systems. In LAC, Peru has pioneered this experience by implementing an evaluation "lab" like those already in effect in Australia, the United Kingdom, and the United States.[8]

The *ensino médio* reform also creates important challenges at the subnational implementation level that translate into opportunities for delivering high-quality and cost-effective education programs. Three important areas of intervention include strengthening M&E and the private sector focus of technical education; supporting the development of socioemotional skills; and piloting and evaluating models for extending the school day.

Strengthening the M&E and private-sector focus in technical education

The provision of technical education in Brazil has strong design features, including good blending across technical and academic knowledge and a vertical permeability, with transitions into higher education. Almeida, Amaral, and Felicio (2015) discuss three main advantages of the Brazilian technical and vocational education and training (TVET) system that should be preserved, as well as strengthened. First, the system displays high levels of vertical permeability across upper secondary and tertiary levels. In other words, those in technical education in Brazil are likely to move from secondary to higher education (which is unusual for technical education in Latin America), so it is not a dead-end track. Second, and related to this, students in upper secondary technical education have greater employability and wage returns than their peers in academic tracks (Almeida, Anazawa, Menezes-Filho, and Vasconcellos 2015). This vertical permeability is important to keep and strengthen further (Almeida, Amaral, and Felicio 2015; Schwartzman and Moura Castro 2013). Third, technical and academic subjects are generally well integrated in the Brazilian system of education, ensuring that students who choose a technical track also have ongoing education in essential foundational subjects, such as math, science, and Portuguese. The three main alternative tracks at the upper secondary level (*integrado, concomitante, and subsequente*) all combine technical courses with general courses.

Moving forward, placing the private sector more squarely at the center of technical education while strengthening the M&E of TVET programs will be essential. While the current reform addresses important issues, including the imbalance in workload across tracks, ample room remains to make curriculum more relevant and its delivery more cost effective during implementation. By rebalancing the workload (in school hours) across technical and academic "itineraries," the reform will promote higher student interest in and take-up of the technical track. But while the current *ensino médio* reform should improve access, there are concerns with the quality and relevance of the contents offered. Almeida, Amaral, and Felicio (2015) and Silva, Almeida, and Strokova (2015) discussed in depth the still-reduced collaborations with the private sector of most public TVET providers across a wide range of program features (such as curricular contents, teacher training opportunities, and internships). Moreover, while the MEC houses comprehensive administrative datasets on TVET, such as the National System of Vocational Education and Information Technology (SISTEC), these data and statistics are not regularly used to track employability of TVET graduates, and/or inform design of TVET policy.

To ensure the quality of technical education and promote public and private partnerships in the formal public school system, more such partnerships need to arise. This will inevitably bring new challenges, including certification and accreditation issues. Almeida, Amaral, and Felicio (2016) have also highlighted the importance of (1) guaranteeing the quality and relevance of program content, including through more innovative curricula and pedagogies and a strong attention to and articulation of core foundational skills (cognitive and socioemotional); (2) better technical preparation for teachers and trainers, including greater linkage with sector experience; and (3) making career guidance available to support students' school-to-work transitions and the sector or job redeployments of older trainees.

Supporting the development of socioemotional skills

Schools in Brazil (especially private schools) are increasingly incorporating socioemotional skills (SESs) into their curricula, with promising results in learning outcomes (Loureiro and Szerman 2017). SESs include competencies related to curiosity, self-regulation, determination—or "grit"—resilience, empathy, and self-esteem, to name a few. While for some youth the optimal age for the development of SESs comes earlier in the life cycle, others best gain these skills in their teenage years.

Multiple types of interventions could be developed to support SESs, including schoolwide approaches, standalone interventions, and post-school programs. Among public schools, the experience of the state of Rio de Janeiro is probably the best known. In a partnership with the Ayrton Senna Institute, the state's education secretary integrated the development of socioemotional skills into the academic curriculum through selected changes.[9] An evaluation showed that participating students performed better on Portuguese and mathematics assessments than comparable students in similar public schools (Ayrton Senna Institute 2014). These encouraging results led to an expansion of this program in 2014 to more than 50 state schools.

The development of SESs has attracted the interest of other LAC policymakers. Mexico and Peru, for example, have experimented with schoolwide approaches by investing in new curricula and accompanying teacher training. As illustrated by box 4.1, such efforts show that, while having a good program design is fundamental, ensuring local capacity and resources to follow through on implementation is also needed. That said, given Brazil's ongoing *ensino médio* reform, the country seems uniquely positioned to consider more systematic reforms to develop social and emotional skills and include them in new learning standards and curricula, as has been done in Colombia and the United States.

How to build 21st-century skills into secondary curriculum: Lessons from Mexico and Peru

With World Bank support, Mexico and Peru designed programs to teach SESs to primary students in (in Peru) and secondary students (in Mexico and Peru). The objective of Escuela Amiga ("Friendly School") in Peru was to improve SESs, school climate, and learning in high-risk urban schools, from grades 1 to 11. It consisted of a socioemotional learning curriculum, teacher training programs, and specialized support by psychologists, pedagogues, and social workers.

Construye-T ("Build-T"), in Mexico, aims to develop SESs in high schools to improve students' present and future well-being. Like Escuela Amiga, it includes a socioemotional curriculum, and it provides virtual courses and online resources and materials for teachers. Both programs focused on developing "intrapersonal" traits (such as self-awareness and self-regulation), "interpersonal" traits (social awareness and positive communication and collaboration), and a goals-oriented mindset ("grit" and responsible decision making). The curriculum proposed series of scripted 50-minute lessons following the SAFE (sequenced, active, focused, and explicit) approach to classroom activities.

The implementation of these programs highlights important lessons. First, while classroom teachers were charged with the task of delivering the sessions, some were less prepared and motivated to do so than others. Offered the opportunity to teach SESs, most teachers took it. This had advantages over hiring external facilitators in terms of costs and connection with students.

Second, making printed materials available for all the students and teachers was challenging. In Peru, toolkits were delivered in the first phase of implementation of *Escuela Amiga*, but later the only available materials were those provided online. Frequently, teachers and schools did not have the resources to print them. In Mexico, the materials are also available online for teachers and schools to print using their own resources, which imposes similar constraints to those seen in Peru.

Third, ensuring timely support and "troubleshooting" mechanisms to help teachers and schools implement the SES *curriculum* proved a challenge. The curriculum required teachers to prioritize listening over lecturing; focus on the students' experiences rather than the teacher's expertise; and build relationships with the students rather than impart concepts and theory. In many cases, this approach conflicted with more traditional ways of teaching.

Teachers also faced the constraints imposed by their own social and emotional skills. The programs found that training all the teachers could be costly, while cascade training might be ineffective and online training insufficient. In addition to any or all these forms of training, having mechanisms in place for teachers to evaluate their experiences of implementing these curricula proved important and to evaluate their own performance proved essential to ensuring the sustainability and adoption of the program. These mechanisms could take the form of support groups within schools, mentoring, or, as in the case of Escuela Amiga, external but regular support, or they could include a combination of all these.

Sources: Kudo 2016 and http://www.construye-t.org.mx/.

Piloting and evaluating models for extending the school day

The FTS reform at the upper secondary level can produce important impacts on education if design and implementation arrangements are made at the subnational level. Recent evaluations in LAC have shown extension of the school day may positively influence dropouts and learning, but success depends on the implementation arrangements (Holland, Evans, and Alfaro 2015).[10] In Brazil, the Mais Educação (More Education) program extended the school day from four and a half to seven hours in public state and municipal *ensino fundamental* schools.[11] But it failed to produce the impacts on dropouts or learning initially expected (see Almeida et al. 2016; Oliveira and Terra 2016).[12] Recent qualitative work led by the World Bank showed substantial heterogeneity in the implementation of the program, as well as in several other subnational experiences (World Bank 2015). Box 4.2 shows the promising implementation lessons for the current reforms learned from selected state- and municipal-level experiences, respectively, in Pernambuco and Rio de Janeiro municipality. There, important determinants of program success are the quality and relevance of the curriculum offered to students; how well the contents of the "extra" school hours are articulated with the contents of the core-mandated curriculum; the quantity and quality of teachers participating in extra time (including whether they have full-time contracts and their career prospects); whether students with learning difficulties have access to tuition programs; and whether additional training is offered to school directors.

BOX 4.2

Promising lessons from the Pernambuco and Rio de Janeiro single-shift program for implementation of the *ensino médio* reform

The Pernambuco and Rio de Janeiro experiences with extending the school day show that any resulting gains in academic learning are likely related to how the additional time is used (through an enriched curriculum strongly related to core curricula) and teachers' time commitment to the project (through the assignment of full-time teachers). In Pernambuco, the extended-day policy has expanded the network of full-time schools in upper secondary education (grades 10–12) through two models: reference schools and technical schools. The target group for both programs are underperforming schools. The extended-time schools have 45 hours of activities per week, of which 35 are dedicated to academic courses and 10 to complementary activities, such as physical education, computer instruction, and science. This expansion of educational, cultural, and athletic and arts experiences is promoted through the assignment

of dedicated full-time teachers focused on improving student motivation and learning.

In Rio de Janeiro, the Single Shift Program (Turno Único) offers additional time (for a total of seven hours daily) that is filled with a diverse and enriched curriculum, including reinforcement classes in basic courses, second languages, computer instruction and science, and extracurricular activities (such as music, arts, and dance). Teachers in Turno Único schools work full-time in one school, an arrangement associated with higher teacher motivation and efficacy. Turno Único also highlights the importance of having adequate and modern infrastructure to support the model. Cruz et al. (2017) has found that when the extra school time is organized within a structured curriculum, a full-time teacher dedicated to a single school and receiving focused training on the extended-day model may have a significant impact on student dropouts and achievement.

Sources: Loureiro and Szerman 2017, and Cruz et al. 2017.

BEYOND THE *ENSINO MÉDIO* REFORM: SUPPORTING EFFECTIVE TEACHERS AND SCHOOL MANAGEMENT FOR HIGHER LEARNING

The WDR (World Bank 2018) highlights three key school-level ingredients for achieving higher learning: prepared learners, effective teaching, and learning-focused inputs, along with a fourth—skilled management and governance—to pull them all together. Brazil has made strong progress in recent decades to encourage attendance, reduce poverty, and improve preparation of learners (with expansion of access through Bolsa Família, among other efforts). The two areas in which Brazil would benefit from bigger and bolder changes are teachers' skills and the quality of school management and governance arrangements to support learning.

Here we argue that the moment is right. Current demographic trends provide a major opportunity to raise teacher standards over the next decade. With the school-aged population in *ensino fundamental* expected to fall by 25 percent from 2010 to 2025, lower-performing teachers can be weeded out through early retirement, new teachers can be recruited to higher standards, and salaries can be made more attractive on average and, importantly, based on performance.

More effective teachers: addressing low teacher preparedness and motivation

Since the early 2000s, Brazil has made important progress in improving its teachers' education. New research prepared for this book, however (Barbosa and Costa 2017), shows no evidence that these efforts have translated into improved secondary student learning. Compelling evidence indicates that teacher quality is the single most important determinant of school systems' ability to raise student learning and that, at the national level, learning outcomes drive the economic and social gains from education.[13] And Brazil has notably improved the initial qualifications of its teachers. The share of those holding college degrees rose from 89 percent in 2002 to 93 percent in 2016. During this period, Brazil progressed in the dispersion of this indicator across states. Barbosa and Costa (2017) assessed whether this trend correlated with improvements in learning. Perhaps surprisingly, they found no evidence of a correlation between increased teacher qualifications—as proxied by the shares of teachers holder tertiary degrees and those holding degrees in their subject areas—and increased student learning in upper secondary school, as proxied by Exame Nacional do Ensino Médio (ENEM), the national high school exam. These results are clearly illustrated by figure 4.4.

Why aren't increases in the share of qualified teachers translating into better learning in *ensino médio*? As discussed by Bruns and Luque (2015) and Barbosa and Costa (2017), one likely explanation is the low quality of applicants to the teaching profession. As in many countries in LAC, teaching does not attract top talent in Brazil. As figure 4.5 shows, the gap in PISA math scores between prospective teachers and prospective engineers is bigger in Brazil than anywhere else in LAC and much worse than in most OECD countries. In addition, Barbosa and Costa (2017) and Louzano et al. (2010) have presented evidence that the upper secondary graduates interested in the teaching profession come disproportionately from among the worse students in their cohorts. In general assessments, the highest scoring candidates for education departments tend to score

FIGURE 4.4

Student proficiency at the end of *ensino médio* and formal teacher qualifications by state, 2009-15

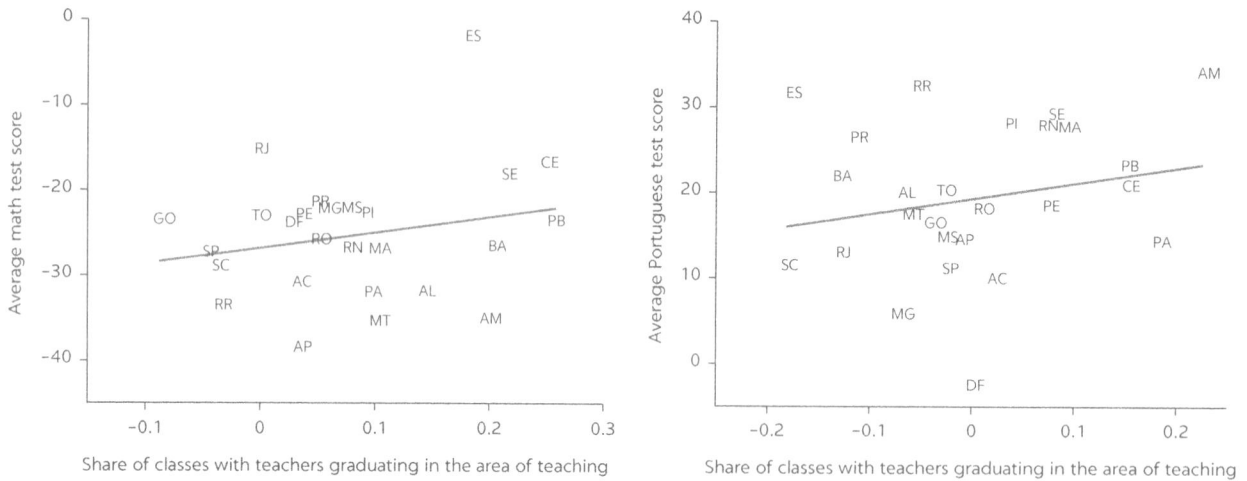

Source: Barbosa and Costa 2017.
Notes: Figure shows the change from 2009 to 2015 in the proficiency in math and language of students from public school at the end of *ensino médio* against teacher formal qualifications.

FIGURE 4.5

Math performance of prospective teachers and engineers

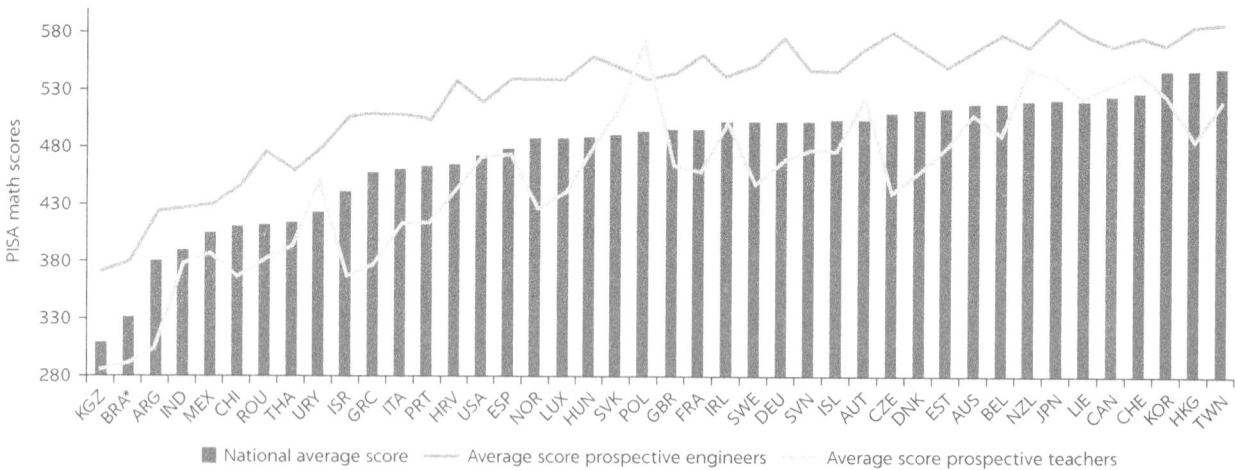

Source: Bruns and Luque 2015.
Note: Based on OECD, PISA, 2000-06. Data are from PISA 2006, except for Brazil (from PISA 2000).

below the worst candidates for medicine, law, and business. The low prestige of the teaching profession, linked to nonselective admission to teacher training and low standards for teacher recruitment, along with flat salary trajectories with no incentives for performance, combine to make the profession unattractive to smart, ambitious individuals.

Furthermore, the recent expansion in initial teacher training, supported partly by the expansion of online courses, is not equipping teachers with adequate skills, either academic or pedagogical. Barbosa and Costa (2017) have shown that more than 70 percent of Brazil's teachers are trained in private and low-quality, virtually unregulated teacher training schools with reduced admission and graduation standards. Many of the courses are based on distance learning, with few opportunities for students to discuss knowledge and contents. In general, the quality of the curricula is poor, and future teachers graduate with weak knowledge in subject areas and no exposure to the best pedagogical skills. In contrast, at the public (or top private) universities, where one out of four teachers is trained, the trainees have greater access to academic resources. Still, anecdotal evidence indicates the curricula at these institutions are very theoretical and divorced from hands-on pedagogical practices. Finally, because the average quality of graduates is low, screening applicants in the formal schooling system as they enter the profession is extremely important in Brazil. Nevertheless, most of the *municípios*, and many smaller states, do not have the capacity to set up competitive recruitment processes.

Further weakening the profession is the failure of most Brazilian states to "groom" the best *ensino médio* teachers with policies that place their motivation at the center. According to Bruns et al. (2015), public school systems cannot raise the average teacher quality unless they have the capacity to do the following:

- Hire carefully by avoiding recruitment mistakes and using probationary periods to monitor and support new teachers over a period of years
- Evaluate individual teachers' performance systematically at regular intervals
- Base promotions, and pay, on skills and performance, rather than years of service
- Dismiss consistently poor performers
- Support good teachers with effective in-service training

Today, no Brazilian school system has a teacher evaluation system that allows for performance-based pay, promotion, and dismissal of ineffective teachers—in fact, rather to the contrary. Barbosa and Costa (2017) have shown that the wage gap between teachers and other professions has been closing since the early 2000s. Salaries are, however, still very far below those paid in professions where the quality of professionals is higher at entry (as proxied by the average student admission tests).

Accountability for developing teacher performance is also low. Absence and tardiness are endemic among teachers (20 percent are absent from school on any given day), and classroom observations (based on the Stallings classroom observation instrument) show that, even when they are not absent, they lose 5 percent of every class hour because they are out of the classroom—arriving late or leaving early.[14] World Bank studies conducted with the states of Ceara, Pernambuco, and Minas and with Rio municipality have shown that teachers lose 20 percent of instructional time—the equivalent of one school day per week—because they cannot manage their classrooms effectively (see figure 4.6). Moreover, they have found teaching practice highly traditional, with heavy reliance on the blackboard and almost no use of information and communication technologies (ICT), and with teachers spending most of their time lecturing or reading aloud rather than questioning students, which research shows is most effective in promoting learning. Like accountability pressure, effective support for teachers, with in-service training, is also low. Brazil spends a lot on in-service training, but most of it is contracted to universities with little interest in raising teachers' effectiveness in the classroom.

The large discrepancies in teacher practices within *municípios*, and even within schools, also pose important challenges to policy. Important facts emerge from classroom observation research documented by Bruns et al. (2015).

FIGURE 4.6

Instructional time use in Brazil, and in Latin America and the Caribbean, 2009–13

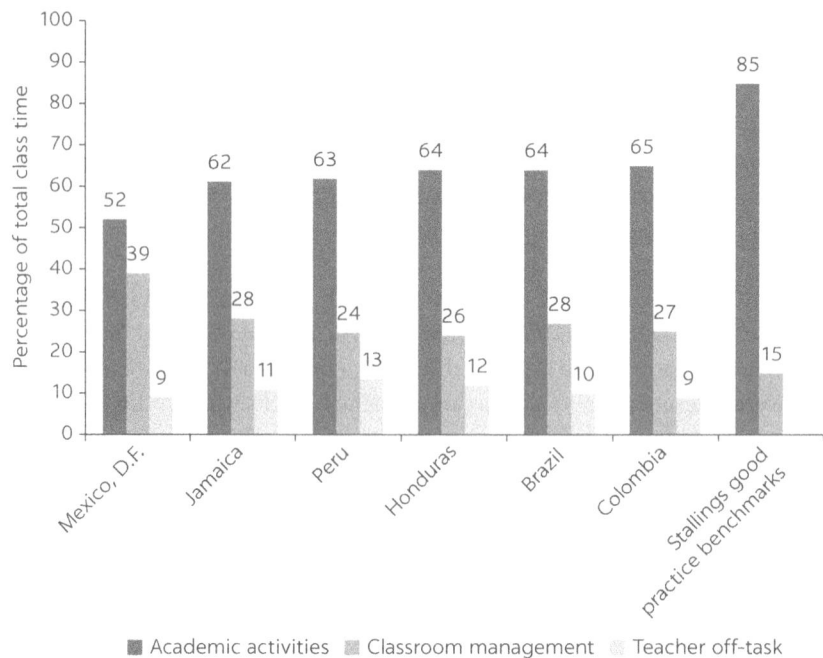

Sources: Bruns and Luque 2015; Stallings and Knight 2003.
Note: Figure reports the results of the application of the Stallings observation instrument in selected LAC countries. The last column reports the values for the proposed "good practice" benchmark resulting from the application of the Stallings instrument in U.S. school districts over several decades, led by Stallings and Knight.

First, teachers with the same formal qualifications and salaries, working within the same schools, often perform very differently. The absence of a teacher evaluation system that can identify and reward the better-performing teachers undermines the long-term incentives for better performance. Second, every school has within it untapped potential for teachers to learn from their peers, but the traditional models of in-service training, delivered by university faculty far offsite, do nothing to catalyze and support this learning. Finally, salary incentives are generally unconnected with teachers' performance.

How can these challenges to improving teacher performance be addressed? At the federal level, having a nationwide teacher entrance exam would be an important initiative. Chile, Colombia, Ecuador, Mexico, and Peru have set national minimum competence standards for teachers and administer an entrance exam to all new teacher graduates that benchmark their readiness to be qualified teachers. The exams generate evidence on the relative quality of different teacher preparation programs and makes it possible to monitor the quality of teacher candidates over time. This reform has been controversial in most countries, especially among teacher unions. The exams are often introduced as voluntary and later made obligatory. Implementing a national exam of this sort in Brazil would send a strong signal that the country is committed to providing all children with good teachers. It would also most benefit the most vulnerable states and *municípios* that do not have the resources to administer their own exams. Another important initiative would be to develop accreditation standards for preservice teacher education schools. Chile and

Peru have made strong efforts to eliminate the lowest quality teacher training schools. In Brazil, university autonomy precludes closing them directly, but accreditation reviews (coupled with poor results on a national teacher entrance exam) would help pressure these deficient training schools out of the market.

Innovative interventions to support the entrance of the "best and brightest" youth into the teaching profession are also promising. Initiatives such as "Teach for All" demonstrate how talented youth can make a difference inside the classroom and can be coupled with more comprehensive teacher evaluations. Well-designed teacher evaluation systems are essential to enable school systems to promote and reward their best teachers and dismiss and/or train their ineffective ones. Brazil has ample room to strengthen its evaluation of secondary school teachers, with the MEC stimulating this progress with financial incentives. A good model is the Race to the Top Program established in the United States by the Barack Obama administration. It awards competitive grants to states and municipalities submitting proposals for new teacher evaluation systems that include assessments of teachers' subject mastery, as well as direct observation of pedagogical practices in the classroom and structured feedback from students, parents, directors, and peers. (Bruns and Luque 2015). Chile, Ecuador, Mexico, and Peru all either have in place or are developing such systems. Some Brazilian states, like Ceará, have also taken important steps in this direction (Bruns, Costa, and Cunha 2017).[15]

Finally, coupling large public investments in in-service teacher training with rigorous impact evaluations is necessary to ensure the cost-effective use of resources. In Brazil, teacher training is mostly the responsibility of the MEC and the states. Some states and municipalities are working with the more promising training approaches, combining in-classroom learning with classroom observation and coaching. The federal government could provide incentives for them to do more evaluations and generate more evidence on which approaches are most cost-effective in their localities. This would make future public spending at all levels of government more efficient. Once successful models are established, the federal government can provide funding and technical support to help the weaker states and municipalities adopt them.

Can technology support teaching and learning?

Can technology support learning in *ensino médio*, especially in more remote areas? Can it be useful in supporting teachers to teach students at the individual level, especially in very diverse classrooms? The greater use of technology in the classrooms is probably the most promising pedagogical intervention in recent years to improve students' outcomes by generating "disruptive innovation" (Glewwe and Muralidharan 2015). Technology-aided instruction, however, has not been always associated with positive impacts on academic outcomes. While some programs have been effective in improving test scores (see, for example, Banerjee et al. 2007; Linden 2008; Lai et al. 2011; and Lai et al. 2012), others have had no impact or even negative impacts (Linden 2008; Barrera-Osorio and Linden 2009; Malamud and Pop-Eleches 2011; Beuermann et al. 2013). Although inconclusive, the evidence suggests that the design and implementation of programs are crucial, and policymakers must be cautious about pronouncing technology interventions effective before scaling them up (Glewwe and Muralidharan 2015).

Technology is already profoundly changing the education sector in Brazil by promoting literacy and equity in access and, one could argue, motivating students and teachers. The main channels through which technology could affect education outcomes include a potentially cost-effective expansion of high-quality instruction using broadcast technology, exposure to better teachers explaining more advanced concepts, additional instruction at home, and interactive instruction with games and puzzles (Glewwe and Muralidharan 2015). Following this international trend, Brazil is committed to implementing further programs that expand access to computers in public schools and incorporate technology into the learning process.

Several states and *municípios* have been using digital technology and have implemented computer-based instruction to individualize the educational process. The early results on learning have been promising. Exposure to technological resources is expected to accommodate individual learning needs better and entice students to pursue higher levels of education. Computer-based instruction can also be used to customize learning plans (World Bank 2018). The Programa Autonomia (Autonomy Program) is one Brazilian example. In partnership with the private sector, this Rio state program aims to reduce age–grade distortion in secondary public schools. It exposes students who are at risk for repeating a grade or of dropping out to technological resources, followed by group discussions. Other states (such as Amazonas or Bahia) exploit technology to provide online lessons to high school students in more remote and rural areas who lack access to physical schools.[16]

Yet rigorous impact evaluations of such initiatives are scarce. One initiative that does attempt such evaluation is underway in an experimental municipal school of the largest favela of Rio de Janeiro. The school is using an innovative pedagogical structure to expose students to educational software that "delivers the entire high-school syllabus in hundreds of digital lessons incorporating text, images, videos and exercises" (Rigby 2016). Online lessons are giving by external lecturers with expertise in advanced topics, and students have individualized learning plans that accommodate their interests and needs. The program "evaluates the students' performance at every step, feeding real-time data to teachers and the school."

Investing in school- and state-level management

Learning in Brazil is undermined by school leaders in most of the secondary schools with weak management skills and low-quality, school-based management practices. The WDR (World Bank 2018) stresses the importance of improving the management aspect of Brazilian schools, which, if it likely does not affect learning directly, does so indirectly, through its impacts on teacher quality and use of learning resources. Substantial reform can happen this area through the promotion of both more effective school-based management models and higher-quality school management.

Recently, the MEC created Plano de Desenvolvimento da Escola (PDE, or the School Development Plan), which is the main federal initiative developed to support school-based management. The purpose of the PDE is to spur innovations at the subnational level to made schools more accountable and orient them toward learning. The efforts include, among others, promoting greater school autonomy, supporting merit-based appointment of school directors, and promoting greater community engagement. The program promotes collaboration across different actors at the local level to help decentralize school management decisions. There, the development of student assessments, complementary to nationwide assessments, has taken place side-by-side with several "results-based" management initiatives at the subnational level. Many systems have designed more targeted training programs for teachers and school leaders, together with other school support programs—for example, the holding of annual meetings between the secretary of education and all school directors in subregional offices to discuss progress and agree on state-level learning targets. During these meetings, regional staff offer technical support on school development plans to school directors of low-performing schools.

Yet these efforts remain isolated and have not been enough to change the poor management practices observed across most systems. Bloom et al. (2014) show that Brazil has struggled to implement effective management practices comparable to those in schools in Canada, Germany, Sweden, the United Kingdom, or the United States. The capacity of school leaders to set and share long-term visions for their schools, as well as to offer feedback to teachers (based on classroom observation) and support them in implementing learning assessments, are important features of the most successful school management models.

The absence of merit-based promotions and the low-quality training programs undermine the quality of school directors. In Brazil, most school directors are middle-aged college-educated women. They receive three times the average salary of teachers, and turnover among them is 20 percent in municipal and 30 percent in state schools. They typically are experienced teachers and hold relatively short job tenures. Reflecting the lack of a federal pre-service strategy for school leaders (directors and pedagogical coordinators), most have never received any school management training. To remedy this, Brazil's Committee of State and Municipal Secretary of Education (CONSED) created Progestão in 2005, as the first national in-service training program targeted to public school leaders. The program expanded rapidly, but its effectiveness has never been evaluated. Other challenges are the lack of merit-based selection of school leaders, the local political influence over their selection, and their low autonomy (Fundação Victor Civita 2009).

Several interventions to improve the quality of school management have been implemented at the subnational level, but few have survived political transitions. Bruns, Filmer, and Patrinos (2011) and Barrera-Osorio et al. (2009) have provided several examples of school-based management reforms. Programs paying bonuses to the best-performing schools have been successfully evaluated in Ceará, Minas Gerais, Pernambuco, and Rio de Janeiro (Vinuela and Zoratto 2013; Bruns, Filmer, and Patrinos 2011). Many certification programs and community consultations were also created to replace the political appointment of most of school directors (Luck 2013). Most of these programs do not continue after governments changed, typically every four years with political elections.

Another challenge to improving school management is the failure to use systematically the administrative and assessment data from Brazil's education system for measuring education results. Brazil's monitoring and information education system is one of the most sophisticated and impressive in the world. The system includes two important features. First, a national annual assessment, "Prova Brasil," measures in a standardized manner student achievement in math and Portuguese. It is administered to all fifth and ninth grade students (when the latter finish *ensino fundamental*). As of 2017, "Prova Brasil" should also be covering all twelfth grade students (in the third cycle of *ensino médio*). Second, Brazil publishes regularly a well-known index of school performance—the Index of Basic Education Development (IDEB)[17]—which combines information on learning with student passing rates across the entire basic education system.[18] Third, ENEM is a nonmandatory standardized student assessment administered in the twelfth grade, when students graduate from high school.[19] Equipped with all this information, Brazil is well positioned to conduct more systematic analysis of the causal factors determining learning performance and to develop learning-oriented reforms, like those already common in several OECD countries, that tackle deeper causes for underperformance and lead to much more effective and results-oriented education management. Brazil is still not systematically using the information, however, to target and monitor education policies.

SUPPORTING RETENTION AND REDUCING DROPOUTS IN *ENSINO MÉDIO:* MOTIVATING AND INFORMING STUDENTS OF THE RETURNS TO EDUCATION

Here we revisit cost-effective interventions intended, first, to reduce the opportunity costs of remaining in school and, second, to increase its perceived benefits. The conceptual framework and evidence discussed in chapters 2 and 3, respectively, highlighted the importance of the opportunity costs of participating in the labor market and/or household tasks, together with the increased opportunity costs associated with teen pregnancy or participation in criminal activities. New evidence also pointed to misinformation on the actual returns on completing *ensino médio* and acknowledged that many students are not motivated by an outdated curriculum. Here we focus on interventions to motivate students to stay in school by reducing teen pregnancy and providing financial support, together with information campaigns on the returns on (or the "value") of education. The discussion draws heavily on Almeida, Fitzsimons, and Rogers (2015) and Loureiro and Szerman (2017), bringing together global experience in dropout prevention for Latin America and for Brazil, respectively.[20]

Motivating students to stay in school: Teen pregnancy prevention and merit scholarships

Despite Brazil's high rates of adolescent pregnancy when compared to peer countries, school-based interventions for preventing it are still rare. The adolescent fertility rate (births per 1,000 females ages 15–19) has been steadily decreasing in Brazil, but, overall, it is still high—in 2015, it was above the average level for LAC, at 66.7 versus 63.7 (Azevedo et al. 2013). The urban/rural divide is also large. Nationwide, 10.5 percent of females 15–19 living in urban areas have had at least one child, compared to 13.2 percent in rural areas.[21] These high rates reduce school attendance and increase the risk of girls dropping out of school. The lack of sex education and limited use of contraceptive methods to prevent pregnancy are likely among the causes. In addition, traditional culture and social norms (especially in rural areas) likely also play a role. Moreover, the most vulnerable youth often lack the motivation and aspirations to continue education and seek entry into the labor market (Machado and Muller 2018).[22] Despite the encouraging evaluation results, success in other countries suggests school-based teen pregnancy prevention programs that are well integrated into secondary school curricula can reduce dropouts, especially among girls. Sex education in the school classrooms, specific support to girls from less structured families, empowerment of the poorest girls, and access to contraceptive methods are among the most common interventions.[23] They aim to address multiple factors that influence teens' decision making relative to pregnancy: sex education and access to information, social norms and gender roles, peer pressure, and socioemotional skills, as well as youth's aspirations toward the future. A regional report on teenage pregnancy for Latin America and the Caribbean reviewed rigorously evaluated interventions to reduce teen pregnancy, including school-based interventions (Azevedo et al. 2012). While such rigorous evaluations are scarce, school-based programs preventing pregnancy and programs encouraging pregnant teens and teen mothers to remain in school seem to reduce dropouts (Steinka-Fry, Wilson, and Tanner-Smith 2013).[24] Brazil still has few interventions to reduce teen pregnancy (Loureiro and Szerman 2017).

Promoting peer support and educating teens on the drivers of their decision making regarding pregnancy and fertility are especially important. The former approach makes use of peer promoters—that is, educators or counselors of similar age and background to those in the target group. The counselors are not professionals but trained volunteers who educate and counsel adolescents in need of reproductive health information and services. Advocates of peer education typically argue that young people relate best to people of their own age with similar backgrounds and interests and who use language and messages meaningful and relevant to them (Azevedo et al. 2012).

Developing higher-level cognitive and socioemotional skills, including higher levels of critical thinking about existing social and gender norms, are other possible ways to reduce teen pregnancy. The first part of this chapter discussed how Brazil can take advantage of the current reform to more strongly emphasize these skills among youth. In addition to basic cognitive competencies (such as literacy and numeracy or information processing) and critical thinking, these include decision making, organization, efficiency, problem solving, and written and oral communications (Cunningham and Villasenor 2014). Box 4.3 discusses successful school-based interventions in Ecuador and the United States for reducing teen pregnancy.

Merit scholarships are another instrument with the potential to motivate and engage youth to stay in school while reducing opportunity costs, especially among girls. Instruments that combine such achievement awards with financial incentives can help the most vulnerable youth overcome financial constraints while motivating them to increase the effort they put into completing secondary education. Brazil is already using conditional cash transfers (such as Bolsa Família) to encourage school attendance; these have proved effective in increasing school enrollment in LAC (Fiszbein et al. 2009).

Several interesting international experiences have shown gender-sensitive results from similar programs. One, implemented in secondary schools in Israel, gives cash rewards to upper secondary students for progressing through the grades and for completing school. Although an evaluation did not show an effect on males, the program did increase completion rates among girls by roughly 10 percentage points (Angrist and Lavy 2009). Similarly, an evaluation of a U.S. program providing cash incentives for graduation, as well as educational support, found female participants enjoyed a short-term gain in high school graduation rates and a long-run gain in postsecondary enrollment; but, again, there was no effect on males (Rodriguez-Planas 2012). Within LAC, the "Ser Pilo Paga" program in Colombia offers incentive to complete high school by providing eligible

BOX 4.3

How to reduce teen pregnancy with school-based interventions? The "Text Me Maybe" program in Ecuador and TOP in the United States

The "Text Me Maybe" program in Ecuador implemented two teenage pregnancy components among public high school students in the academic year 2013–14. The first was a "peer-to-peer" education program in municipal schools, in which student leaders were trained on topics of sexual and reproductive health, gender roles, and prejudices and stereotypes. These students provided information to peers through adolescent-friendly events, including customized workshops, games, and other interactive activities. In the second, behavioral component, information was sent via cell phone text messages at crucial times, including weekend evenings, to remind teenagers of their long-term aspirations. Using a randomized controlled trial (RCT), Cuevas et al. (2015) found that attending a school with the Text Me Maybe program increased the proportion of individuals currently studying (86 percent in control schools, as compared to 89 percent in treatment schools) and reduced teenage pregnancy by 3 percentage points. No reduction in teen pregnancy was found to be associated specifically with the text message intervention.

The "Teen Outreach Program" (TOP) has been implemented in various U.S. cities. TOP is a high school–level teenage pregnancy and school dropout prevention program that specifically targets students at high risk of dropping out for teenage mothering or fathering. The program has three components, which are implemented over a nine-month time frame: community service to empower youth to succeed; classroom discussions about their volunteer experiences; and socioemotional skill development (which the program calls "life skills"). The TOP curriculum covers such topics as values, human growth and development, relationships, coping with family stress, and other social and emotional issues relevant to youth transitions from adolescence to adulthood. Evaluations of TOP show participants have lower rates of risky behaviors, such as failing classes, being suspended from school, dropping out of school, and becoming pregnant in adolescence (Frost and Forrest 1995; Allen 2001). In an evaluation conducted by Allen (2001), participants in TOP had half the risk of pregnancy of the comparison group, and participants who were already mothers or fathers showed one-fifth the risk of a repeat pregnancy.

Source: Busso et al. 2017.

students with college loans that are forgiven upon college graduation (Busso et al. 2017; Londono-Velez, Rodriguez, and Sanchez 2017).

Remedial academic support, CBT, and the value of information

At the subnational level, remedial education prevention programs for lagging students may be a means of reducing dropouts from *ensino médio*. This chapter has already discussed in detail the remarkably high rates of age–grade distortion and grade repetition in Brazil, as well as the large within-country inequities in these regards. Remedial instruction can help students, especially disadvantaged ones, catch up to their peers by strengthening their proficiency levels in basic subjects, thus keeping them in the formal education system. Several states and municipalities have developed their own remedial programs (Loureiro and Szerman 2017). Among them are the Rio de Janeiro program "Reforço Escola" and the Ceara state program "Aprender para Valer." The former provides two weeks of intensive tutoring to students who are identified as functional illiterates at the primary level, while the latter aims to bring high school students' knowledge up to age–grade levels by providing supplementary learning time and materials.

To promote remedial education, local and state governments have formed partnerships with educational nongovernmental organizations (NGOs) and the private sector. The Ayrton Senna Institute, together with subnational governments, has implemented several programs to reduce age–grade distortion rates and in primary schools. Two examples are the Acelera Brasil (Speed Up Brazil) program helping students who have repeated a grade in primary education by accelerating their learning to established proficiency levels, and Se Liga" [Come On], targeting illiterate students in their first years of primary education (Loureiro and Szerman 2017). Both use specific remedial learning material and include systematic support from teachers and a school coordinator. While both seem to be showing positive results, rigorous evaluations of their impacts on age–grade distortion have yet to be done.

Programs based on cognitive behavioral therapy (CBT) can support changes in thoughts and behaviors, especially among the most vulnerable high school students. Typically, these programs aim to improve the social skills and problem-solving abilities young people need to cope with life and to reduce violence and/or depression. Students learn to recognize difficult situations that have provoked negative responses in the past and to identify and implement acceptable responses. By practicing these skills through various teaching and role-playing activities, they learn to engage in appropriate behavior more consistently in such situations.

CBT techniques delivered to at-risk youth can reduce depression and anxiety, ultimately preventing dropout. Little rigorous evaluation evidence is as yet available on CBT-based interventions with young people in secondary schools, and well-conducted randomized controlled trials are clearly needed. One large RCT was conducted by Heller et al. (2013) for Becoming a Man (BAM), an intervention for disadvantaged male youth in grades 7–10 from high-crime neighborhoods in Chicago. BAM included regular interactions with psychologists, after-school programming, and in-school programming designed to reduce common problems related to judgment and decision making, and the study found its effects were quite substantial. Program participation reduced violent-crime arrests during the program year by 8.1 per 100 youth (a 44 percent reduction). It also generated sustained gains in schooling outcomes equal to 0.14 standard deviations during the program year and 0.19 standard deviations during the follow-up year, which, the authors estimated, could lead to higher graduation rates of 3–10 percentage points (equal to gains of 7–22 percent, because of the low baseline rate).

Turning to another form of intervention, Brazil is very well positioned to take advantage of its world-class education M&E system to invest in information campaigns to parents on the value of attending school and of education. The Dominican Republic invested in such a program with positive returns (see, Jensen 2010).[25] By contrast, an experiment with upper secondary students in Mexico found no effect of information campaigns (Avitabile and De Hoyos Navarro 2015). These outcomes suggest that information-based programs work better at preventing dropout where students are initially less informed—most likely in poorer areas—and where the information intervention is supported by financing for students from poor households.

Finally, Brazil can also make use of its M&E information system to predict dropouts at the school level, creating, in effect, an early warning system. Many OECD countries, including European countries and the United States, have already developed such systems with success, and some middle-income countries in LAC are now considering them (see Adelman et al. 2017).

SUPPORTING TRANSITIONS INTO HIGHER EDUCATION

An expansion in access to higher education that has been going on in Brazil since the early 2000s was motivated in part by large wage returns on having a college degree. On average, the monthly earnings of workers with degrees from higher education institutions are more than double those of high school graduate workers. According to Ferreyra et al. (2017), the economic returns associated with higher education degrees in Brazil, at 130 percent, are among the highest in the region, well above the LAC average of 102 percent.

The expansion was also supported by new student financing programs, including the well-known Financing of Higher Education (FIES) program and ProUni, which are described in detail in a background paper prepared for this book (Verhire and Nascimento 2017). ProUni is a federal scholarship program, created in 2005, that gives tax incentives to private providers who offer full or partial scholarships to low-income students.[26] FIES is a federal student loan program, but, unlike similar programs found in many countries, it gives the loan directly to the institution at which the student is enrolled. To participate, a student must obtain a passing grade on the national test for secondary school students (the ENEM), and the institution needs to be approved by the MEC's national evaluation system for higher education (Sistema Nacional de Avaliação da Educação Superior, or SINAES).[27] Over one million students are in FIES, and 1.7 million have so far benefited from ProUni.

Finally, the expansion in access to higher education has also been supported by affirmative action programs for the lowest income students).[28] As of 2013, students from the bottom half of the income distribution in Brazil accounted for 19 percent of all the enrollments (Ferreyra et al. 2017).

Despite this increased access for lower-income youth, those from higher-income backgrounds still hold a significant advantage in obtaining higher education and are more likely to complete their degrees than their lower-income peers. Brazilian youth among the bottom quintile of the income distribution still have less access to higher education than those in the top quintile; 10 percent versus 55 percent, respectively, go to college. Once in college, lower-income youth are also less likely to complete their undergraduate degrees, in part because of their less adequate academic readiness (Ferreyra et al. 2017). Although little empirical evidence is available on dropout rates in higher education in Brazil, some estimates put it between 25 and 50 percent of students. This failure to complete is likely related to affordability, students' transitions to the labor market, and poor academic preparation. Research on the link between student aid and college completion has demonstrated that aid tends to improve student performance and reduce dropouts. (Bettinger 2015). This seems to be also true for Brazil, where evidence indicates FIES and ProUni students who graduated from high school between 2003 and 2005 were 25–67 percent more likely to complete college (Xavier 2014).

Many lower-income youth attend short-duration and market-oriented technological courses provided mostly by private universities in the areas of business administration, finance, human resources, logistics, and marketing; evidence shows these can be a good option to support employability among students who are not necessarily in the top ability distribution. In a background paper prepared for this book, Almeida et al. (2016) quantified the private wage returns on technological courses after accounting for differences in students' aptitude and an extensive set of observable characteristics at entry.[29] Their comparison of the labor market performance of students who enrolled in these two-year courses in 2011 and 2012 with that of those never attended higher education during 2010–15 showed substantial heterogeneity in the returns across courses, and generally higher returns on finance-related courses.[30]

Concerns with the high noncompletion rates among the poorest youth in Brazil have prompted reforms in federal subsidy programs. Overall, public financing of higher education accounts for 30 percent of the overall budget and is in line with peer countries (World Bank 2017). But this spending is mostly concentrated among the higher-income groups, who are more likely to complete high school with high enough grades to qualify for admission to college. Reforms in FIES and ProUni have aimed to reduce public financing while increasing the quality of education by raising the threshold (in the test scores) for students to gain access to these subsidies. In addition, a policy reform disqualified lower-quality higher-education providers—that is, those with Index of Courses (IGC) evaluations of less than 3 out of 5—from receiving FIES funding and required that students have a minimum score of 450 on the ENEM. In 2015, the FIES interest rate also increased, from 3.4 percent to 6.5 percent. Together, these reforms caused the number of new loan contracts to fall. While the unbalanced public spending across basic and higher education, and the high inefficiencies in the basic education system, may be acknowledged as the main reasons higher-education spending has been focused on the better-off students, room still remains to rethink the design of student financing programs.

Although the quality assurance of the higher education system is well-grounded on a set of sophisticated student and provider information, it, too, can be strengthened by including a stronger focus on relevance and labor market insertion of graduates. The higher-education National Assessment of Student Achievement (ENADE) assesses the knowledge of students in undergraduate programs when they finish their courses.[31] Courses are also evaluated by the Brazilian Higher Education Evaluation Commission (Comissão Nacional de Avaliação do Ensino Superior, or CONAES), based on data from the National System of Evaluation of Higher Education (SINAES). Instituto Nacional de Estudos e Pesquisas Educacionais Anísio Teixeira (INEP) collects and publishes these data, and the MEC publishes the results of the annual evaluations regularly. Nevertheless, more can be done by including measures of graduation rates and labor market outcomes in SINAES and by focusing the criteria used in the M&E system to measure the relevance and quality of providers more on these areas.

Also advisable would be to make available to youth more and better information on the employability and earnings of graduates of different higher education providers, which today are assessed and disclosed by only a few. Providers could, for instance, follow the example of Italy, where universities and private business work together to make academic information available to students that they can upload to individual digital files to help match them to jobs. Since Brazil has solid data sets on education (such as Census Escolar and ENEM) and its labor market (RAIS) that can be used to compute the learning and labor market "value added" of higher education, more such information could be systematically produced and publicly disclosed to inform meaningfully student choices. This is especially important in light of the heterogeneity of the labor market returns across socioeconomic backgrounds, courses, and providers, as documented above. The Italian consortium AlmaLaurea, described in box 4.4, which offers systematic M&E at the university level, might be adaptable to technical education. AlmaLaurea successfully integrates the collection of student data, labor market outcomes, and curricula vitae to provide the relevant stakeholders with a suite of services.

More broadly, at the federal level, the MEC can work on a more systematic effort to understand what jobs are being created in Brazil's economy and which skills are most in demand to determine which courses and programs would be most effective.

BOX 4.4

AlmaLaurea in Italy: Emphasizing labor market intermediation

AlmaLaurea is an interuniversity consortium that emerged in Italy in 1994 from the collaborative efforts of a group of researchers at the University of Bologna. They had set up a databank of students' curricula vitae (CVs) to aid in the evaluation of the role universities play in youth employability. Today, the consortium comprises 64 Italian universities and the Italian Ministry of Education, University, and Research (MIUR), as well as companies and institutions that use AlmaLaurea's databank and services. AlmaLaurea has also signed agreements with other European universities. In Asia Latin America, it facilitates the mobility of both the Italian and foreign students in its networks in the international labor market.

Since 1994, AlmaLaurea's portfolio of services has expanded from its start as a CV databank. Its approach to the provision of data, information, and career guidance to connect universities, students, and the labor market rests on three pillars:

- *Graduates' Profile*—an annual survey and report on the internal efficiency of the higher education system
- *Graduates' Employment Conditions*—an annual survey and report on the external efficiency of the higher education system

- The online databank of graduates' curricula vitae—a tool that improves the match between supply and demand of graduates and facilitates their transnational mobility. In Italy, the databank covers approximately 78 percent of Italian graduates and includes more than 1.72 million university-certified curricula vitae, which are translated into English.

AlmaLaurea supplies reliable data to the governing bodies of the consortium universities, as well as the assessment units and committees dealing with teaching activities and career guidance. AlmaLaurea's data serve as a basis for national- and university-level policymaking and activity planning, especially in the development and improvement of training activities and services that target students. Moreover, AlmaLaurea creates more equal conditions for young people to get access to both the Italian and international labor markets. In 2007, an impact study of AlmaLaurea concluded that graduates of universities in the consortium had more than a 2 percent higher chance of finding a job and a 3 percent higher average monthly income, and were 2.5 percent more satisfied with their jobs, than graduates who were not part of the consortium (see Bagues and Labini 2009).

Sources: Almeida, Amaral, and Felicio 2015; Bagues and Labini 2009.

TABLE 4.1 Reforms to Brazil's education policies likely improving completion and transitions to higher education or back into the education system

PROGRAMS	MAIN CHALLENGES	PROPOSED REFORMS	ANTICIPATED IMPACT
Subnational implementation of the *ensino médio* reform (new competence-based curriculum and full-time school model)	• Increased inequalities in access to good-quality education • Technical education that does not meet business needs • Lack of socioemotional skills among teenagers • Extended-day schools without improved educational outcomes • World-class monitoring and evaluation system in education rarely used to inform policies	• Increased staffing and trainings for technical staff at MEC to monitor and supervise implementation of the *ensino médio* reform at the subnational level (including inputs and outputs) • Creation of an Edu-lab within MEC, promoting the use of innovative and cost-effective programs in the execution of selected aspects of the reform (for example, developing SESs and delivery of FTS) • Strengthened partnerships with private sector in the delivery of TVET (in the design of the curriculum, apprenticeship opportunities, and teacher training) • Systematic analysis of learning assessments to inform design and implementation of policies at national and subnational levels	• Increased student learning, reduced grade repetition, and reduction in dropout rates • Strengthened institutional capacity to support states in the implementation of the *ensino médio* reform • Move toward evidence-based decision making
Teacher and school management reforms	• Low teacher preparedness and motivation • Political appointments of school principals	• Development of accreditation standards for preservice teacher trainings including training in academic subjects but also in SESs and pedagogical practices • Piloting and evaluation of ICT interventions supporting customized teaching and learning at the "right" level • Creation of a nationwide teacher entrance exam • Development of more comprehensive teacher evaluation systems, including school-based classroom observation tools • Merit-based selection of school principals and more effective in-service training programs	• Increased student learning
Complementary programs to reduce dropouts from *ensino médio*	• High teenage pregnancy rates • Misinformation on the returns on education • Low retention and completion rates in *ensino médio*	• Use of school-based informational programs on teen pregnancy • Regular computing and dissemination of information on the returns to students on formal academic and technical education • Conditioning of merit scholarships on student performance • Provision of remedial education on core academic subjects, complemented by SES interventions	• Reduced teen pregnancy rates • Improved knowledge on the incentives to invest in human capital • Reduced dropouts from *ensino médio* and increased completion rates

NOTES

1. This chapter relies on several sources, including new background papers prepared especially for this book. These include Loureiro and Szerman's (2017) assessment of the patterns in youth dropouts in *ensino médio* in Brazil and discussion of promising national interventions to mitigate them; Barbosa and Costa's (2017) evaluation of the outcomes of increased education for teachers; Machado and Muller's (2018) documenting of new qualitative work exploring the drivers and consequences of gender differences in the patterns of youth dropout; and Gukovas and Kejsefman's (2017) proposal of new evidence on the returns on education among Brazilian teenagers and the incentives to remain in school. The chapter also benefited from analytical work led by the WBG Education Global practice, including Almeida, Fitzsimons, and Rodgers (2015); Almeida et al. (2016); the education background paper prepared for the WBG Brazil Systematic Country Diagnostic; and the education chapter in the *Brazil Expenditure Review* (World Bank 2017).

2. The Programme for International Student Assessment (PISA), led by the OECD, is a worldwide project intended to evaluate education systems by measuring the performance of 15-year-old students on mathematics, science, and reading.

3. Figure 4.2 reports statistics for students in the last year of *ensino medio* taking the Exame Nacional do Ensino Médio (ENEM) between 2009 and 2015. ENEM is a nonmandatory, standardized national exam that evaluates high school students in Brazil. Since 2009, ENEM has been used both as an admissions test for enrollment in higher education and for high school certification.

4. The decision to drop out of school in Brazil is usually made in critical moments, such as during family struggles, transition into high school, or family shocks. For young men, the transition into adulthood is expressed in their increased focus on their work lives in search of financial independence. For young women, it is expressed in their desire to form their own families. In both cases, these transitions represent a shift in the meaning of education in their lives.

5. The NEP establishes that, by 2024, at least 25 percent of all students enrolled in public upper secondary education in Brazil must attend full-time schools.

6. The Ministry of Education (Ministério da Educação, or MEC) is supporting the state education secretariats (Secretaria Estadual Educação, or SEE) in the introduction of full-time school in 1,088 targeted schools throughout the country (8 percent of total public upper secondary enrollment). Schools are selected based on four conditions, two of which were set to foster equity: (1) a minimum of 120 enrollments in the first year of upper secondary; (2) high socioeconomic vulnerability in the student population relative to the respective education network, taking into consideration a socioeconomic indicator disaggregated by school; (3) the existence of at least four of the six infrastructure items; and (4) location in the more disadvantaged states (measured as low learning/high dropout).

7. The MEC, through the Basic Education Secretariat (Secretaria Educação Basica, or SEB) leads the process for the development of the BNCC, sets curricular guidelines, and offers technical support to states in curricular design. At the time of the completion of this book, the BNCC was under consultation with the civil society. Once approved, the states' curricula will be redesigned to align with it.

8. For more information, see http://www.minedu.gob.pe/minedulab/.

9. In the Rio model to develop SESs, teachers support students in various ways. During guided study periods, they help them search for information of interest and synthetize it. They also hold meetings with small groups of students to discuss their academic or personal concerns. During self-management periods, students are granted autonomy to decide which activities to participate in (artistic activities, sports, workshops, and so on); during intervention project and research periods, they are organized into groups to develop projects related to real-life experiences (InnoveEdu).

10. The global review also shows that full-time schools, although expensive, can be cost-effective models for improving student learning and school dropout rates in upper secondary education if they are well designed and implemented (Holland, Evans, and Alfaro 2015). In some cases, the intervention raises test scores or improves other outcomes; rigorously obtained evidence has shown effects on attainment and dropout rates in Argentina (Llach, Gigaglia, and Orgales 2009) and Brazil (Dias 2011) and in Chile (Pires and Urzua 2010), with an especially large increase of 21 percent in graduation rates in Argentina. The review

concludes that positive effects are often especially large for at-risk students; it also cautions, however, that full-time schooling problems are quite expensive to address, so these benefits should be weighed against the costs.

11. The program started in 2008 with 1,380 schools, and, by 2013, more than 65 percent of the Brazilian municipalities had schools participating in the program.

12. Almeida et al. (2016) evaluated the program's impact in its first years of implementation between 2008 and 2011. They found, on average, no impact on dropout rates; but cities with higher gross domestic product (GDP) per capita did experience reductions. Focusing on urban schools that implemented the program in 2012, Oliveira and Terra (2016) also did not find any effect on dropout rates. Almeida et al. (2016) found the expansion of the program associated with a negative impact on mathematics test scores for both fifth and ninth graders, but these effects tended to fade away over time; no impact on Portuguese test scores was found. Almeida et al. (2016) attributed the lack of significant impact to initial challenges in the implementation of the program, which required changes for students, teachers, and schools. As long as the initiative consolidated, the negative effects tended to diminish and ultimately be reversed. Oliveira and Terra (2016) did not find any impact on test scores.

13. See Hanushek and Woessman (2012), Hanushek, Peterson, and Woessmann (2012), and Chetty, Friedman, and Rockoff (2014a; 2014b). Qualitative research in Machado and Muller (2018) also stresses the role teachers can play in defining the value students attribute to education and securing youth's engagement with the education system.

14. For details, see Bruns and Luque (2015). The Stallings observation instrument was applied in selected LAC countries, including Brazil, between 2009 and 2013. This was a large-scale effort to build reliable, globally comparable data on teacher classroom practice covering more than 150,000 different "snapshots" of classrooms in over 3,000 schools in seven different countries. In addition to Brazil, participating countries included Colombia, Honduras, Jamaica, Mexico, and Peru, and a pilot effort was carried out in the Dominican Republic (not reported). In Colombia, Honduras, Jamaica, and Peru, school samples were representative at the national level. The samples in Brazil and Mexico were representative at the level of participating subnational governments: the states of Pernambuco and Minas Gerais and the municipality of Rio de Janeiro in Brazil and the Federal District (Distrito Federal, or D.F.) in Mexico. High-performing schools achieve an average of 85 percent of class time spent on instruction, which is taken as a benchmark for good classroom practice.

15. Bruns, Costa, and Cunha (2017) have evaluated a program to improve teachers' effectiveness by using an information "shock" (benchmarked feedback) and expert coaching to promote increased professional interaction among teachers within schools. The program significantly increased teachers' use of class time for instruction and, consistent with its objective of fostering interaction among them, reduced the variation in their practices.

16. Loureiro and Szerman (2017) describe the initiatives in the Amazonas state, with the Educational Media Center of Amazonas (Centro de Mídias de Educação do Amazonas), and in the state of Bahia, with the High School with Technological Intervention (Ensino Médio com Mediação Tecnológica).

17. In Brazil, basic education includes fundamental education (with low fundamental education covering grades 1–5 and high fundamental education covering grades 6–9). Upper secondary education (or *ensino médio*) covers grades 10–12.

18. IDEB shows how well students are learning and how efficiently their schools or school systems are performing (Bruns, Filmer, and Patrinos 2011). IDEB scores are available for approximately 5,200 municipal school systems, 26 state systems, and the federal district. Hence, every segment of the Brazilian education system can be benchmarked.

19. Although not mandatory, the ENEM is used to determine entry into university. The assessment covers student performance in different fields, including science, Portuguese, math, and general knowledge.

20. Almeida, Fitzsimons, and Rogers (2015) reviewed the evidence on programs to prevent dropouts around the world at the upper secondary level using a rigorous empirical strategy with well-defined counterfactuals (including randomized controlled trials), quasi-experimental studies, and well-designed matching studies. Loureiro and Szerman (2017) is a complementary paper to this one, focused specifically on evidence for Brazil at secondary schools. Drawing on rigorous studies to support policy recommendations is especially important in this area. Brazilian youth who drop out of school are clearly different from those who

graduate from *ensino médio* in their socioeconomic backgrounds, local and school environments, and individual motivations, among other characteristics.

21. In the North, the shares are 14.9 percent in urban and 18.9 percent in rural areas (see Azevedo et al. 2012).

22. Women's aspirations are usually related to "happiness in family life," and the partners' and communities' control over their mobility creates additional barriers. Many teenage girls do not feel motivated enough to continue studying, and some prefer to anticipate motherhood.

23. Aspirations and "grit" among young women can be shaped by exposing them to female role models and mentors, as well as by supporting their negotiation of household responsibilities and offering positive coping strategies to deal with negative community and family attitudes toward their work, education, and mobility.

24. Much less rigorous evidence is available on the relationship between programs to prevent teen fatherhood and boys' likelihood of dropping out of school.

25. Youth who were given information on the actual returns to education substantially increased their attainment. The effects were strongest for students from less poor households.

26. To qualify for a full exemption from four different types of taxes, private higher education institutions must offer scholarships equivalent to 8.5 percent of their annual revenue. Priority must be given to full scholarships, with a required ratio of at least one scholarship student to every 22 paying students. If full scholarships provided to students do not meet the 8.5 percent requirement, private institutions are allowed to complement their count with half scholarships until the threshold is met.

27. Created in 1998, FIES expanded after 2005. In 2014, FIES loans benefited more than 500,000 students enrolled in private institutions. In addition to funds provided by the MEC, FIES is supported by government bonds and contributions from a national lottery.

28. Evidence presented by Waltenberg and Carvalho (2012) shows these actions have been successful in improving the chances of lower-income youth to get access to all types of higher education institutions, public and private.

29. Almeida, Caseiro, Maciente, and Nascimento (2017) used unique administrative data sets and PSM methodology to compute the labor earnings of selected higher-education courses during 2009–14. They combined data sets collected by INEP with data from the ENEM (2009–10), the National Higher Education Performance Exam (ENADE 2012), the Higher Education Census (2010–14), and the Annual Social Information Registry (RAIS 2009–14).

30. According to Ferreyra et al. (2017), in Chile and Peru, fields such as education and humanities provide either close to zero or negative net returns, while engineering, law, and business provide returns much more than double than those of a high school diploma.

31. Each program is assessed every three years, and the assessment is compulsory.

REFERENCES

Adelman, Melissa, Francisco Haimovich, Andres Ham, and Emmanuel Vazquez. 2017. "Predicting School Dropout with Administrative Data: New Evidence from Guatemala and Honduras." Policy Research Working Paper 8142. World Bank, Washington, DC.

Alfaro, Pablo, David Evans, and Peter Anthony Holland. 2015. "Extending the School Day in Latin America and the Caribbean (English)." Policy Research Working Paper WPS 7309, Impact Evaluation series. World Bank Group, Washington, DC.

Allen, Anita. 2001. "Is Privacy Now Possible? A Brief History of an Obsession." *Social Research: An International Quarterly* 68 (1): 301–5.

Almeida, R., N. Amaral, and F. de Felicio. 2016. "Assessing Advances and Challenges in Technical Education in Brazil." Publication 22726, World Bank, Washington, DC, January. https://openknowledge.worldbank.org/handle/10986/22726.

Almeida, R., L. Caseiro, A. Maciente, and P. Nascimento. "Wages and Employability of Higher Education Graduates in Brazil: Evidence from Matched Employer-Employee Data." Unpublished presentation, World Bank, Washington, DC.

Almeida, R., A. Loureiro, L. Costa, M. Drabble, and B. Bruns. 2016. Unpublished background education paper to the Brazil Systematic Country Diagnostic. Mimeo. World Bank. World Bank, Washington, DC.

Almeida, R., N. Amaral, and F. Felicio. 2015. "Assessing Advances and Challenges in Technical Education in Brazil." World Bank, Washington, DC.

Almeida, Rita Kullberg, Leandro Anazawa, Naercio Menezes Filho, Ligia Maria De Vasconcellos. 2015. Investing in Technical & Vocational Education and Training: Does It Yield Large Economic Returns in Brazil? (English). Policy Research working paper; no. WPS 7246. Washington, DC: World Bank. http://documents.worldbank.org/curated/en/46598146 8181787054/Investing-in-technical-vocational-education-and-training-does-it-yield-large -economic-returns-in-Brazil.

Almeida, R., E. Fitzsimons, and H. Rogers. 2015. "How to Prevent Secondary-School Drop-Outs: Evidence from Rigorous Evaluations." World Bank, Washington, DC.

Angrist, J., and V. Lavy. 2009. "The Effects of High Stakes High School Achievement Awards: Evidence from a Randomized Trial." *American Economic Review*, 99 (4): 1384–1414.

Avitabile, Ciro, and Rafael E. De Hoyos Navarro. 2015. "The Heterogeneous Effect of Information on Student Performance: Evidence from a Randomized Control Trial in Mexico (English)." Policy Research Working Paper WPS 7422. World Bank Group, Washington, DC.

Ayrton Senna Institute. 2014. Annual results report working paper.

Azevedo, J.P., M. E. Dávalos, C. Diaz-Bonilla, B. Atuesta, and R.A. Castañeda. (2013). "Fifteen Years of Inequality in Latin America: How Have Labor Markets Helped?" Policy Research Working Paper 6384, World Bank, Washington, DC.

Azevedo, Joao Pedro, M. Favara, S. E. Haddock, Luis F. Lopez-Calva, Miriam Muller, and Elizaveta Perova. 2012. "Teenage Pregnancy and Opportunities in Latin America and the Caribbean: On Teenage Fertility Decisions, Poverty and Economic Achievement." World Bank, Washington, DC.

Bagues, M. F., and M. Sylos Labini. 2009. "Do Online Labor Market Intermediaries Matter? The Impact of AlmaLaurea on the University-to-Work Transition." In *Studies of Labor Market Intermediation*. Chicago: University of Chicago Press.

Banerjee, A., S. Cole, E. Duflo, and L. Linden. 2007. "Remedying Education: Evidence from Two Randomized Experiments in India." *Quarterly Journal of Economics* 122 (3): 1235–64.

Barbosa, M., and L. Costa. 2017. "Formação dos professores e aprendizagem nas escolas de *Ensino Médio* da rede pública." Mimeo. World Bank Group, Washington, DC.

Barrera-Osorio, Felipe, Tazeen Fasih, Harry Anthony Patrinos, and Lucrecia Santibáñez. 2009. "Decentralized Decision-Making in Schools: The Theory and Evidence on School-Based Management." Directions in Development: Human Development. World Bank, Washington, DC.

Barrera-Osorio, Felipe, and Leigh L. Linden. 2009. "The Use and Misuse of Computers in Education: Evidence from a Randomized Experiment in Colombia." Impact Evaluation series; no. IE 29. Policy Research working paper WPS 4836. World Bank, Washington, DC.

Barros, R., M. Carvalho, S. Franco, and R. Mendonça. 2010. "Markets, the State, and the Dynamics of Inequality in Brazil." In *Declining Inequality in Latin America: A Decade of Progress?* edited by Luis F. Lopez-Calva and Nora Lustig, 134–74. Washington, DC: Brookings Institution and United Nations Development Programme.

Bettinger, E. 2015. "Need-Based Aid and College Persistence: The Effects of the Ohio College Opportunity Grant." *Educational Evaluation and Policy Analysis* 37 (1S): 102–19S.

Beuermann, D., J. P. Cristia, Y. Cruz-Aguayo, S. Cueto, and O. Malamud. 2013. "Home Computers and Child Outcomes: Short-Term Impacts from a Randomized Experiment in Peru." NBER Working Paper No. 18818.

Bloom, N., R. Lemos, R. Sadun, and J. Van Reenen. 2014. "Does Management Matter in Schools?" CEP Discussion Paper 1312. Centre for Economic Performance, London.

Bruns, B., D. Evans, and J. Luque. 2012. "Achieving World-Class Education in Brazil: The Next Agenda." Directions in Development Series. Washington, DC: World Bank.

Bruns, B., D. Filmer, and H. A. Patrinos. 2011. "Making Schools Work: New Evidence on Accountability Reforms." Human Development Perspectives. Washington DC: World Bank Group.

Bruns, Barbara, Leandro Costa, and Nina Cunha. 2017. "Through the Looking Glass: Can Classroom Observation and Coaching Improve Teacher Performance in Brazil?" Policy Research Working Paper 8156. World Bank, Washington, DC.

Bruns, Barbara, and Javier Luque. 2015. "Great Teachers: How to Raise Student Learning in Latin America and the Caribbean." World Bank, Washington, DC. https://openknowledge .worldbank.org/handle/10986/20488.

Busso, M., J. Cristia, D. Hincapié, J. Messina, and L. Ripani. 2017. "Learning Better: Public Policy for Skills Development." Inter-American Development Bank, Washington DC.

Chetty, R., J. N. Friedman, and J. E. Rockoff. 2014a. "Measuring the Impacts of Teachers I: Evaluating Bias in Teacher Value-Added Estimates." *American Economic Review* 104 (9): 2593–2632

———. 2014b. "Measuring the Impacts of Teachers II: Teacher Value-Added and Student Outcomes in Adulthood." *American Economic Review* 104 (9): 2633–79.

Cruz, Tassia, Andre Loureiro, and Eduardo Sa. 2017. "Full-Time Teachers, Students, and Curriculum: The Single-Shift Model in Rio de Janeiro." Policy Research Working Paper WPS 8086. World Bank, Washington, DC. https://openknowledge.worldbank.org/handle/10986/27286.

Cuevas, Pablo Facundo, Marta Favara, and Megan Zella Rounseville. 2015. *Piloting a New Intervention for Teenage Pregnancy Prevention: Impact Evaluation Report.* Washington, DC: World Bank. https://hubs.worldbank.org/docs/imagebank/pages/docprofile.aspx ?nodeid=25692397

Cunningham, Wendy, and Paula Villasenor. 2014. "Employer Voices, Employer Demands, and Implications for Public Skills Development Policy." Policy Research Working Paper WPS 6853. World Bank, Washington, DC.

Ferreyra, M., Ciro Avitabile, Javier Botero Álvarez, Francisco Haimovich Paz, and Sergio Urzúa. 2017. "At a Crossroads: Higher Education in Latin America and the Caribbean." Directions in Development: Human Development. World Bank, Washington, DC.

Fiszbein, A., N. Schady, F. Ferreira, H. G. Francisco, M. Grosh, N. Keleher, P. Olinto, and E. Skoufias. 2009. "Conditional Cash Transfers: Reducing Present and Future Poverty." World Bank Policy Research Report. World Bank, Washington, DC.

Frost, J. J., and J. D. Forrest. 1995. "Understanding the Impact of Effective Teenage Pregnancy Prevention Programs." *Family Planning Perspectives* 27: 188–95.

Fundação Civita Foundation. 2009. "Gestão Escolar nas Escolas Públicas de Ensino Básico das principais capitais brasileiras: o perfil do protagonista. Estudos e Pesquisas Educacionais" [School Management in Basic Education Public Schools among the Brazilian Main Capital Cities"] Estudos e Pesquisas, Fundação Victor Civita, São Paulo, Brazil.

Glewwe, Paul, and Karthik Muralidharan. 2015. "Improving School Education Outcomes in Developing Countries." RISE Working Paper 15/001. Rise Programme.

Hanushek, E., P. Peterson, and L. Woessmann. 2012. "Achievement Growth: International and U.S. State Trends in Student Performance." PEPG Report 12-03, Program on Education Policy and Governance, Harvard University, Cambridge, MA.

Hanushek, E. A., and L. Woessmann. 2008. "The Role of Cognitive Skills in Economic Development." *Journal of Economic Literature* 46 (3): 607–68.

———. 2012. "Schooling, Educational Achievement, and the Latin American Growth Puzzle." *Journal of Development Economics* 99 (2): 497–512.

Holland, P., P. Alfaro, and D. Evans. 2015. "Extending the School Day in Latin America and the Caribbean." Policy Research Working Paper WPS 7309. Impact Evaluation series. World Bank Group, Washington, DC.

IBGE (Brazilian Institute of Geography and Statistics). 2004–15. "*Pesquisa Nacional por Amostra de Domicílios* (PNAD)."

Jensen, Robert. 2010. "The (Perceived) Returns to Education and the Demand for Schooling." *Quarterly Journal of Economics* 125 (2): 515–48.

Kudo, Ines. 2017. "Build Yourself Step by Step: Designing SEL Interventions in Peru & Mexico." Unpublished presentation for the Korean Skills Workshop, Seoul, Korea. World Bank Group, Washington, DC.

Lai, M. C., M. V. Lombardo, B. Chakrabarti, C. Ecker, S. A. Sadek, S. J. Wheelwright, D. G. M. Murphy, J. Suckling, E. T. Bullmore. MRC AIMS Consortium, and Baron-Cohen. 2012. "Individual Differences in Brain Structure Underpin Empathizing-Systemizing Cognitive Styles in Male Adults. *Neuroimage* 61: 1347–54.

Lai, M. C., M. V. Lombardo, G. Pasco, A. N. V. Ruigrok, S. J. Wheelwright, S. A. Sadek, B. Chakrabarti. MRC AIMS Consortium, and Simon Baron-Cohen. "A Behavioral Comparison of Male and Female Adults with High Functioning Autism Spectrum Conditions." *PLOS ONE.* June 13. https://doi.org/10.1371/journal.pone.0020835.

Linden, Leigh L. 2008. "Complement or Substitute? The Effect of Technology on Student Achievement in India (English)." InfoDev working paper no. 17. World Bank, Washington, DC. http://documents.worldbank.org/curated/en/804371468034237060/Complement-or -substitute-The-effect-of-technology-on-student-achievement-in-India.

Llach, J. J., C. Adrogué, and M. E. Gigaglia. 2009. "Do Longer School Days Have Enduring Educational, Occupational or Income Effects? A Natural Experiment on the Effects of Lengthening Primary School Days in Buenos Aires, Argentina." *Economía* 10 (1): 1–39.

Londono-Velez, J., C. Rodriguez, and F. Sánchez. 2017. "The Intended and Unintended Impacts of a Merit-Based Financial Aid Program for the Poor: The Case of Ser Pilo Paga." Documento CEDE No. 2017-24.

Loureiro, Andre, and C. Szerman. 2017. "Increasing School Engagement in Brazil: Stylized Facts and Relevant Policies." Mimeo. World Bank, Washington, DC.

Louzano, P., et al. 2010, "Quem quer ser professor? Atratividade, seleção e formação docente no Brasil" [Who Wants to Be a Teacher? The Attractiveness, Selection, and Training of Teachers in Brazil]. *Estudos em Avaliação Educacional* 21 (4): 543–68.

Lück, H. 2011. "Mapeamento De Práticas De Seleção E Capacitação De Diretores Escolares." Relatório Final. Estudos e Pesquisas, Fundação Victor Civita, São Paulo, Brazil.

Malamud, Ofer, and Cristian Pop-Eleches. 2011. "Home Computer Use and the Development of Human Capital." *Quarterly Journal of Economics* 126 (2): 987–1027.

Machado, Ana Luiza, and Miriam Muller. 2018. "'If It's Already Tough, Imagine for Me...:' A Qualitative Perspective on Youth Out of School and Out of Work in Brazil." Policy Research Working Paper; No. 8358. Washington, DC: World Bank. https://openknowledge.worldbank .org/handle/10986/29424

Nascimento, Paulo. 2017. "Looking at Higher Education Access, Conclusion, Relevance, Employability—and Finance." Mimeo. PPT prepared for the author's workshop, "Brazil Skills and Jobs." World Bank, Washington DC.

Neri, Marcelo. 2009. "A educação professional e você no mercado de trabalho" [Technical and Professional Education and You in the Labor Market]. Centro de Politicas Sociais, FGV, Brazil. http://portal.mec.gov.br/index.php?option=com_docman&view=download&alias=5300 -eduprofi-texto-neri-20100526-formatado&Itemid=30192.

Oliveira, Luis Felipe Batista, and Rafael Terra. 2016. "Impact of School Day Extension on Educational Outcomes: Evidence from Mais Educação in Brazil." IPC-IG Working Paper No. 147. International Policy Centre for Inclusive Growth, Brasília.

Pires, T., and S. Urzua. 2014. "Longer School Days, Better Outcomes?" Mimeo. University of Maryland.

Rigby, Claire. 2016. "How Software Learns As It Teaches Is Upgrading Brazilian Education." *The Guardian*, January 10. https://www.theguardian.com/technology/2016/jan/10/geekie -educational-software-brazil-machine-learning.

Rodríguez-Planas, Núria. 2012. "Longer-Term Impacts of Mentoring, Educational Services, and Learning Incentives: Evidence from a Randomized Trial in the United States." *American Economic Journal: Applied Economics* 4 (4): 121–39.

Schwartzman, S., and Cláudio de Moura Castro. 2013. "Ensino, Formação Profissional e a Questão da Mão de Obra Ensaio." *Avaliação e Políticas Públicas em Educação* 21 (80): 563–624.

Silva, J., R. Almeida, and V. Strokova. 2015. "Sustaining Employment and Wage Gains in Brazil." World Bank. Washington, DC.

Steinka-Fry, K., S. Wilson, and E. Tanner-Smith. 2013. "Effects of School Dropout Prevention Programs for Pregnant and Parenting Adolescents: A Meta-Analytic Review." *Journal of the Society for Social Work and Research* 4 (4): 373–89.

Verhine, R., and P. Nascimento. 2017. "Mapping of Higher Education Institutions in Brazil: Access and Relevance." Unpublished presentation and paper. World Bank, Washington, DC.

Vinuela, Lorena, and Laura Zoratto. 2013. *Review and Research Agenda on Results-Based Management in Brazilian States*. Washington, DC: World Bank Group. https://hubs .worldbank.org/docs/ImageBank/Pages/DocProfile.aspx?nodeid=18740788.

Waltenberg, F., and M. Carvalho. 2012. "Cotas aumentam a diversidade sem comprometer o desempenho." *Sinais Socias*, September–December.

World Bank. 2014. "Implications of a Changing China for Brazil: A New Window of Opportunity?" World Bank, Washington, DC.

——. 2015. "Completion Report for the Non-Lending Technical Assistance on the Extension of the School Day in Brazil." World Bank, Washington, DC.

Xavier, T. 2014. "Improving College Completion in Brazil: An Examination of Government-Subsidized Aid Programs." Master of Arts paper, International Comparative Education, Graduate School of Education, Stanford University.

5 Labor Market Policies and Youth Employment Prospects

ABSTRACT This chapter covers the labor market policies that shape incentives for young people to look for work and for firms to hire youth. These policies also help to determine the quality of matches between firms and young workers.[1] In this chapter, we argue that Brazil's labor market policies have long privileged (mainly older) "insiders" at the expense of opportunities for young people with little prior experience or who enter the labor force for the first time. The chapter points to policy solutions to this problem and recommends structural changes to improve the efficiency of the labor market. Also discussed are reforms to the labor code that were legislated in 2017 and their potential impact on the prospects of working youth. The 2017 reforms constitute an ambitious step in the right direction that could lower insider advantages, increase the share of formally employed young people, and improve the quality of labor market matches. Much more can still be done, however. The chapter closes with proposals for changes to the policies and programs that the 2017 reforms left untouched, which create perverse incentives that constrain human capital creation and could, in aggregate, lower the speed limit on Brazil's economic growth already imposed by an aging population.

Human capital is the most important asset in which households can invest, and the labor market is where people go to seek a return on that investment. Like many markets, the labor market has imperfections and failures that motivate actions by government to help improve people's prospects. These policies vary widely across countries in their character, the combination in which they are deployed, and the extent to which the authorities have implementation, monitoring, and enforcement capacity to make the measures amount to more than just pages in the labor code (World Bank 2012). The objectives of most governments in deploying labor market policies are similar, however—that is, to ensure the labor market is safe, fair, and a place where people's skills and enterprise are rewarded. Having these assurances is particularly important for the newest entrants to the labor market, who may be fresh from full-time education but lacking in real-world experience.

Policymakers help shape people's labor market prospects with a range of instruments. To provide a better understanding of labor market policy in Brazil, we employ in this chapter a useful typology of policy instruments first used in the World Bank and IPEA's 2002 *Brazil Jobs Report*: labor regulations, interventions, and institutions. *Regulations* correct uneven market power between those selling and those seeking labor by setting the rules and key parameters of employment agreements in the form of statutory wage "floors," restrictions on hiring and dismissals, and firms' other human resource decisions. The costs of regulations are borne mainly by employers and workers. *Interventions* are deployed by governments to make up for other market shortcomings, such as the inability of insurance markets to pool the risk of losses from unemployment, and consequences of information problems. In contrast to regulations, the costs of interventions are borne almost entirely by a country's general budget and, thus, by all taxpayers, whether they participate in the labor market or not. Interventions can also have a stabilizing effect during economic downturns, acting as so-called "automatic stabilizers." Finally, *institutions* are the norms, structures, and agreed-upon procedures by which stakeholders exert influence and make, carry out, and enforce decisions that shape regulations and interventions. The best example of an institution according to this typology is the space afforded in the legal code of many countries for collective bargaining. Another salient example of an institution are the structures and procedures for resolving labor disputes, which in Brazil are prominent in the form of a dedicated branch of the judicial system.

Although the labor market can appear dynamic by many measures, labor policies and programs may be holding back Brazil's performance. The assertion that Brazil's labor market is among the most rigidly regulated in the world is not immediately or obviously reflected in the broadly used benchmark indicators of de jure employment protection. Even outcome measures such as the employment rate, rate of unemployment, earnings differentials, and the share of workers with legal employment contracts suggest that the usual policy constraints on performance of the labor market did not hold back job creation during the decade of high growth that ended abruptly in 2014 (Silva, Almeida, and Strokova 2015). And although the number of jobs has fallen and open unemployment risen sharply since then, the importance of labor market policies relative to broader economic forces in determining these outcomes is a matter of debate. In contrast to some of the countries of Southern and Central Europe, structural unemployment in Brazil has been relatively low, firms find it fairly easy to dismiss workers, and people move across jobs and in and out of the labor market frequently.

While the usual symptoms of labor policy rigidity are not immediately apparent and are often masked by the economic cycle, some relatively persistent outcome indicators have long warned that Brazil's policies could be a source of problems. The most apparent are a persistently substantial share of the labor force working informally, particularly young people; unusually high rates of churn even among people with formal jobs; a court system congested with cases; and low labor productivity.

In the first half of 2017, Brazil legislated changes to its labor market policies.[2] The reforms were designed to give greater freedom to firms in how they employ people and organize their workforces, improve collective bargaining institutions, extend access to worker protection, and lower the uncertain costs of resolving labor disputes. Specific aims of the reforms were to make it easier for firms to bring more working women and young people into formal employment, extend access to worker protection, and reduce the uncertain costs of resolving labor disputes.

The 2017 labor market reforms are controversial, and their impact on outcomes in the short term are uncertain; but they are a step in the right direction. Because they make no direct changes to the main policy drivers of labor costs, however, it is difficult to predict what their impact will be on labor demand and job creation in the short term, given the fragile recovery from the 2015–16 recession. The reform package can be expected to increase efficiency of the labor market in the medium and longer term. It offers firms and individuals more options for entering regulated and protected ("formal") work arrangements; it provides greater flexibility by shifting the weight of labor outcomes away from legislation towards the bargaining table; it creates incentives for unions to be more responsive and accountable to members; and it lowers the legal uncertainty and other costs of resolving labor disputes. All this should help improve job matches particularly for labor market outsiders such as the youth, reduce informality and thus encourage investment and job creation. However, the reforms' impact in the short run is more uncertain. First, the application of the law by the labor courts remains contested and a period of uncertainty over its implementation is likely. Second, in the context of the tepid economic recovery, job creation has continued to remain mostly informal, with a growing number of self-employed. This may reflect voluntary outsourcing to ease workers' integration into the labor market, but likely is also a reflection of arbitrage to reduce the burden of social security and income taxes and thus of potential abuse or insufficient clarity of new outsourcing rules. If the trend is persistent, it could negatively affect the sustainability of social security. Third, it is likely to take some time for unions to reorganize themselves, leaving workers without strong representation precisely at a time when their bargaining power is weakened by the lingering recession.

In addition to the above concerns, the package of labor market reforms has not fundamentally altered the potential mismatch between wage costs and productivity for the young and unskilled, of which rising informality may be one symptom. To improve labor market outcomes for working youth further,

TABLE 5.1 A typology of labor market policy instruments

REGULATIONS: ADDRESS IMBALANCES IN MARKET POWER AND SET LEGAL EMPLOYMENT CONDITIONS; DIRECT COSTS BORNE MAINLY BY FIRMS	INTERVENTIONS: CORRECT OTHER MARKET FAILURES; DIRECT COSTS BORNE MAINLY BY THE BUDGET/TAXPAYERS	INSTITUTIONS: FORMULATE, ENFORCE, AND IMPLEMENT REGULATIONS AND INTERVENTIONS; DIRECT COSTS BORNE MAINLY BY THE BUDGET/TAXPAYERS
• Statutory wage "floors"	• Earned income tax credits	• Formation and financing of unions
• Mandated individual savings	• Wage (hiring and/or retention) subsidies	• Scope and coverage of collective agreements
• Restrictions on hiring/contracting	• Unemployment insurance	• Jurisdiction of labor courts
• Restrictions on dismissal	• Unemployment "safety net" benefit	• Role of social partners in governance of political parties
• Procedural requirements for dismissals	• Intermediation and other job search assistance	• Role of social partners in the legislative process
• Financial obligations upon dismissal	• Public employment programs	

Source: World Bank and IPEA 2002.

however, more reforms to government interventions will be required. Although politically very difficult, further reforms of Brazil's labor policies will be vital to ease the transition of young people from full-time study into full-time work and to raise their likelihood of entering formal employment. Changes to federal minimum wage adjustment policies—and perhaps even to how statutory minimum earnings are mandated for the youngest members of the labor force—could encourage more employers to hire young people legally. Reorganizing the structure and changing the parameters of the Fundo de Garantia por Tempo de Servico (FGTS), the Seguro Desemprego, and the fines (*multas*) on employers for nondisciplinary dismissals could reduce the perverse incentives that encourage churn and prevent the formation of firm-specific human capital needed by businesses to become more productive. An ambitious reorganization of income and job search support interventions is urgently required. The large but relatively regressive wage supplement program, Abono Salarial, could be restructured into a wage subsidy and provide an incentive for employers to hire young people entering the market for the first time or unemployed people who try but struggle to find jobs.

Along with an upgrade of intermediation and job-search support programs and more adequate funding of these "active labor market programs," at levels in line with Organisation of Economic Co-operation and Development (OECD) member countries, these changes could substantially improve the prospects of young jobseekers. This chapter presents an agenda of further reforms to Brazil's unemployment income and job search support policies, based on the positive outcomes of policy reform simulations, that the government should consider. It motivates them by presenting evidence on how current policies can hamper the labor market prospects of young people and, by doing so, constrain Brazil's productivity potential.

THE STATUTORY MINIMUM WAGE

The objective of most governments that legislate a statutory minimum wage (SMW) floor is to ensure workers are paid fairly according to their productivity. In the often-imperfect labor market, where the bargaining power of employers (the "purchasers" of labor time and skills) and workers (who are seeking to sell their labor time and skills) is uneven, a statutory minimum wage is an important policy instrument deployed to ensure a "fairer" distribution of marginal product. It can be even more important to the employment outcomes of young people with little experience and relatively few skills who struggle against even greater constraints on their bargaining power with employers. When firms have "buying power" in the labor market (that is, monopsony power), a statutory minimum wage can lower the risk of exploitation by raising the pay of people who would otherwise earn very low wages (that is, below their marginal productivity). The empirical evidence from high- and middle-income countries of the impact of statutory minimum wages on labor market outcomes, however, continues to be mixed. Much of the evidence showing a positive impact from minimum wage increases comes from the United States, where enforcement is effective and compliance is high (Card 1992; Allegretto, Dube, and Reich 2011; Liu, Hyclak, and Regmi 2016). An increase in the minimum wage of 10 percent can lead to an increase in earnings of 1.2–2.5 percent. (Neumark and Wascher 2007; Sabia, Burkhauser, and Hansen 2012).

Increases in statutory minimum wages can, however, lower the likelihood of employment, particularly among people with lower levels of completed education and limited work experience. An early survey of the literature by Brown et al. (1982) initially established that a minimum wage increase of 10 percent reduces the probability of employment for teenagers by 1–3 percent. Moreover, if the statutory minimum wage is set too high—that is, above the productivity of workers at the lower end of the earnings distribution—minimum wages can hurt the lowest productivity workers more than they help. Negative employment effects ranging from 2–3 percent have been found in studies of Peru (Céspedes-Reynaga and Sanchez 2013), Chile (Grau and Landerretche 2011), and Brazil (Jales 2015), while no effects were found in China (Huang, Loungani, and Wang 2014), Ecuador (Canelas 2014), or Mexico (Campos et al. 2015). The impact of minimum wage increases can vary across workers in different types of firms. Alatas and Cameron (2008) found minimum wage hikes in Indonesia from 1990 to 1996 had no negative employment impact on workers in large establishments but adverse impacts on those in small, domestic firms. Similarly, Del Carpio et al. (2012) found varying impacts on employment in Indonesia, with increases having a negative impact on people working in small firms and on less educated workers.

High statutory minimum wages can increase the likelihood that people will be employed informally. The main effects of a minimum wage that is set too high (see box 5.1) are increased evasion of taxes, regulatory restrictions, and so on; undeclared working arrangements (either in underreported hours or in terms of reporting earnings); employers' substitution of higher productivity for lower productivity workers; firms choosing to invest more in capital—particularly in labor savings technology and automation—to reduce their use of labor; job destruction and longer spells of unemployment, particularly for people with little prior work experience. While these adverse effects can be small for the labor force as a whole, they can affect certain groups more acutely, including women, people with less education, and young people who have not yet accumulated work experience and can present risker prospects to employers.

A large body of evidence from middle-income countries supports the conclusion that, when set at high levels (relative to median wages), minimum wages harm employment prospects for youth, particularly the youngest and least skilled workers. In the United States, many researchers have estimated a 10 percent hike in minimum wages reduces the probability that teenagers will be employed by 1–4 percent. Although these conclusions are contested (Allegretto, Dube, and Reich 2011), the weight of the evidence suggests that minimum wage hikes are particularly disadvantageous to the employment prospects of young people, particularly those who have not completed secondary education (Clemens 2015; Liu, Hyclak, and Regmi 2015; Sabia, Burkhauser, and Hansen 2012). The published evidence from middle-income countries (tabulated in appendix A) is more conclusive. Most of the studies show minimum wage rises associated with reductions in young people's probability of being employed. The size of these effects varies substantially, from 0.08 percent in China to 0.78 percent in Brazil, with most effects hovering around 2–3 percent. In Indonesia, minimum wage hikes are estimated to have a negative impact on employment for those 15–24 years of age (SMERU 2001), especially lower-skilled and part-time workers (Surhayadi et al. 2003). Recent meta-analyses of evidence from emerging economies find no overall effects, but acknowledge that youth and low-skilled members of the workforce are more negatively affected by minimum wage increases (Chletsos and Giorgis 2015; Broecke et al. 2017).

Analysis of minimum wages in Brazil has found more consistent, negative employment impacts on young people. For Brazil's labor force overall, empirical evidence of the impact of minimum wages on employment outcomes has been ambiguous. While some researchers have found negative employment effects from minimum wage increases (Foguel 1998; Neumark, Salas, and Wascher 2014; Ulyssea and Foguel 2006; Foguel, Ramos, and Carneiro 2015; Jales 2015), others have found no such significant effects (Lemos 2004, 2009; Broecke, Forti, and Vandeweyer 2015). The evidence of consistent, negative impacts on the job prospects of young people in particular, however, is clearer. Fajnzylber (2001) found an increase of 10 percent in the minimum wage to be associated with a decrease in employment of 3.8 percent. Gonçalvez and Menezes-Filho (2016) found that minimum wage increases reduced the likelihood of teenagers' working by 3 percent (although they attributed the reduction to an intrahousehold reallocation of labor). Broecke and Vandeweyer (2015) found a larger effect of 7.8 percent. (When hours worked were used as the dependent variable, the magnitude and significance of this effect diminished.) They also found an increase of 10 percent in the minimum wage as a share of the average wage to be associated with a decline in formality by 3–4 percent, on average. Similarly, Foguel et al. (2014) found that minimum wage hikes increase young people's transitions from employment into inactivity and into unemployment. These transitions and the negative effects of minimum wages are amplified during economic downturns.

While most analysis of statutory wage floors has focused on short-term employment and other adjustment effects, evidence is growing that high statutory minimum wages can have longer-term adverse impacts on the labor market outcomes of young people, as well (see box 5.1). Neumark and Nizalova (2007)

BOX 5.1

Statutory wage floors: Impact on the skills and jobs of young people

Few instruments of labor market policy have been scrutinized and debated as heatedly and for as long as the statutory minimum wage. First introduced in 1894 as an official structure for the resolution of industrial disputes by a government in New Zealand, the instrument grew in popularity and became widely deployed, starting in late–industrial era European countries and during the period of turbulent industrial relations in the Americas between the two world wars (Neumark and Wascher 2007). In Latin America, Mexico was the first country to establish a minimum wage policy. Its example was followed by Brazil in 1938.

As enduring and as plainly heated as the policy debate on the merits and costs of this policy instrument has been, it also appears to be maturing. It is now rare to hear the polarized positions taken by many economists in the 1980s and 1990s. Those in the broadening "mainstream" of the profession have tended to debate *how* a statutory minimum wage should be imposed and managed, rather than *whether* it should. Another welcome sign of maturity in the discussion is that an appeal to evidence has become expected. For this reason, the body of empirical evidence on the impact of wage floors and the minutiae of their implementation is far larger and more expansive in the countries it covers than, for example, evidence of the impact of regulations on hiring and dismissals or unionization and collective bargaining. Key pieces of this evidence have been cited earlier in this chapter—specifically, the impact of statutory wage floors on labor market opportunities and outcomes for young people.

continued

Box 5.1, *continued*

Recent reviews by World Bank staff (see Del Carpio and Pabon 2014, 2017; Cunningham et al. 2016) of the impact of minimum wages in countries with large, unregulated, "informal" economies merit special mention in a discussion of building skills and ensuring human capital is fully engaged. In these reviews of experiences in several East Asian and Latin American countries, the authors have charted and organized empirical evidence on the relationship between the minimum wage and unemployment and informal employment and systematically categorized the potential effects of increasing the minimum wage on outcomes that include skills development. Following the evolution of the debate, these papers tended to focus on the size of adjustments in the level of statutory wage floors and the institutions countries have in place to make these decisions.

In general, the empirical literature shows that firms use one or a combination of five channels to absorb the added labor costs of a rise in the statutory wage floor: (1) absorbing costs by accepting lower profits; (2) raising the prices for their outputs (or reducing their quality) and reducing nonwage costs, such as worker training; (3) restructuring their workforces; (4) informalizing labor inputs, partly or entirely; and (5) upgrading capital (broadly defined to include physical capital, technology, business processes, and human capital). The second, third, and fourth channels directly undermine the process and threaten the quality of human capital built in the workplace. The fifth will be advantageous to jobseekers with higher levels of formal education and more years of experience but, as a consequence, will adversely shape the opportunities of first-time jobseekers, those with limited market experience, and those with less or poor-quality education.

Most of the evidence cited in these reviews suggests sizable increases in the minimum wage are likely to exacerbate unemployment and the prevalence of informal employment, which could have negative consequences for labor productivity and businesses as a result of reduced investment in employee training and the loss of productive workers. While most of the empirical evidence suggests the effects of minimum wage increase on unemployment and the demand for labor are unclear in aggregate, those affected by minimum wage increases tend to be the least qualified and often also the youngest workers. In many countries in Latin American and East Asia where rigorous analysis has been carried out, differences in the effects of minimum wage increases and which of the channels of adjustment is dominant depend largely on the size and types of firms. Given the characteristics of the labor market in emerging economies, businesses faced with increased labor costs will likely resort to less than optimal channels, which will tend to affect their productivity and the labor market in general.

found that exposure to high minimum wages for teenagers and young adults reduced their earnings and the probability of their being employed in the longer run. These effects were proportional to age: those exposed to higher minimum wages in their teenage years (independent of their participation in the labor market) experienced larger reductions in wages at the ages of 25–29 than those exposed during ages 20–24. Neumark and Nizlova's initial estimates suggested about a third of the earnings reduction was due to the reduction in schooling (that is, young people were enticed away from school by a higher minimum wage), as well as foregone experience and reduced training. Building on this work, Cardoso (2009) delved deeper into the causes of these longer-term SMW effects by assessing actual exposure to SMW in Portugal. She found ambiguous effects: that workers exposed to high SMW when young earned an overall wage premium of 1–4 percent in the long run (as employers raised investment in general training), but also experienced lower returns on seniority within the firm (as employers reduced firm-specific training).

Historically, little evidence has been found in Brazil of the segmentation sometimes caused in other countries by statutory minimum wages. Analyzing the impact of minimum wage increases in Brazil has been tricky, given the unification of regional minimum wages in 1984, as well as the linkage of minimum wages to inflation and the growth in gross domestic product (GDP) since 2005 (Jales 2017). In 2002, the World Bank and IPEA's *Brazil Jobs Report* found little evidence of the labor market segmentation usually attributable to statutory minimum wages that is sometimes found in other countries. The report cited an "*efeito farol*" (the so-called "lighthouse" effect), in which informal employment agreements appeared to be informed by the level of the statutory minimum wage (Neri, Gonzaga, and Camargo 2001; Fajnzylber 2001). Indeed, analysis of the earnings distribution of formal and informal workers in Brazil over the period 2001–15 shows that, while the share of informally employed people earning less than the minimum wage has always been substantial, the statutory minimum continues to shape the earnings of people working informally (see figure 5.1).

Minimum wage policy in Brazil has a long history, dating to 1936, when President Getulio Vargas established "salary commissions," which were responsible for setting the minimum wage in each of the country's 22 states. Commission members were drawn from among employers and worker organizations within their areas of jurisdiction. Once determined, the level of the minimum wage became the legal "floor" on wages for three years and could only be modified during that period by at least a three-quarters majority vote of the commission. While the federal statutory minimum wage continues to be the legal floor on wages throughout the country, several states—Paraná, Rio de Janeiro, Rio Grande do Sul, Santa Catarina, and São Paulo—set their statutory minimum wages higher. Since the establishment of Brazil's 1988 constitution, the fiscal consequences of the link between the value of social insurance benefits (that is, old-age, survivor, and disability pensions) and the statutory minimum wage has acted as a powerful restraint on political pressures to raise the minimum wage. The policy link to social insurance, thus, kept the minimum wage at relatively benign levels.

The introduction of new adjustment policies has caused the statutory minimum wage to rise rapidly. Since 2003, Brazil has followed a "minimum wage valuation policy" that entails annual adjustments of the national minimum wage based on predetermined rules, including an explicit formula. Brazil's statutory minimum wage is adjusted by the inflation rate in the previous year, plus the real rate of GDP growth two years previously. The adjustment rule was extended in 2015 for the period 2016–19. The valuation policy and adjustment rule have delivered a real rise in the minimum wage of more than 77 percent over the period 2003–16 (see figure 5.2). Even in the midst of a deep recession, its nominal value increased from R$678 per month in 2013 to R$937 in 2017.[3]

At 70 percent of the median wage, Brazil's minimum wage also appears high by international benchmark levels. The average statutory minimum wage among OECD-member countries has remained stable, at between 45 percent and 50 percent of median wages. Some other countries in Latin America (Colombia, Chile, and Cosa Rica) have higher minimum wages than Brazil by this metric. When demand for labor slackens, real labor costs adjust downward to contain unemployment. The new adjustment policies prevent that from happening in Brazil. Unfortunately, after a long period of decline, the share of working people earning less than the minimum wage in the country is rising again, along with unemployment. The rise has been steepest for Brazilian youth (see figure 5.3).

FIGURE 5.1

Wage distribution of the formally and informally employed and the statutory minimum wage, 2001–15

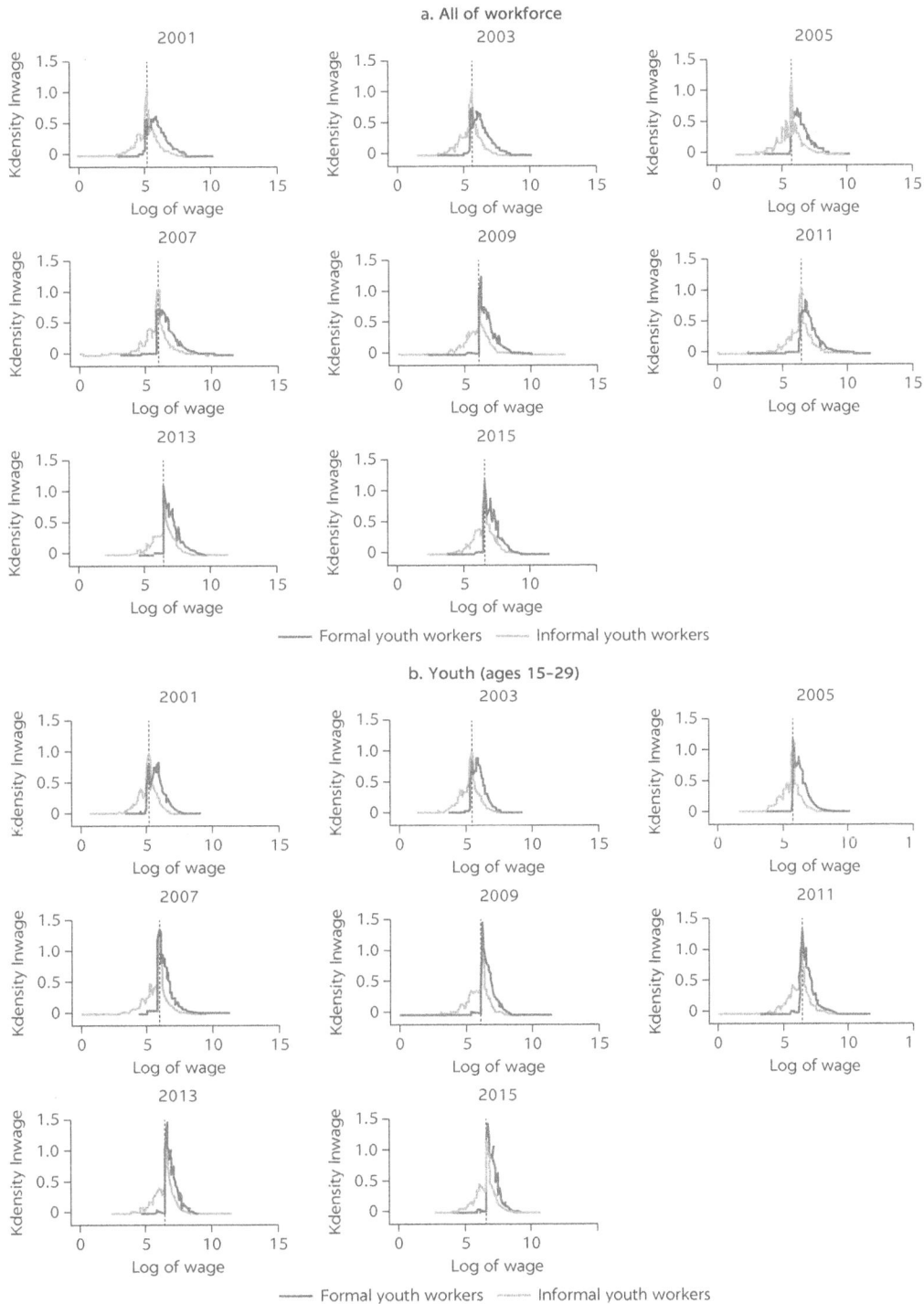

a. All of workforce

— Formal youth workers   — Informal youth workers

b. Youth (ages 15–29)

— Formal youth workers   — Informal youth workers

Source: Based on *Pesquisa Nacional por Amostra de Domicílios* (PNAD), 2001–15.
Notes: Due to the Demographic Census, PNAD was not held in 2010.

FIGURE 5.2

Real hourly minimum wages (PPP US$), Brazil and selected peers, 2000–16

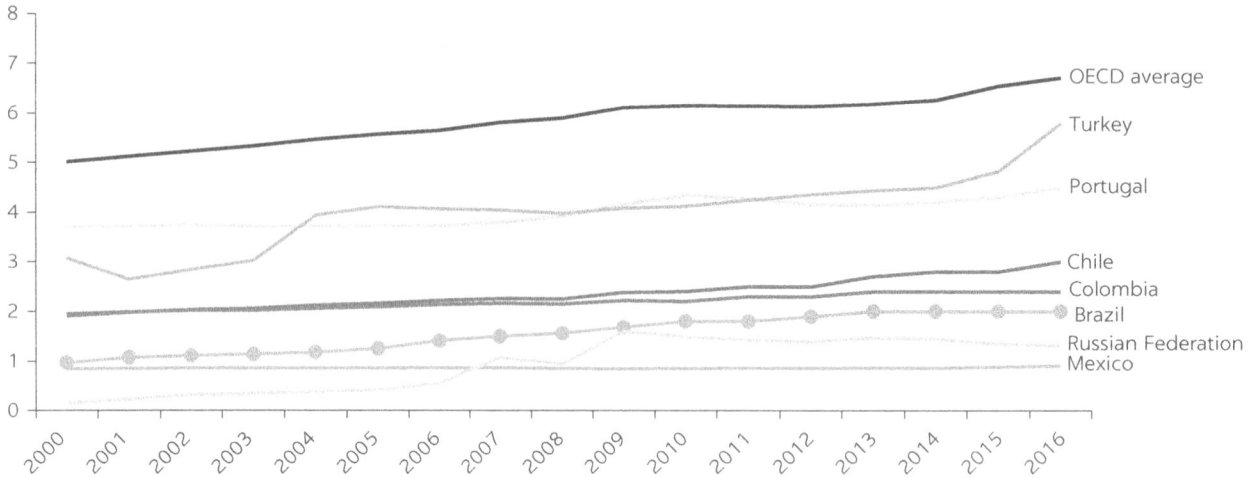

Source: OECD 2016, OECD Stata (https://data.oecd.org).
Note: Figure shows real hourly minimum wage in 2015 constant prices at 2015 US$ PPPs.

FIGURE 5.3

Unemployment and workers' earnings less than the minimum wage, by age group

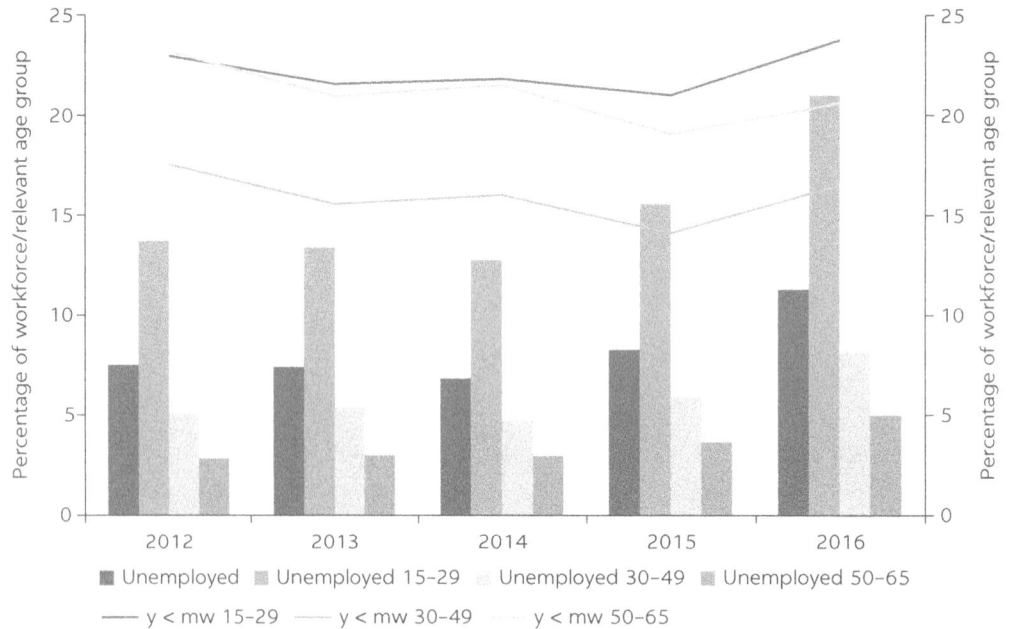

Source: Based on *Pesquisa Nacional por Amostra de Domicílios* (PNAD), 2001–15.

EMPLOYMENT PROTECTION

Employment protection legislation (EPL) is a broad category of regulation that governs the hiring and dismissal practices of firms. The intent of employment protection legislation is to improve workers' welfare by establishing some degree of job security and improving their bargaining power vis-à-vis employers. EPL typically achieves these goals by regulating employer behavior—for example, setting conditions for fair and unfair dismissal of permanent employees and limiting the use of temporary contracts; mandating certain benefits, such as severance payments to employees; and prescribing the necessary procedures to be followed when employment is commenced or terminated.

The effects of employment protection on labor market outcomes is theoretically ambiguous. On the one hand, strict protection is expected to reduce job destruction and, hence, reduce flows into unemployment, leading to greater employment stability over the business cycle. On the other, employment protection can reduce job creation and flows into employment if the high statutory costs of dismissing workers cause firms to hesitate before hiring, prolonging unemployment spells in the economy (Bertola 1990). The aggregate effect on the overall level of employment at any point in time, therefore, depends on the rate of hiring relative to the rate of dismissals.

Empirical evidence of the impact of employment protection on labor market outcomes is similarly mixed. The earliest comparative studies across OECD member countries (Scarpetta 1996; Nickell 1997; OECD 1999) and on countries in Latin America (Heckman and Pagés 2000) found negative, although weak, employment effects. More recent cross-country studies following a similar approach, however, have failed to find significant impacts on employment (Baccaro and Rei 2005; Bassanini and Duvall 2006; Heckman and Pagés 2004). This ambiguity in the empirical literature shows the weakness of composite measures of employment protection that package a wide range of regulatory restrictions and costs into summary indices. Narrower analysis of specific components of dismissal costs and restrictions on hiring are more conclusive. Increasing severance provisions, for example, had sizable and significant negative effects on employment in Argentina (Mondino and Montoya 2004) and Peru (Saavedra and Torero 2004), although similar measures did not appear to have any effect in Brazil (Paes de Barros and Corseuil 2004). Greater restrictions on the use of temporary contracts appears to reduce employment in Colombia (Kugler 2004). In India, where employment protection and dismissal costs vary widely from state to state, evidence of negative effects has been found not just on employment, but also on firms' investments and productivity (Besley and Burgess 2004; Schwab 2015).

Consensus is greater that employment protection regulations also have a stronger negative impact on the job prospects of youth than on those of older workers. As new entrants to the labor market, youth are less skilled and less productive than more experienced, prime-age workers. All else being equal, younger workers can be riskier for employers to take on. More stringent employment protection regulations can make firms reluctant to hire young people if they remain unproductive and are difficult to dismiss, for example. Tenure-based restrictions on dismissal can also make firms reluctant to fire existing, older workers in response to an economic contraction, even if they are less productive, and instead to let younger workers go. The empirical literature shows that more restrictive regulations adversely affect those for whom labor demand is more elastic (that is, less-skilled groups), including young people (Bassanini and Duvall 2006). The effect is substantial: Bassanini and Duvall (2006) found a decline in the OECD's employment protection legislation (EPL) indicator by two standard deviations to be associated with an increase of four percentage points in youth employment. For Chile, Montenegro and Pagés (2004; 2007) found job security provisions lowered the probability for youth (as well as less-skilled workers and women) to be employed. As a result of high levels of employment protection for workers with indefinite contracts, youth are more likely to be offered informal jobs or only temporary employment (Kahn 2012). In OECD countries in 2012, nearly a quarter of workers 15–24 years of age were employed in temporary jobs.

If temporary jobs serve as stepping-stones to more stable employment, flexible forms of hiring can be advantageous to young people as a way for them to gain experience. A growing number of studies conclude, however, that where tight restrictions and protections remain in place for workers on indefinite contracts, accepting a contingent job may, in fact, delay the transitions of young people into more permanent employment and reduce their human capital development and earnings prospects (Yu 2012).

Although its statutory requirements for dismissing formal workers on indefinite contracts are lighter than those of OECD member countries and its neighbors, Brazil has had very stringent restrictions on firms' use of flexible forms of hiring. True, measures of de jure employment protection applied to people with "regular" (that is, indefinite) labor contracts suggest Brazil has few restrictions on dismissals (even if the direct costs paid by employer in fines, or *multas*, for non-disciplinary, involuntary separations can be high). But comparisons of measures of regulation on employers' decisions to use outsourcing and fixed term and temporary forms of employment show firms to have been far more restricted (see figure 5.4). Prior to the 2017 labor reforms, this extreme regulatory stance could be particularly damaging to the prospects of young people, who are more likely to prefer or need part-time and flexible employment than people of prime working age. These restrictions are also severely constraining to productivity, as they make it difficult for firms to innovate, experiment with new technology and business processes, or adjust their labor and skills inputs to rapidly shifting market demands.

Furthermore, restrictions on the use of part-time and flexible hiring increase the likelihood of informal employment. The tight restrictions on when firms can use outsourced labor, as well as the limitations on the use of fixed-term and less than full-time employment, have forced most firms to engage these human resources informally. This has been bad for firms, which have had to spend time and resources avoiding detection and enforcement; it has been bad for working people who have a preference for flexibility, including not only young people who might want to combine work with study and training, but also young parents who need to balance market and household responsibilities; and it has ultimately been bad for society, in that it has forced firms and households that are reasonably pursuing economic opportunities into evasion of laws and regulations.

INCOME SUPPORT AND JOB SEARCH ASSISTANCE FOR THE UNEMPLOYED

The deployment of labor market interventions in Brazil is weighted heavily toward "passive" income support programs for people who lose formal jobs, which account for 83 percent of total labor program expenditure, and away from "active" intermediation and job search assistance programs (see figure 5.5). Most labor market interventions are financed from the federal budget or dedicated levies and funds (specifically, Fundo de Amparo ao Trabalhador, or FAT, a fund financed from statutory payroll contributions that finances unemployment insurance and other labor programs). As shown in the *Brazil Expenditure Review* (World Bank 2017) the bulk of public spending on labor market programs goes to people who already have formal jobs

FIGURE 5.4

Employment protection legislations in Brazil and comparator countries, ca. 2013

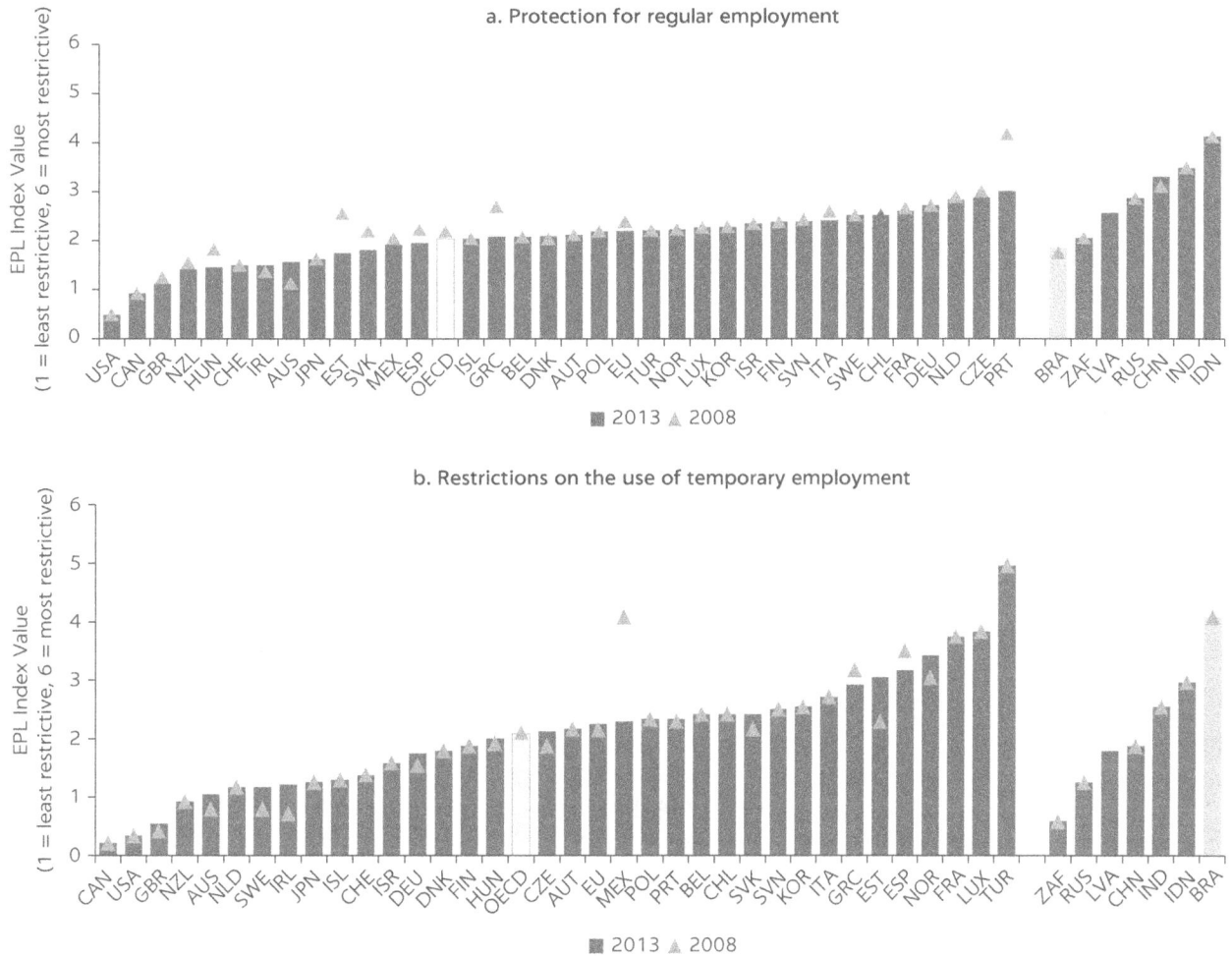

a. Protection for regular employment

b. Restrictions on the use of temporary employment

Source: OECD 2016.

rather than to jobseekers. The policies and programs Brazil puts in place to help correct failures of the labor market are skewed away from the intermediation services that could improve the quality of matches between firms and jobseekers. Although still modest relative to public spending on pensions for the elderly and people living with disabilities, public spending on labor market programs has been rising in recent years. Drawing on the World Bank's recent review of Brazil's federal budget (World Bank 2017), while public spending on labor programs in 2000 was historically low, at 0.4 percent of GDP, this category of social expenditure grew hand in hand with the relatively high levels of employment creation until 2014, reaching 0.85 percent of GDP in 2011 and 0.99 percent in 2014. In 2015, expenditure accelerated to 1.1 percent of GDP as the country slipped into economic crisis and unemployment began to surge. The contributory nature of the labor programs, which were historically limited in scope to the large formal companies and the public sector, means the system benefits almost exclusively relatively well-off, formally employed workers; only 1.8 percent of labor program expenditure is accessible to workers who are not necessarily formalized—that is, workers without signed contracts, referred to in Brazil as "*sem carteira assinada.*"

FIGURE 5.5

Public spending on labor market programs is weighted heavily to "passive" income support, over the "active" services that help people find jobs

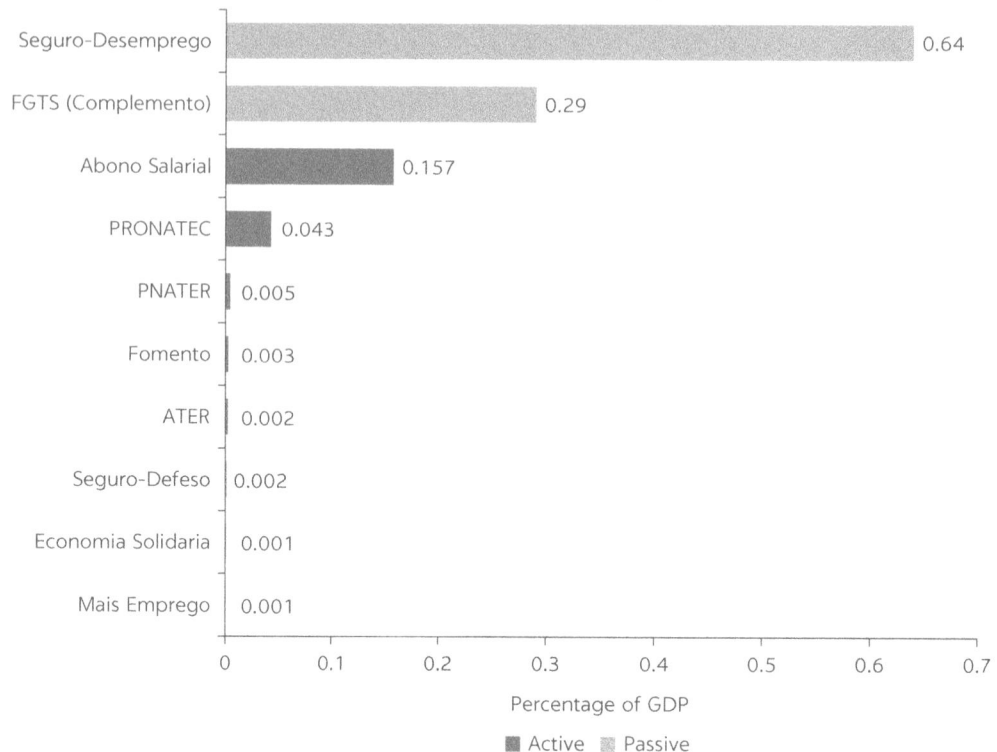

Source: World Bank 2017.

Public spending on programs that actively promote labor market insertion of the unemployed and economically inactive remains very small, even after taking into account the recent increased spending on skills training. A wage top-up program, Abono Salarial, is meant to provide incentive for formal employment. By design, however, it does not play an explicit role in activating the out-of-work, since it requires a five-year history of employment for eligibility. Other Brazilian programs that fall squarely under the internationally used definition of "active labor market programs" are training for vulnerable groups and the unemployed (BSM and Pronatec-Seguro Desemprego, Projovem), public employment services (Mais Pronatec Emprego), and entrepreneurship programs (Programa de Fomento de Atividades Produtivas Rurais, Asistência Técnica e Extensão Rural). Although it has received significant attention because of its rapid growth since 2011, Pronatec was only a modest driver of expenditure on labor programs, and it continues to represent a small share of the total (3.8 percent in 2015).[4] Federal spending on labor market intermediation services represented by the Sistema Nacional de Emprego (SINE) has remained persistently low, and it is probably the least adequately financed labor function in the Brazilian social protection and labor policy architecture.

The heavy reliance on income top-up wage subsidies is a unique feature of Brazil's approach to active labor market programs. Brazil spends about 90 percent of its active labor market program (ALMP) resources on employment incentives. The highest ratio of spending among OECD countries, by Luxembourg, is only 60 percent. Hence, the composition of active labor market expenditures in Brazil is out of line with comparator countries in the OECD and in Latin America. Brazil's spending goes mostly to Abono Salarial; if it were excluded from the list of active labor programs—due to its limited functions as a work incentive—Brazil's expenditure on ALMPs would be lower than that of all OECD member countries.

Brazil's labor market programs may be providing incentive for too much churn in the labor market. Policymakers concerned about labor market opportunity and productivity in most middle-income countries worry about a lack of dynamism or a stagnation of labor and skills. In Brazil, however, the worry is that labor is too mobile. About 23 percent of working Brazilians have been in the same firm or institution for a year or less. Fully 38 percent have worked in the same firm for up to two years. Over half (58 percent) have been working in the same establishment for less than five years (Silva, Almeida, and Strokova 2015). Brazil's rate of turnover is higher than those of almost all OECD-member countries, with the exception of the United States. But whereas in the United States the movement of labor across geography and sectors is ample (although slowing), in Brazil most turnover is within the same geographical area, sector, and industry. Furthermore, in many middle-income countries, high turnover rates are observed among people who are informally employed and self-employed. What sets Brazil apart is that labor in the formal sector appears to be just as mobile. And whereas in most countries informal employment spells are considerably shorter and less stable than in formal employment, Zylberstajn and Silva (2015) have shown turnover in Brazil is as high among formally as among informally employed.

FIGURE 5.6

Public expenditure categorized as "active" is mostly in the form of salary top-ups

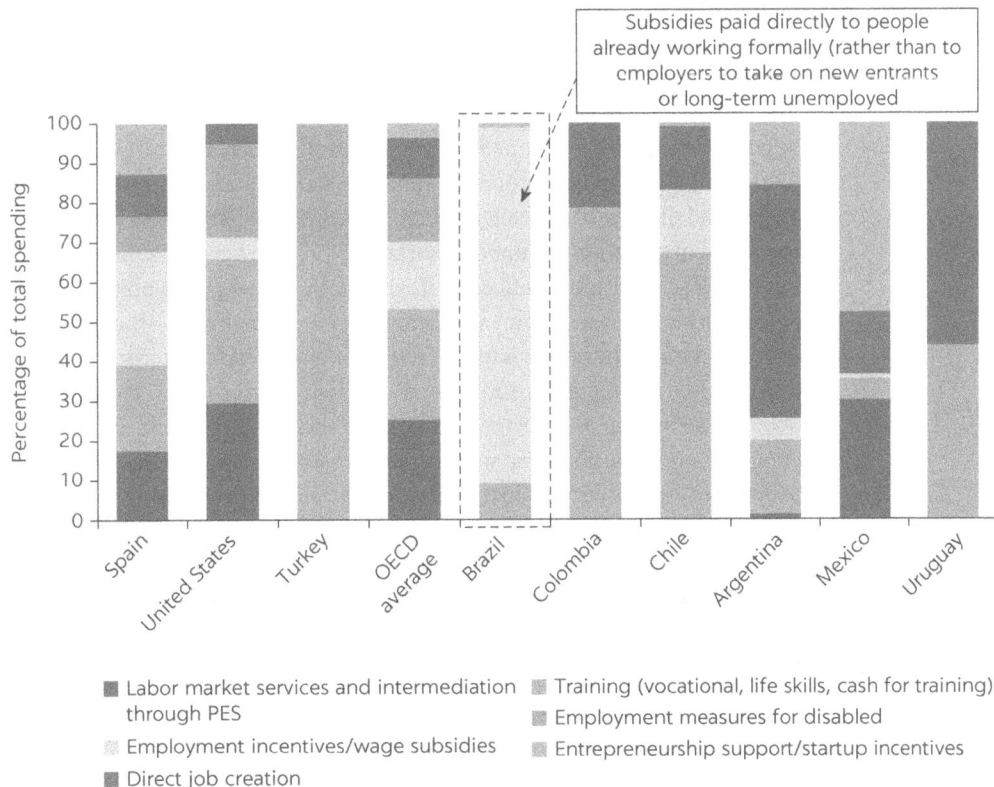

Subsidies paid directly to people already working formally (rather than to employers to take on new entrants or long-term unemployed)

- Labor market services and intermediation through PES
- Employment incentives/wage subsidies
- Direct job creation
- Training (vocational, life skills, cash for training)
- Employment measures for disabled
- Entrepreneurship support/startup incentives

Source: World Bank 2017.

High levels of churn may reveal perverse incentives created by the generosity, duplication, and incoherence of Brazil's income support programs for workers who lose formal jobs. A debate as to why turnover is so high has been going on among labor economists in Brazil for years. Although the evidence is not yet definitive, a strong link between worker movements and the system of entitlements, such as access to unemployment income support, has become apparent. Zylberstajn and Silva (2015), for example, have shown high turnover despite earnings losses in the destination workplace. Pinto (2015) has found evidence of induced dismissals, including a spike in the share of dismissals at the de jure vesting period for unemployment insurance and the return of 6 percent of those dismissed "without just cause" to the same firm after a period similar to that for the maximum payout for unemployment insurance.

The parameters of Brazil's passive labor programs may encourage these high levels of turnover. Multiple benefits are triggered when a person in formal work loses his or her job. Brazil's Seguro Desemprego (unemployment insurance), for example, is quite generous, with replacement rates—the benefit received relative to the unemployed person's last wage—between 68 and 80 percent, even if capped at 2.1 times the statutory minimum wage; this stands in contrast to replacement rates of 50 percent in Argentina and 70 percent in Chile, and an average of 60 percent among countries of the OECD. Another unusual feature of Brazil's unemployment insurance benefits is that they do not decline over the payout period. In Chile, for instance, payments decline by 10 percent per month. Considerable empirical evidence indicates the generosity of unemployment benefits has an impact on job search efforts and a person's likelihood of accepting a new job. The progressive decline of the benefit serves as an incentive to reduce the reservation wage of the unemployed, while preserving at least some of the protective function of the benefits (Vodopivec 2004). The relatively high replacement rates, lax requirements to search for jobs, and, especially, the few requirements to accept job offers, along with the relatively low vesting periods for this right, could explain the very high rotation rates in and out of formal employment in Brazil (Portela et al. 2016; Corseuil, Foguel, Gonzaga, and Ribeiro 2014).

Incentives can also be shaped by the size of Brazil's mandatory employer-financed individual savings program (Fundo de Garantia por Tempo de Servico, or FGTS) and the way in which it is administered. The FGTS plays a vital role as a passive labor program to support workers, who gain access to their savings when they lose their jobs. Reflecting its originally stated policy objectives—to support workers whose employment contracts are terminated—the most frequent reason for withdrawals is involuntary, nondisciplinary dismissal "without just cause" (*sem justa causa*). In 2014, total withdrawals from the FGTS amounted to about R$86 billion, or 1.6 percent of GDP. Of these, 62.9 percent, about 1 percent of GDP, were for dismissal without just cause. The law requires employers who dismiss workers without just cause to pay a penalty (or *multa*) as a deterrent to dismissals. The *multa* is analogous to the "risk-rated" contributions paid in the unemployment insurance program of the United States, which adjusts the "premium" for the likelihood of dismissals in a particular sector. In Brazil, however, instead of supplementing the finances of the Seguro Desemprego, the bulk of the *multa* is received by the dismissed employee at the time of dismissal. This additional penalty payment from employers can reach up to 40 percent of the total FGTS withdrawal.[5]

Poor coordination of Seguro Desemprego and the FGTS further distort incentives and contribute to high turnover. First, the coverage conditions (for example, the minimum period of contribution prior to job loss) and other eligibility requirements for the Seguro are lighter than those of similar programs in neighboring countries and among Brazil's peers. And although the maximum period over which a benefit is paid out is shorter, the benefit amount is relatively generous. Second, FGTS accounts managed by Caixa Econômica Federal earn only a statutory—and below-market—rate of interest. In an economy with a history of high inflation and prone to inflation spurts, relatively low returns on compulsory savings can raise the financial repression felt by households and create urgency to get access to their savings. And because most of the *multa* is paid to workers, the risk-pooling fund for FAT receives only a small fraction of the penalty amount. Combined with limited monitoring capacity, these features create a potential bonanza payment for those who lose formal jobs and strong incentives for workers and employers to collude to game the programs.

Another problem constraining Brazil's productivity potential is its high and uncertain nonwage labor costs. De jure, nonwage unit labor costs in Brazil are very high compared to those of benchmark countries. Most of these costs—contributions to social insurance pensions, FGTS savings, and other employment-related benefits—are the sole statutory responsibility of employers. As discussed previously, total labor costs have been rising, driven by growth in the national statutory minimum wage. What has now become a relatively high statutory minimum wage is accompanied by one of the highest mandatory contribution rates for social insurance, and rationed, mandatory savings, in Latin America and among comparator countries.

These factors combine to limit formal job offers, especially to young people, by keeping unit labor costs high. Not all formal jobs are productive, and not all informal jobs are unproductive. That said, when firms are confronted with high mandated labor costs and the complexity of the labor regulation and worker protection systems in Brazil, they could reasonably choose to forego operating at larger, more efficient scale to escape enforcement of these regulations. Their choice to "stay small" to avoid detection can have an aggregate, negative drag on the country's productivity and growth. As already pointed out, the statutory minimum wage has been growing rapidly since changes to the adjustment formula were made in 2012, and with little reference to the conditions created by Brazil's current downturn. Most nonwage labor costs from other regulatory instruments or benefits are linked to the minimum wage. When combined with relatively high mandatory contributions from employers for social insurance and FGTS savings accounts and the threat of formal dispute in Brazil's system of labor courts, firms may be reasonably wary of creating formal jobs.

Public spending on labor market intermediation and public employment services is very low in Brazil compared to OECD countries but comparable to that of other countries in Latin America. Whether compared to countries that share similar labor policy institutional features (such as Italy and Portugal) or similar levels of labor program spending (Poland and New Zealand) or are aspirational comparators (France and Spain), the dominance of wage subsidies in Brazil's total labor program expenditure stands out. Intermediation is a critical component of labor market systems in advanced countries, where public employment services (PESs) connect jobseekers to employers by offering it, along with training and other services. They also function as a gateway mechanism to control access to—and prevent the abuse of—unemployment benefits and other social programs.

Giving relatively less emphasis to PESs is common in Latin America and can be explained by the institutional history of labor policy developments in the region. Among Brazil's peers in Latin America, only Mexico allocates a significant portion of expenditure (about 30 percent) to labor market intermediation. Another distinguishing feature of Latin American countries' approach to active labor programs, including Brazil's, is the significant investment in entrepreneurship programs, which remain limited in most member countries of the OECD. Spending is heavily concentrated on wage supplements to people already formally employed rather than on labor activation support. This spending is inefficient, in the sense that large overlaps occur between programs, and the subsidies are of limited effectiveness for bringing workers into formal jobs.

As the economy struggles to create new jobs, Brazil's lack of active intermediation and job search assistance is dangerous. While spending on wage top-ups seems excessive, programs that actively help the unemployed or inactive individuals to prepare for and find work (training, job search assistance, intermediation) receive only about 4 percent of total labor spending. This leaves people who are unemployed—and particularly first-time jobseekers—particularly vulnerable, raising the likelihood of long unemployment spells, consequent depreciation of human capital, and "scarring" effects that can last for years. The solution is not *just* to increase spending on intermediation services and job search assistance, but to modernize these services to perform at the level of active labor market programs in some of the leading-practice countries, such as Australia, the United Kingdom, and the United States.

THE 2017 REFORMS: STRENGTHS AND WEAKNESSES

In the first half of 2017, Brazil's government legislated changes to its labor market policies, presenting them as a long overdue "modernization" to bring its policies up to date with those in other countries. The stated objectives were to increase labor market flexibility; broaden access to worker rights and protections; improve workplace relations; and lower the uncertainties that motivate most labor disputes. If successful in meeting these objectives, the government expects the reforms will eventually increase the share of formal employment in the labor force, improve the quality of matches between workers and firms, raise productivity, and help chip away at *custo Brasil*. The reform's designers claim the measures will do the following:

- Create more legal forms for structuring individual work relationships
- Increase the penalty for not registering employees
- Ensure minimum pay, rights, and mandated benefits are pro-rata and proportional to time worked, regardless of contracting arrangements
- Shift primary responsibility for key employment conditions to firm-level bargaining
- Grant primacy to firm-level collective agreements
- Increase worker choice for collective representation by making union membership and the payment of union fees strictly voluntary
- Assign penalties for frivolous court claims and cases brought to courts in "bad faith"
- Institute other measures to lower the likelihood of disputes ending up in the courts

Table 5.2 provides a detailed—though not exhaustive—presentation of the specific measures included in the labor market reforms. These selected measures are mapped following the typology of policy instruments presented earlier.

It is reasonable to expect efficiency savings from the reforms in the medium and long terms. Insofar as the package offers firms and individuals more

TABLE 5.2 **Brazil's 2017 labor policy reforms: Main measures**

REGULATIONS	INTERVENTIONS	INSTITUTIONS
• Restrictions lifted on working hours, while maintaining the maximum weekly and monthly hours worked	• More stringent job-search requirements for recipients of unemployment insurance benefits	• Expansion of the set of issues relating to employment conditions (pay, working hours, overtime, paid leave, productivity bonuses, within-firm mobility) that can be negotiated through collective bargaining at the firm level
• Relaxation of requirements on how much paid leave can be taken at a time	• Modification (rise) of the rate of return earned by individuals' savings in FGTS accounts	• "Prevalence" (that is, primacy) given to firm-level agreements over other collective agreements and the labor law on these matters
• Increase in total hours a week that a person can work for an employer less than full time	• Access granted to individuals' savings in "inactive," dormant FGTS accounts	• Payment of union dues only with individuals' prior, explicit consent
• Expansion of the set of firm activities/parts of the production process that can be performed by people on fixed-term contracts and by outsourced (agency) workers	• [PENDING, PL No. 5278/2016] More financing and improved resource sharing arrangements for Brazil's principal intermediation service, SINE (Site Nacional de Empregos)	• Restrictions on permissible court claims on matters clearly set in the labor code and/or covered by firm-level agreements
• Extension of the maximum period (180 days, with renewal for up to 90 days for a maximum 270 days) a person can be kept on a fixed-term contract by the same employer		• Burden of proof on both parties to the dispute
• Creation of "intermittent" (on-call or "zero-hour") employment contracts		• Losing party made responsible for the costs of legal advice/services
• Allowance of differentiated pay according to productivity/performance, and bonuses		• Fines imposed for labor court claims made in bad faith
• Requirement of pro rata proportional remuneration, all other benefits, rights, protections and entitlements, for people working on less-than-full time, fixed-term, and intermittent contracts		• Lower income threshold to qualify for free legal advice/services ("legal aid")
• Creation of a new "*mutually agreed*" separation, with access to 80 percent of FGTS savings accumulated over the employment period ending and half the fine (*multa*) paid for involuntary dismissal		• Labor regulation applicable regardless of whether contract is between employer and employee or firm and sole trader company • Missed INSS contributions included in the settlement
• Allowance of remote ("tele-"') employment		• Updating of labor claims by lower rate (TR/Bacen)
		• Labor court decides when to ratify extrajudicial settlements
		• Increase in fines for employing people informally

Source: Morgandi, Battaglin Schwengber, and Packard 2017.

options to enter regulated and protected ("formal") work arrangements; provides greater flexibility by shifting weight away from legislation and toward the bargaining table; creates incentives for unions to be more responsive and accountable to members; and lowers the legal uncertainty and other costs of resolving labor disputes, then the reforms should help the labor market create better matches, fewer matches outside the legal framework, and less adversarial workplace relations and reduce deterrents to investment. It is also reasonable to expect that if all these positive outcomes obtain, better matches will lead to longer employment spells and lower the high rate of labor turnover. That said, eliminating the perverse incentives created by Brazil's passive labor programs could further increase the likelihood of these outcomes.

The government is keen to avoid segmentation of the formal labor market. Given that many of the benefits and protections discussed in earlier sections of this chapter remain intact, a key feature of the 2017 reforms is that they are also required for outsourced labor and for employees engaged with fixed-term contracts and in part-time employment. The reforms clearly require they be made available on proportional, pro-rata terms and should help Brazil avoid the outcomes that followed labor code reforms in some European and Latin American countries. The changes Brazil's reforms have also enacted to collective bargaining and workplace conditions are expected to give firms greater certainty about labor costs and lower the risks of time-consuming legal actions.

The 2017 labor market reforms aim mainly at relaxing regulations, and improving the function of institutions, with relatively few measures to improve interventions. That said, and as noted in the *Brazil Expenditure Review* (World Bank 2017), a proposed increase of resources to Brazil's main intermediation and job search assistance service, SINE, is probably justified (although still pending passage of PL No. 5278/2016), given years of funding well below spending levels on comparable programs in other countries.

Notable by its absence from a package of reforms focused mainly on labor regulation is any change to how the national statutory minimum wage is set and adjusted. In the current context of price stability relative to past periods of crisis and recovery, the upward pressure of the minimum wage has been forcing firms to adjust either by informalizing jobs or dismissing workers outright. Indeed, the percentage of people employed and earning less than the minimum wage has been rising, along with the rate of unemployment, for all age groups. Even with no statutory changes to the minimum wage, the 2017 reforms might introduce greater earnings flexibility at the lower level of the productivity distribution of workers, where the minimum wage has started to bind. Although less-than-full-time employment was possible prior to reforms, the changes legislated in 2017 are expected to make it easier for employers to make these and other nonstandard employment offers. This could increase knowledge and use of proportional pay, benefits, and rights and give firms more flexibility to adjust on pay rather than the number of jobs.

Will the 2017 labor market reforms improve employment, welfare, and productivity? Unfortunately, the answer is not straightforward, and it will probably be equally or more directly determined by the health and contestability of Brazil's other factor and product markets, where misallocations and competitiveness are a far greater problem than in the labor market. The complexity of the package of measures that has passed raises myriad questions, but there are notable strengths and weaknesses in the reform.

Will new flexibility in contracting increase or sacrifice equity of labor rights, protections, and benefits?

The changes in permissible contracting and working hours formalize within the legal framework many of the practices to which working people and firms have long had to resort, and which have become the norms of doing business. Compliance costs have been too high for most firms to remain viable. Anecdotes abound of the contortions employers and individuals have had to make to avoid or evade Brazil's expansive, detailed, and rigid labor code. When firms did comply, it was with the letter of the law, and for many compliance could come at the cost of formal employment offers to people performing more routine tasks (Almeida, Corseuil, and Poole 2017). Widespread disregard and outright evasion of the law is an unsatisfactory and unsustainable equilibrium, even when the costs of compliance are prohibitive to business. Respect for and compliance with laws help build and reinforce good governance, which has a widely recognized, public-good benefit to growth. Thus, by bringing many of firms' and workers' actual labor market practices in from the shadows of the informal economy, the reform has made a clear advance. Greater freedom and a broader range of choices for how firms employ people should give businesses more flexibility to experiment with different processes, innovate by adopting new production models and new technology, and adjust with greater agility to the cycle and shifting economic demands, particularly in fast-changing export markets.

The risk is that Brazil's reform will repeat the experience of other countries (notably Italy, Portugal, and Spain), whose reforms that created new, more flexible ways of legally employing people ended up segmenting the formal labor force. Argentina and Chile have had similar reform experiences. And an outcome of these reforms has often been the unexpected emergence of a formal underclass of temporary workers, made up mainly of young people with few pathways to indefinite employment. This segmentation is worse if the protections of people already in indefinite employment, which originally created the need for greater flexibility, and the policy interventions that accompany these protections have been left intact rather than restructured.

A lesson to draw from the experience of earlier reforms is that employers will gravitate to the lowest risk option. Brazilian employers tend to prefer the contracting forms that incur the least explicit nonwage labor costs during workers' tenure and the lowest costs at the point of dismissal. They also consider the value of flexibility to be greater than the risk of losing workers on temporary contracts, especially in industries with lower value-added, for which people with the required skills are relatively easy to find. Only when the labor market tightens do employers have a strong incentive to offer indefinite employment contracts to retain workers with valuable skills. Fixed-term contracts are more advantageous to firms in pretty much any other circumstance.

Because Brazil has fewer restrictions on dismissal, the danger of segmentation of formal employment and the "insider-outsider" dynamics observed in Europe in the 1990s poses less of a risk. The government has stated its policy intention that firms' contracting decisions should not be driven by differences in the per-hour wage and nonwage labor costs. The measures in Law 13.426 include requirements to extend mandated parameters of pay, leave, access to savings and insurance, and any other rights and worker protections to *all* the new contracting arrangements permitted by the labor code after the reform (with the exception of *contratos intermitentes*). An additional regulation was proposed through

Provisional Decree 808 to address benefits and regulation for more flexible types of contracts, particularly intermittent (that is, "zero hour") and *autônomos exclusivos* (for certain occupations, specifically truck drivers, and people working on commission) and increase social security contributions emphasizing these as the responsibility of the employer. Achieving this proportionality presents implementation challenges for employers, as well as monitoring and enforcement costs for regulators. The direct employers (that is, the agency) of outsourced workers are responsible for their rights and worker protections. The risk of employer coercion of current employees into an outsourced employment arrangement is attenuated by an 18-month restriction on a person's returning to work as an outsourced worker at a firm he or she left as a direct employee. This safeguard against arbitrage is temporary, however, extending until December 31, 2020.[6]

Despite proportionally guaranteed worker protections and benefits, risks of arbitrage remain. Even though the reforms introduced greater contracting choice and flexibility, along with the careful requirements for proportional pay and worker protections, there are still some causes for concern. More could be done to ensure a truly level playing field across contracting types. Apparently, for example, the employer-paid *multas* only apply to people who hold indefinite contracts, and there does not appear to be any active incentive for employers to put people on a pathway to indefinite employment. Evidence from several countries shows that placing indefinite employment out of reach affects long-term decisions of the household that entail risk-taking and commitment—for example, the purchase of a home or the decision to have children.

Also, the external costs that greater flexibility might impose do not appear to have been considered. Since workers on fixed-term contracts remain eligible for unemployment insurance, and Brazil's Seguro Desemprego is not actuarially financed, a potentially larger share of Seguro claimants could impose additional fiscal costs (although see discussion of provisional decree, below). The intent of employer-paid fines for involuntary, nondisciplinary dismissals in most countries is to help society recoup the costs of high turnover. But where they are effective, these fines are paid to the public pooled fund that finances unemployment insurance and job-search assistance programs.

A more fundamental concern arises from the ambiguity created by the combination of the outsourcing law and the labor reform law. Specifically, there doesn't appear to be a clear distinction between what is autonomous work and what is subordinated employment and no requirements or guidance to firms as to what tasks or parts of the production process are more suitable to one or the other form of engaging work. This matters to the extent that there are statutory differences between the two regarding rights and protections and differences in who bears financial responsibility for these rights and protections. When these statutory differences are substantial, firms' and individuals' labor market decisions are affected. And there are consequences for work to be deemed either self-employment or subordinated, dependent employment.

Where the reform raises the most concern is an apparent lack of clarity about what constitutes a relationship between businesses—for example, a firm and a self-employed, sole-trader provider of services—and what is an employer–employee relationship. This opens the opportunity for employers with monopsony power to coerce people into what the International Labour Organization calls "disguised employment," and, in so doing, to abscond legally from their financial responsibilities for worker protection (ILO 2016).

Will the 2017 reforms strengthen or weaken collective bargaining?

Advocates of the reforms expect more harmonious workplace relations from the measures, brought about by collective bargaining between employers and more professional and accountable labor unions. Opponents retort that, by eliminating the secure source of financing unions could count on from mandatory worker contributions, the legislation weakens the bargaining position of working people in the face of employers with monopsony power and widespread oligopolistic product markets. A weaker bargaining position could raise the risks of segmentation and the abuses just discussed.

The reforms have, unquestionably, given workers and employers more things to bargain over that were previously mandated in the labor code. Deals struck at the firm level on a specified set of workplace matters—including pay, working conditions, and leave, among others—now have primacy (*prevalência*) over agreements negotiated at any other (sectoral or municipal) level and, indeed, even over stipulations on these matters in the labor code. If they have more to negotiate and their negotiated agreements are given greater weight, the parties are expected to take collective bargaining more seriously and to come up with a greater array of creative, "win–win" agreements better suited to the specific needs of the firm and its workforce. With greater responsibility to advocate for their members' well-being at work, and potentially more to show for their efforts, unions would attract and be held accountable by voluntarily-paying members.[7] Importantly, the matters unions are permitted to bargain over have been more clearly defined, and for workplaces of 200 or more workers a new entity has been created: the *comissão de representantes dos empregados*. This new worker-representative body can negotiate over certain aspects of workplace conditions but cannot take up issues clearly reserved (by article 8 of the constitution) for labor unions.

Many who are skeptical of the reforms point out the "free rider" problems that arise when union dues are voluntary. Because in most countries and jurisdictions it is common for the law to require "nondiscrimination" (that is, equal pay and benefits for people doing the same job in the same place), the benefits unions negotiate have to be extended to members and nonmembers alike. This may explain how unions—particularly those that represent workers in the public sector—have an impact on workplace conditions disproportionate to the share of the workforce they directly represent. But the requirement of equal pay and conditions also lowers the incentives of working people to join unions and pay union fees. This rationale has become the basis for mandating payment of dues (or "agency fees") to cover the costs unions incur to negotiate for the benefit of all. In places where membership and/or fees are voluntary, even people who value the benefits unions win are less likely to join and pay dues, which threatens an "undersupply" of unions' collective representation and advocacy services.

Workers' ability to associate and bargain collectively is a vital complement to an efficient, contestable, and equitable labor market. And diminished representation and advocacy services incur costs. Whether the free rider problems actually lead to diminished or undersupplied advocacy services, however, is determined by the extent to which alternatives and competition can provide those services. If more options are available to people in a workplace—including that of self-representation—it is reasonable to expect workers to join and pay the dues of the union that gives them the best deal, and for this to be the one with the greatest bargaining power. And in firms where a small number of workers would make competition between providers of representation services unviable, exclusive representation rights could be granted to a single union; that the exclusive provider bear the cost of the free riders is a usual concession. These matters do not, however, appear to be acknowledged or addressed with provisions for exclusive representation. Furthermore, many large sectors of the Brazilian economy are, indeed, dominated by employers with monopsony power (such as in agriculture and mining).

Will the reduction in judicial uncertainty encourage investment in job creation?

As noted in the *Brazil Jobs Report* of 2002 (World Bank and IPEA 2002), the labor courts system had a systemic tendency to favor plaintiff employees over employers. Brazil was not unique in having a dedicated branch of its judiciary to hear and rule on labor disputes, but it was among the countries where court action was most frequently taken. As more formal employment relationships were formed over the high-growth period in Brazil, the number of cases brought to the labor courts rose, and the rise has accelerated since the start of the recession in 2014. The report noted some exceptional features of the system: hearing cases brought by employees even if they could not produce documentation of their employment relationships; a burden on employers to prove their innocence of the infractions they were accused of; no clear assignment of court costs; and a cost burden that fell exclusively to the employer. The uncertainty raised by these features was a deterrent to job creation and increased the cost of doing business, including the cost of failure when firms would take risks by innovating with new technology or production processes.

As the reforms widen the space for collective bargaining and give primacy to firm-level agreements, the set of disputes that can now be heard in court is narrower. The courts will also have less discretion in interpreting the law and will be restricted from creating new rights with their decisions. While these changes are intended to give firms greater certainty, a long period of adjustment may ensue before this certainty is had. Also creating uncertainty for a time may be the greater complexity of the new contracting forms brought about to give firms more flexibility, as they struggle to learn their new responsibilities and discourage job offers. Yet these uncertainties are only to be expected with the passage of such a structural reform, and the government can counter them with measures to inform and educate all parties on their new rights and responsibilities.

The body of anecdotal evidence of frivolous, opportunistic, and even strategically motivated complaints filed in the labor courts is sufficiently large to justify the new deterrents passed in 2017. The reforms have enacted fines and clearly assigned court costs in an attempt to make disputes less likely be taken to court. The backlog of cases in the labor courts is itself evidence alternative dispute resolution structures are to be systematically encouraged. Indeed, in the short period since the labor reform was legislated, there has been a sharp drop in cases, which is a tentatively positive sign that the reform may be having its intended impact. That said, the reforms lowered the income threshold below which people qualify for legal financial assistance. As with the potential for abuse of contracting, the monopsony power of firms in many of Brazil's largest sectors raises concern for the workers for whom the changes in eligibility or legal aid may have put the courts out of reach.

THE PENDING LABOR REFORM AGENDA

A formidable agenda of reform to labor market policies and programs could still be pursued to raise Brazil's productivity potential by better engaging its young people. The remainder of this chapter proposes several policy options on which a government concerned with the labor market prospects of its young people could draw. None of the ideas proposed is easy, and they differ considerably in procedural and legislative difficulty. Any of those put forward would face enormous political resistance. To realize the full potential of the labor market reforms it legislated in 2017, however, Brazil will need to do more to give its young people a better chance of contesting and succeeding in the labor market.

Statutory minimum wage-setting and adjustment process

The distortions of a statutory minimum wage can be minimized if adjustments are made with greater reference to changes in workers' productivity. In Brazil, however, the federal minimum wage has been increasing faster than labor productivity for many years.

Several methods are used around the world to set the level of statutory minimum wages, some more discretionary and others more formula-based. Brazil has one of the more rigid systems for setting its federal minimum wage, which raises the risk of harmful distortions. The minimum wage is adjusted based on inflation of the previous year and real GDP growth of the year prior to that, if the GDP growth was positive. The real level of the minimum wage can only rise. This adjustment policy has two fundamental problems. First, the formula allows minimum wages to rise faster than workers' productivity, especially when economic and labor productivity growth rise at the same pace. As the minimum wage is frequently used as a benchmark for the earnings of all workers, this can push up labor costs or compress wages across the entire wage distribution. Second, the adjustment formula creates the risk of countercyclical, upward adjustments. The lag between observed rates of economic growth and the adjustment required by the formula creates the possibility that the minimum wage will increase at times of economic slowdown, as happened in 2015–16. Brazil could consider scrutinizing the current formula and accompanying adjustment institutions and make changes to lower the risks of mechanical adjustments that are unresponsive to current economic conditions. Creating institutions that engage stakeholders in a continuous and flexible process is now considered leading practice (box 5.2).

BOX 5.2

Wage floor adjustment formulas: Respectability, with a productivity argument

As with statutory wage floors generally, the debate on how the level of the minimum wage should be adjusted has evolved from an exchange of arguments on "whether" to arguments on "how." The old debates pitted ardent proponents of discretion and flexibility in the face of uncertain future economic circumstances against equally passionate advocates for transparency and predictability in how wage policy is carried out. The latter argued for clear, undiscriminating adjustment formulas and their technical value in places with weak or opaque governance institutions that are vulnerable to capture by one or another party. The former feared that the hand of policy on the level of statutory wage floors would be pushed or pulled mechanically, and with little

continued

Box 5.2, *continued*

reference to circumstances and unforeseen events. In countries prone to price instability, critics of adjustment formulas had the added ammunition of so-called "wage-price spirals," a notion they used very effectively in these debates. But adjustment formulas for the level of statutory minimum wages are newly *en vogue*.

The current debate is duller but also more useful. The value of a transparently designed and managed adjustment formula is clearly recognized, but just as important are the voices of stakeholders and government, interacting regularly through permanent institutions. The debate is over the relative weights of stakeholder and government input and formula outcomes. In their review of leading practices, Del Carpio and Pabon (2014, 2017) conclude it is best to have a clear formula that avoids excessive rigidity in the process and is easy for all stakeholders to understand, apply, and discuss. The idea is to construct the formula to reflect policy objectives agreed upon by stakeholders and government (for example, to lower income inequality or ensure workers in uncompetitive labor markets are fairly remunerated, per their contributions to firms' and the economy's productivity) and so the resulting levels serve as a technically derived "starting position" in regular negotiations, rather than a predetermined and uncontestable outcome.

Additionally, in this new debate, "productivity and growth" appear to sit equally alongside "risk management" and "social justice" objectives. When adjustment formulas include arguments to reflect labor's marginal product, a large part of the distortion imposed by a wage floor can be mitigated. Cunningham et al. (2016) present wage-setting and adjustment formulas they use to calculate an adjustment path for minimum wages that takes better account of economic conditions, including the extent of informal employment. Their methodology starts with a formula to set the level of a basic minimum wage as a function of the median wage and the poverty line. The outcome is adjusted for labor productivity, the unemployment rate, and the cost of living index. A second formula is defined to adjust the level of the minimum wage annually by the cost of living, labor productivity, the employment rate, and the rate of informal employment. The steps are as follows.

Setting the level: The starting level of the minimum wage is a simple average of the poverty line per worker (P) and the median salary of workers in the lower half of the wage distribution. This ensures the minimum wage is always above the poverty line. The second argument in the formula takes account of productivity (P), the consumer price index (CPI), and the rate of unemployment (U), which allows the level of the minimum to keep pace with salaries in the rest of the economy.

$$MW_i = \left[Average\left(P_i + \left(Median\ wage \right) \right) \right] * \left[1 + \left(\frac{P_i}{100} \right) + \left(\frac{CPI_i}{100} \right) - \left(\frac{U_i}{100} \right) \right]$$

The annual adjustment: A second formula determines annual adjustment, using four arguments: the Consumer Price Index (CPI), workers'

productivity (LP), the share of workers in the informal sector (INF), and the employment rate (EMP).

$$\Delta\% MW_{t-t_1} = +\beta_1 \% CPI_{t-t_1} + \beta_2 \% \Delta LP_{t-t_1} -(\beta_4)\% \Delta INF_{t-trend} +(\beta_5)\% \Delta EMP_{t-trend}$$

The coefficients β_1 and β_2 are set by negotiation among stakeholders. The coefficients β_4 and β_5 are calculated using elasticities of employment with respect to the minimum wage and the rate of informal employment.

The positive sign on the CPI reflects the increases required to maintain workers' purchasing power. Productivity also enters the formula positively, reflecting a greater contribution of workers to GDP. The positive sign on the employment parameter is associated with the possibility of raising the minimum wage when doing so contributes to employment growth.

The coefficient on the rate of informality is negative, reflecting the tendency of rises in the level of the minimum wage to increase informal work.

More important than the specific arguments in the formula and the signs they carry, the advantage of this approach is to leave the value of specific coefficients to negotiation among stakeholders, which acts as a device to keep them engaged. If a national wage floor is kept sufficiently low in the statute, this same procedure can be followed at the subnational and firm levels in the collective bargaining process to negotiate wages above the mandatory minimum.

Lower statutory minimums for younger working people

There is encouraging evidence that setting a lower minimum wage for the young-est workers that rises with age can reduce the many negative employment effects of a statutory minimum wage. If minimum wages are set lower for youth than for adults, then, from the perspective of hiring firms, the labor costs of engaging young people are lower, and the employment effects offsetting a statutory wage floor become more ambiguous. The experiences of European and other OECD coun-tries with age-differentiated minimum wages have been quite successful. Dickens et al. (2014) found that when low-skilled individuals in the United Kingdom turned 22 years of age and moved from the youth to the adult minimum wage, their rate of employment increased by about 3–4 percentage points. Contrary to what the classical economic models predict, this suggests firms may not see those below the age threshold as perfect substitutes for those above it. The increase in wages may induce more young people to participate in the labor market or increase the inten-sity of their job searches. Similarly, in Greece, Yannelis (2014) and Karakitsios (2016) found a reduction in the minimum wage for people under age 25 increased their probability of being employed. In New Zealand, Hyslop and Stillman (2004) found that decreasing the statutory minimum by 41 percent for 16–17-year-olds resulted in a slightly positive impact on their employment probability (employ-ment elasticity of 0.25), while decreasing the minimum by 69 percent for 18–19-year-olds also resulted in positive, though smaller, employment effects for that group (employment elasticity of 0.08).

Critically, reforms to minimum wages have to be made paying close attention to the profile of workers who earn the minimum. In many high-income coun-tries, adults who are parents or otherwise responsible for dependent household members are less likely to be in jobs that pay the minimum wage. So-called "sec-ondary earners"—that is, those whose earned income is not the primary source for financing essential household consumption—are more likely to hold jobs that pay the minimum wage. This can, of course, vary substantially across households according to composition, wealth, and geography. In lower-income countries, jobs paying the minimum wage are among the most stable and sought after. The key question that has to be answered is in how many cases working people earn-ing the minimum wage are a main or even the only source of market income for their households. Using the narrower age definition of youth (15–24), the highest share of those earning one minimum wage (about 34 percent) is in the third income quintile. This is followed by about 26 percent of youth earning one min-imum wage in the second quintile, and just under 10 percent in the poorest quin-tile (where many working people earn less than the minimum wage). Among youth who are heads of households or working spouses of the household heads and who earn one minimum wage, the largest portion (about 40 percent) are in the poorest quintile. This represents a substantial number of people who would be affected by a policy to lower the minimum wage for youth. The possible gains form this policy could, however, justify focused compensation for those adversely affected, and Brazil performs far better than most of its peers in identifying and responding to households in need of income support.

Care also has to be taken in setting the minimum wage not to provide incen-tive for dropping out of school or create abrupt increases in labor costs as youth move from one age to the next. Kábatek (2015) indicated that the Dutch model of incremental minimum wage increases from ages 15 to 23 may be having some unintended consequences. He showed that for workers ages 16–23, the probability of job separation increased by 1–2 percent in the three months preceding their birthdays (when they move to a higher minimum wage tier). These results contradicted those found in Portugal by Cardoso (2006), who found the teenage share of job separations fell by about 15 percent in response to increases in the minimum wage (by 33–50 percent) for 17–19-year-olds in 1987, despite the reduction in relative demand for teenage labor. In Denmark, Kreiner et al. (2017) used regression discontinuity to show employment falls by 33 percent when the hourly wage rate jumps by 40 percent as individuals turn 18 years old. This decline is almost entirely driven by job losses that are likely to be motivated by higher labor costs. Finally, Larrain and Poblete (2007) showed that while relaxing the minimum wage solely for young workers reduced youth unemployment, doing so might force less skilled workers to remain longer in the uncovered sector. On the basis of this evidence, a reduced but rising statutory minimum would ideally be implemented in small increments.

Reforms to unemployment income support

Brazil's government can build on its labor reforms with supportive changes to unemployment income support programs. Although a step in the right direction, the outsourcing and labor reforms passed in the first half of 2017 are not enough to encourage longer employment spells, with more opportunities to build critical skills and achieve higher productivity. Brazil's main unemployment support programs, the Seguro Desemprego and FGTS, and the fines (multas) paid by employers for involuntary, nondisciplinary dismissal, are likely to continue creating perverse incentives for high rates of unproductive churn.

Changes could be made to the parameters of FGTS and Seguro Desemprego to lower perverse incentives and improve the programs' effectiveness. The most urgent and important measure would be to sequence workers' access to the two. Rather than being entitled to gain access simultaneously to their individual savings (FGTS) and the risk-pooling benefit (Seguro) upon involuntary separation, workers could be required to exhaust their savings before receiving Seguro. A limit on how much of their savings could be withdrawn for every month of the unemployment period could be imposed, and this maximum benefit could decline over time. Indeed, most modern unemployment insurance programs feature a declining benefit rate of replacement over the total payout period. Requiring workers to draw down their own savings creates urgency that can counter the "moral hazard" of income support during unemployment spells.

With this sequencing proposal, Seguro Desemprego could underpin the FGTS and, in doing so, provide more support to lower-earners and those who find it more difficult to find new jobs. It also has the merit of reserving the public resources that finance Seguro Desemprego for those likely to run down their *FGTS* savings fastest or who take longer to find new jobs. These are the people with fewer sought-after skills; lower-income earners who are not able to accumulate large balances in individual accounts; or people who have suffered repeated employment shocks. As in countries that combine individual savings with risk pooling, the number of times an individual can get access to benefits from the unemployment insurance risk pool could be limited in any given period; could be conditioned on the intensity of job search, acceptance of job offers, and take-up of training, counseling, or other support services; or could depend on a combination of these public employment services.

Coordinating workers' access to FTGS and Seguro Desemprego would offer households a more resilient set of tools to manage a diverse set of risks to employment. In any country, even in times of economic stability and growth, an efficient level of turnover exists, as workers move from one job to another, and as firms go out of and come into existence. As mentioned previously, Brazil stands out for turnover higher than that observed among its peers, which may partly explain its low levels of productivity. Turnover may be faster than it should be because of the generosity created by the current overlap of passive income support programs. Sequencing access to FTGS and Seguro Desemprego would provide actuarial benefits and could contribute to productivity by providing support for individual mobility following an idiosyncratic, or even a predictable, employment disruption and augmenting this support when unemployment spells are longer or the shock to the economy is systemic, as is the case in the wake of a crisis or long recession. Chile's mixed unemployment protection system includes triggers that can lengthen the total payout period when the country's unemployment rate rises above a certain level.

The proposed measures to give greater coherence to unemployment support programs could substantially lengthen employment spells and benefit productivity. Table 5.3 sets out the main labor market programs deployed by the federal

TABLE 5.3 Reforms to Brazil's labor programs likely to improve labor market incentives and outcomes

PROGRAMS	CURRENT PROBLEMS	PROPOSED REFORM	ANTICIPATED IMPACT
Wage supplements (Abono Salarial & Salario Família)	• Abono Salarial: Regressively distributed • Poor "formalization" incentives • Overlap and duplication between programs => unnecessary overspending	• Convert Abono Salarial into a wage subsidy paid to employers to encourage formal hiring of inexperienced/low skilled/unemployed. • Pay Salario Família allowance to lower earners, taking account of dependents in the household and consistent with Bolsa Familia	• Improved distribution of transfers • Improved incentives to formalize and remain formally employed • Fiscal savings from eliminating spending on duplicated/overlapping programs
Mandated individual savings for income support during unemployment (FGTS)	• Strong incentive to gain access to savings (large saving ratio and low returns)	• Raise rate of return on FGTS accounts • Limit access to FGTS forced savings to involuntary, nondisciplinary separations • Require a structured drawdown of savings before giving access to Seguro Desemprego	• Less incentive to become unemployed • Longer employment spells • Shorter unemployment spells
Risk pooling to mitigate losses from job separation during unemployment spells (Seguro Desemprego)	• Relatively easy to vest • Generous benefits • Short payout period • "Flat" benefit payout structure • Weak job search requirements	• Lower initial benefits (replacement rate of salary lost) • Lengthen the maximum payout period • Institute reclining benefit level (replacement rate of salary lost) • Impose stringent job search and training requirements, especially for individuals who repeatedly require access to Seguro Desemprego	• More progressive distribution of Fundo de Amparo ao Trabalhador (FAT) allocations • Stronger incentives to find new job • More and higher-quality matches • Self-targeted job search assistance to the most difficult to place
Removal of incentives to dismiss workers from/allocation of its cost to employer	• Large portion of taxes on individual, nondisciplinary dismissals (*multas*) is paid to the person dismissed • No way to capture external costs (public bads) of job destruction • Perverse penalties of (*multa*) award structure	• Pay 100 percent of *multas* to FAT	• Lower perverse incentives for employees to seek frequent involuntary dismissal • Longer duration of formal employment spells

government and the problems they create. The last two columns of the table propose reforms and provide the expected impact of the proposed measures. The same proposals are made in the World Bank's *Brazil Expenditure Review* (2017), but there they are mainly motivated to achieve a better distribution of public spending and some fiscal savings. The emphasis of these reforms in this book is on the anticipated improvement in incentives. Simulations of their impact conducted for both the *Brazil Expenditure Review* and this book (see figure 5.7) show a small, but statistically significant, increase in the duration of formal employment and a similarly small but significant decrease in the duration of unemployment after the loss of a formal job. Moreover, readers should note that, although the changes shown by the simulations are small,

FIGURE 5.7

Proposed reforms to labor programs reduce the number of formal workers who are unemployed and average duration of unemployment, and increase the share of unemployed who go into formal jobs

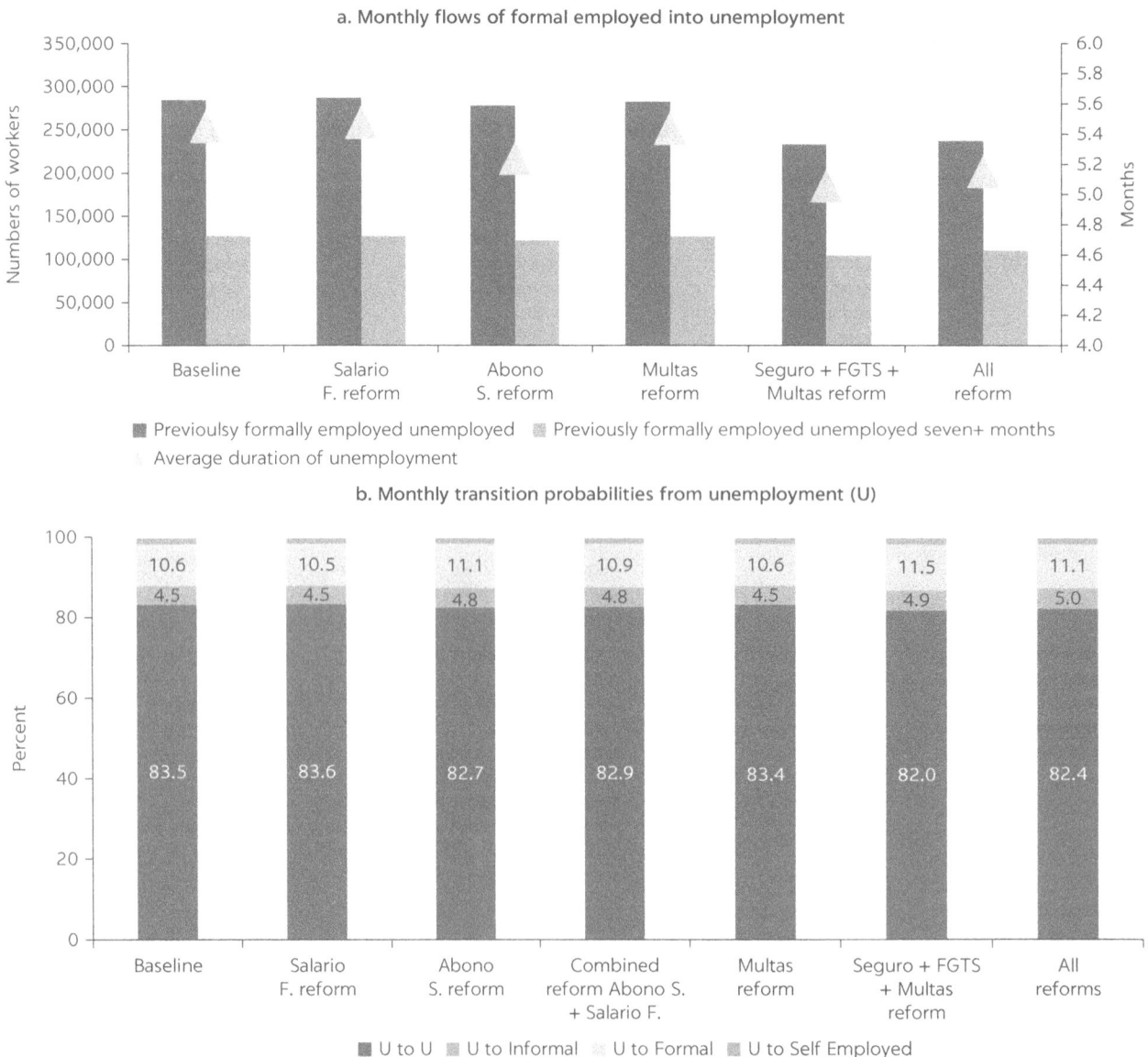

a. Monthly flows of formal employed into unemployment

- Previoulsy formally employed unemployed
- Previously formally employed unemployed seven+ months
- Average duration of unemployment

b. Monthly transition probabilities from unemployment (U)

- U to U
- U to Informal
- U to Formal
- U to Self Employed

Source: Reform simulations based on *Pesquisa Mensal de Emprego* (PME), May 2015.
Notes: Figures shows the simulated impact of Brazil labor market program reform using World Bank's SimPLE model.

the analysis was limited to the panel data available, specifically the PME, which has a limited sample. The results are sufficiently promising to merit a more thorough analysis of reform options along the lines described above.

NOTES

1. This chapter draws heavily on a review of empirical literature conducted by Pui Shen Yoong and included in appendix B of this book. The chapter also draws on work carried out by World Bank staff and consultants for the chapter on labor market programs in "A Just Adjustment," *Brazil Expenditure Review* (World Bank 2017), as well as on the first policy report from the Bank's Brazil Skills and Jobs analytical and advisory program (see Silva, Almeida, and Strokova 2015). Supporting analysis presented in this chapter was conducted by Matteo Morgandi, Vanessa Moreira da Silva, Michael Weber, Rovane Battaglin Schwengber, Renata Gukovas, and Raquel Tsukada.
2. Law No. 13.429 on outsourcing (*Lei da terceirização*) in March 2017; Law No. 13.446 (*Rentabilidade de contas FGTS*) in May; Law No. 13.456 (*Programa Seguro-Emprego prazo de vigência*) in June 2017; and Law No. 13.467 to the labor code (*Reforma trabalhista*) in July 2017.
3. https://direitosbrasil.com/salario-minimo-2018/
4. Part of the reason is that Sistema S, which offers many of the training courses that are now financed by Pronatec, now also has to provide courses to the same type of beneficiaries with its own (levy-financed) revenues.
5. The law requires payment of a *multa* equivalent to 50 percent of the employer's total contributions to the worker's FGTS account *during the worker's tenure in the specific job* (Portela et al. 2016). The worker retains 80 percent of this *multa*. While termination-related withdrawals from FGTS accounts in 2014 amounted to 1 percent of GDP, it is difficult to determine what share was from *multas*, since the tenure of the workers in their companies at time of dismissal is unknown.
6. http://www.planalto.gov.br/ccivil_03/Decreto-Lei/Del5452.htm, l, art. 452g. *"Até 31 de dezembro de 2020, o empregado registrado por meio de contrato de trabalho por prazo indeterminado demitido não poderá prestar serviços para o mesmo empregador por meio de contrato de trabalho intermitente pelo prazo de dezoito meses, contado da data da demissão do empregado."*
7. http://www.planalto.gov.br/ccivil_03/Decreto-Lei/Del5452.htm, l, art 510e. *"A comissão de representantes dos empregados não substituirá a função do sindicato de defender os direitos e os interesses coletivos ou individuais da categoria, inclusive em questões judiciais ou administrativas, hipótese em que será obrigatória a participação dos sindicatos em negociações coletivas de trabalho, nos termos do incisos III e VI do caput do art. 8° da Constituição."*

REFERENCES

Alatas, Vivi, and Lisa A. Cameron. 2008. "The Impact of Minimum Wages on Employment in a Low-Income Country: A Quasi-Natural Experiment in Indonesia", ILR Review, Vol. 61, No. 2 Cornell University: Ithaca, NY.

Allegretto, S. A., A. Dube, and M. Reich. 2011. "Do Minimum Wages Really Reduce Teen Employment? Accounting for Heterogeneity and Selectivity in State Panel Data." *Industrial Relations: A Journal of Economy and Society* 50 (2): 205–40.

Almeida, Rita Kullberg, Carlos H. L. Corseuil, and Jennifer Pamela Poole. 2017. "The Impact of Digital Technologies on Routine Tasks: Do Labor Policies Matter?" Policy Research Working Paper 8187. World Bank, Washington, DC.

Baccaro, L., and D. Rei. 2005. "Institutional Determinants of Unemployment in OECD Countries: A Time Series Cross-Section Analysis (1960–98)." International Institute for Labour Studies, Geneva.

Bassanini, A., and R. Duval. 2006. "The Determinants of Unemployment across OECD Countries: Reassessing the Role of Policies and Institutions." *OECD Economic Studies* 42 (1): 7.

Bertola, G. 1990. "Job Security, Employment and Wages." *European Economic Review* 34 (4): 851–79.

Besley, T. J., and R. Burgess. 2004. "Can Labour Regulation Hinder Economic Performance? Evidence from India." *The Quarterly Journal of Economics* 119(1): 91–134.

Broecke, Stijn, Alessia Forti, and Marieke Vandeweyer. 2017. "The Effects of Minimum Wages on Employment in Emerging Economies: A Literature Review."

Broecke, S., and M. Vandeweyer. 2015. "Doubling the Minimum Wage and Its Effect on Labor Market Outcomes: Evidence from Brazil."

Campos, R.M., G. Esquivel, and A.S. Santillán. 2015. "El impacto del salario mínimo en los ingresos y el empleo en México." *Serie Estudios y Perspectivas 162*. Mexico: CEPAL.

Canelas, C. 2014. "Minimum wage and informality in Ecuador." WIDERWorking Paper 2014/006, United Nations University World Institute for Development Economics Research. Helsinki: UNU-WIDER.

Card, D. 1992. "Do Minimum Wages Reduce Employment? A Case Study of California, 1987–89." *Industrial and Labor Relations Review* 46 (1): 38–54.

Cardoso, A.R. 2009. "Long-Term Impact of Youth Minimum Wages: Evidence from Two Decades of Individual Longitudinal Data." IZA Discussion Paper No. 4236, Institute for the Study of Labor (IZA). Bonn, Germany: IZA.

Céspedes, N., and A. Sánchez. 2013. "Minimum Wage and Job Mobility." Working Papers 2013-012, Banco Central de Reserva del Perú. Retrieved from: https://ideas.repec.org/p/rbp/wpaper/2013-012.html.

Chletsos, Michael, and Georgios P. Giotis. 2015. "The Employment Effect of Minimum Wage Using 77 International Studies since 1992: A Meta-Analysis." MPRA Paper 61321, University Library of Munich, Germany.

Clemens, J. 2015. "The Minimum Wage and the Great Recession: Evidence from the Current Population Survey." NBER Working Paper 21830. Cambridge, MA: National Bureau of Economic Research.

Corseuil, C., M. Foguel, G. Gonzaga, and E. Ribeiro. 2014. "Youth Turnover in Brazil: Job and Worker Flows and an Evaluation of a Youth-Targeted Training Program." Universidad Nacional de La Plata, La Plata, Argentina.

Cunningham, Wendy, Ximena Vanessa Del Carpio, Leonardo Iacovone, Juan Martin Moreno, Laura Milena Pabon Alvarado, and Elizaveta Perova. 2016. *El salario mínimo y la productividad empresarial, laboral, y general con un enfoque en el caso de México*. Washington, DC: World Bank.

Del Carpio, Ximena, and Laura Pabon. 2014. *Minimum wage policy: Lessons with a Focus on the ASEAN Region*. Washington, DC: World Bank. https://hubs.worldbank.org/docs/imagebank/pages/docprofile.aspx?nodeid=19457058.

Del Carpio, Ximena Vanessa, and Laura M. Pabon. 2017. *Implications of Minimum Wage Increases on Labor Market Dynamics Lessons for Emerging Economies*. Policy Research working paper, no. WPS 8030. Washington, DC: World Bank. https://hubs.worldbank.org/docs/imagebank/pages/docprofile.aspx?nodeid=27370704.

Del Carpio, X., H. Nguyen, and L.C. Wang. 2012. "Does the Minimum Wage Affect Employment? Evidence from the Manufacturing Sector in Indonesia." Policy Research Working Paper, no. 6147. Washington, DC: World Bank.

Dickens, R., R. Riley, and D. Wilkinson. 2014. "The UK Minimum Wage at 22 Years of Age: A Regression Discontinuity Approach." *Journal of the Royal Statistical Society: Series A (Statistics in Society)*, 177(1): 95–114.

Fajnzylber, P. 2001. "Minimum Wage Effects throughout the Wage Distribution: Evidence from Brazil's Formal and Informal Sectors." No. td151. Universidade Federal de Minas Gerais, Cedeplar.

Foguel, M.N. 1998. "Uma Avaliação dos Efeitos do Salário Mínimo sobre o Mercado de Trabalho no Brasil." Texto para discussão IPEA. Brasília: IPEA.

Foguel, M., G. Ulyssea, and C.H. Corseuil. "Salário Mínimo e Mercado do Trabalho no Brasil." Chapter 14 in *Brasil em Desenvolvimento 2014: Estado, Planejamento e Políticas Públicas*, Vol. 1. Eds. Monasterio, L.M., M. Côrtes Neri, and S. Soares. Brasília: IPEA.

Foguel, Miguel, Lauro Ramos, and Francisco Carneiro. 2015. "Impacts of the Minimum Wage on the Labor Market, Poverty and Fiscal Budget in Brazil." Discussion paper 108, Instituto de Pesquisa Econômica Aplicada (IPEA). https://econpapers.repec.org/paper/ipeipetds/.

Grau, N., and O. Landerretche. 2011. "The Labor Impact of Minimum Wages: A Method for Estimating the Effect in Emerging Economies Using Chilean Panel Data." Working Papers, University of Chile, Department of Economics. Retrieved from: http://www.econ.uchile.cl/uploads/publicacion/80a7ba9cf917b18adfa52210cde6a29bac9e0849.pdf.

Heckman, J. J., and C. Pagés. 2000. "The Cost of Job Security Regulation: Evidence from Latin American Labor Markets." No. w7773. National Bureau of Economic Research.

Heckman, J. and C. Pagés, eds. 2004. *Law and Employment: Lessons from Latin America and the Caribbean*, 183–228. Chicago: University of Chicago Press.

Huang, Y., P. Loungani, and G. Wang. 2014. "Minimum Wages and Firm Employment: Evidence from China." Federal Reserve Bank of Dallas Globalization and Monetary Policy Institute Working Paper No. 173. Retrieved from: <https://www.dallasfed.org/~/media/documents/institute/wpapers/2014/0173.pdf>

Hyslop, D., and S. Stillman. 2004. "Youth Minimum Wage Reform and the Labour Market." IZA Discussion Paper No. 1091. Bonn: Institute for the Study of Labor.

IBGE (Brazilian Institute of Geography and Statistics). 2004–15. *Pesquisa Nacional por Amostra de Domicílios* (PNAD).

Jales, H. 2015. "Estimating the effects of the minimum wage in a developing country: a density discontinuity design approach." Global Labour Organization (GLO) Discussion Paper, No. 54. Retrieved from: http://hdl.handle.net/10419/156725.

———. 2017. "Estimating the Effects of the Minimum Wage in a Developing Country: A Density Discontinuity Design Approach." *Journal of Applied Econometrics* 33 (1): 29–51.

Kabátek, J. 2015. "Happy Birthday, You're Fired! The Effects of Age-Dependent Minimum Wage on Youth Employment Flows in the Netherlands." IZA Discussion Paper 9528. Bonn: Institute for the Study of Labor.

Kahn, L. M. 2012. "Labor Market Policy: A Comparative View on the Costs and Benefits of Labor Market Flexibility." *Journal of Policy Analysis and* Management 31(1): 94–110.

Karakitsios, A. 2016. "The Effect of Subminimum Wage Introduction on Employment in Greece." Athens University of Economics and Business, mimeo. Retrieved from: http://www.lse.ac.uk/europeanInstitute/research/hellenicObservatory/Events/HO%20PhD%20Symposia/7th-Symposium/Documents/Papers/Karakitsios%20Alexandros.pdf.

Komatsu, Bruno, and Naercio Menezes-Filho, 2016. "Does the Rise of the Minimum Wage Explain the Fall of Wage Inequality in Brazil?", Policy Paper No. 16, June. INSPER Centro de Politicas Publicas: São Paulo.

Kreiner, C.T., D. Reck, and P.E. Skov. 2017. "Do Lower Minimum Wages for Young Workers Raise their Employment? Evidence from a Danish Discontinuity." CEPRDiscussion Papers 12359, Center for Economic Policy Research.

Kugler, A. D. 2004. "The Effect of Job Security Regulations on Labor Market Flexibility: Evidence from the Colombian Labor Market Reform." In *Law and Employment: Lessons from Latin America and the Caribbean*, edited by James J. Heckman and Carmen Pagés, 183–228. Chicago: University of Chicago Press.

Larraín, M., and J. Poblete. 2007. "Age-differentiated minimum wages in developing countries." *Journal of Development Economics* 84: 777–797.

Lemos, S. 2004. "The Effects of the Minimum Wage on the Formal and Informal Sectors in Brazil." IZA Discussion Paper No. 1089. Bonn: Institute for the Study of Labor.

Lemos, S. 2009. "Minimum Wage Effects in a Developing Country." *Labour Economics* 16 (2): 224–37.

Liu, S., T. J. Hyclak, and K. Regmi. 2016. "Impact of the Minimum Wage on Youth Labor Markets." *Labour* 30 (1): 18–37.

Morgandi, Matteo, Rovane Battaglin Schwengber, and Truman Packard. 2017. "An Assessment of Brazil's 2017 Labor Reform" unpublished mimeo, Social Protection and Jobs Global Practice, World Bank: Washington, DC.

Neri, Marcelo, Gustavo Gonzaga, and José Márcio Camargo. 2001. "Salário mínimo, 'efeito farol' e pobreza." *Revista de Economia Politica* 21 (2): 82.

Neumark, D., and O. Nizalova. 2007. "Minimum Wage Effects in the Longer Run." *Journal of Human Resources* 42 (2); 435–52.

Neumark, D., J. I. Salas, and W. Wascher. 2014. "Revisiting the Minimum Wage—Employment Debate: Throwing Out the Baby with the Bathwater?" *Industrial & Labor Relations Review* 67 (3 suppl): 608–48.

Neumark, D., and W. Wascher. 2007. "Minimum Wages, the Earned Income Tax Credit, and Employment: Evidence from the Post-Welfare Reform Era." IZA Discussion Paper 2610. Bonn: Institute for the Study of Labor.

Nickell, S. 1997. Unemployment and Labor Market Rigidities: Europe versus North America." *Journal of Economic Perspectives* 11 (3): 55–74.

OECD. 1999. "Employment Protection Regulation and Labour Market Performance." *OECD Employment Outlook* (June): 49–130. Paris: OECD.

OECD. 2016. "Economic Policy Reforms: Going for Growth," OECD: Paris, http://www.oecd.org/eco/growth/going-for-growth-2016.htm.

Paes de Barros, R. P., and C. H. Corseuil. 2004. "The Impact of Regulations on Brazilian Labor Market Performance." In *Law and Employment: Lessons from Latin America and the Caribbean*, pp. 273–350. (eds.) J. Heckman and C. Páges. Chicago: University of Chicago Press.

Pesquisa Mensal de Emprego (PME). 2015. Instituto Brasileiro de Geografia e Estatística, IBGE.

Pinto, Rafael de Carvalho Cayres. 2015. "Three Essays on Labor Market Institutions and Labor Turnover in Brazil." Pontifícia Universidade Católica do Rio de Janeiro. Departamento de Economia, Rio de Janeiro.

Portela Souza, Andre, Gabriel Ulyssea, Ricardo Paes de Barros, Diana Coutinho, Lucas Finamor, Lycia Lima. 2016. "Rede de Proteção ao Trabalhador no Brasil: Avaliação Ex-Ante e Proposta de Redesenho", mimeo, FGV ESSP & CLEAR, Sao Paulo.

Portugal, P., and A.R. Cardoso. 2006. "Disentangling the Minimum Wage Puzzle: An Analysis of Worker Accessions and Separations." *Journal of the European Economic Association* 4(5): 988–1013.

Saavedra, J., and M. Torero. 2004. "Labor Market Reforms and Their Impact over Formal Labor Demand and Job Market Turnover: The Case of Peru." In *Law and Employment: Lessons from Latin America and the Caribbean*, edited by James J. Heckman and Carmen Pagés, 131–82. Chicago: University of Chicago Press.

Sabia, Joseph J., Richard V. Burkhauser, and Benjamin Hansen. 2012. "Are the Effects of Minimum Wage Increases Always Small? New Evidence from a Case Study of New York State." Industrial and Labor Relations Review, vol. 65, no. 2, pp. 350–376.

Scarpetta, S. 1996. Assessing the Role of Labour Market Policies and Institutional Settings on Unemployment: A Cross-Country Study. *OECD Economic Studies* 26 (1): 43–98.

Schwab, D. 2015. "Employment Protection and the Labor Informality of the Youth: Evidence from India." Job Market Paper, Boston University. https://sites.google.com/site/danielwschwab/home/research.

Silva, J., R. Almeida, and V. Strokova. 2015. "Sustaining Employment and Wage Gains in Brazil." World Bank, Washington, DC.

Suryahadi, A., W. Widyanti, D. Perwira, S. Sumarto. 2003. "Minimum Wage Policy and Its Impact on Employment in the Urban Formal Sector." *Bulletin of Indonesian Economic Studies* 39 (1): 29–50.

Ulyssea, G., and M. N. Foguel. 2006. "Efeitos do salário mínimo sobre o mercado de trabalho Brasileiro." Rio de Janeiro, February. Discussion text 1168, Instituto de Pesquisa Econômica Aplicada (IPEA).

World Bank. 2012. *World Development Report 2013: Jobs*. Washington, DC: World Bank

———. 2017. *Brazil Expenditure Review*. Washington, DC: World Bank Group.

World Bank and IPEA (Instituto de Pesquisa Económica Aplicada). 2002. *Brazil: Jobs Report*. Social Protection and Labor, Regional Office for Latin America and Caribbean. Washington, DC: World Bank.

Vodopivec, Milan. 2013. "Introducing Unemployment Insurance to Developing Countries." *IZA Journal of Labor Policy*, 2 (1): 1.

Yannelis, C. 2014. "The Minimum Wage and Employment Dynamics: Evidence from an Age Based Reform in Greece." Royal Economic Society Annual Conference. Retrieved from: http://www.sole-jole.org/14015.pdf.

Yu, W.-h. 2012. "Better Off Jobless? Scarring Effects of Contingent Employment in Japan." *Social Forces* 90 (3): 735–68.

Zylberstajn, Eduardo, and Joana Silva. 2015. "Earnings Consequences of Labor Turnover: The Case of Brazil." Research paper—background paper for this report, World Bank, Washington, DC.

6 Supporting Employability and Labor Mobility for Out-of-School Youth

ABSTRACT This chapter discusses skills and active labor measures for youth in Brazil who are already out of the formal schooling system but need additional support to quickly find higher-productivity jobs. These young people might be holding low-productivity jobs and in need of programs to upgrade their skills, or they might be unemployed or inactive and in need of other active measures. Recognizing that what is most likely to work will depend on the profiles of these groups, the chapter focuses on concrete areas for reform in Brazil across two main types of policies. First, it discusses "second-chance" and short-term training programs for a large cohort of youth that is already out of the formal schooling system and requires skills upgrading. For them, the challenge is to provide incentives to either return to the formal schooling system and/or complete training and to acquire relevant foundational and technical skills. Second, the chapter discusses other active labor market measures, beyond training, to help youth find better employment matches sooner and, ultimately, to avoid the depreciation of their already acquired skills. The most promising intervention is stronger, youth-focused, and modernized public employment services. The chapter concludes with concrete recommendations for reform.

SECOND-CHANCE PROGRAMS

For those who have dropped out of the school system, "second-chance" programs are a way to encourage youth to complete formal education or training. Although illiteracy has declined in Brazil since 2004, every year approximately 1.5 percent of youth ages 15–29 remain illiterate and leave school without basic foundational skills (see figure 6.1). The Brazilian Youth and Adult Education (EJA) program is the best-known intervention for those out of school. This federal program is targeted to those ages 15 or 18 years old who do not complete their lower or upper

FIGURE 6.1

Illiteracy rates in Brazil, trends and youth subgroups

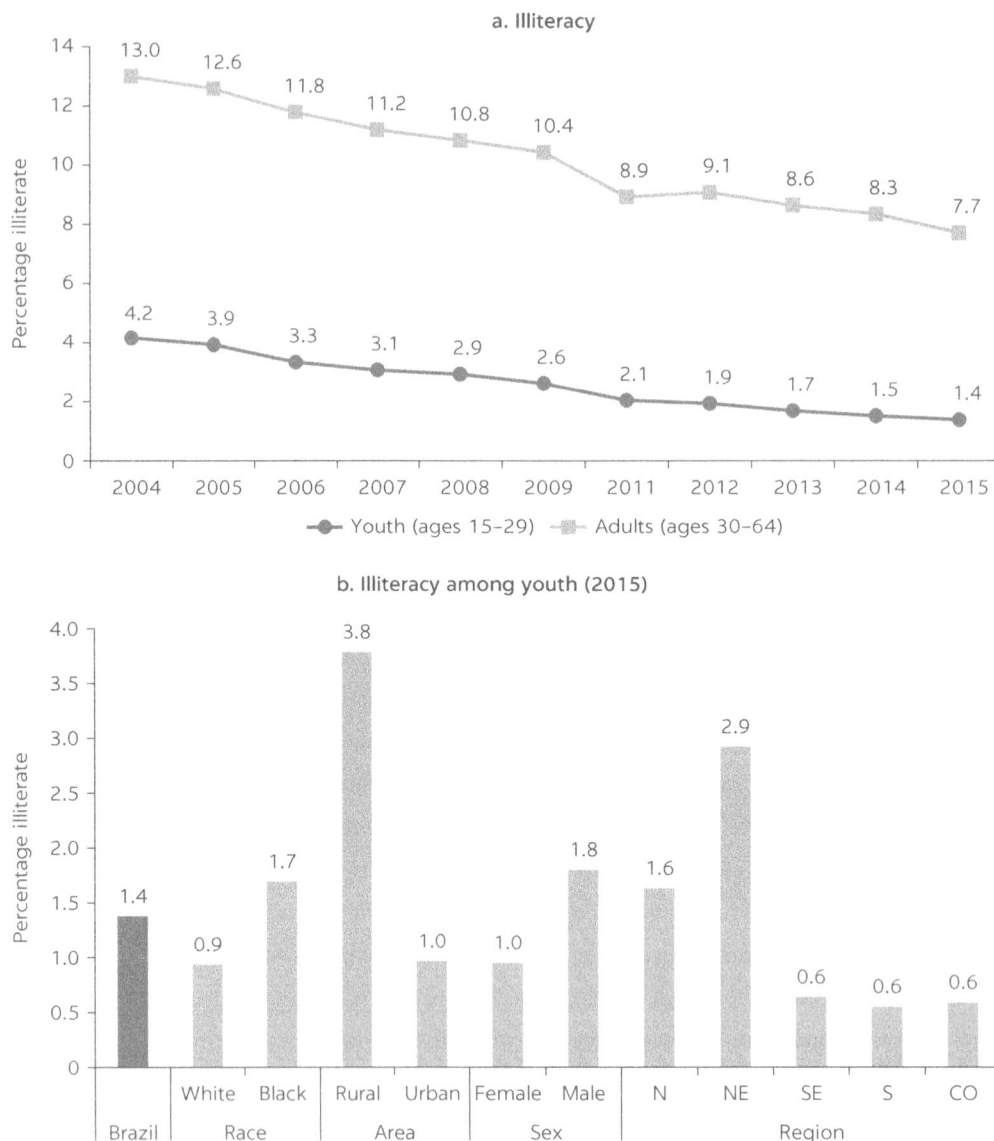

Source: Based on *Pesquisa Nacional por Amostra de Domicílios* (PNAD), 2004–15. PNAD is not available in 2010, when the demographic census was collected.
Notes: Youth illiteracy rates are presented by youth subgroups. The black race category includes self-reported races *preta* and *parda*. Other races (indigenous and East-Asian origin) are not reported due to very low frequencies (less than 1 percent of the sample combined).

secondary education. It aims to increase their educational attainment by providing incentives to go back to the formal schooling system. EJA programs are typically more flexible than the regular courses, combining classroom-based and distance learning. Over the past years, while building foundational skills, the programs have been increasingly integrating technical components to alleviate lack of skills for the labor market. Because classes are offered at night, they pose lower opportunity costs for working people than regular schools.

Evidence shows, however, that the EJA program, which was initially targeted to adults who had already dropped out of school, often attracts high school students who could be enrolled in regular education. As the quality of the EJA courses is often lower than in the regular courses, this is of concern (see Tavares et al. 2014).

TRAINING AND OTHER ACTIVE LABOR MARKET MEASURES: A LOOK INTO THE YOUTH POLICY PORTFOLIO

Although historically low—at just 0.4 percent of gross domestic product (GDP) in 2000—and modest relative to spending on other social functions (for example, pensions), Brazil's public spending on labor policy and programs has lately been on the rise. Growing hand in hand with the relatively high levels of employment creation in the early 2000s, it reached 0.85 percent of GDP in 2011 and 0.99 percent in 2014. In 2015, as the country slipped into economic crisis and unemployment began to surge, expenditure accelerated to 1.1 percent of GDP.

Chapter 5 has documented, however, how the policies in place to help correct failures of the labor market have been skewed away from the intermediation services that could improve the quality of matches between firms and jobseekers. Instead, they are dominated by "passive" labor market programs (PLMPs), which constitute 83 percent of expenditure, and are directed mainly to income protection. In addition, the programs, which were historically limited in scope to the large formal companies and the public sector, are contributory in nature— that is, eligibility is based on statutory employer and employee contributions. This means the system benefits almost exclusively relatively well-off formal workers; only 1.8 percent of expenditure is accessible to workers who are not necessarily formalized (those without signed contracts), who are referred to in Brazil as *carteira assinada*.

Public expenditures on programs that actively promote labor market insertion of the jobless and economically inactive remain very small, including for youth, even after recent increased spending on skills development programs. A wage top-up program, Abono Salarial, is meant to provide incentive for "formal" (registered, regulated, and taxed) employment. By design, however, it does not play an explicit role in activating the out of work, since eligibility requires a five-year history of employment. Other Brazilian programs that fall squarely in the classical, internationally used definition of "active labor market programs" (ALMPs) include training for vulnerable groups and the unemployed (Pronatec-BSM and Pronatec-Seguro Desemprego; Projovem), public employment services (Mais Emprego), and entrepreneurship support programs (Programa de Fomento de Atividades Produtivas Rurais and Asistência Técnica e Extensão Rural). Its rapid growth since 2011 has brought Brazil's flagship Program for Access to Technical Education and Employment, (Pronatec), significant attention; even so, in terms of total spending, it has been a modest driver of expenditure, and it continues to represent only a small share of total spending in labor programs (3.8 percent in 2015).[1] Federal spending on labor market intermediation services, represented by the Sistema Nacional de Emprego (SINE), remained persistently low, and it is probably the least adequately financed labor function in Brazil's social protection and labor policy architecture.

The heavy reliance on income "top-up" wage supplements is a unique feature of Brazil's approach to active labor market programs. Brazil spends about 90 percent of its ALMP resources on employment incentives (mostly Abono Salarial), more than any Organisation for Economic Co-operation and Development (OECD) country. Hence, the composition of active labor market expenditures in Brazil is out of line with comparator countries in both the OECD and Latin America. If Abono Salarial were excluded from the list of active labor programs—because of its limited function as a work incentive—Brazil's expenditure on ALMPs would be lower than those of all the member countries of the OECD.

Brazil also has a host of short-term training programs with very diverse quality, some aimed specifically at youth—either those in school or recently graduated—and the unemployed, to create better matches between jobseekers and jobs by providing the necessary skills. Among them are Cursos FIC and Formação Inicial e Continuada (Initial and Continuing Training Programs), which are usually directed at improving workers' existing qualifications and are not tied to the formal education system.[2] The many strengths of the technical and vocational education and training (TVET) system include a well-coordinated set of diverse, short-duration courses that often yield good—although heterogeneous—employability and productivity results (Silva, Gukovas, and Caruso 2015). The TVET system might effectively promote even higher employability and productivity if it were not hampered by the persistent weaknesses in the general education system, discussed in chapter 4, that lead to deficient learning trajectories in academic, cognitive, and socioemotional core skills.

Brazil's creation of Pronatec has given a policy push to increasing access to these short-term training programs, including for youth. Significant investment in vocational training and TEC since 2011 has been aimed at fostering economic opportunities for all—especially young people from the poorest and most vulnerable households, who often drop out of formal schooling. Pronatec is an umbrella program that coordinates a variety of previously existing and new vocational education and training policies, including short and longer courses. Under it, the Ministry of Education (MEC) has established partnerships with several other ministries, covering industrial development, social development, labor and employment, tourism, and communication, to identify and select potential trainees for technical courses. Between 2011 and 2014, Pronatec offered 8.8 million training places, and, with its primary focus on reaching poor and disadvantaged populations, the program disrupted the traditional panorama of TVET in Brazil, where TEC had primarily reached students of high socioeconomic backgrounds and vocational training was geared toward the needs of larger firms (Canali and Barbosa 2009; Silva, Almeida, and Strokova 2015).

With some exceptions, however, the short-term training programs for youth have several design and implementation issues that hinder their efficiency and are holding back their effectiveness. In their close analysis of Brazil's short-term training, Almeida, Anazawa, Menezes-Filho, and Vasconcellos (2015) documented large heterogeneity within Brazil in the wage returns on these courses. For people who received short-term training from public providers, the returns could even be very close to zero. The researchers also showed the labor market returns on these courses tended to be higher for youth, and for those graduates who found jobs in areas that matched the technical content of the training programs from which they graduated. Courses provided by private provider Sistema S, on the other hand, have shown large, positive returns, as documented by Silva, Gukovas, and Caruso (2015). Sistema S is run by industry to meet the demands of industry, and to a very high standard. Most Pronatec expansion happened through the Sistema S network of course providers, but future reliance on the network is constrained by its capacity (Silva, Almeida, and Strokova 2016). Overall, most of the public TVET providers seem to offer little coordination with the private sector (Almeida, Amaral, and Felicio 2015). Good administrative databases are neither regularly updated nor used to track employability or to inform policy. There are also many accounts, albeit anecdotal, of supply-side pressures for students to take courses with little likely applicability in the labor market.

ProJovem is one of the largest education and training programs targeted especially to Brazilian youth. ProJovem Integrado (Integrated National Program for Youth Inclusion) offers opportunities to gain professional qualifications while also encouraging the completion of foundational education. Managed by different line ministries, ProJovem is an entirely classroom-based training program that prioritizes educational attainment to ensure youth are receiving basic qualifications and will be able to meet the basic demands of the labor market. The program consists of four separate initiatives that were consolidated in 2008 under ProJovem Integrado and refocused to improve its coordination and efficiency; the four components are ProJovem Adolescente, ProJovem Urbano, ProJovem Campo, and ProJovem Trabalhador.[3] While each has a slightly different objective, all use some combination of vocational training with, at times, other "social" modules as a way to bring disadvantaged youth back into the fold of the education system.

The component of ProJovem Integrado especially relevant to promoting employability among the most vulnerable is ProJovem Trabalhador, which targets unemployed youth from families who live on less than one minimum wage per month. The program offers 350 hours of training, comprising 250 hours of professional training and 100 hours of a "social" module that covers such topics as ethics, citizenship, personal hygiene, occupational health and safety, and entrepreneurship (OECD 2014). Qualified participants receive a monthly stipend of R$100 for up to six months as an incentive to enroll and remain enrolled. The desired outcome for youth who graduate from ProJovem Trabalhador is that they be more prepared for life beyond the relatively friendly confines of the structured educational system and feel comfortable navigating the labor market. In short, the program is charged with turning vulnerable youth into confident young adults.

Despite its importance, ProJovem still has many design and implementation flaws. Perhaps the most glaring is that it does not incorporate any work-based learning opportunities. Even ProJovem Trabalhador, arguably Brazil's most employment-oriented youth program, has no on-the-job training components. Furthermore, although the intention behind consolidating the ProJovem programs into Projovem Integrado in 2008 was to streamline and avoid any fragmentation or duplication among them, the ProJovem components today are seemingly as dispersed as ever among different authoritative entities that work independently of one another (ProJovem Adolescente within the Ministry of Social Development, ProJovem Urbano and ProJovem Campo under the Ministry of Education, and ProJovem Trabalhador under the Ministry of Labor and Employment). Making matters worse is that the now-consolidated ProJovem programs have no evaluation system in place to assess the effectiveness of the consolidation or of the program components themselves. Low enrollment is also a hindrance to success, since few youth report even knowing about the programs (OECD 2014). A reform package that includes a new central authority to run the ProJovem package, work-based training components in ProJovem Trabalhador, a robust evaluation system overall, and renewed educational outreach programs could go a long way to revive and strengthen a promising program for youth.

Another important initiative to support the employability of youth is Lei do Aprendiz (Apprenticeship Law), which was enacted in 2000 to offer a flexible way for medium and large firms to hire those between the ages of 14 and 24 under special employment contracts for periods of up to two years. Policymakers intended the law to promote a smoother school-to-work transition by combining academic learning with hands-on job experience. The program provides youth with training in specific technical skills while on the job, along with practical experience that can help them start their professional careers.[4] Apprentices must attend technical and professional skills-building workshops throughout their stints and be enrolled in accredited training courses (provided by Sistema S or others).[5] On the flipside, the law gives businesses incentive to hire apprentices under temporary contracts by conceding payroll subsidies and by waiving enforcement of dismissal costs for apprentices. The goal set by the law was eventually to have 5 to 15 percent of the workforce in apprenticeships. The policy has produced some successes but also some notable failures, now that it has been on the books for nearly two decades.

The Apprenticeship Law is an effective tool to help youth make the transition from school to work, but questions remain about the lasting impact of apprenticeships on labor market outcomes later in life. Corseuil et al. (2012) showed positive labor market impacts for apprentices: participating youth had a 5 percent higher probability of getting non-temporary jobs in the two to three years after their apprenticeships than youth of similar ages who did not go through the program. The program had only a small positive effect on future wages, however, indicating the law does not provide sustainable results in terms of longer-term labor earnings (and possibly increased labor productivity). Qualitative data from the apprentices following completion of the program indicate they perceive themselves as better prepared for the labor market. Despite these positive conclusions, the number of apprenticeships remains low in Brazil, registering only 1 percent of eligible youth (ages 14–24 years) working as apprentices in 2012 (OECD 2014).

In addition, the law does not yet provide firms with sufficient incentives to hire apprentices, which has limited program adoption. After being in place for nearly two full decades, the law has consistently fallen far short of reaching the 5 percent minimum apprentice-to-workforce ratio. Although the program in 2010 boasted nearly 250,000 workers—up from 57,000 in 2007—and firms hired 335,800 apprentices in 2013, full compliance would have meant at least 1.24 million apprentices hired in 2013 (Marra et al. 2015). In that snapshot in time, only 23 percent of the potential youth apprentices in Brazil were hired. The number of apprenticeships rose to 404,000 in 2014, before falling to 379,000 in 2015 as the Brazilian economy started to contract, and it has remained at about the same level since. Increasing the law's effectiveness and flexibility will require a better understanding of business needs, better screening of the existing youth candidate pool, and better data on youth who have gone through the program. In addition, better enforcement of the Apprenticeship Law, along with additional financial incentives to firms to hire apprentices, could increase compliance and opportunities for youth to gain on-the-job experience.

As noted earlier, Brazil's labor market intermediation service, Sistema Nacional de Emprego (SINE) remains a small part of the social protection and labor policy architecture. Created in 1975, SINE provides labor intermediation services to all Brazilians who seek them. It aims specifically to assist those facing unique obstacles to employment, including youth. Its core function is offering job placement services to both jobseekers and employers, facilitated by computerized information services for making job matches. SINE is quite decentralized compared to similar programs in OECD countries, with over 2,200 offices across the country administered by state and local governments. It also lacks any significant empirical evidence on its effectiveness, which creates an obstacle to any push to expand the service. According to McKenzie [2017], evidence from other countries suggests labor intermediation provided by programs such as SINE is the most cost-effective form of active labor market assistance, with high success rates in job placement.

Despite being the foremost labor intermediation service in Brazil, SINE is allocated substantially lower public funding than similar programs in OECD countries. As noted earlier, whether compared to countries with similar labor policy institutional features (such as Italy and Portugal) or similar levels of labor program spending (New Zealand and Poland) or to countries that are aspirational comparators (France and Spain), Brazil stands out in terms of the underfunding of labor market intermediation services as a share of total labor program expenditure. Intermediation is a critical component of labor market systems in advanced countries, where public employment services (PESs) connect jobseekers to employers by offering it, along with training and other services. They also function as a gateway mechanism to control access to—and prevent the abuse of—unemployment benefits and other social programs.

As the economy struggles to create new jobs, the lack of active intermediation and job search assistance is dangerous. While spending on wage top-ups seems excessive, programs that actively help the unemployed or inactive individuals to prepare for and find work (training, job search assistance, intermediation) receive only about 4 percent of total labor spending. This leaves people who are unemployed—and particularly first-time jobseekers—particularly vulnerable, raising the likelihood of long unemployment spells, consequent depreciation of human capital, and "scarring" effects that can last for years.

REVISITING REFORM PRIORITIES FROM THE YOUTH PERSPECTIVE

The large number of youth who leave the formal schooling system with low foundational skills and the large opportunity costs of returning to full-time study faced by this group create an urgency to strengthen the quality of EJA. Many questions remain open on what is the most effective way to give young adults incentive to return to education and, once they are there, to help them learn effectively. Aker and Sawyer (2017) highlight two core constraints for this group. The high opportunity cost of time for older youth means most learning has to happen at night. And the well-documented lower plasticity of the adult brain compared to the brain in childhood and early adolescence means the learning process is more difficult and time consuming. To address these and other challenges, Brazil could apply three principles to rethinking its second-chance programs: development of a proper sequencing of course contents for improved comprehension; support for more practice and application of concepts through increased opportunities for group discussion; and focus on the development of higher-order cognitive skills. International evidence shows a second-chance program is most effective in promoting skills and employability when it leads to a certification as it shows proof to the potential employer that the person has acquired basic skills.[6] This mitigates problems youth may have signaling their qualifications in the labor market (Crawford and Mogollon 2010).

Among middle-income countries, Chile's Chilecalifica stands out for its success in providing a successful "second chance". It is designed to provide beneficiaries with basic education and/or technical and vocational training. Unlike a GED, the degree in Chile is indistinguishable from an ordinary school diploma. That the initiative is free, well-promoted, and publicly supported, with its own course materials and flexible services customized to poor youngsters and adults, proves that formal education is considered key in Chile in training for work. Preliminary impact evaluation results suggest Chilecalifica leads to an increase in wages for and greater post-program schooling of beneficiaries, particularly women (although the results may be positively biased by the study's small sample size and selectivity issues; Santiago Consultores 2009).

Brazil has a solid package of activation programs—mostly active—to help youth make the transition to work. The barriers and challenges faced by youth in finding good jobs in the labor market are often multidimensional. Youth often lack job-relevant skills, including basic, technical, and behavioral skills, and they can be limited in their job searches by lack of access to information about job openings or difficulties in communicating their skills to potential employers. Some are constrained from starting their own businesses by lack of entrepreneurial knowledge or access to financial capital or business networks. Chapter 4 also discussed the important social constraints, including social norms, that especially limit the skills development or labor market entry of women.

On a positive note, Brazil's current portfolio of youth ALMPs does acknowledge this diversity of constraints on employability faced by youth and offers a wide range of services, including Pronatec, ProJovem, Lei do Aprendiz, and SINE, among others, although the portfolio could stand to be improved in terms of matching beneficiaries with their needs, and it seems excessively biased toward training programs. Furthermore, the design and implementation of the programs too often do not address the most pressing needs of the most vulnerable youth.

A formidable reform agenda of policy changes to these youth-focused skills development and labor market programs could be pursued to raise Brazil's productivity potential. In light of the issues raised here, further action can be taken in pursuit of two major objectives. First, Brazil must ensure its youth attain the skills required for a modern workforce through the existing skills training system; this is critical, so the country can produce workers with the skills that firms are seeking and keep pace with the shifting demands of firms in a globally competitive economy. Second, Brazil must support jobseekers and improve the matches between firms and workers through modern intermediation services.

In the push to expand active labor programs beyond just training, the opportunity to reform and improve programs such as Pronatec, Lei do Aprendiz, and ProJovem must not be overlooked. Vocational education and training are still vitally important policy options with a role to play in preparing youth for the labor market. Should labor intermediation fail to match a jobseeker with a job, for instance, effective programs must be in place to which the jobseeker can be referred, and these programs need to be relevant to and flexible for the 21st century labor market. Brazil currently has a set of policies and programs in place that accomplish these goals to a certain extent, but much more can be done to update them. Some existing programs have important failures in design or flaws that prevent them from reaching their potential. ProJovem, the youth-specific education training program, and the Lei do Aprendiz for apprenticeships, for example, both could benefit from tweaks that could make a large impact.

Giving industry a leading role in the skills development system

A more modern approach to youth-focused skills development programs entails giving industry a (the) leading role in vocational education, training programs, and in apprenticeships. An ambitious reform agenda to improve the efficiency and quality of secondary education was outlined in chapter 3 and is vital, as the quality of basic education is the essential foundation for further human capital development and the sort of life-long re-skilling and upskilling increasingly demanded by a globally integrated, competitive economy. When the government has met expectations for the quality of the mandatory education system, the stage is then set for industry to take a more active role in ensuring the workforce has the skills firms demand. Where industry already takes a lead in Brazil's skills development system—for example, in Sistema S—high-quality courses that impart in-demand skills are on offer. But Sistema S is just a small segment of the overall TVET system in Brazil. Today the TVET system is still quite supply driven, and many argue that the push to expand the flagship Pronatec has aggravated this problem. Recent evidence for Brazil (see, for example, Silva, Almeida, and Strokova 2015 and O'Connell et al. 2017) shows that putting industry in a leading role can improve results. Findings from an evaluation carried out by Brazil's Ministry of Industry and Trade (MDIC) of the Pronatec initiative in 2014–15 were also encouraging. When firms were given several opportunities to state their needed skills and engage in the design of curriculum, as well as meet and get to know the recipients of training, the program outperformed a parallel Pronatec program that did not have the same demand-informed features.

International experiences also suggest the effectiveness of worker training can be dramatically increased when industry has direct input into the curricula. As discussed by Silva, Almeida, and Strokova (2016) and Almeida, Amaral, and Felicio (2015), substantial room remains to improve partnerships among public TVET providers with employers regarding the relevance of both curriculum and materials. A modern curriculum is needed that combines attention to core foundational skills with promoting hands-on learning. Rarely do TVET pedagogies use real-life case studies, as they do in the United Kingdom, or focus on solving firms' real-world challenges, as they do in Norway. Technical education in Brazil also rarely incorporates the latest technologies, nor does it offer a set of physical tools that enable students to apply their learning in new and innovative ways; curricula and pedagogies should incorporate the latest technologies. Brazil could also take better advantage of access to the relatively low-cost but high-tech infrastructure that is increasingly available through "maker-space" and "fab-lab" laboratories, either being built in house or linked to by many technical schools and universities around the world (see Silva, Almeida, and Strokova 2015).

TVET programs can also build more partnerships with employers to create more workplace learning opportunities, including periods of on-the-job learning as a mandatory part of the curriculum. Workplace learning stands out as one of the best ways to promote TVET learning that both is aligned with labor market needs and builds and strengthens socioemotional skills. For the student, the workplace provides a strong learning environment because it offers real, on-the-job training experience that makes it easier to acquire both hard and soft skills. It also facilitates the exchange of information between potential employers and employees, making recruitment less costly to the employer.

Another way to bolster the TVET programs is to increase collaborations with employers for improving teacher preparedness and development.

The challenges in maintaining and training the existing pool of teachers in Brazil's education system are difficult and persistent. Add in the government's increased education spending and expanded programs, and the challenge of finding good instructors becomes a real problem. One of the biggest challenges is finding teachers with the appropriate amount of education training as well as practical knowledge and skills. This is especially an issue in vocational programs, where a background in research and publications may not be as appropriate as having innovation and entrepreneurial skills. Encouraging teachers to spend time in industry could have practical benefits down the line, as would

BOX 6.1

National apprenticeship policies: Lessons from leading practice countries

Official apprentice programs at the country level used to train youth for the labor market are not new and constitute a policy tool increasingly in use around the world. In fact, codified laws detailing how youth should be hired and trained are a hallmark of most advanced economies today. While the success and depth of such programs vary internationally, some common elements across the board determine their success. These distinctive elements can be broken down into four essential components: (1) the program has a formal training plan for apprentices; (2) that plan combines classroom-based and on-the-job training; (3) a written contract states the benefits of the program to both parties and makes the arrangement official; and (4) some sort of recognized certification is awarded upon completion of the apprenticeship.

Australia is known for its longstanding Australian Apprenticeships (AA) program, which is unique in that it is available without pre-entry qualification to people of all ages, not just youth in the school-to-work transition period. In fact, 10 percent of those enrolled are over age 45. Besides incorporating the four components above, AA does a substantial job of involving multiple stakeholders from various government ministries at both state and local levels and public–private groups, such as the technical and further education (TAFE) institutes, as well as private industry groups and employers, including registered training organizations (RTOs), group training organizations (GTOs), and industry skills councils (ISCs). Of particular note are the ten ISCs, which provide industry intelligence and advice to GTOs and RTOs on workforce

development and skills needs. This method of setting the curriculum and implementation of AA places the program on the cutting edge of innovation and makes Australia's workforce competitive in the ever-globalizing and changing labor market. Participation rates in AA are exceptionally high when compared internationally. Additionally, the rigorous monitoring and evaluation system present at every step of AA has allowed the Australian government to make informed, modest improvements in recent years to address weaknesses, such as low completion rates.

In Germany, apprenticeships became an official component of the system of public employment services as far back as 1969 with the Vocational Training Act, or the *Berufsbildungsgesetz*. That act enshrined the shared responsibility of all parties involved, including the state, unions, associations, industry, and chambers of trade, giving them all a pivotal stake in the future of skilled labor supply. Today Germany has a dual education system that includes formal classroom-based learning with on-the-job training for all youth. Germany has nearly 350 recognized trades in which apprenticeships can be completed. Some simply recommend that applicants complete apprenticeships, while others, such as in the sciences and engineering fields, go as far as to make them mandatory before entry. Most apprenticeships last around three years. Because of their central role, employers determine the content of the training, which makes the system highly responsive to changes in the labor market. Overall, the system is highly regulated and comprehensively organized, with high participation rates of over 50 percent of youth.

continued

Box 6.1, *continued*

Registered apprenticeships (RAs) in the United States were established in 1937 under the National Apprenticeship Act, following the successful first registered apprenticeship program in Wisconsin in 1911. Today the program stands out for it sheer size across industries. Apprenticeship programs are offered in nearly 1,000 occupations and include close to 30,000 programs, involving 250,000 employers. The number of apprentices has increased dramatically from 375,000 in 2014 to 500,000 in 2016, with a goal of nearly 1,000,000 by 2020. Like other advanced economies, the United States relies heavily on private sector involvement in determining the content of the training and education. In 2015, the government introduced apprenticeship grants to support public–private initiatives, including apprenticeship programs in high-growth industries and expanded apprenticeship opportunities for women, youth, and minorities.

Sources: Fazio, Fernandez-Coto, and Ripani 2016; U.S. Department of Labor 2015.

making it easier for industry workers to become educators. Almeida, Amaral, and Felicio (2015) discuss how lessons from Switzerland could be relevant for Brazil in this regard.

Finally, finding ways to increase the effectiveness and flexibility of the Apprentice Law is essential to increasing the impact of ALMPs on youth engagement. Doing so will require a better understanding of the business needs of firms and the existing candidate pool of youths and better data on youth who have gone through the program. Better enforcement of the law, along with additional (financial) incentives to firms to hire apprentices, could increase both compliance and opportunities for youth to gain on-the-job experience. While the law reduces the costs for a firm of dismissing apprentices when necessary, the hiring costs are still the same as for regular employees. Thus, despite the high proven returns on training apprentices, some firms could be deterred by the seemingly high upfront costs (Fazio, Fernandez-Coto, and Ripani 2016). Finding a way to remove or lower these costs legally could go a long way in pushing firms to achieve the 5 percent mandate.

Strengthen intermediation assistance support for youth to help them find and retain high-productivity jobs

Brazil, like many of its neighbors in Latin America, will need to shift greater public support to labor market intermediation and job search assistance. An analysis of spending on labor market programs in the *Brazil Expenditure Review* (World Bank 2017) showed a clear pattern in the structure and financing of labor market programs in Latin America that favors passive income support for the unemployed over more active intermediation and job search assistance measures. This bias in the orientation of government interventions, which contrasts sharply with member countries of the OECD, is not about the volume of spending, but about what sort of programs are given greater emphasis.

The lack of emphasis on active labor market support—particularly job search assistance and intermediation—is a weakness of Brazil's approach to labor programs and should be corrected to support innovation. While evidence of the efficacy and efficiency of skills training programs for vulnerable job seekers is mixed at best (Dar and Gill 1998; Dar and Tzannatos 1999), public employment services, intermediation, counseling, and coaching have been found to be cost effective (Betcherman 2012). The skewed approach taken by Brazil and the weakness of its intermediation institutions will constrain the government's ability to respond effectively to rising levels of unemployment and, hence, its ability to contain spending on passive labor market support. In a more integrated economy, unemployment and job searching are likely to become more frequent "disruptions." Transitions across firms, sectors, and occupations could become the new normal for many people. Brazil, like its neighbors, will need to shift the emphasis of its labor market programs to be ready.

As a first step, current spending on wage top-ups for people already in formal employment could be shifted to provide incentive to employers to offer jobs. The *Brazil Expenditure Review* (World Bank 2017) also found that spending on the largest category of ALMPs—the Abono Salarial—was relatively regressive. This finding is not surprising, given that the so-called wage subsidy is paid to workers already in formal jobs. Similar subsidies in OECD member countries are typically paid to employers, as incentive and as compensation for taking the risk of hiring people who have been unemployed for a long period, or who have entered the labor market for the first time.

Strengthening intermediation support will include reforming SINE, the main provider of public labor intermediation services in Brazil—a vital program for youth, who rarely have the job search skills or experience necessary to navigate the labor market. OECD countries spend, on average, 10 percent of their active labor program budgets on placement and related services, resulting in much higher spending as a share of gross domestic product. Brazil's spending on public employment services barely registers at .01 percent of GDP (Silva, Almeida, and Strokova 2015). SINE can be strengthened to facilitate job searches and matches by adopting a management approach more focused on actual job placements, rather than simple registrations and matches. Some changes that appeal directly to youth could help, too, such as support on resume writing, interview skills, and job search strategies. Streamlining SINE, along with other public employment services, into a "one-stop shop" could be an attractive option that opens all opportunities to all beneficiaries. This would allow jobseekers, especially youth, to see the programs and options available to them, with SINE intermediation services as the foremost option. International experience has proved that public employment services and other SINE-equivalent programs are efficient in placing jobseekers with good jobs and are particularly effective in increasing placements for the poor and youth.

Also crucial to producing well-rounded job candidates who can handle unforeseen and abrupt changes in the labor market is adding more on-the-job training opportunities and "soft-skills" modules to training programs for youth-targeted programs, such as ProJovem and Pronatec. While technical skills are necessary for youth to meet the basic requirement thresholds for most jobs openings, more personal (or "life") skills can make a tremendous difference, as well. From personal budgeting to conflict management to office dynamics navigation, life skills can bolster candidates' resumes and make them more marketable as well-rounded candidates, while also making them more adaptable and flexible in a labor market landscape that is changing rapidly. Such skills may not always be transferable to a resume, but they still have job-specific benefits in that they can help employees keep their jobs once they have them. Finally, the value of life skills, by definition, goes beyond just time spent on the job and can be

BOX 6.2

Labor intermediation services: Best practices for youth

Seeking solutions to one of the worst recessions in modern European history, the European Council knew it needed to reform public employment services (PESs) drastically throughout member states to arm youth and the most vulnerable for the tough labor markets ahead. The fate of future economic growth and well-being in the European Union depended on how the current problem of youth unemployment and inactivity was addressed. In 2013, the EU adopted the Youth Guarantee, ensuring the commitment to the reception by every youth under age 25 of a good offer of employment, continued education, or an apprenticeship within four months of leaving formal education or becoming unemployed. This guarantee also asked all member states to submit implementation plans that would work toward achieving this goal. The Council did not require any strict, across-the-board policies but, rather, offered information and data on proven techniques and gave each member state flexibility in how to go about implementation. Some of the best practices observed after implementation of the Youth Guarantee have included extensive engagement in cross-PES collaboration and interaction with industry. Such engagement improves youth's access to information on the options available to them, both in the specific programs aimed to help them and

employment, education, and training possibilities. Under the new approach, programs were to complement and supplement each other where possible, rather than be in competition, often offering redundant services. Partnerships with industry would facilitate opportunities for hands-on training and apprenticeships that place youth directly into the labor market and give them relevant skills for jobs today.

Other best practices include engaging youth early, with a strong focus on upfront job matching. Working with students while they are still in the structured setting of their secondary education to prepare them for the labor market or higher education is far more effective than waiting until they are several years removed from high school and possibly unemployed. Additionally, eliminating as many bureaucratic steps as possible in connecting youth quickly with PES can reduce stints of unemployment; PESs within the Youth Guarantee aim for placement in as little as four months. With a quick job-matching process, youth are less likely to become discouraged and more likely to maintain their confidence in the system and in themselves. Core interventions to accomplish this include face-to-face career guidance and counseling, individual action plans, support for geographical mobility, and entrepreneurial training.

Source: European Network of Public Employment Services 2015.

deployed outside of work. Well-developed personal skills can have positive spillover effects into many aspects of life, benefiting not only the employee but his or her family and society as whole. ALMPs that build life skills as well as technical skills provide youth with the ability to help themselves in the future and still help satisfy the immediate need of job placement.

Fortunately, policymakers in Brazil do not need to start from scratch in attempting to achieve efficient and effective labor market training programs. Rather, investing in improving the existing structure of active measures and focusing them more on youth will accomplish much in closing the gap for the young and most vulnerable. In improving these youth-targeted policies, several components are essential to success: (1) greater investment in labor intermediation and job search services as an effective low-cost tool; 2) a new emphasis is needed on building personal skills and hands-on learning, not just technical skills; and (3) greater attention needs to be paid to complementary policies for entrepreneurship, in both training and financing aspects. Overall, the programs need to be cost effective, with robust monitoring and evaluation components to ensure that.

Simply increasing funding for existing programs is not enough, however. These active labor market measures urgently need to be redesigned to prioritize youth needs for higher engagement and opportunity and improve their implementation. In particular, they need to be more cost effective; reform in addition to increased investment is likely the combination that will yield the best results. Adding assessment tools to evaluate their impact can help provide data-based evidence that the policies are working (or not working), which is pivotal for future expansion opportunities.

In short, improving existing active labor market measures in Brazil need not be exceptionally resource intensive; a concentrated focus on the combination of cost-effective programs, working in tandem with layers of evaluation at each stage of implementation, can be enough. Tilting these much-needed reforms toward youth can go a long way toward positively engaging them and pulling them back into the fold of a flourishing economy.

NOTES

1. Part of the reason is that Sistema S, which offers many of the training courses now financed by Pronatec, now must also provide courses to the same type of beneficiaries with its own (levy-financed) revenues.
2. FIC courses are offered by a variety of training providers, including Sistema S and other private providers. The longer-term technical and technological courses that are part of the secondary and higher education curricula were discussed in chapter 4.
3. ProJovem Adolescente, which is aimed at 15–17-year-olds in social assistance programs, places them in structured activities that center on six themes: human rights and social welfare, work, culture, the environment, health and sports, and leisure. ProJovem Urbano targets 18–29-year-olds who have not completed their fundamental education. Through this component, youth go through 2,000 hours of education, training for professional qualifications, and citizenship training. ProJovem Campo is specifically for rural youth who have not completed their formal educations, while ProJovem Trabalhador works with unemployed youth and includes a work-based component.
4. For examples of courses, see http://site.aprendizlegal.org.br/cursos.
5. The training courses must be at least 400 hours long, and the daily workload for apprentices should total no more than six hours when the apprentice is still enrolled in school and no more than eight when the apprentice has already graduated.
6. The best-documented and most-analyzed second-chance programs are those in OECD countries (Mattero 2010).

REFERENCES

Aker, Jenny C., and Melita Sawyer. 2017. "Adult Learning in Sub-Saharan Africa: What Do and Don't We Know?" Background paper for the World Bank Africa Regional Study on Skills. Mimeo. World Bank Group, Washington, DC.

Almeida, Rita; Leandro Anazawa, Naercio Menezes Filho, Ligia Vasconcellos. 2015. Investing in Technical and Vocational Education and Training: Does It Yield Large Economic Returns in Brazil? Policy Research Working Paper, No. 7246. Washington, DC: World Bank. https://openknowledge.worldbank.org/handle/10986/21861.

Almeida, Rita; Nicole Amaral, Fabiana de Felicio. 2016. Assessing Advances and Challenges in Technical Education in Brazil. World Bank Study. Washington, DC: World Bank. https://openknowledge.worldbank.org/handle/10986/22726.

Betcherman, G. 2012. "Labor Market Institutions: A Review of the Literature." World Development Report background papers. World Bank, Washington, DC.

Canali, H., and H. Barbosa. 2009. "A trajetória da educação profissional no Brasil e os desafios da construção de um *Ensino Médio* integrado à educação profissional." [The Path of Vocational Education in Brazil and Challenges of a Middle School Integrated into Professional Education.] Unpublished manuscript. FAE–UFMG University Belo Horizonte, Brazil.

Corseuil, Carlos Henrique L., M. Foguel, G. Gonzaga, and E. Pontual Ribeiro. 2012. "The Effects of a Youth Training Program on Youth Turnover in Brazil." Network of Applied Economics Working Paper 042 (Rede de Economia Aplicada, REAP), São Paulo.

Crawford, M., and M. P. Mogollon. 2010. "Literature Review: Labor Competency Certification for Private Sector Employees." Latin America and Caribbean Education Working Paper Series 17, World Bank, Washington, DC.

Dar, A., and I. Gill. 1998. "Evaluating Retraining Programs in OECD Countries: Lessons Learned." *World Bank Research Observer* 13 (1): 79–101.

Dar, A., and Z. Tzannatos. 1999. "Active Labor Market Programs: A Review of the Evidence from Evaluations." World Bank, Washington, DC.

European Network of Public Employment Services. 2015. "Report on PES Implementation of the Youth Guarantee: Brussels." European Commission, Belgium.

Fazio, M. V., R. Fernandez-Coto, and L. Ripani. 2016. "Apprenticeships for the XXI Century: A Model for Latin America and the Carribean?" Inter-American Development Bank, Washington DC.

IBGE (Brazilian Institute of Geography and Statistics). 2004–15. "*Pesquisa Nacional por Amostra de Domicílios* (PNAD)."

Marra, K., J. Luz, J. Silva, and R. Gukovas. 2015. "Mapping of the Current Network of Active Labor Market Programs (ALMPs)." Policy report. World Bank, Washington, DC.

Mattero, M. 2010. "Second Chance Education: A Conceptual Framework and Review of Programs." Human Development Network, Washington, DC: World Bank.

McKenzie, David J. 2017. "How Effective Are Active Labor Market Policies in Developing Countries? A Critical Review of Recent Evidence (English)." Policy Research Working Paper WPS 8011. Impact Evaluation series. World Bank Group, Washington, DC. http://documents .worldbank.org/curated/en/256001490191438119/How-effective-are-active-labor-market -policies-in-developing-countries-a-critical review-of-recent-evidence.

O'Connell, S., L. F. Mation, J. Bevilaqua Teixeira Basto, and M. Dutz. 2017. "Can Business Input Improve the Effectiveness of Worker Training? Evidence from Brazil's Pronatec-MDIC." Policy Research Working Paper WPS 8155. World Bank, Washington, DC.

OECD (Organisation for Economic Co-operation and Development). 2014. "Investing in Youth: Brazil." Paris, France: OECD Publishing. http://dx.doi.org/10.1787/9789264208988-en.

Santiago Consultores. 2009. "Minuta Ejecutiva: Evaluación en Profundidad Chilecalifica." Ministerio de Educación, Ministerio del Trabajo y Previsión Social.

Silva, J., R. Almeida, and V. Strokova. 2015. "Sustaining Employment and Wage Gains in Brazil: A Skills and Jobs Agenda." Directions in Development: Human Development. World Bank, Washington, DC. https://openknowledge.worldbank.org/handle/10986/22545.

Silva, J., R. Gukovas, and L. Caruso. 2015. "The Wage Returns and Employability of Vocational Training in Brazil: Evidence from Matched Provider-Employer Administrative Data." Research paper. Mimeo. World Bank, Washington, DC.

Tavares, Priscilla, André Portela de Souza, and Vladimir Ponczek. "Uma análise dos fatores associados à frequência ao ensino médio na educação de jovens e adultos (EJA) no Brasil." Instituto de Pesquisa Econômica Aplicada, Artigo de Pesquisa (2014).

U.S. Department of Labor. 2015. "Annual Report: Employment and Training Administration." Employment and Training Administration. https://oa.doleta.gov/.

World Bank. 2017. *Brazil Expenditure Review*. Washington, DC: World Bank Group.

Appendix A

HOW DO LABOR MARKET INSTITUTIONS,
REGULATIONS, AND INTERVENTIONS
AFFECT YOUTH? A REVIEW OF THE
EVIDENCE IN BRAZIL AND GLOBALLY

MOTIVATION AND SCOPE OF THIS REVIEW

Young people worldwide face challenging prospects in the labor market. A decade after the Global Financial Crisis, unemployment rates for youth (about 21 percent) are still almost three times the adult unemployment rate in the Euro-area. In emerging economy countries, about 14 percent or more than 53 million youth are unemployed (ILO 2017). More worryingly, about a third of young people worldwide can be classified as "NEET": that is, *not in education, employment nor training* (S4YE 2015). The situation for those who are already engaged in employment is not much better: the ILO (2017) estimates that nearly 38 percent of working youth in emerging countries are in extreme or moderate poverty, compared to 26 percent of working adults. These statistics do not only reflect transitional challenges, but also belie important structural issues in the labor market.

Brazilian youth face similar challenges despite experiencing a "golden decade" of higher-than-average growth and advances in shared prosperity. From 2003 to 2014, the participation of youth[1] (15–29 years) in the labor market declined by about 8 percentage points to about 49 percent, most notably among those without even a primary school education. The ongoing economic crisis has exacerbated youth unemployment (27 percent in 2016), as well as youth inactivity (over 20 percent). Even if they are employed, the labor market for youth is characterized by high turnover, high incidence of informal work and poor remuneration (OECD 2014). Moreover, these challenges disproportionately affect those who already face multiple disadvantages due to their ethnicity, gender, income or geography, reflecting existing inequities in education.

Governments have tried to tackle these structural issues through a variety of regulatory reforms and active labor market programs (ALMP). Many European countries have introduced or modified subminimum wages for youth and relaxed restrictions on worker protection to make it easier for firms to hire youth through temporary contracts. There is skepticism, however, over the effectiveness of deregulation on labor market outcomes for youth (Barbieri 2009).

This review was conducted by Pui Shen Yoong, Economist, Macroeconomics, Trade, and Investment Global Practice, World Bank.

Further, analysis of recent labor market reforms worldwide indicates that not many emerging economies engage in regulatory reform (Adascalitei et al. 2015), perhaps for political economy reasons. In Brazil, a country with strong union presence and historically rigid labor laws up until recently, recent reforms to facilitate the use of temporary contracts and outsourcing elicited significant public protests. ALMP are often a more palatable option, but there is increasing skepticism over their effectiveness (Kluve et al. 2016; McKenzie 2017).

In short, there is still plenty of debate over how labor market policies can help or hinder labor market outcomes for youth. This appendix A provides a review of what is known about the impacts of labor market policies on youth on a global scale, contrasting the evidence in advanced and emerging economies. Given the motivation of the review, particular attention is paid to evidence from Brazil and her structural peers (Colombia, Mexico, Indonesia, South Africa, Turkey). This review encompasses evidence on the effects of a) labor market *regulations* such as minimum wages and employment protection legislation, which set the legal parameters of employment, b) *institutions* such as unions and collective bargaining, which set the terms by which interested parties exert their influence in the labor market, and c) active labor market *interventions*, through governments try to generate more and better employment opportunities. These regulations, institutions and interventions can shape the supply and demand for young workers in a variety of ways. On one hand, such policies may incentivize employers to provide productive opportunities to youth; on the other, improperly designed or implemented policies might have detrimental effects on youths' prospects in the labor market—and not only in the short term. Ample research has found that exposure to higher levels of unemployment and poor quality/informal employment during one's youth has scarring effects on labor market outcomes later in life, whether in the form of shorter employment spells and/or lower wages (Cruces et al. 2012 for Argentina/Brazil; Naidoo et al. 2015 for Indonesia; Yu 2012 for Japan).

This review differs from existing work in several ways. First, while there have been recent meta-analyses and reviews of labor market regulations (Betcherman 2015; Broecke, Forti and Vandeweyer 2015; Neumark et al. 2014) and ALMPs (Card, Kluve, and Weber 2010; McKenzie 2017), few focus specifically on youth (exceptions include Kluve et al. 2016 and Vezza 2014 on ALMPs). This review differentiates between overall and youth-specific impacts, in the interest of understanding if and why these effects might differ. Second, the review distinguishes between the evidence in advanced versus emerging economies, with particular attention to Brazil. The impact of labor market policies may differ when there is a scarcity of skilled labor, large informal sectors and relatively weaker institutional capacity for monitoring and enforcement (Betcherman 2015). Third, the review pays particular attention to differences in profiles across the youth population. Teenagers and young adults differ in terms of tenure and time allocation decisions, and therefore may require different interventions to ensure better labor market outcomes. Teenagers are more likely to require education policy instruments to facilitate smooth transitions from school to work, whereas young adults may require more active labor market interventions (OECD 2006).

An overall finding is that the specific effects of labor market policies on youth cannot be ignored, and that there is ample room for further research, especially in emerging economies. The effects of labor market policies on youth are not always straightforward, and may differ from aggregate effects on the overall labor market. Some cases are more clear cut in terms of policy prescriptions—stringent rules on hiring and firing, for example, are almost unanimously found to reduce the probability of employment for the youth cohort. The effects of some policies, such as subsidized employment and other mandated benefits, would benefit from further research before more conclusive findings can be drawn.

Two caveats are worth stating. First, although this review focuses on the impacts of the specific labor market policies in isolation, the overall effect of a country's labor market policy is clearly influenced by the interactions between these different instruments. Second, the estimates presented refer to youth overall, it is worth noting that youth who are already disadvantaged in other aspects (due to one's gender, income, geography or other factors beyond one's control) are likely to suffer more disproportionately from detrimental consequences of labor market policies. Although the review does not exclusively focus on disadvantaged youth, it does point out that certain interventions are more effective for this group than others (see Blattman and Ralston, for example).

METHODOLOGY

This literature review set out to find studies that assess the impact of labor market regulations, institutions and interventions on young people's labor market performance. Eligible studies investigated at least one of the labor market policies and outcomes of interest in Table A.1.

Studies were taken into account if they included age-specific results that captured the youth cohort (15–29 years old) regardless of whether they focused on labor market outcomes for youth. These age-specific effects are important because labor market reforms may have important unintended consequences on youth even when they are not the target of the policy. In addition, guidelines for inclusion were as follows:

- Evidence (papers and notes, including comments and rebuttals) published in refereed academic journals
- Evidence using data sets gathered since 1995 (studies that do not meet this criteria are mentioned for context)
- Books citing articles published in refereed academic journals, or that presented primary evidence that has been refereed
- As yet unpublished working papers of high technical quality, only if they presented relatively recent (i.e., since 2010) and compelling evidence from Brazil, middle or upper-middle income countries, or particularly from Brazil's "structural peers" (Colombia, Mexico, Indonesia, South Africa, and Turkey).

TABLE A.1 **Scope of the review**

LABOR MARKET POLICY	OUTCOME VARIABLES
Minimum wage	Employment probability
Employment protection legislation	Unemployment probability
Unions and collective bargaining	Hours worked
Active labor market programs	Unemployment duration
Training	Earnings/income
Entrepreneurship	Salary/wages
Employment services	
Workfare	
Wage subsidies	

Source: World Bank.

The primary search was conducted electronically using a desktop review from May to August 2016, and updated in June 2017. Studies were identified using keywords in English, Spanish and Portuguese in Google Scholar, IDEAS, REPEC and similar databases. A supplementary search reviewed recently-published meta analyses and systematic reviews to identify other suitable references. The main results of these analyses are summarized in Table A.2. All in all, the review encompasses 171 studies, almost equally divided between advanced and emerging economies (Table A.3). Most work centers on the minimum wage and on evaluations of training programs, as studies on these policies have

TABLE A.2 **Existing meta-analyses generally find minimal effects of labor market policies**

AUTHOR(S)/YEAR	INDEPENDENT VARIABLE(S)	DEPENDENT VARIABLE(S)	OVERALL FINDING
Broecke, Forti, and Vandeweyer (2017)	Minimum wage	Employment Formality	Increases in the minimum wage have a minimal or no impact on employment in 14 major emerging economies. Vulnerable groups (youth, low-skilled) marginally more negatively affected, and some indication of higher informality.
Betcherman (2012)	Minimum wages Employment protection legislation Unions & collective bargaining	Employment Earnings Productivity Social cohesion	Regulations have modest and mixed effects on economic efficiency, but clearer distributional effects that may harm uncovered workers (often youth, women, and the less skilled).
Freeman (2009)	Minimum wage Mandated benefits Unions & collective bargaining	Employment Wages	Minimum wages generally help the low-paid as wage effects dominate employment effects. Overall, modest effects on labor market outcomes.
Betcherman et al. (2007)	ALMP	Employment Earnings	About 60 percent of programs analyzed had positive labor market outcomes for youth, but only a third were also cost-effective.
Kluve, et al. (2016)	ALMP	Employment Earnings Business performance	Overall positive and statistically significant impacts on youth employment and earnings.
McKenzie (2017)	ALMP	Employment Earnings	Traditional ALMPs (skill training, wage subsidies, job search assistance) have at best modest impacts. Policies that help overcome structural and spatial mismatches in labor, and less traditional approaches, are more promising.

Source: World Bank.
Note: ALMP = active labor market programs.

TABLE A.3 **Almost an equal number of studies in advanced and emerging economies**

	DEVELOPED	EMERGING (EXCL. BRAZIL)	BRAZIL	TOTAL
Minimum wage	21	12	5	38
Employment protection legislation	12	1	0	13
Unions and collective bargaining	9	1	0	10
Active labor market programs	16	36	3	55
Training	5	18	3	26
Entrepreneurship	0	6	0	6
Employment services	3	4	0	7
Workfare	3	2	0	5
Wage subsidies	5	6	0	11
Total	**58**	**50**	**11**	**171**

Source: World Bank.

increased in emerging economies in recent years. By contrast, virtually all eligible studies on employment protection legislation are from advanced economies, especially Europe. There is a notable absence of empirical studies on unions and collective bargaining regardless of country income level.

The following sections analyze the global evidence on each type of labor market policy, starting with regulations before moving to institutions and interventions. It contrasts overall and youth-specific effects, advanced versus emerging economies, and highlights differences between Brazil and other peers where present.

REGULATIONS

Labor market regulations may allow for greater flexibility and reduce segmentation. The problem is that it creates a dual effect, often benefiting those who are covered by the regulation versus those who are not. Youth are more likely to fall in the latter category and take up informal, low-skilled jobs. Even among those who are covered by a particular policy, Heckman and Pagés (2000) find that the unemployment effect of stricter regulations is almost twice as large for youth than for adult workers.

Investigating the importance of labor market regulations is particularly important for Brazil, one of the least flexible labor markets in the world. The 1988 Constitution enshrines a high degree of worker protection and dispenses generous benefits, and firing workers is especially costly. High severance payments also distort incentives for workers, who force their own dismissal. Almeida and Carneiro (2009) find that a higher level of enforcement corresponds to lower informal employment, higher unemployment, lower income inequality and lower poverty. They also find that mandated benefits may encourage those who are low-skilled and self-employed to search for employment in the formal sector.

This section reviews the impacts of statutory minimum wages (SMW) and employment protection legislation on labor markets outcomes for young workers. While the employment effects of minimum wages are a longstanding subject of debate, there is strong evidence that they adversely affect the employment prospects of young workers both in advanced and in emerging economies. There is also substantial evidence that stringent employment protection legislation (EPL) harms the employment prospects of young workers, at least in advanced economies. More research is needed on the effects of EPL in emerging economies.

Statutory minimum wage

Minimum wages are a popular policy tool aimed at establishing a minimum standard of living for all workers. Almost all countries have minimum wages, and many have special subminimum wages for special groups such as youth and low-skilled workers. In most cases, minimum wages are "statutory"—that is, set through a process of collective bargaining between workers and employers. The idea is that establishing a wage floor will prevent firms from exploiting workers and encourage workers to increase their efforts, while boosting purchasing power and increasing aggregate demand. Raising minimum wages are therefore a common feature of political rhetoric,[2] with the argument that doing so will increase incomes of low-paid workers and reduce poverty.

In general, minimum wage hikes have positive effects on the earnings of employed youth, both in advanced and emerging economies. Studies that control for state and year fixed effects find that minimum wages increase formal sector earnings for teenagers (16–19 year olds) in the United States (Allegretto, Dube, and Reich 2011; Card 1992; Liu, Hyclak, and Regmi 2015). An increase in the minimum wage of 10 percent is expected to lead to an increase in American teenagers' earnings by 1.2–1.5 percent (Table A.4). Neumark and Wascher (2007) estimate a larger response at 2.5 percent, while Sabia et al. (2012) find slightly smaller effects from a sample of 16–19 year olds without a high school degree. However, minimum wages appear to have no statistically significant effects on the earnings of older youth cohorts in the United States (Liu, Hyclak, and Regmi 2015; Neumark and Wascher 2007; Sabia et al. 2012), suggesting that the impact is greatest where the minimum wage "bites." Studies that focus exclusively on teenagers in emerging economies are not available, but minimum wages lead to positive earnings elasticities are found for 15–29 year olds in South Africa, Thailand, Indonesia and Brazil (Table A.5). Increases in wages tend to be larger for youth than for adults; in Indonesia, this differential effect is estimated to be 7 times larger (SMERU 2001). In Brazil, there is also some evidence of a "lighthouse" effect where informal sector salaries also rise along with increases in the statutory minimum (Fajnzylber 2001).

Imposing or increasing SMW, however, do not automatically imply an increase in living standards for workers, especially not for those who are low-skilled. In the standard textbook model of competitive labor markets with an upward-sloping supply curve, setting a wage floor will lead the quantity of labor employed to fall as the marginal cost of workers increase. Firms are expected to substitute away from labor towards other inputs, as employment falls and wages increase (for those who remain employed). In other words, groups that the minimum wage intends to help—low-skilled, low-income, or least experienced workers (including youth)—may end up harmed by the policy. This is not to say

TABLE A.4 **Higher minimum wages increase teenage earnings by 1–3 percent in the United States**

AUTHOR (PUBLICATION YEAR)	PERIOD	EARNINGS ELASTICITY (%)
Liu, Hyclak, and Regmi (2015)[a]	2000–09	+0.127
Sabia, Burkhauser, and Hansen (2012)	2004–06	+0.104
Allegretto, Dube, and Reich (2011)	1990–2009	+0.149
Neumark and Wascher (2007)	1997–2005	+0.254
Sabia (2009)	1979–2004	+0.159

Source: World Bank.
a. Teenagers here refer to 14–18 year olds. Other studies refer to 16–19 year olds.

TABLE A.5 **Statutory minimum wages generally increase the earnings of 15–29 year olds in emerging economies**

COUNTRY	AUTHOR (PUBLICATION YEAR)	PERIOD	EARNINGS ELASTICITY (%)
South Africa	Bhorat, et al. (2016)	2000–07	+0.1154
Thailand	Del Carpio, Messina, Sanz-de-Galdeano	1990–2009	+0.5162
Indonesia	SMERU (2001)	1988–2000	+0.0834
Brazil	Fajnzylber (2001)	1982–97	+0.139

Source: World Bank.

that minimum wages are not a valid labor market instrument, but they may have unintended consequences and may not be effective in alleviating poverty (Betcherman 2012; Neumark et al. 2014; Pães de Barros et al. 2006). The aggregate effects of minimum wages on labor markets therefore depend on the combination of wage and employment effects.

If minimum wages have negative effects on employment overall as the standard model predicts, their effects on youth are likely to be equally, if not more perverse. While minimum wages may benefit youth in terms of higher earnings (if they are earning below the wage floor before the implementation of the policy), they may result in negative consequences for youth on aggregate. First, minimum wage increases may make it more difficult for young people to obtain employment, or increase unemployment if young people are laid off. This is because employers may be more reluctant to bear the higher cost of hiring a less experienced worker. Young people are also relatively lower skilled than older workers, so demand for them is highly elastic and they are more dispensable in the event of a minimum wage increase. Second, minimum wage increases may affect the accumulation of skills and experience by young people. They may be tempted to drop out of school to work, affecting their chances of being employed in high-skill industries in the future, or experience fewer on-the-job-training opportunities. Cardoso (2009) provides a more detailed discussion of these human capital effects.

Whether minimum wages help or hinder the employment prospects of young people remains a subject of intense debate. An early survey of the literature by Brown, Gilroy, and Kohen (1982) initially established a consensus that a minimum wage hike of 10 percent reduces the probability of employment for teenagers by 1–3 percent. "New minimum wage research" abolished this consensus, showing that higher minimum wages do not necessarily harm teenage employment. Exploiting state-level variation in minimum wages and longer sample periods, studies found significant and positive employment effects, with elasticities ranging from 0.35 to 2.65 (Card 1992; Card and Krueger 1994; Katz and Krueger 1992). These results pointed to the presence of monopsony in the labor market, but the choice of control groups and the reliability of the data were questioned.[3] Surveying several industrialized and developing countries, Neumark and Wascher (2007) countered that the majority of studies focusing on broader groups (rather than a narrow industry) show negative employment effects, at least for low-skilled workers. A recent, third wave of studies further argue that once spatial correlation is controlled for, the minimum wage has no effect on teenage employment, at least in the United States (Allegretto, Dube, and Reich 2011; Dube et al. 2010). This "synthetic control" approach is not without controversy (see the debates in Neumark et al. 2014 and Allegretto et al. 2017). Reich et al. (2017) use this method to show that raising the minimum wage to $13 in Seattle had no effect on employment in the food services industry, but Jardim et al. (2017) argue that low-skilled workers were adversely affected.

Studies on minimum wage effects in emerging economies similarly find mixed results. Negative employment effects ranging from 2–3 percent are found in Peru (Céspedes-Reynaga and Sanchez 2013), Chile (Grau and Landerretche 2011) and Brazil (Jales 2015), while no effects are found in China (Huang, Loungani, and Wang 2014), Ecuador (Canelas 2014) and Mexico (Campos et al. 2015). Nonetheless, even if there are no overall effects, there may be important distributional effects of minimum wages. Alatas and Cameron (2008) find that minimum wage hikes in Indonesia from 1990 to 1996 had no negative employment impact for large establishments, but may have adversely impacted workers in smaller, domestic establishments. Similarly, Del Carpio et al. (2012) also find heterogeneous employment impacts in Indonesia, with negative effects for small firms and less educated workers, but not large firms and workers with at least a high school education. In fact, Huang et al. (2014) find that Chinese firms with high wages and large profit margins increase employment following minimum wage hikes, while those with low wages and small profit margins downsize.

The majority of studies reviewed find that minimum wages harm employment prospects for youth, particularly the youngest and least-skilled workers. In the United States, most studies had estimated that a 10 percent hike in minimum wages reduce the employment probability of teenagers by 1–4 percent (Table A.6). These findings are disputed by Allegretto, Dube, and Reich (2011) and others who argue that the estimates are biased by spatial correlation, and that minimum wages have no effect on overall teenage employment. However, a number of studies find that minimum wage hikes are particularly disadvantageous to the employment prospects of American teenagers without a high school degree (Clemens 2015; Liu, Hyclak, and Regmi 2015; Sabia, Burkhauser and Hansen 2012). This suggests that even if the overall impact is negligible, there may be adverse impacts on those who are the least-skilled.

It is unclear whether minimum wage hikes disproportionately affect teenagers more than older youth (see table A.7). Similar to the earnings effects, minimum wages may only hurt where they "bite" and hence have no detectable effects on older youth. Liu, Hyclak, and Regmi (2015) find that this is true for the USA, where the minimum wage reduces the probability of employment of 14–18 year olds but has no significant impact on 19–21 and 22–24 year olds. Similarly, Meer and West (2013) find that minimum wages have large negative effects on net job growth for 14–18 year olds that decrease in magnitude for each subsequent age bracket. Neumark and Wascher (2007) find that older youth still suffer a small negative effect; a 10 percent increase in the minimum wage decreases the probability of employment by 0.4 percent for 20–24 year olds on average. The size of this effect is larger for young minority men and females without a high school education (Neumark and Wascher 2007).

Studies on minimum wage effects on youth in emerging economies also mostly show negative employment effects, albeit for a broader age cohort. Most of the studies selected for this review show that minimum wage hikes are associated with reductions in the probability of being employed for young people (Table A.8). The size of these effects varies substantially from 0.08 percent in China to 0.78 percent in Brazil, with most effects hovering around 2–3 percent. In Indonesia, minimum wage hikes are estimated to have a negative impact on

TABLE A.6 **Minimum wages appear to hurt U.S. teenage employment (1–4%)**

AUTHOR (PUBLICATION YEAR)	PERIOD	EMPLOYMENT ELASTICITY (%)
Allegretto, Dube, and Reich (2011)	1990–2009	0
Fadlon (2015)	1997–2010	−0.412
Thompson (2009)	1996–2000	−0.26
Sabia (2009)	1979–2004	−0.126
Neumark and Wascher (2007)	1997–2005	−0.158

Source: World Bank.

TABLE A.7 **The disemployment effects for 20–24 year olds may be smaller than for teenagers**

COUNTRY	AUTHOR (PUBLICATION YEAR)	PERIOD	EMPLOYMENT ELASTICITY (%)
Europe	Arpaia, et al. (2017)	n.a.	−0.317
United States	Liu, Hyclak, and Regmi (2015)	n.a.	0
United States	Neumark and Wascher (2007)	1997–2005	−0.041
United States	Sabia, Burkhauser, Hansen (2012)	2004–06	−0.887

Source: World Bank.
n.a. = not applicable.

TABLE A.8 **Most studies in emerging economies find negative employment effects for youth**

COUNTRY	AUTHOR (PUBLICATION YEAR)	AGE RANGE	PERIOD	EMPLOYMENT ELASTICITY (%)
Brazil	Broecke and Vandeweyer (2015)	15–24	2003–14	−0.78
Brazil	Fajnzylber (2001)	15–20	1982–97	−0.38
Brazil	Gonçalvez and Menezes-Filho (2016)	14–22	2012–15	−0.3
Brazil	Lemos (2009)	10–24	1982–2004	0
China	Fang and Lin (2013)	15–29	2004–09	−0.088
Colombia	Arango and Pachon (2004)	12–22	1984–2001	−0.252
Colombia	Hernandez and Lasso (2003)	12–24	1984–2000	0
Indonesia	SMERU (2001)	15–24	1988–2000	−0.307
Russian Federation	Muravyev and Oshchepkov (2013)	16–24	2001–10	−0.12[a]
South Africa	Bhorat et al. (2016)	15–29	2000–07	−0.462[b]
Thailand	Del Carpio, Messina, and Sanz-de-Galdeano	15–24	1998–2010	0
Thailand	Lathapipat and Poggi (2017)	15–24	2002–13	−0.47
Turkey	Papps (2012)	16–29	2002–05	−0.283
Turkey	Pelek (2015)	15–29	2004–14	0

Source: World Bank.
a. The dependent variable here is unemployment.
b. Averaged across sectors. Positive employment probability in taxi and retail, but large disemployment effects in agriculture.

employment for 15–24 year olds (SMERU 2001), especially for lower-skilled and part-time workers (Surhayadi et al. 2003). In some countries—Brazil, Colombia, Thailand and Turkey—the evidence is notably more mixed, with some finding negative effects and others no effects. Recent meta-analyses in emerging economies also find no overall effects, but acknowledge that youth and low-skilled groups are marginally more negatively affected by minimum wages (Broecke, Forti and Vandeweyer 2017; Chletsos and Giorgis 2015).

Although minimum wage research on Brazil also yields mixed results, more negative employment effects tend to be found for youth. Investigating the effects of minimum wage increases in Brazil has been tricky given the unification of regional minimum wages in 1984, as well as the linking of minimum wages to inflation and GDP growth since 2005 (Jales 2015). Some researchers have found that minimum wage increases led to negative employment effects overall (Foguel 1998; Foguel, Ramos and Carneiro 2015; Jales 2015; Neumark and Wascher (2007); Ulyssea and Foguel 2006) while others have found no effect (Broecke and Vandeweyer 2015; Lemos 2004, 2009). For youth, however, there is stronger evidence of negative effects. Fajnzylber (2001) finds that an increase in the minimum wage of 10 percent is associated with a decrease in employment of 3.8 percent. Gonçalvez and Menezes-Filho (2016) also find that minimum wage hikes reduce the likelihood of teenagers working by 3 percent, although this is due to an intrahousehold reallocation of labor. Broecke and Vandeweyer (2015) find a larger effect of 7.8 percent, but when hours worked are used as the dependent variable, the magnitude and significance of this effect diminishes. They also find that an increase in the Kaitz index by 10 percent is associated with a decline in formality by 3–4 percent on average. Similarly, Foguel et al. (2014) find that minimum wage hikes increase young people's transitions from employment into inactivity and into unemployment. These transitions and the negative effects of minimum wages may be amplified in recessionary times, as demonstrated by Dolton and Rosazzza Bondibene (2012) for Europe.

There are several reasons for these heterogeneous results. First, improvements in data collection and accuracy over time or other methodological differences lead to different results. Many of these studies measure employment probability rather than hours worked, which may be a more accurate measure of employment (Betcherman 2015). Second, the precise effects of SMW vary depending on the design of SMW policy (the process by which minimum wages are determined, the level at which SMW are set, etc.), as well as the effectiveness of its implementation. Further, the effects of SMW may differ by industry, region or target group, especially when there are differentiated rates for certain groups (such as youth). In emerging economies with large informal sectors, the minimum wage is often not "binding," and regulations are not always monitored or enforced. Moreover, the differences could be due to the interaction effects with other regulations/institutions. Neumark and Wascher (2004) find that the disemployment effects of minimum wages are particularly strong where there is higher union coverage and more restrictive labor standards, perhaps because employers have little room to adjust apart from hiring fewer workers. Conversely, active labor market policies reduce disemployment effects, likely because they absorb displaced workers or because they enable low-skilled workers to raise their productivity. In Brazil's case, there may also be a cyclical component to the findings, in that when an economy is booming (as Brazil's had from 2003–14), demand for labor will be high and employers are ready to pay wages to scarce labor that are higher than the statutory minimum. At times like these, the minimum wage is not "binding" and becomes irrelevant.

Despite the plethora of studies on SMW, few examine their longer-term effects on labor market outcomes for youth. Almost all the studies reviewed thus far focus on short-term effects; however, there is some indication that minimum wages can have long-term effects as well. Neumark and Nizalova (2007) find that exposure to high SMW for teenagers and young adults reduce their earnings and the probability that they are employed in the longer run. These effects are proportional to age; those exposed to higher minimum wages in their teenage years (independent of their participation in the labor market) experience larger reductions in wages at the age of 25–29 compared to those exposed during the ages 20–24. Initial estimates suggest that about a third of the earnings reduction is due to the reduction in schooling (enticed by a higher SMW), as well as due to foregone experience and reduced training. Building on this work, Cardoso (2009) delves deeper into the causes of these longer-term SMW effects by assessing actual exposure to SMW in Portugal. She finds that workers exposed to high MW as youth earn an overall wage premium of 1–4 percent in the long run (as employers raise investment in general training), but also experience lower returns to seniority within the firm (as employers reduce firm-specific training). Although not focusing on youth per se, Aaronson et al. (2017) use a putty-clay approach to show that the long-run disemployment effects of minimum wage increases can be larger than the short-run effects. The longer-term effects of SMW on youth thus merit further investigation in emerging economies.

There is encouraging evidence that youth subminimum wages may attenuate the expected negative employment effects. If minimum wages are set at a lower level for youth than for adults, then their labor costs decrease in the firm's perspective, and the employment effects become more ambiguous. The experiences of European and OECD countries with age-differentiated minimum wages have been quite successful. Dickens et al. (2014) find that when low-skilled individuals turn 22 years of age and transition from the youth to the adult SMW wage in the UK, their rate of employment increases by about 3–4 percentage points. Contrary to what the standard model predicts, this suggests that firms may not see those below the cutoff as perfect substitutes of those above the cutoff. The authors also suggest that the increase in wages may induce more young people to participate in the labor market or increase their job search intensity. Similarly, in Greece, Yannelis (2014) and Karakitsios (2016) find that the larger minimum wage cut for under-25 year olds benefited their probability of being employed. In New Zealand, Hyslop and Stillman (2004) find increasing the SMW by 41 percent for 16–17 year olds resulted in a slightly positive impact on the employment probability of 16–17 year olds (employment elasticity of 0.25), while increasing the SMW by 69 percent for 18–19 year olds also resulted in positive, though smaller employment effects (employment elasticity of 0.08).

Not all the evidence concerning youth subminimum wages is positive. Despite the positive effects on earnings and employment, Hyslop and Stillman (2004) find some evidence of a decline in educational enrolment and an increase in unemployment/inactivity. More recently, Kábatek (2015) indicates that the Dutch model of incremental minimum wage increases from 15 to 23 may have some unintended consequences. He shows that for workers aged 16–23, the probability of job separation increases by 1–2 percent in the three months preceding their birthdays (at which they move to a higher minimum wage tier). These results contradict those found by Portugal and Cardoso (2006), who find that the teenage share of job separations fell by about 15 percent in response to increases in the SMW (by 33–50 percent) for 17–19 year olds in 1987, despite the reduction in relative demand for teenage labor. In Denmark, Kreiner et al. (2017) also use regression discontinuity to show that employment falls by 33 percent when the hourly wage rate jumps by 40 percent as individuals turn 18 years old. This decline is almost entirely driven by job losses that are likely to be motivated by higher labor costs. Finally, Larrain and Poblete (2007) show that while relaxing the minimum wage solely for young workers reduces youth unemployment, doing so may force less skilled workers to remain longer in the uncovered sector.

Employment protection legislation

Employment protection legislation (EPL) refers to the rules and regulations that govern the hiring and dismissal of workers. The intent of such legislation is to improve workers' welfare by establishing some degree of job security and improving their bargaining power vis-à-vis employers. EPL typically achieves these goals by: a) regulating employer behavior, for example, setting conditions for fair and unfair dismissal of permanent employees and limiting the use of temporary contracts, b) mandating certain benefits such as severance payments to employees; and c) prescribing the necessary procedures to be followed in the case of commencement or termination of employment. Countries vary in their requirements of employers and employees for each of these components.

The effects of EPL on labor market outcomes in general are theoretically ambiguous. On one hand, strict EPL is expected to reduce job destruction and hence reduce flows into unemployment, leading to greater employment stability over the business cycle; on the other, strict EPL reduces job creation and reduces flows into employment, thus prolonging unemployment spells (Bertola 1990). The aggregate effect on the overall level of employment at any point in time is therefore ambiguous, depending on the relative rates of hiring and firing. The coverage of EPL is also important: if employers revert to hiring workers on a fixed-term or temporary basis to circumvent the high costs of permanent employees, this may affect lifetime earnings and employment. Workers who enjoy increased job security may also reduce their effort level and hence their productivity, which would lead to efficiency losses from maintaining unproductive workers in their roles. Moreover, stringent EPL may also induce firms to operate in the informal sector in order to avoid the high costs generated by labor regulations, contributing to the formation of a dual labor market and exacerbating the inequality between those who are covered versus those who are not.

These unintended negative consequences may be particularly acute for youth, those who are and other groups that are disadvantaged in the labor market. First, as new entrants to the labor market, youth are relatively low skilled and hence incur higher training costs for employers. More stringent regulations are thus likely to make firms more reluctant to hire young workers since they cannot be easily dismissed if they remain unproductive. Second, high costs of firing can also make firms more reluctant to fire existing workers even if they are unproductive. In addition, youth are more likely to work in informal or temporary employment as a result of strict EPL (Kahn 2012). In OECD countries, nearly a quarter of youth aged 15–24 years were employed in temporary work in 2012. While such opportunities may serve as stepping-stones to more permanent positions, studies suggest that accepting a contingent job may in fact delay individuals' transitions to standard employment and reduce the longer-term quality of their employment, wages and human capital development (Yu 2012). EPL may therefore not only impact short-term employment, but also labor market outcomes for youth in the longer term.

Available evidence suggests, with some caveats, that more flexible EPL is desirable for the overall labor market. There is some indication that strict EPL has a negative effect on aggregate employment (see table A.9), but the results are sensitive to different specifications, particularly the measurement of EPL (Betcherman 2015). Earlier cross-country studies of EPL across OECD countries (Nickell 1997; OECD 1999; Scarpetta 1996) and in Latin America (Heckman and Pagés 2000) found negative, albeit weak employment effects, but more recent studies with similar approaches in these regions do not yield any significant impact on employment (Baccaro and Rei 2005; Bassanini and Duvall). The evidence is also divided between negative effects and no effect when one examines single country studies in Latin America. Although increasing severance

TABLE A.9 **Stricter EPL may reduce employment in emerging economies**

COUNTRY	OVERALL EMPLOYMENT EFFECT	YOUTH-SPECIFIC EMPLOYMENT EFFECT
Advanced	Negative or no effect	Negative
Emerging	Mostly negative, but limited to Latin America, India	Stronger negative effects, but limited to Latin America, India
Brazil	Negative, but very limited evidence	n.a.

Source: World Bank.
n.a. = not applicable.

payments had sizeable and significant negative effects on employment in Argentina (Mondino and Montoya 2004) and Peru (Saavedra and Torero 2004), doing so did not appear to have any effect in Brazil (Paes de Barros and Corseuil 2004). Composite measures of EPL also did not appear to have any effect on aggregate employment in Caribbean countries (Downes, Mamingi, and Antoine 2004). More restrictions on the use of temporary contracts, however, appeared to reduce employment in Colombia (Kugler 2004); Second, the geographic scope of studies on EPL is largely limited to developed countries. Aside from Latin America, most of the literature on EPL for developing countries is limited to India, where there is stronger evidence of negative effects (Schwab 2015), not just on employment, but also productivity, investment and output (Besley and Burgess 2004). This heterogeneity of results can partly be explained by methodological and data issues, as well as institutional differences across countries (Betcherman 2015).

Limiting the analysis to impacts on youth, there is a stronger consensus that stringent EPL harms youth employment. Most studies largely support the theory that more restrictive regulations adversely affect those for whom labor demand is more elastic (i.e., less-skilled groups), at least in OECD countries (Bassanini and Duvall 2006; OECD 1996, 1999). The effect is quite large: Bassanini and Duvall (2006) find that a decline in the OECD EPL indicator by two standard deviations is associated with a 4 percentage point increase in youth employment on average. Nonetheless, it is unclear which component of EPL is most pernicious. Many studies emphasize the role of job security provisions (Breen 2005; Esping-Andersen 2000); in Chile, Montenegro and Pagés (2004) find that job security provisions (mandated benefits) adversely impact the employment probability for youth, as well as less skilled workers and women. A later study (2007) by the same authors estimate that doubling severance pay for workers would reduce the wage employment to population rates for young workers by 1.6 percentage points due to their shorter tenure. However, Skedinger (2011) argues that it is the stringent regulation of permanent work that tends to lead to a higher incidence of involuntary temporary employment, especially among those aged 15–24 years old, as well as among women, immigrants and those with low cognitive ability (Kahn 2007).

While there is no consensus on which component of EPL is most harmful to labor market outcomes for youth if it is too restrictive, several studies have attempted to study the effects of deregulation efforts. Feldman (2009) finds that more flexible hiring and firing rules reduce the youth unemployment rate by 9 percentage points, whereas reducing payroll taxes and dismissal costs increased the employment of young workers on permanent contracts in Spain (Kugler et al. 2003). Meanwhile, Noelke (2015) finds that while job security provisions per se do not always have the intended benefits for youth, deregulating temporary contracts at high levels of job security provisions has the opposite effect of what is desired—doing so increases youth unemployment rates and lowers youth employment rates. The author's conclusions are, like most of the literature, centered on OECD countries; hence, little is known about the effects of deregulation in emerging economies.

INSTITUTIONS

Labor market institutions refer to legislated structures, norms and procedures in a country through which interested parties make and implement decisions that shape regulations and interventions. These include collective bargaining mechanisms, labor unions and employer associations. By increasing the bargaining power of those they represent, labor market institutions have the potential to improve the welfare of certain groups of workers. Unions may, for example, exert collective pressure for higher earnings, better quality jobs or more secure jobs. They also tend to play a significant role in wage-setting, especially in negotiating or enforcing the minimum wage.

The theoretical effects of unions on labor market outcomes are ambiguous. On one hand, unions may increase the wages of workers in the affected sector/industry by improving their bargaining power vis-à-vis employers. Assuming perfect labor mobility, the Harris-Tadaro-Calvo framework predicts that the union relative wage effect, or the union wage premium, encourages individuals to move from uncovered to unionized sectors. Unemployment in uncovered sectors thus increases until expected wages are equalized across sectors. However, the precise effects can vary: as displaced workers move to non-union sectors, wages fall, but nonunion employers may also increase wages to prevent workers from becoming unionized (Freeman and Medoff 1984). Other important factors that influence the behavior of unions are the level of rent-seeking/competition, the extent to which government intervention influences behavior and representation, and the degree of centralization (Pierre and Scarpetta 2007).

There are a variety of ways in which unions may benefit young people. Given that youth face discrimination in the labor market due to lack of experience, we can expect that unions raise youths' wages on aggregate. Unions can also play a role in ensuring that apprenticeships are a success by participating in consultations, defining working conditions of apprentices, or providing the apprenticeship in consortium with employers and training institutions. In Germany, for example, trade unions are heavily involved in developing the structure and content of apprenticeship schemes (see O'Higgins 2001). Since they represent workers across the country and across firms, unions are well-positioned to identify and train workers for in-demand skills (Fazio, Fernandez-Coto, and Ripani 2016).

However, unions appear to be increasingly less popular among youth worldwide. It is unlikely that unions have a large impact on labor market outcomes given the low participation of young workers in such institutions. Although limited data is available, the decline in trade union membership worldwide appears to be even more pronounced for youth (Blanchflower 2006). Only 4.2 percent of youth are affiliated with unions in the United States, similar to the UK (5 percent). The rate of unionization among young workers is slightly higher in developing countries, but remains low. In Brazil, only 9 percent of working youth are affiliated with unions (ILO 2015), and only 4 percent of youth respondents in the World Values Survey (2014) identify as an active member. This is despite moderately high union membership overall: there are nearly 11,000 workers' unions representing 16.2 percent of the total labor force (Campos 2016). Youth tend to be indifferent towards trade unions or have low confidence in them (Fontes and Margolies 2010; OIT 2015; Serrano Pascual and Waddington 2000), and are hence less likely to join unions (Blanchflower and Freeman 2000; Johnson and Jarley 2005; Waddington and Kerr 2002). Such negative perceptions of labor unions may be influenced by the tendency of unions in developing countries to play a political role above all else.

Although very few studies examine the specific impact of unions on young workers, existing evidence indicates that unions have positive effects on their earnings, at least in developed countries. An early study by Freeman and Medoff (1984) found that private sector unions raise wages most for the young, the least tenured, the least educated, blue-collar workers and for men in largely unorganized regions of the USA. Reassessing these findings using data from 1996 to 2001, Blanchflower and Bryson (2003) find that the U-shaped relationship between unions and age has disappeared because there has been a precipitous decline in the premium for the youngest workers (from 32 percent to 19 percent), while the older workers' wage gap has remained roughly constant. However, young workers still benefit the most from unionization. Schmitt (2008) also finds a small but positive effect on hourly wages for unionized young workers in low-wage occupations in the USA. He estimates that the union wage premium is about 12.4 percent (14 percent for men, 10 percent for women), and that younger workers benefit even more from health insurance and pension coverage. He also finds that unionization raises wages by about 10 percent for younger workers in the 15 lowest-paying occupations. All in all, estimates of the union wage premium range from 5 to 15 percent in developed countries (Aidt and Tzannatos 2002).

It is unclear whether unions similarly benefit the earnings of young workers in emerging economies (see table A.10). Analyzing school-to-work transition surveys of 15–29 year olds in South Asia and the Middle East, Matsumoto and Elder (2010) find that there does not appear to be a positive relationship between trade union membership and earnings. Freeman (2010) also finds that unions have more varied effects on wages and on wage dispersion in developing countries, ranging from negative wage gaps in Ghana, Senegal and Zimbabwe to large positive wage gaps in South Africa. The wages of union members of young South African males are estimated to be 145 percent higher than comparable nonunion workers in the bottom decile of distribution and 19 percent higher in the top decile of the wage distribution (Schultz and Mwabu 1998). In Latin America, wage premiums are estimated to be positive but modest: 7 percent in Uruguay (Cassoni, Labadie, and Fachola 2005), 11 percent in Bolivia and 14 percent in Chile (Rios-Avila and Hirsch 2013). In Brazil, the estimated wage gap is larger at about 15–18 percent (Arbache 1998) but the evidence is somewhat dated.

The effects on unions and collective bargaining on employment are more ambiguous, depending on the independent variable in question (see table A.11 and table A.12). Jimeno and Rodriguez-Palenzuela (2002) find that *union*

TABLE A.10 **Limited evidence suggests that unions have positive effects on young people's earnings**

COUNTRY	AUTHOR (PUBLICATION YEAR)	PERIOD	EFFECT ON EARNINGS
United States	Schmitt (2008)	2004–07	+0.124
United States	Blanchflower and Bryson (2003)	1996–2001	+0.171
South Africa	Schultz and Mwabu (1998)	1993–95	+1.45

Source: World Bank.

TABLE A.11 **Union coverage has mostly negative employment effects for young people**

COUNTRY	AUTHOR (PUBLICATION YEAR)	PERIOD	EFFECT ON EMPLOYMENT
OECD	Jimeno and Rodriguez-Palenzuela (2002)	1968–96	−0.78
OECD	Traxler and Brandl (2009)	1980–2000	−0.06
OECD	Bertola, Blau, and Kahn (2007)	1960–96	−0.0902 (M); −0.1996 (F)
Europe	Baranowska and Gebel (2010)	2004	0.93
South Africa	Schultz and Mwabu (1998)	1993–95	−0.056

Source: World Bank.
OECD = Organisation for Economic Co-operation and Development.

TABLE A.12 **Union density has mixed effects on employment for young people**

COUNTRY	AUTHOR (PUBLICATION YEAR)	PERIOD	EFFECT ON EMPLOYMENT
OECD	Jimeno and Rodriguez-Palenzuela (2002)	1968–96	+0.016
OECD	Neumark and Wascher (2004)	1975–2000	−0.24 to -0.3
OECD	Van der Velden and Wolbers (2003)	1992–97	0

Source: World Bank.
OECD = Organisation for Economic Co-operation and Development.

coverage[4] increases the unemployment rate of women aged 15–24 by 7.8 percent and have no significant effects on young males, but *union density*[5] increases the unemployment rate for men aged 15–24 by 0.16 percent and has no significant effect on young females. Moreover, an increase in the degree of coordination increases the unemployment rate for males and females aged 15–24 by 0.227 and 0.294 respectively. Similarly, Nickell (1997) find that both union coverage and density are positively related with unemployment, whereas Belot and Van Ours (2000) find that this association is only true for union density in OECD countries. Overall, studies are roughly divided between those that find that unions increase unemployment (Baccaro and Rei 2005; Bertola, Blau, and Kahn 2002; Nickell, Nunziata, and Ochel 2005) and those that find no significant effect (Aidt and Tzannatos 2002; Bassanini and Duvall 2006; Eurofound 2012). However, this research is mostly limited to OECD countries.

Studies that find that unions adversely impact youth employment outcomes disagree over the cause. While Jimeno and Rodriguez-Palenzuela argue that unionization rates reduce youth employment due to wage compression, Bertola, Blau, and Kahn (2007) suggest that this is because unions bargain to protect their core members, who are usually prime-age males. They find that higher unionization (an index of union density, union coverage and collective bargaining) is associated with decreased employment for groups with relatively elastic labor supply—youth, older individuals, and women—that have better/more uniform alternatives to paid employment (e.g., schooling, retirement and home production). Moreover, the effects of unions on employment outcomes for youth could also differ according to age cohort. Neumark and Wascher (2004) find that unionization has a negative effect on youth employment as a whole, but a positive effect if only looking at teenagers. Similarly, Bassanini and Duvall (2006) find that union density has a positive but insignificant effect on unemployment for 20–24 year olds in OECD countries.

TABLE A.13 **Unions and collective bargaining have diverse effects on the labor market for young people, depending on the independent variable**

	UNION DENSITY	UNION COVERAGE	DEGREE OF CENTRALIZATION
Employment	−0.1103 (3)	+0.038 (2)	−1.123 (2)
Unemployment	+0.016 (1)	+0.36 (2)	+0.2605 (1)
Wages	n.a.	+0.787 (2)	n.a.

Source: World Bank.
n.a. = not applicable.

One possibility is that greater coordination and/or centralization of the bargaining process attenuates the unemployment effects of unions. Aidt and Tzannatos (2002) find that OECD countries with highly coordinated bargaining tend to have lower unemployment rates. A number of other studies (Baccaro and Rei 2005; Bassanini and Duvall 2006) similarly conclude that the negative effect of union density/coverage on unemployment may be reduced by coordinated bargaining (Baccaro and Rei 2005). If bargaining takes place at the firm level, as opposed to the state or the national level, then wage increases tend to be limited to productivity levels, thus resulting in less of a negative impact on overall employment/unemployment (Banerji et al., 2014). Baranowska and Gebel (2010) find that in European countries where centralized bargaining is high, those aged 15–24 are 0.93 percentage points more likely to experience temporary employment relative to prime-aged workers.

Again, there is extremely limited evidence on the employment effects of unions for young people in developing countries. Schultz and Mwabu (1998) find that a 10 pp increase in union workers' wages is associated with a weakly significant decline in employment by 5.6 percent for young men in South Africa. Although they find similarly negative effects on young women, none of them are significant. They estimate that halving the union wage differential would increase overall employment by 2 percentage points, with a smaller but still positive effect on youth. The review did not find eligible empirical studies on unions and youth in Brazil or Latin America despite the historical presence of unions in the region (see Rios-Avila and Hirsch 2013). In general, there remains ample room for further research on the impact of unions and collective bargaining on youth in non-OECD countries.

INTERVENTIONS

The importance of sustained job creation for economic growth and social cohesion has encouraged governments to assist groups that face difficulties in finding employment. These interventions can be classified as "active" or "passive," depending on their objectives and the ways in which they are implemented. Active labor market policies (ALMPs) typically aim to reduce unemployment by improving the quality of the labor supply or by directly creating job opportunities for workers.

This section considers the overall impact of both types of policies on the labor market outcomes for youth. Although they are in many ways complements to one another, and are often used in combination, the discussion only considers the separate effects of individual policies.

Active labor market policies

ALMPs have become increasingly important since the 1990s—not only as a tool to address challenges faced by youth in the labor market, but also by other groups that face difficulties in finding employment. Although initially popular in OECD countries, low- and middle-income countries have started to experiment more with ALMPs over the past decade, especially with skills training and labor intermediation services in Latin America and the Caribbean. ALMPs aim to address structural or cyclical unemployment by improving the quality of the labor force, thus increasing job seekers' likelihood of employment, rather than by reducing the supply of workers. They may also target those who already have jobs in order to boost their productivity and earnings. ALMPs can therefore be characterized as a combination of supply and demand-side labor market policies.

Despite their popularity, systematic reviews of ALMPs have found lukewarm evidence of their effectiveness (Betcherman et al. 2004; Card, Kluve, and Weber 2010; Dar and Tzannatos 1999). Examining over 200 evaluations of such programs, Card, Kluve, and Weber (2010) conclude that the average impact of ALMPs is close to zero in the short run, although they become more positive 2–3 years after the program. The authors also find that ALMPs targeted at younger people are generally less successful than those that target older people, reinforcing earlier conclusions from the literature (Kluve 2006). ALMPs, however, have attracted renewed attention following the Global Financial Crisis, particularly in OECD countries. The Banerji et al. (2014) estimates that increasing ALMP spending per unemployed person in Italy/Portugal/Spain to average European levels is associated with lower unemployment rates by 1–5 pp, ceteris paribus (assuming they are well targeted and implemented). More recent evaluations from low and middle-income countries suggest that youth-targeted ALMPs are more likely to have substantial effects on the probability of employment and earnings, but less on other labor market outcomes (Kluve et al. 2016).

It is difficult to isolate the impact of ALMPs because they often utilize a combination of instruments (for example, combining training and employment services), and are hence difficult to compare justifiably across countries (Betcherman 2004; Kluve et al. 2016). Moreover, interventions are not often rigorously evaluated, especially in developing countries. Only a quarter of 200+ interventions evaluated by Betcherman (2007) use a control group methodology to estimate the net impact of the program in question. Nonetheless, an independent evaluation of World Bank and IFC support for ALMPs (IEG 2015) find that these comprehensive interventions that combine different instruments tend to be more effective than isolated components, reinforcing the conclusions of Betcherman (2004) and Vezza (2014).

This section evaluates the effectiveness of commonly used ALMPs in improving labor market outcomes for youth. Although categorizations of ALMPs vary, the following are considered: a) labor market training; b) entrepreneurship support programs, c) employment services and d) subsidized employment, which includes workfare programs and wage subsidies.

Skills training

Training programs are the most widely used youth employment intervention worldwide, and the most evaluated type of ALMP to date. They are used alone or in combination with other interventions (most frequently on-the-job training and entrepreneurship promotion), and often target specific groups who are relatively lower-skilled and/or have difficulty finding employment. Beneficiaries of training programs therefore often include youth, especially in Latin America, where most countries implement some form of skills training program for youth (Jovenes) or subsidize training (e.g., Lei do Aprendiz in Brazil). Although the content of training programs varies widely, they typically encompass some vocational element and soft skills. Entrepreneurial or management skills have also become more popular, although in this review they are covered separately (see next section).

The majority of training programs implemented in the recent decade have had a positive effect on the employability of youth in the short term. A recent meta-analysis by Kluve et al. (2015) found that skills training interventions raise the probability of being employed by 3.35 percentage points and lead to higher earnings in aggregate by 0.01 standard mean deviations. Statistically significant effects are found for a range of countries across the income spectrum, from high-income countries such as the USA (Frumento et al. 2012; Schochet et al. 2001) and Germany (Ehlert, Kluve, and Schaffner 2012) to middle income ones such as Mexico (Delajara, Freije, and Soloaga 2006) and Peru (Díaz and Jaramillo 2006) and lower-income countries such as the Republic of Yemen (McKenzie et al. 2016) and Liberia (Adoho et al. 2014). Although the programs reviewed are not directly comparable, large positive effects were found particularly in contexts that targeted disadvantaged groups. In Nepal, training increased non-farm employment by 15–16 percentage points or 50 percent, with larger effects for women (regardless of age) rather than men (Chakravarty et al. 2015). In Liberia, the EPAG program increased employment by about 47 percent (Adoho et al. 2014). As in Uganda, where training led to an increase in income-generating activities among eligible female participants (Bandiera et al. 2014), most of the increase in employment was due to new entrants in the labor force. Some programs have also had impact on the quality of employment (i.e., the probability of finding formal employment), for example, Jovenes-type programs in the Dominican Republic (Ibarrán et al. 2015), Argentina (Alzuá and Brassiolo 2006) and Peru (Díaz and Jaramillo 2006).

A number of evaluations find that training had no effect on employment even in the short or medium term, and the aggregate impact of training programs worldwide is small. Training had no significant effects on the likelihood of youth having a job in the Dominican Republic (Card et al. 2011), Kenya (Hicks et al. 2013) and Argentina (Alzuá and Brassiolo 2006; Elías et al. 2004), as well as OECD countries such as France (Fougere, Kramarz, and Magnac 2000) and Germany (Caliendo, Kunn and Schmidl 2011). The findings of these studies suggest that the impact of training programs depends heavily on the content, the context in which the program is implemented and the target group. Moreover, even if these programs are effective, they are not necessarily cost-effective (Blattman and Ralston 2015). McKenzie (2017) finds that training programs cost an average of US$17,000–US$60,000 per additional person employed, which is a fairly inefficient outcome.

The persistence of these positive effects on youths' employability in the longer term is questionable. In general, the effects of skills training dissipate over time. Ibarrán et al. (2015) find no impact on average employment six years after the training was administered in the Dominican Republic. Similarly, Ehlert, Kluve, and Schaffner (2012) find positive effects on employment probability in Germany after six months, but these become insignificant at 18 months. In Turkey, Hirshleifer et al. (2015) also find significant positive impacts on the likelihood of employment for males aged 25 years and younger, but these effects do not persist over time. However, there are a few exceptions. In India, for example, Maitra and Mani (2015) find that training had positive and sustained effects on probability of employment and self-employment for low-income women. Being offered training in Colombia increases the probability that a young person will have a formal job by 5.3 percentage points, and the probability of paid employment by 6.8 percent (Attanasio, Kugler, and Meghir 2009) in the short term, but also had a positive and sustained impact on the duration of formal sector employment (Kugler et al. 2015). Some positive effects are also found from a similar training program in Peru after three years, although these are more heterogeneous (Díaz and Rosas Shady 2016).

The effects of training programs on youth labor market outcomes are highly dependent on the gender, age and educational level of beneficiaries. Several studies show that training is less beneficial for women than for men; in Malawi, for example, women are more constrained when it comes to participating in training and therefore tend to drop out and not put their newfound knowledge into practice as much as men do (Cho et al. 2013). Similarly, Honorati (2015) finds that training in Kenya increased current employment among male participants, but had no effect on females. Several evaluations from Latin America (Entra 21, Especial de Jovenes and Juventud y Empleo) also find no effects on job quality for women, but positive effects for men (see Vezza 2014). Moreover, training is more effective for those with higher levels of education (Delajara, Freije, and Soloaga 2006). It may also be more beneficial for those who are currently enrolled in school: in an evaluation of the Projoven program in Peru, Díaz and Jaramillo (2006) find that the likelihood of being a paid worker increased for females and for 16–20 year olds, but not for 21–25 year olds.

Overall, training programs seem to have an overwhelmingly positive effect on young people's wages. Although some evaluations find that training has had a negligible impact on the income of trainees (Alzuá and Brassiolo 2006) or no effect at all (Cho et al. 2013), the majority of training programs reviewed have helped to boost participants' earnings in Liberia (Adoho et al. 2014), Argentina (Aedo and Núñez 2004) and Colombia (Attanasio, Kugler, and Meghir 2009). It is not always clear, however, whether the gains in earnings are from self-employment or from wage employment. An evaluation of a training program in Uganda found positive impact on reported earnings from self-employment but no effect on wage employment (Bandiera et al. 2014), whereas in Kenya (Hicks et al. 2013) and Colombia (Kugler et al. 2015), the gains were entirely from formal wage employment. There is also some evidence of persistence in wage gains over time in Peru (Díaz and Jaramillo 2006), Colombia (Kugler et al. 2015) and India (Maitra and Mani 2015). In the USA, sustained impacts on earnings are only found for always-employed compliers at all time periods (Frumento et al. 2012).

Nonetheless, the magnitude of the wage gain from training programs differs depending on gender and age. Several program evaluations find that females increase their earnings disproportionately more than other groups as a result of participating in training. This is true in Kenya, where wage earnings increased especially for females and older males (Hicks et al. 2013), Colombia (Attanasio, Kugler, and Meghir 2009) and Argentina (Elías et al. 2004). Moreover, Ibarrán et al. (2015) find that training only benefited women's wages in Santo Domingo, and had no effect elsewhere. Additionally, differential impacts by age can be found: in the USA, beneficiaries of Job Corps experienced a 12 percent gain in weekly earnings, but young adults experienced larger average effects compared to 16–19 year olds (Schochet, Burghardt, and Glazerman 2001). In the Dominican Republic, however, the situation was the reverse; conditional on being employed, training had a marginally significant and positive impact on wages only for male teens, and not for women or for young adults (Card et al. 2011). Brazil's apprenticeship program also appears to have led to an increase in real hourly wage levels in the short and medium run for 17–18 year old beneficiaries (Corseuil et al. 2012).

Entrepreneurship support programs

Initiatives to promote entrepreneurship have become an increasingly important instrument for job creation. This is true not only in developing countries with barriers to formal wage employment, but also in developed countries that are struggling to restart the job growth engine following large economic shocks. Although it is difficult to define entrepreneurship support programmes (ESP), they generally feature one or a combination of the following elements: business/financial skills training, advisory services (coaching, mentoring and access to networks), and access to finance (including microcredit, cash, grants, and microfranchising). They also tend to have dual objectives of job creation and social protection, and therefore target groups that are vulnerable to unemployment or underemployment: youth, women, low-skilled/unskilled individuals and rural dwellers.

Such heterogeneity in terms of content and participants make it difficult to compare across countries and disentangle what works for whom. From the few studies that exist, it is not clear that ESP as a whole significantly improves labor market income or activity in developing countries. In an evaluation of ESP in developing countries, Cho and Honorati (2013) find that programs do not affect startup rates or income. These results are in spite of the fact that that ESP have positive but small impacts on business practices, suggesting that these changes are not disruptive enough to lead to significant increases in income. Focusing exclusively on business training programs, McKenzie and Woodruff (2013) find similarly positive and small effects on business practices, but no effects on overall employment, profits or sales. They do, however, find that programs increase the rate of new business creation in the short term.

Nonetheless, there is some evidence that ESP lead to improved labor market income and activity for youth (Cho and Honorati 2013). In Liberia, the EPAG program, targeted at females aged 16–27, increased the likelihood of working by 18 percentage points (nearly 50 percent increase from the baseline). Similarly, Blattman, Fiala, and Martinez (2012) find that the Youth Opportunities Program in Uganda increased beneficiaries' hours in employment outside the home from 14 to 25 per week. Although both of these studies focus on vulnerable youth in conflict-affected areas, there is some indication of positive effects in other settings. In Tunisia, Premand et al. (2012) find that participating in an entrepreneurship track rather than an academic one in the final year of university rather than an academic one in the final year of university leads to an increase in self-employment rates for males (6 percent) and females (3 percent) one year later. It must be noted, however, that these programs may not necessarily have an impact on aggregate youth employment; Premand et al. (2012), for instance, finds evidence of a substitution effect from wage employment to self-employment, echoing de Mel et al. (2014).

These programs also have positive impacts on earnings, although it is not always clear why this occurs and to what extent. The World Bank (2015) finds that the EPAG program increased beneficiaries' weekly earnings by approximately (US$8) relative to the control group, primarily due to new labor market entrants, whereas Blattman et al. (2013) find large and significant impacts of the YOP in Uganda. Conversely, Blattman et al. (2013) find a small increase in monthly income and consumption for the median WINGS beneficiary in Uganda.

The differential impacts for youth may be the case because young (potential) entrepreneurs may benefit more than their older counterparts from skills training or mentoring owing to unobserved differences in their receptivity to new ideas and business practices. There is some indication that this occurs; McKenzie and Woodruff (2013) find that practicing entrepreneurs do not benefit from training programs. Youth may also benefit disproportionately more from interventions that improve access to finance, given their limited bandwidth to borrow and save. Further, they may also benefit more in the longer term from their exposure to mentors, networks and training early on in their careers.

A number of caveats apply to these results. First, the positive effects that are found in meta-analyses of entrepreneurship support programs are driven strongly by a few studies[6] in highly specific, typically conflict-affected settings and on disadvantaged groups (see Cho and Honorati 2013; Kluve et al. 2015; Mckenzie and Woodruff 2013). These studies also tend to be quite recent, and do not track effects over a longer period of time. Moreover, the positive results of some programs may be driven by program-specific characteristics that are not always accounted for. The EPAG program in Liberia, for instance, is unique in its high participation rate (95 percent) and low attrition, which is in part due to the presence of incentives for beneficiaries.

There is ample scope for research before more conclusive findings about the effect of entrepreneurship programs on youth labor market outcomes can be drawn. First, not much is known about the long-term impacts of ESP. This is particularly important for studies that evaluate the impact of ESP on secondary and tertiary students, since most existing ones focus on the knowledge, attitudes and intentions of starting a business, rather than on specific labor market outcomes (Valerio, Parton, and Robb 2014). However, entrepreneurship education[7] programs may encourage those in secondary or tertiary institutions to start new businesses, these effects may not materialize immediately after an intervention as youth seek further education or opt for wage employment before pursuing self-employment later on in life. Moreover, few studies consider general equilibrium effects or include cost-benefit analyses, so it is difficult to assess how much policymakers should invest in youth-targeted entrepreneurship initiatives vis-à-vis other means of activation.

Employment services

Employment services, or labor intermediation services, address problems in matching workers to jobs and vice versa. Such services range from job counseling, job search assistance and mentoring services to more direct support such as job placement and financial assistance for job search activities. By providing these services, governments—by themselves or in partnership with private entities—can tackle structural issues that certain individuals may have in looking for jobs, such as imperfect information about vacancies due to their lack of networks or knowledge of how to connect with employers, or difficulties in signaling their skills/credentials to employers.

Employment services therefore have a range of potential positive effects on labor market outcomes, although perhaps not for vulnerable youth.

They may not only reduce the length and incidence of unemployment by helping unemployed individuals find work faster than they would otherwise, but also increase the quality of eventual employment and wages by reducing the chance of mismatches between employer and employee. The latter effect is not likely to happen, however, if barriers to workers' productivity have to do with poor quality jobs or poor skills rather than structural barriers in information (Barros and Carvalho 2002). Since youth are likely to fall in the first category, the potential of such services to help youth find employment or improve their performance in the labor market is thus limited.

Nonetheless, there is some evidence that such services help youth get jobs in high-income countries. An early study by Heckman, LaLonde and Smith (1999) was pessimistic about the impact of such services, but later evidence about the impact of the UK's New Deal found that unemployed young men who receive job search assistance and other services are 20 percent more likely to be employed than the control group. About a fifth of this effect was due to the job search component of the intervention (Blundell et al. 2004; Van Reenen 2003). Evaluations in the United States by Decker et al. (2000), Jacobson and Petta (2000) also find positive impacts on the speed of re-employment, earnings and the reduction of unemployment benefits. There is similarly positive evidence in Canada and Sweden about the effect of employment services; a simulation by Boone and Van Ours (2004) find that public employment services reduce unemployment in OECD countries. Though not focused on youth per se, employment services also reduced the duration of unemployment and increased employment and earnings in Romania (Rodriguez-Planas 2007).

Although the majority of studies concern interventions in developed or transition economies, recent work suggests that employment services also play an important role in helping youth find jobs in more disadvantaged settings. Recent empirical evaluations of programs that address structural barriers that make it difficult for youth to obtain employment have yielded positive results. Simply providing information about jobs in the business process outsourcing (BPO) sector and basic knowledge of interview skills to young females living in rural areas of India, for example, increased their employment, and not just in the BPO sector (Jensen 2012). Likewise, transport subsidies that help young Ethiopians travel to areas where there are new jobs have a positive effect on employment overall (Franklin 2014).

It is worth noting, however, that the impact of employment services differs depending on the profile of beneficiaries and the reasons why they are unemployed. More educated, urban youth may have less success with employment services due to higher reservation wages (voluntary unemployment) rather than the failure of the service to match job seekers and employers. In Amman, Jordan, approximately a third of young job candidates turned down the opportunity to have an interview when matched with a job, and the overwhelming majority of young job candidates (83 percent) rejected job offers that were made through the service. Moreover, employment services are likely to be effective only to the extent that beneficiaries are actually looking for employment. Saniter and Siedler (2014) find that mandatory visits to job information centers for high school students in Germany resulted in a smoother transition to the labor market, but had no apparent effects on the likelihood of having a full-time job five years later, nor on the number of hours worked or first job earnings. Taken together, these studies suggest that employment services are more effective if they target specific groups of youth who face tangible barriers in accessing jobs.

Three final caveats are important in evaluating the effectiveness of employment services. First, there may be substantial negative externalities that may emerge due to the program. In the Netherlands, for example, employment services led to a substitution from unmonitored, informal search activities to monitored, more formal search activities, but no change in overall employment (Van den Berg and Van der Klaauw 2006). Moreover, Crépon et al. (2013) find that eligible unemployed youths who received job placement assistance were significantly more likely to have found a stable job than those in the control group, but that these gains came at the expense of the control group and were not sustained over time. There are also likely to be deadweight losses that are not always accounted for in existing studies, that is, many of those who enrolled in employment services and found jobs may have done so in absence of the program. Few studies take these general equilibrium effects into consideration. Second, employment services may be cost-effective, but they may not work for everyone. Robalino et al. (2013) point out that such programs need high institutional capacity in order to succeed. Third, different target groups make the comparison across programs and countries quite difficult. Blundell et al. (2004) point out that those who benefited from the UK's New Deal are less disadvantaged than comparable programs in the United States.

Subsidized employment: Workfare programs

Workfare programs focus on the direct creation and provision of public works or other activities that produce public goods or services. Governments typically launch large-scale public works programs to provide temporary employment to disadvantaged, unskilled or long-term unemployed individuals while they search for better-paid jobs. Public works programs can thus be targeted towards youth, although this is not common. In fact, with the exception of India and Bangladesh, which have had such programs for decades, most low- and middle-income countries have only recently started to introduce public works programs.

Unlike other active labor market interventions discussed previously, public works programs have a strong social safety net component. They are intended to mitigate the consequences of covariate and idiosyncratic shocks, and provide poverty relief in the short term. Nonetheless, their labor market objectives are also important. Public works may serve as a bridge to permanent employment, provide a "floor" to the wage rates of unskilled labor, and, in the longer term, improve the incidence and quality of post-program employment if there are returns to additional work experience. On the other hand, public works programs may generate potentially negative effects if they are not carefully designed and implemented. Apart from the substitution, displacement and deadweight losses described earlier, public works programs may create welfare dependency and harm future labor market outcomes if employers associate such programs with lower potential productivity.

Overall, international experience with public works suggests that they are not very effective at improving labor market outcomes overall. Meta-analyses consistently find that they have no effect and even negative effects on employment and earnings (Card et al. 2015, reinforcing conclusions in Betcherman, Dar, and Olivas 2004 and Dar and Tzannatos 1999). Negative effects are found in both high-income and transition economies. Caliendo, Kunn and Schmidl (2011) find that public works harm beneficiaries' post-program employment prospects in Germany, while Rodriguez-Planas and Benus (2010) find no impact in Romania, that is, public works beneficiaries do not exhibit higher rate of employment. They do, however, find a modest reduction in the duration of unemployment. There is some indication of gender effects as well, although it is not clear why: Kluve et al. (1999) and Puhani (1999) find that public works programs in Poland only have negative effects on exiting unemployment for men, but little effect on employment overall. Even where positive effects on transitioning to employment are found in Slovenia (Vodopivec 1999) and Ukraine (Olga 2000), there are indications that these effects are not sustained in the medium or longer term.

Nonetheless, public works programs may have positive, though mostly small effects on labor market outcomes in developing countries. In an evaluation of Argentina's Jefes program, Galasso and Ravallion (2004) find that female beneficiaries worked more hours per week and had higher labor force participation than non-beneficiaries. Elsewhere in the region, public works programs also had positive effects on employment in Chile, Mexico and Colombia (Grosh et al. 2008). Programs appear to have a limited effect in reducing unemployment in the cases of Argentina (Galasso and Ravallion 2004) and South Africa (Expanded Public Works Programme 2008). Apart from questions of design[8] and implementation, the economic context and objectives of these programs also matter. There is more promising evidence for the role of public works programs that have a rural or agricultural focus, such as India's National Rural Employment Guarantee Act (see Azam 2012; Berg et al. 2012; Imbert and Papps 2015) and Bangladesh (Mujeri 2002), which find substantial positive effects on employment and wages. Similarly, labor-intensive programs may have greater chances of success in lifting beneficiaries' prospects. Christian et al. (2015) find that the Labor Intensive Works program in the Republic of Yemen increased the total number of days worked, average wages, and the probability of female employment, and shifted the structure of the workforce away from lowest-paid sectors.

Public works programs typically do not target youth, although they are eligible in many cases. From the limited evidence available, there is some indication that targeted public works programs can be effective in boosting youths' performance in the labor market, at least in the short term. Subsidized part-time employment increased the likelihood of employment for disadvantaged young females in Belgium (Cockx, Goebel, and Robin 2010), and Bulgaria's temporary employment program had a small, positive effect on the chance of having a normal job for those aged less than 30 years (Walsh et al. 2011). It may also be the case that programs specifically targeted towards youth are more effective in the short term. The New York City Summer Employment Program, for example, substantially increased participants' probability of employment and average earnings in the year of program participation, but had no effect on employment and a negative effect on earnings three years following the program (Gelber, Isen, and Kessler 2014).

More recent evidence suggests that workfare programs may have more lasting positive effects on youth if they are combined with skills training and employment services (Acosta and Ramírez 2004). Several countries have begun to experiment with such "public works plus" programs. South Africa's public works program, for example, provides training opportunities beyond skills acquired on the job to prepare participants for longer-term employment, self-employment and/or further education or training. Preliminary results from Cote d'Ivoire suggest that these combined interventions can be effective. Bertrand et al. (2016) find small and positive effects on overall employment and number of hours worked weekly and a strong effect on total earnings for beneficiaries.

Despite the emergence of several new studies since the review by Betcherman et al. (2004), there is still a paucity of evaluations of workfare programs, particularly in low and middle-income countries. Moreover, most public employment programs do not explicitly target youth, and few studies disaggregate the impacts by age cohort to allow for a closer examination of their potential to boost youth employment and labor force participation. Further research could look at factors that influence youth participation in workfare programs, a closer examination of young beneficiaries, and the impact of these programs on their skills development, employability and job quality in the medium and longer term.

Subsidized employment: Wage subsidies

Another way of subsidizing youth employment is to give wage subsidies, either to employers (to reduce the cost of labor) or to workers (to increase their take-home pay). These can take the form of direct transfers or vouchers, reductions in social security contributions or tax credits. The objective is to make the labor market more accessible for groups that have difficulties securing employment, that is, the long-term unemployed, welfare recipients, disabled individuals, underprivileged youth and females. The wage subsidy acts as an incentive for employers to hire members of a certain group by compensating them for the elevated risk and/or training costs of taking them on. Subsidies may therefore increase current employment and earnings for groups whose productivity is expected to be lower than the market wage. They might also have longer-term effects on future employment and earnings, to the extent that on-the-job training is useful. On the other hand, wage subsidies might hurt future employment and earnings prospects if they signal a potential employee's low productivity, and result in the negative externalities described earlier.

Overall, wage subsidies have positive effects on employment in industrialized countries, particularly the United States where several government schemes have been introduced. The Targeted Jobs Tax Credit scheme increased employment of disadvantaged 23–24 year olds by 3.4 pp or 7.7 percent in the late 1980s (Katz 1998), largely due to a significant windfall effect (Bishop and Montgomery 1993). The Earned Income Tax Credit scheme was similarly successful, leading to a 3.4 percent increase in disposable income and 5.6 percent increase in employment for welfare recipients with more than two children (Hotz, Imbens, and Klerman 2006). Similar payroll tax credit schemes have boosted employment in Belgium (Goos and Konings 2007), and reduced unemployment in Sweden (Carling and Richardson; Forslund, Johansson, and Lindqvist 2004; Fredriksson and Johansson 2003; Sianesi 2004), Germany (Eichler and Lechner 2000) and Switzerland (Gerfin and Lechner 2002). One caveat, however, is that jobs created may not necessarily be of high quality. Crepon and Desplatz find that larger subsidies in France are associated with faster growth in total employment, but they cannot distinguish between low-wage and high-wage job growth. An earlier study of the same scheme by Kramarz and Philippon (2001) found no evidence of increased employment when the payroll tax subsidy was increased. Similarly, Huttunen, Pirttilä, and Uusitalo (2010) find that wage subsidies have no effect on employment in Finland, but are associated with a small increase in hours worked in the industrial sector.

Few studies consider the effect of wage subsidies in transition and developing economies, and available evidence presents a mixed record. Wage subsidies have no effect on employment in the Slovak Republic and Poland, and in some cases a negative effect on transitioning to employment. On the other hand, an evaluation of the Proempleo program in Argentina found that receiving wage subsidy vouchers significantly increased employment in the first 18 months by 8–9 percentage points and reduced reliance on workfare by a similar magnitude for women and youth (Galasso, Ravallion, and Salvia 2004).

Despite the limited evidence, the effects of wage subsidies on labor market outcomes for youth appear to be promising. The wage subsidy component of the New Deal program in the UK drove most of success of the program in reducing unemployment rates among young males aged 18–24 years (Blundell et al. 2004; Van Reenen 2003). Evaluations of wage subsidies in Sweden have also found positive though small effects on the employment probability and earnings of similarly aged youths.

Although most studies do not disaggregate the impacts by age, there is some indication that wage subsidies may be more effective for older cohorts who are more likely to be in tertiary rather than secondary education. Payroll tax subsidies are found to have the largest positive effects on the employment probabilities of low-wage workers aged 25–30 compared to younger groups in France (Fougere, Kramarz, and Magnac 2000). Similarly, Chile's Subsidio al Empleo Joven had more positive effects on the likelihood of securing a formal job and labor force participation on those aged 20–24 compared to those aged 18–19 years (Universidad de Chile 2012). Similarly, Levinsohn et al. (2014) finds that workers aged 20–24 benefit substantially in terms of wage employment from South Africa's wage subsidies, although the program had no effect on the aggregate group aged 18–29. These findings suggest that wage subsidies may be effective in helping disadvantaged workers find employment, but that their low skill levels will most likely be a barrier in finding better-paid jobs. Indeed, most studies of wage subsidy schemes find no significant impact on earnings or current incomes in South Africa and Argentina (Galasso, Ravallion, and Salvia 2004; Levinsohn et al. 2014). It is possible, however, that they have an impact on groups that would otherwise not be working at all; Egebark and Kaunitz (2014) find that the Job Training Partnership Act did not change earnings of youth or adult men, but raised women's earnings by about 15 percent over 30-month period—especially for welfare recipients.

Even if wage subsidies have the potential to boost labor market outcomes for youth, it is important to note that these effects may not be sustained in the medium and long term. In a recent study of wage subsidy vouchers in Jordan, Groh et al. (2016) conclude that the program had a substantial impact on employment in the short run, but this effect dissipates and becomes insignificant after the vouchers expire. By contrast, Levinsohn et al. (2014) find a positive and substantial effect on wage employment in South Africa that is sustained two years later. Further research on the substitution and displacement effects of these programs is also needed. Dar and Tzannatos (1999) and Martin (2000) conclude that wage and employment subsidies have substantial deadweight and substitution risks, and there is some evidence that the Subsidio al Empleo Joven displaced older workers, especially in microenterprises.

NOTES

1. Although the standard OECD definition of youth spans individuals aged 18–24 years old, Brazil's Youth Statute (2013) defines youth as those aged 15–29 years old. This review takes varying definitions of youth into account, but ensures that studies are comparable as much as possible in terms of age cohort.

2. See, for example, the Fight for 15 campaign, which aims to raise the minimum wage to $15 an hour in all U.S. states. http://fightfor15.org/.

3. See the discussion in Neumark and Wascher (2007).

4. The percentage of workforce covered by collective agreements, which can cover non-union members and unaffiliated employers.

5. The percentage of the workforce in unions.

6. Meta-analyses of entrepreneurship support programs are generally restricted to 15 or fewer studies (see) and few of these studies focus exclusively on youth.

7. Valerio et al (2014) distinguish between *entrepreneurship education*, which aims to build entrepreneurial mindsets or skills among students of secondary and tertiary education for general purposes, and *entrepreneurship training*, which focuses more specifically on potential/current entrepreneurs i.e. those who are already keen to start a new or expand an existing business. Youth who are neither in education nor training are more likely to fall into the second category, whereas those who are in tertiary education may benefit from either type of program.

8. Some design challenges include the wage rate, number of hours worked, labor intensity, targeting method, timing, gender sensitivity, community involvement, financing and implementation responsibilities and local government involvement.

BIBLIOGRAPHY

Aaronson, D., E. French, I. Sorkin, and T. To. 2017. "Industry Dynamics and the Minimum Wage: A Putty-Clay Approach." *International Economic Review* 59:51–84. doi:10.1111/iere.12262.

Acosta, O., and J.C. Ramírez. 2004. "Las redes de protección social: modelo incompleto." Financiamiento del desarrollo series, No. 141 (LC/L.2067-P), Santiago, Chile, Economic Commission for Latin America and the Caribbean (ECLAC). United Nations publication, Sales No.S.04.II.G.10.

Adascalitei, D., S. Khatiwada, M.A. Malo, and C. Pigatti Morano. 2015. "Employment Protection and Collective Bargaining During the Great Recession: A Comprehensive Review of International Evidence." *Revista de Economía Laboral* 12: 50–87.

Adoho, F., S. Chakravarty, D. T. Korkoyah Jr, M. Lundberg and A. Tasneem. 2014. The Impact of an Adolescent Girls Employment Program: The EPAG Project in Liberia. World Bank Policy Research Working Paper 6832, World Bank.

Aedo, C. and S. Núñez. 2004. "The Impact of Training Policies in Latin America and the Caribbean: The Case of Programa Joven." IDB Working Paper No. 188. Retrieved from: https://dx.doi.org/10.2139/ssrn.1814739.

Aidt, T., and Z. Tzannatos. 2002. *Unions and Collective Bargaining. Economic Effects in a Global Environment*. Washington DC: World Bank.

Alatas, V. and L.A. Cameron. 2008. "The Impact of Minimum Wages on Employment in a Low-Income Country: A Quasi-Natural Experiment in Indonesia." *Industrial and Labor Relations Review* 61(2): 201–223.

Allegretto, S. A., A. Dube, and M. Reich. 2011. "Do Minimum Wages Really Reduce Teen Employment? Accounting for Heterogeneity and Selectivity in State Panel Data." *Industrial Relations: A Journal of Economy and Society* 50 (2): 205–40.

Allegretto, S., A. Dube, M. Reich, and B. Zipperer. 2017. "Credible Research Designs for Minimum Wage Studies: A Response to Neumark, Salas and Wascher." *Industrial and Labor Relations Review* 70(3): 559–592.

Almeida, Rita, and Pedro Carneiro. 2009. "Mandated Benefits, Employment, and Inequality in a Dual Economy." Policy Research Working Paper Series 5119, The World Bank. https://openknowledge.worldbank.org/handle/10986/4311.

Alzúa, M. L., and P. Brassiolo. 2006. *The Impact of Training Policies in Argentina: An Evaluation of Proyecto Joven*. Inter-American Development Bank. Washington DC: Inter-American Development Bank.

Arango, C. A. A., and A. Pachón. 2004. *Minimum Wages in Colombia: Holding the Middle with a Bite on the Poor*. Banco de la República. Retrieved from http://www.banrep.gov.co/docum/ftp/borra280.pdf.

Arbache, J.S. 1998. "The Impact of Unions on Wages in Brazilian Manufacturing." Studies in Economics 9805, School of Economics, University of Kent. Retrieved from: https://ideas .repec.org/p/ukc/ukcedp/9805.html.

Arpaia, A., P. Cardoso, A. Kiss, K. Van Herck, and A. Vandeplas. 2017. "Statutory Minimum Wages in the EU: Institutional Settings and Macroeconomic Implications." IZA Policy Paper No. 124. Bonn: Institute for the Study of Labor.

Arulampalam, W., P. Gregg, and M. Gregory. 2001. "Unemployment Scarring." *Economic Journal* 111 (475): 577–84.

Attanasio, O., A. Kugler, and C. Meghir. 2011. "Subsidizing Vocational Training for Disadvantaged Youth in Colombia: Evidence from a Randomized Trial." *American Economic Journal: Applied Economics* 3 (3): 188–220.

Azam, M. 2012. "The Impact of Indian Job Guarantee Scheme on Labor Market Outcomes: Evidence from a Natural Experiment." IZA DP 6548, Bonn: Institute for the Study of Labor. Institute for the Study of Labor.

Baccaro, L., and D. Rei. 2005. *Institutional Determinants of Unemployment in OECD Countries: A Time Series Cross-Section Analysis (1960-98)*. Geneva: International Institute for Labour Studies.

Bandiera, O., N. Buehren, R. Burgess, M. Goldstein, S. Gulesci, I. Rasul, and M. Sulaiman. 2014. "Women's Empowerment in Action: Evidence from a Randomized Control Trial in Africa." Suntory and Toyota International Centres for Economics and Related Disciplines, LSE. Retrieved from: http://www.ucl.ac.uk/~uctpimr/research/ELA.pdf.

Banerji, A., S. Saksonovs, H. Lin, and R. Blavy. 2014. "Youth Unemployment in Advanced Economies in Europe: Searching for Solutions." IMF Staff Discussion Note SDN/14/11. Washington, DC: International Monetary Fund.

Baranowska, A., and M. Gebel. 2010. "The Determinants of Youth Temporary Employment in the Enlarged Europe." *European Societies* 12(3): 367–390.

Barros, R. P. D., and M. D. Carvalho. 2002. *Políticas ativas de emprego e renda*. Nota Tecnica, Mercado de Trabalho, Instituto de Pesquisa de Economia Aplicada (IPEA). http:// repositorio.ipea.gov.br/handle/11058/5542.

Barbieri, P. 2009. "Flexible employment and inequality in Europe." *European Sociological Review* 25(6):621–628.

Bassanini, A., and R. Duval. 2006. The Determinants of Unemployment across OECD Countries: Reassessing the Role of Policies and Institutions. *OECD Economic Studies* 42 (1): 7.

Belot, M. and J.C. van Ours.

Bertola, G., F.D. Blau, and L.M. Kahn. 2002. "Labor market institutions and demographic employment patterns." NBER Working paper 9043. Cambridge, MA: NBER.

Berg, E., S. Bhattacharyya, R. Durgam, and M. Ramachandra. 2012. "Can Rural Public Works Affect Agricultural Wages? Evidence from India." Work.

Bertola, G. 1990. "Job Security, Employment and Wages." *European Economic Review* 34 (4): 851–79.

Bertola, G., F. D. Blau, and L. M. Kahn. 2007. Labor Market Institutions and Demographic Employment Patterns." *Journal of Population Economics* 20 (4): 833–67.

Bertrand, M., B. Crépon, A. Marguerie, and P. Premand. 2016. "Short Term Impacts of Labour Intensive Public Works for Youths in Cote d'Ivoire." Slides prepared for Workshop on Evidence from Randomized Control Trials in Youth Employment. ILO, Geneva, July 12. http://www.ilo .org/wcmsp5/groups/public/---ed_emp/documents/presentation/wcms_506174.pdf.

Besley, T. J., and R. Burgess. 2004. "Can Labour Regulation Hinder Economic Performance? Evidence from India." *The Quarterly Journal of Economics* 119(1): 91–134.

Betcherman, G. 2012. "Labor Market Institutions: A review of the Literature." World Bank Policy research Working Paper 6276. Washington DC: World Bank.

——. 2015. "Labor Market regulations: What Do We know about their Impacts in Developing Countries?" *The World Bank Research Observer* 30 (1): 124–53.

Betcherman, G., M. Godfrey, S. Puerto, F. Rother, A. Stavreska. "A Review of Interventions to Support Young Workers: Findings of the Youth Employment Inventory." World Bank SP Discussion Paper No. 0715, Washington, DC: World Bank.

Betcherman, G., M. Godfrey, S. Puerto, F. rother, and A. Stavreska. 2007. *Global Inventory of Interventions to Support Young Workers: Synthesis Report*. Washington, DC: The World Bank.

Betcherman, G., A. Dar, and K. Olivas. 2004. *Impacts of Active Labor Market Programs: New Evidence from Evaluations with Particular Attention to Developing and Transition Countries*. Social Protection, World Bank. Washington, DC: World Bank.

Bhorat, H., A. Cassim, R. Kanbur, B. Stanwix, and D. Yu. 2016. "Minimum Wages and Youth: the Case of South Africa." *Journal of African Economies*, 25(1): 61–102.

Bishop, J. H., and M. Montgomery. 1993. "Does the Targeted Jobs Tax Credit Create Jobs at Subsidized Firms?" *Industrial Relations: A Journal of Economy and Society* 32 (3): 289–306.

Blanchflower, D.G., and R.B. Freeman. 2000. "The Declining Economic Status of Young Workers in OECD Countries." In Youth Employment and Joblessness in Advanced Countries, eds. Blanchflower, D.G., and R.B. Freeman. Chicago: University of Chicago Press: 19–56.

Blanchflower, D. G. 2006. "A Cross-Country Study of Union Membership," Discussion Paper Series IZA DP 2016, Bonn: Institute for the Study of Labor.

Blanchflower, D. G., and A. Bryson. 2003. "What Effect Do Unions Have on Wages Now and Would 'What Do Unions Do' Be Surprised?" w9973, National Bureau of Economic Research. Cambridge, MA: NBER.

Blattman, C., N. Fiala, and S. Martinez. 2012. "Employment Generation in Rural Africa: Mid-Term Results from an Experimental Evaluation of the Youth Opportunities Program in Northern Uganda." DIW Berlin Discussion Paper 1201. Retrieved from: https://ssrn.com/abstract=2030866.

Blattman, C., E. Green, J. Annan, and J. Jamison. 2013. "Building Women's Economic and Social Empowerment through Enterprise: An Experimental Assessment of the Women's Income Generating Support (WINGS) Program in Uganda." LOGICA Study Series No. 1. Washington, DC: World Bank.

———.2014. "Generating Skilled Self-Employment in Developing Countries: Experimental Evidence from Uganda." *The Quarterly Journal of Economics* 697: 752.

Blattman, C., and L. Ralston. 2015. "Generating Employment in Poor and Fragile States: Evidence from Labor Market and Entrepreneurship Programs." Retrieved from: https://papers.ssrn.com/sol3/papers.cfm?abstract_id=2622220.

Blundell, R., M. C. Dias, C. Meghir, and J. Reenen. 2004. "Evaluating the Employment Impact of a Mandatory Job Search Program." *Journal of the European Economic Association* 2 (4): 569–606.

Boone, J. and J. Van Ours. 2004. "Effective Active Labor Market Policies." IZA DP 1335, Bonn: Institute for the Study of Labor.

Breen, R. 2005. "Explaining Cross-National Variation in Youth Unemployment. Market and Institutional Factors." *European Sociology Review* 21(2): 125–134.

Broecke, Stijn, Forti Alessia, and Marieke Vandeweyer. 2017. "The Effects of Minimum Wages on Employment in Emerging Economies: A Literature Review."

Broecke, S., and M. Vandeweyer. 2015. "Doubling the Minimum Wage and its Effect on Labor Market Outcomes: Evidence from Brazil." Mimeo. Retrieved from: http://conference.iza.org/conference_files/worldb2015/broecke_s8754.pdf.

Brown, C., C. Gilroy, and A. Kohen. 1982. "The Effect of the Minimum Wage on Employment and Unemployment." *Journal of Economic literature* 20 (2): 487–528.

Bustamante, N.R., A. M. Uribe, and C. O. Vargas. 2015. "Maternity and Labor Markets: Impact of Legislation in Colombia." IDB Working Paper Series IDB-WP-583, Inter-American Development Bank. Washington DC.

Caliendo, M., S. Künn, and R. Schmidl. 2011. "Fighting Youth Unemployment: The Effects of Active Labor Market Policies." IZA DP 6222, Institute for the Study of Labor. Bonn.

Campolieti, M., T. Fang, and M. Gunderson. 2005. "Minimum Wage Impacts on Youth Employment Transitions, 1993–1999." *Canadian Journal of Economics/Revue canadienne d'économique* 38 (1): 81–104.

Campos, R.M., G. Esquivel, and A.S. Santillán. 2015. "El impacto del salario mínimo en los ingresos y el empleo en México." *Serie Estudios y Perspectivas 162*. Mexico: CEPAL.

Campos. A.G. 2016. "Sindicatos no Brasil: o que esperar no futuro próximo?" Texto para discussão 2262. Brasília: IPEA.

Canelas, C. 2014. "Minimum wage and informality in Ecuador." WIDER Working Paper 2014/006, United Nations University World Institute for Development Economics Research. Helsinki: UNU-WIDER.

Card, D. 1992. "Do Minimum Wages Reduce Employment? A Case Study of California, 1987–89." *Industrial & Labor Relations Review* 46 (1): 38–54.

Card, D., and A. B. Krueger. 1994. "Minimum Wages and Employment: A Case Study of the Fast-Food Industry in New Jersey and Pennsylvania." *The American Economic Review* 84 (4): 772–93.

Card, D., J. Kluve, and A. Weber. 2010. "Active Labour Market Policy Evaluations: A Meta-Analysis." *The Economic Journal* 120 (548): F452–77.

Card, D., P. Ibarrarán, F. Regalia, D. Rosas-Shady, and Y. Soares. 2011. The Labor Market Impacts of Youth Training in the Dominican Republic." *Journal of Labor Economics* 29 (2): 267–300.

Card, D., J. Kluve, and A. Weber. 2015. "What Works? A Meta Analysis of Recent Active Labor Market Program Evaluations." IZA Discussion Paper 9236. Bonn: Institute for the Study of Labor.

Cardoso, A.R. 2009. "Long-Term Impact of Youth Minimum Wages: Evidence from Two Decades of Individual Longitudinal Data." IZA Discussion Paper No. 4236, Institute for the Study of Labor (IZA). Bonn, Germany: IZA.

Cassoni, A., S.G. Allen, and G.J. Labadie. "Unions and Employment in Uruguay." Chapter 8 in Law and Employment: Lessons from Latin America and the Caribbean, eds. Heckman, J., and C. Pagés. Chicago: University of Chicago Press.

Céspedes, N. and A. Sánchez. 2013. "Minimum Wage and Job Mobility." Working Papers 2013-012, Banco Central de Reserva del Perú. Retrieved from: https://ideas.repec.org/p/rbp /wpaper/2013-012.html.

Chakravarty, S., M. Lundberg, P. N. Danchev, and J. Zenker. 2015. *The Role of Training Programs for Youth Employment in Nepal: Impact Evaluation Report on the Employment Fund*. Washington, DC: World Bank.

Chletsos, Michael and Georgios P. Giotis. 2015. "The Employment Effect of Minimum Wage Using 77 International Studies since 1992: A Meta-Analysis." MPRA Paper 61321, University Library of Munich, Germany.

Cho, Y., and M. Honorati. 2014. "Entrepreneurship Programs in Developing Countries: A Meta Regression Analysis." *Labour Economics* 28: 110–30.

Cho, Y., D. Kalomba, A. M. Mobarak, and V. Orozco. 2013. "Gender Differences in the Effects of Vocational Training: Constraints on Women and Drop-Out Behavior." IZA DP 7408, Institute for the Study of Labor. Bonn.

Christian, S., A. de Janvry, D. Egel, and E. Sadoulet. 2015. "Quantitative Evaluation of the Social Fund for Development Labor Intensive Works Program (LIWP)." Department of Agricultural and Resource Economics, UC Berkeley, Working Paper Series. Retrieved from: http://escholarship.org/uc/item/2s5230h2.

Clemens, J. 2015. "The Minimum Wage and the Great Recession: Evidence from the Current Population Survey." NBER Working Paper 21830. Cambridge, MA: National Bureau of Economic Research.

Cockx, B., C. Goebel, and S. Robin. 2013. "Can Income Support for Part-Time Workers Serve as a Stepping-Stone to Regular Jobs? An Application to Young Long-Term Unemployed Women." *Empirical Economics* 44 (1): 189–229.

Corseuil, C. H., M. Foguel, G. Gonzaga, and E. P. Ribeiro. 2012, "The Effect of an Apprenticeship Program on Labor Market Outcomes of Youth in Brazil." Mimeo presented in the 7th IZA/ World Bank Conference: Employment and Development, New Delhi. November 6, 2012.

Crépon, B. and R. Desplatz. 2002. *Evaluation of the Effects of Payroll Tax Subsidies for Low Wage Workers*. CREST-INSEE. www.crest.fr/pageperso/dr/crepon/payrolltax.pdf.

Crépon, B., E. Duflo, M. Gurgand, R. Rathelot, and P. Zamora. 2013, "Do Labour Market Policies Have Displacement Effects? Evidence from a Clustered Randomized Experiment." *Quarterly Journal of Economics* 128 (2): 531–580.

Cruces, G., A. Ham, and M. Viollaz. 2012. "Scarring effects of youth unemployment and informality: Evidence from Argentina and Brazil." CEDLAS, Universidad Nacional de La Plata. Retrieved from: http://conference.iza.org/conference_files/YULMI2012/viollaz_m8017.pdf.

Dar, A., and Z. Tzannatos, Z. 1999. *Active Labor Market Programs: A Review of the Evidence from Evaluations*. Social Protection, World Bank. Washington DC: World Bank.

De Mel, S., D. McKenzie, and C. Woodruff. 2014. "Business Training and Female Enterprise Start-Up, Growth, and Dynamics: Experimental Evidence from Sri Lanka." *Journal of Development Economics* 106: 199–210.

Decker, P. T., R. B. Olson, L. Freeman, and D. H. Klepinger. 2000. Assisting Unemployment Insurance Claimants: the Long-Term Impact of the Job Search Assistance Demonstration." Report prepared for the U.S. Department of Labor, Employment and Training Amdinistration, Unemployment Insurance Service. https://wdr.doleta.gov/owsdrr/00-2/00-02.pdf.

Delajara, M., S. Freije, and I. Soloaga. 2006. "An Evaluation of Training for the Unemployed in Mexico." Working Paper OVE/WP-09/06. Washington, DC: Inter-American Development Bank.

Dickens, R., R. Riley, and D. Wilkinson. 2014. "The UK minimum wage at 22 years of age: a regression discontinuity approach." *Journal of the Royal Statistical Society: Series A (Statistics in Society)*, 177(1): 95–114.

Díaz, J. J., and M. Jaramillo. 2006. "An Evaluation of the Peruvian Youth Labor Training Program - PROJOVEN." Working Paper: OVE/WP-10/06. Washington, DC: Inter-American Development Bank.

Díaz, J. J., and D. Rosas Shady. 2016. "Impact Evaluation of the Job Youth Training Program Projoven." IDB Working Paper Series 693. Washington, DC: Inter-American Development Bank.

Del Carpio, X., H. Nguyen, and L.C. Wang. 2012. "Does the Minimum Wage Affect Employment? Evidence from the Manufacturing Sector in Indonesia." Policy Research Working Paper, no. 6147. Washington, DC: World Bank.

Downes, A., N. Mamingi, and R. M. B. Antoine. 2004. Labor Market Regulation and Employment in the Caribbean. In *Law and Employment: Lessons from Latin America and the Caribbean*, pp. 517–52. (eds) J. Heckman and C. Páges. Chicago: University of Chicago Press.

Dube, A., W. Lester, and M. Reich. 2010. "Minimum Wage Effects Across State Borders: Estimates Using Contiguous Countries." The Review of Economics and Statistics 92(4): 945–964. Cambridge, MA: MIT Press.

Egebark, J. and N. Kaunitz. 2013. "Do Payroll Tax Cuts Raise Youth Employment?" Working Paper Series 2013:27, IFAU—Institute for Evaluation of Labour Market and Education Policy. Retrieved from: https://papers.ssrn.com/sol3/papers.cfm?abstract_id=2369989.

Ehlert, C. R., J. Kluve, and S. Schaffner. 2012. "Temporary Work as an Active Labor Market Policy: Evaluating an Innovative Program for Disadvantage Youths." IZA Discussion Paper 6670. Bonn: Institute for the Study of Labor.

Eichler, M. and M. Lechner. 2000. "Some Econometric Evidence on the Effectiveness of Active Labour Market Programmes in East Germany." Working Paper 318, William Davidson Institute. https://core.ac.uk/download/pdf/3102800.pdf.

Elias, Victor, Fernando Ruiz, Ricardo Cossa, and David Bravo. 2004. "An Econometric Cost-Benefit Analysis of Argentina's Youth Training Program." IDB Working Paper R-482. Washington, DC: Inter-American Development Bank.

Esping-Andersen, G. 2000. "Who Is Harmed by Labour Market Regulations? Quantitative Evidence." In *Why deregulate labour markets?* Oxford University Press: 66–98.

Eurofound. 2012. "NEETS Young people not in employment, education or training: Characteristics, costs and policy responses in Europe." Luxembourg: Publications Office of the European Union.

Fadlon, Y. 2015. "The Effects of an Increase in Minimum Wage on Labor Market Transitions: Evidence from NLSY." Retrieved from: http://sites.cgu.edu/fadlony/files/2013/10/ILRR_2015.pdf.

Fajnzylber, P. 2001. "Minimum Wage Effects throughout the Wage Distribution: Evidence from Brazil's Formal and Informal Sectors." Cedeplar Working Paper 151, Universidade Federal de Minas Gerais. Fajnzylber, Pablo, Minimum Wage Effects Throughout the Wage Distribution: Evidence from Brazil's Formal and Informal Sectors (May 2001). CEDEPLAR Working Paper No. 151. Retrieved from: https://ssrn.com/abstract=269622.

Fang, T. and C. Lin. 2013. "Minimum Wages and Employment in China." IZA Discussion Paper No. 7813. Bonn: Institute of Labor Economics.

Fazio, M. V., R. Fernández-Coto, and L. Ripani. 2016. *Apprenticeships for the XXI Century: A Model for Latin America and the Caribbean?* Washington, DC: Inter-American Development Bank.

Feldman, H. 2009. "The unemployment effects of labor regulation around the world." *Journal of Comparative Economics* 37: 76–90.

Foguel, M.N. 1998. "Uma Avaliação dos Efeitos do Salário Mínimo sobre o Mercado de Trabalho no Brasil." Texto para discussão IPEA. Brasília: IPEA.

Foguel, M., G. Ulyssea, and C.H. Corseuil. "Salário Mínimo e Mercado do Trabalho no Brasil." Chapter 14 in *Brasil em Desenvolvimento 2014: Estado, Planejamento e Políticas Públicas*, Vol. 1. Eds. Monasterio, L.M., M. Côrtes Neri, and S. Soares. Brasília: IPEA.

Fontes, M., and K. Margolies. 2010. "Youth and Unions." Retrieved 25 July 2016 from Cornell University, ILR School site: http://digitalcommons.ilr.cornell.edu/workingpapers/104.

Forslund, A., P. Johansson, and L. Lindqvist. 2004. "Employment Subsidies-A Fast Lane from Unemployment to Work?" Institute for Labour Market Policy Evaluation (IFAU). Retrieved from: https://econpapers.repec.org/paper/hhsifauwp/2004_5f018.htm.

Fougere, D., F. Kramarz, and T. Magnac. 2000. "Youth Employment Policies in France." *European Economic Review* 44 (4): 928–42.

Franklin, S. 2014. "Location, Search Costs and Youth Unemployment: The Impact of a Randomized Transport Subsidy in Urban Ethiopia." Retrieved from: http://sites.bu.edu/neudc/files/2014/10/paper_375.pdf.

Fredriksson, P., and P. Johansson. 2003. "Employment, Mobility and Active Labor Market Programs." Working Paper Series No. 2003:3, IFAU - Institute for Evaluation of Labour Market and Education Policy. Retrieved from: https://EconPapers.repec.org/RePEc:hhs:ifauwp:2003_003.

Freeman, R. B. 2009. "Labor Regulations, Unions, and Social Protection in Developing Countries: Market Distortions or Efficient Institutions?" w14789, National Bureau of Economic Research.

Freeman, R. B., and J. L. Medoff. 1984. "What Do Unions Do." *Industrial and Labor Relations Review* 38: 244.

Freeman, R.B. 2010. "Labor Regulations, Unions and Social Protection in Developing Countries: Market Distortions or Efficient Institutions?" In Dani Rodrik and Mark Rosenszweig (eds.), Handbook of Development Economics Vol. 5: 4657-4702. Amsterdam: Elsevier.

Frumento, P., F. Mealli, B. Pacini, and D. B. Rubin. 2012. "Evaluating the Effect of Training on Wages in the Presence of Noncompliance, Nonemployment, and Missing Outcome Data." *Journal of the American Statistical Association* 107 (498): 450–66.

Galasso, E., and M. Ravallion. 2004. "Social Protection in a Crisis: Argentina's Plan Jefes y Jefas." *The World Bank Economic Review* 18 (3): 367–99.

Galasso, E., M. Ravallion, and A. Salvia. 2004. Assisting the Transition from Workfare to Work: A Randomized Experiment. *Industrial and Labor Relations Review* 58 (1): 128–42.

Gelber, A., A. Isen, and J. B. Kessler. 2014. "The Effects of Youth Employment: Evidence from New York City Summer Youth Employment Program Lotteries." Working Paper 20810, National Bureau of Economic Research. Cambridge, MA: NBER.

Gerfin, M., and M. Lechner. 2002. "A Microeconometric Evaluation of the Active Labour Market Policy in Switzerland." *The Economic Journal* 112 (482): 854–93.

Gonçalves, S. and N.A. Menezes Filho. 2016. "O salário mínimo e a oferta de trabalho das famílias pobres: uma abordagem coletiva com os dados da PNAD Contínua (2012-2015)." Anais do XLIII Encontro Nacional de Economia 237, ANPEC. Retrieved from: https://ideas.repec.org/p/anp/en2015/237.html.

Goos, M. and J. Konings. 2007. "The Impact of Payroll Tax Reductions on Employment and Wages: A Natural Experiment Using Firm Level Data." Discussion Paper 178/2007, LICOS Centre for Institutions and Economic Performance, Leuven, Belgium.

Gorry, A. 2013. "Minimum Wages and Youth Unemployment." *European Economic Review* 64: 57–75.

Groh, M., N. Krishnan, D. McKenzie, and T. Vishwanath, T. 2016. "The Impact of Soft Skills Training on Female Youth Employment: Evidence from a Randomized Experiment in Jordan." *IZA Journal of Labor and Development* 5: 9.

Grau, N. and O. Landerretche. 2011. "The Labor Impact of Minimum Wages: A Method for Estimating the Effect in Emerging Economies Using Chilean Panel Data." Working Papers, University of Chile, Department of Economics. Retrieved from: http://www.econ.uchile.cl /uploads/publicacion/80a7ba9cf917b18adfa52210cde6a29bac9e0849.pdf

Grosh, M., C. Del Ninno, E. Tesliuc, and A. Ouerghi. 2008. *For Protection and Promotion: The Design and Implementation of Effective Safety Nets*. World Bank. Washington, DC: World Bank.

Heckman, J. J., R. J. LaLonde, and J. A. Smith. 1999. "The Economics and Econometrics of Active Labor Market Programs." *Handbook of Labor Economics* 3: 1865–2097.

Heckman, J. J. and C. Pagés. 2000. "The Cost of Job Security Regulation: Evidence from Latin American Labor Markets." *Journal of the Latin American and Caribbean Economic Association* 1, 1(Fall 2000): 109–154.

Hernández, G., and F. J. Lasso. 2003. "Estimación de la relación entre salario mínimo y empleo en Colombia: 1984-2000." *Revista de Economía del Rosario* 6 (2). Retrieved from: https:// revistas.urosario.edu.co/index.php/economia/article/view/1018.

Hernández Diaz, G., and E. Pinzon Garcia. 2006. "El efecto del salario mínimo sobre el empleo y los ingresos." *Archivos de economía* 316, Departamento Nacional de Planeación. Retrieved from: https://ideas.repec.org/p/col/000118/011229.html.

Hicks, J. H., M. Kremer, I. Mbiti, and E. Miguel. 2013. "Vocational Education in Kenya: Evidence from a Randomized Evaluation among Youth." Nashville, TN: Vanderbilt University.

Hirshleifer, S., D. McKenzie, R. Almeida, and C. Ridao-Cano. 2015. "The Impact of Vocational Training for the Unemployed: Experimental Evidence from Turkey." *Economic Journal* 126(597): 2115–2146.

Honorati, M. 2015. "The Impact of Private Sector Internship and Training on Urban Youth in Kenya." World Bank Policy Research Working Paper 7404. Washington, DC: World Bank.

Hotz, V. J., G. W. Imbens, and J. A. Klerman. 2006. "Evaluating the Differential Effects of Alternative Welfare-to-Work Training Components: A Re-Analysis of the California GAIN Program." w11939, National Bureau of Economic Research. Cambridge, MA: NBER.

Huang, Y., P. Loungani, and G. Wang. 2014. "Minimum Wages and Firm Employment: Evidence from China." Federal Reserve Bank of Dallas Globalization and Monetary Policy Institute Working Paper No. 173. Retrieved from: https://www.dallasfed.org/~/media/documents /institute/wpapers/2014/0173.pdf.

Huttunen, K., J. Pirttilä, and R. Uusitalo. 2013. "The Employment Effects of Low-Wage Subsidies." *Journal of Public Economics* 97: 49–60.

Hyslop, D. and S. Stillman. 2004. "Youth Minimum Wage Reform and the Labour Market." IZA Discussion Paper No. 1091. Bonn: Institute for the Study of Labor.

Ibarrarán, P., J. Kluve, L. Ripani, and D. Rosas Shady. 2015. *Experimental Evidence on the Long Term Impacts of a Youth Training Program*. IDB Working Paper Series, No. 657. Washington, DC: Inter-American Development Bank.

ILO. (2015). Juventud y Organizaciones Sindicales en América Latina y el Caribe. Retrieved from: http://www.ilo.org/americas/temas/tripartismo/WCMS_380963/lang--es/index .htm.

Imbert, C. and J. Papps. 2015. "Labor Market Effects of Social Programs: Evidence from India's Employment Guarantee." *American Economic Journal: Applied Economics* 7 (2): 233–63.

Independent Evaluation Group. 2013. "Youth Employment Programs: An Evaluation of World Bank and IFC Support." Washington, DC: World Bank.

International Labour Organization, (ILO). 2017. *Global Employment Trends for Youth 2017: Paths to a better working future*. International Labour Office, Geneva.

Jacobson, L., and I. Petta. 2000. "Measuring the Effect of Public Labor Exchange (PLX) Referrals and Placements in Washington and Oregon." OWS Occasional Paper 6, Prepared for Washington State Employment Security Department. Retrieved from: https://ows.doleta.gov/dmstree/op/op2k/op_06-00.pdf

Jales, H. 2015. "Estimating the effects of the minimum wage in a developing country: a density discontinuity design approach." Global Labour Organization (GLO) Discussion Paper, No. 54. Retrieved from: http://hdl.handle.net/10419/156725.

Jardim, E., M.C. Long, R. Plotnick, E. van Inwegen, J. Vigdor, and H. Wething. 2017. "Minimum Wage Increases, Wages and Low-wage Employment: Evidence from Seattle." NBER Working Paper No, 23532. Cambridge, MA: NBER.

Jensen, R. 2012. "Do Labor Market Opportunities Affect Young Women's Work and Family Decisions? Experimental Evidence from India." *The Quarterly Journal of Economics* 127(2): 753–792.

Jimeno, J.F., and D. Rodriguez-Palenzuela. 2002. "Youth Employment in the OECD: Demographic Shifts, Labour Market Institutions and Macroeconomic Shocks." Working Paper No. 155. Frankfurt: European Central Bank.

Johnson, N., and P. Jarley. 2005. "Unions as social capital: the impact of trade union youth programmes on young workers' political and community engagement." Transfer: *European Review of Labour and Research* 11(4): 605–616.

Kabátek, J. 2015. "Happy Birthday, You're Fired! The Effects of Age-Dependent Minimum Wage on Youth Employment Flows in the Netherlands." IZA Discussion Paper 9528. Bonn: Institute for the Study of Labor.

Kahn, L.M. 2007. "The Impact of Employment Protection Mandates on Demographic Temporary Employment Patterns: International Microeconomic Evidence." *The Economic Journal* 117(521): 333–356.

Kahn, L. M. 2012. "Labor Market Policy: A Comparative View on the Costs and Benefits of Labor Market Flexibility." *Journal of Policy Analysis and Management* 31 (1): 94–110.

Kalenkoski, Charlene. 2016. "The Effects of Minimum Wages on Youth Employment and Income." *IZA World of Labor* 243.

Karakitsios, A. 2016. "The Effect of Subminimum Wage Introduction on Employment in Greece." Athens University of Economics and Business, mimeo. Retrieved from: http://www.lse.ac.uk/europeanInstitute/research/hellenicObservatory/Events/HO%20PhD%20Symposia/7th-Symposium/Documents/Papers/Karakitsios%20Alexandros.pdf.

Katz, Larry. 1998. "Wage Subsidies for the Disadvantaged." In *Generating Jobs*, (eds) R. Freeman and P. Gottschalk. pp. 21–53. New York: Russell Sage Foundation.

Katz, L. F., and A. B. Krueger. 1992. "The Effect of the Minimum Wage on the Fast-Food Industry." *Industrial & Labor Relations Review* 46 (1): 6–21.

Kluve, J., H. Lehmann, and C. Schmidt. 1999. "Active Labor Market Policies in Poland: Human Capital Enhancement, Stigmatization or Benefit Churning?" *Journal of Comparative Economics* 27(1): 61–89.

Kluve, J., H. Lehmann, and C. M. Schmidt. 1999. "Active Labor Market Policies in Poland: Human Capital Enhancement, Stigmatization, or Benefit Churning?" *Journal of Comparative Economics* 27 (1): 61–89.

Kluve, J. 2006. "The Effectiveness of European Active Labor Market Policy." IZA DP 2018, Bonn: Institute for the Study of Labor.

Kluve, J., S. Puerto, D. Robalino, J. M. Romero, F. Rother, J. Stoterau, F. Widenkaff, M. Witte. 2016. "Do Youth Employment Programs Improve Labor Market Outcomes? A Systematic Review." Washington DC: World Bank.

Kramarz, F., and T. Philippon. 2001. "The Impact of Differential Payroll Tax Subsidies on Minimum Wage Employment." *Journal of Public Economics* 82 (1): 115–46.

Kreiner, C.T., D. Reck, and P.E. Skov. 2017. "Do Lower Minimum Wages for Young Workers Raise their Employment? Evidence from a Danish Discontinuity." CEPR Discussion Papers 12359, Center for Economic Policy Research.

Krueger, A. B., and A. Mueller. 2010. "Job Search and Unemployment Insurance: New Evidence from Time Use Data." *Journal of Public Economics* 94 (3): 298–307.

Kugler, A., M. Kugler, J. Saavedra, and L. O. H. Prada. 2015. "Long-Term Direct and Spillover Effects of Job Training: Experimental Evidence from Colombia." NBER Working Paper 21607. Cambridge, MA: NBER.

Kugler, A. D. 2004. "The Effect of Job Security Regulations on Labor Market Flexibility. Evidence from the Colombian Labor Market Reform." In *Law and Employment: Lessons from Latin America and the Caribbean*, pp. 183–228. eds. J. Heckman and C. Páges. Chicago: University of Chicago Press.

Kugler, A. D., J. F. Jimeno-Serrano, and V. Hernanz. 2003. "Employment Consequences of Restrictive Permanent Contracts: Evidence from Spanish Labour Market Reforms." IZA Discussion Paper No. 657, Universitat Pompeu Fabra, Economics and Business Working Paper No. 651. Retrieved from: https://ssrn.com/abstract=372463.

Larraín, M. and J. Poblete. 2007. "Age-differentiated minimum wages in developing countries." *Journal of Development Economics* 84: 777–797.

Lathapipat, D. and C. Poggi. 2017. "From Many to One: Minimum Wage Effects in Thailand." Discussion Paper No. 41, Puey Ungphakorn Institute for Economic Research. Retrieved from: https://EconPapers.repec.org/RePEc:pui:dpaper:41.

Lemos, S. 2004. "The Effects of the Minimum Wage on the Formal and Informal Sectors in Brazil." IZA Discussion Paper No. 1089. Bonn: Institute for the Study of Labor.

Lemos, S. 2009. "Minimum Wage Effects in a Developing Country." *Labour Economics* 16 (2): 224–37.

Levinsohn, J., N. Rankin, G. Roberts, and V. Schoer. 2014. "Wage Subsidies and Youth Employment in South Africa: Evidence from a Randomized Control Trial." Stellenbosch Economic Working Papers 02/14. Retrieved from: https://www.ekon.sun.ac.za/wpapers/2014/wp022014/wp-02-2014.pdf.

Liu, S., T. J. Hyclak, and K. Regmi. 2016. "Impact of the Minimum Wage on Youth Labor Markets." *Labour* 30 (1): 18–37.

Lynch, L. M. 1983. "Job Search and Youth Unemployment." *Oxford Economic Papers* 35: 271–82.

Martin, J.P. (2000). "What works among active labor market policies: Evidence from OECD countries' experiences." *OECD Economic Studies 30*. Paris: OECD.

Maitra, P. and S. Mani. 2012. "Learning and Earning: Evidence from a Randomized Evaluation in India." Monash Economics Working Papers 44-12, Monash University, Department of Economics. Retrieved from: https://papers.ssrn.com/sol3/papers.cfm?abstract_id=2341125.

Matsumoto, M., and S. Elder. 2010. "Characterizing the school-to-work transitions of young men and women: Evidence from the ILO School-to-work transition surveys." Employment Working Paper No. 51. Geneva: ILO.

McKenzie, D., and C. Woodruff. 2013. "What Are We Learning from Business Training and Entrepreneurship Evaluations around the Developing World?" *The World Bank Research Observer* 29(1): 48–82.

McKenzie, D. J., N. Assaf, and A. Cusolito. 2015. "The Additionality Impact of a Matching Grant Program for Small Firms: Experimental Evidence from Yemen." World Bank Policy Research Working Paper 7462. Washington DC: World Bank.

McKenzie, D., N. Assaf, and A.P. Cusolito. 2016. "The demand for, and impact of, youth internships: evidence from a randomized experiment in Yemen." *Journal of Labor & Development* 5(1).

McKenzie, D. 2017. "How Effective Are Active Labor Market Policies in Developing Countries? A Critical Review of Recent Evidence." Policy Research working paper, no. WPS 8011; Impact Evaluation series. Washington, DC: World Bank Group.

Meer, J. and J. West. 2013. "Effects of the Minimum Wage on Employment Dynamics." NBER Working Paper No. 19262. Cambridge, MA: NBER.

Mondino, G., and S. Montoya. 2004. "The Effects of Labor Market Regulations on Employment Decisions by Firms. Empirical Evidence for Argentina." In *Law and Employment: Lessons from Latin America and the Caribbean*, pp. 351–400. (eds.) J. Heckman and C. Páges. Chicago: University of Chicago Press.

Montenegro, C. and C. Pagés. 2004. "Who Benefits from Labor Market Regulations? Chile, 1960–1998." In *Law and Employment: Lessons from Latin America and the Caribbean*, NBER Chapters, p. 401–34. (eds.) J. Heckman and C. Páges. Chicago: University of Chicago Press.

——. 2007. "Job Security and the Age-Composition of Employment: Evidence from Chile." *Estudios de Economia* 34 (December): 109–39.

Mujeri, M. K. 2002. "Bangladesh: Bringing Poverty Focus in Rural Infrastructure Development." ILO Issues in Employment and Poverty Discussion Paper 6. Geneva: ILO.

Muravyev, A., and A. Oshchepkov. 2013. "Minimum Wages, Unemployment and Informality: Evidence from Panel Data on Russian Regions." IZA Discussion Paper 7878, Bonn: Institute for the Study of Labor.

Naidoo, D., T. Packard, I. Auwalin. 2015. "Mobility, Scarring and Job Quality in Indonesia's Labor Market." Policy Research Working Paper, no. 7484. Washington, DC: World Bank.

Nekoei, A. and A. Weber. 2015. "Does Extending Unemployment Benefits Improve Job Quality?" CEPR Discussion Paper DP10568, SSRN. http://ssrn.com/abstract=2602805.

Neumark, D., and O. Nizalova. 2007. "Minimum Wage Effects in the Longer Run." *Journal of Human Resources* 42 (2); 435–52.

Neumark, D., J. I. Salas, and W. Wascher. 2014. "Revisiting the Minimum Wage—Employment Debate: Throwing Out the Baby with the Bathwater?" *Industrial & Labor Relations Review* 67 (3 Suppl): 608–48.

Neumark, D., and W. Wascher. 2004. "Minimum Wages, Labor Market Institutions, and Youth Employment: A Cross-National Analysis." *Industrial & Labor Relations Review* 57 (2): 223–48.

——. 2007. "Minimum Wages, the Earned Income Tax Credit, and Employment: Evidence from the Post-Welfare Reform Era." IZA Discussion Paper 2610. Bonn: Institute for the Study of Labor.

Nickell, S. 1997. "Unemployment and Labor Market Rigidities: Europe versus North America." *The Journal of Economic Perspectives* 11 (3): 55–74.

Nickell, S., L. Nunziata, and W. Ochel. 2005. "Unemployment in the OECD since the 1960s: What Do We Know?" *The Economic Journal* 115(500): 1–27.

Noelke, C. 2015. "Employment Protection Legislation and the Youth Labour Market." *European Sociological Review* 32(4): 471–485.

O'Higgins, N. 2001. "Youth Unemployment and Employment Policy: A Global Perspective." Geneva: International Labour Organization.

Olga, K. 2000. "The Impact of Active Labor Market Policies on the Outflows from Unemployment to Regular Jobs in Ukraine." Doctoral dissertation, National University.

OECD. 1996. "Employment Protection Regulation and Labour Market Performance." *OECD Employment Outlook (July)*. Paris: OECD.

OECD, 2014. *Investing in Youth: Brazil*. Paris: OECD Publishing.

——. 1999. "Employment Protection Regulation and Labour Market Performance." *OECD Employment Outlook* (June): 49–130. Paris: OECD.

——. 2006. *Boosting Jobs and Incomes: Policy Lessons from Reassessing the OECD Jobs Strategy*. Paris: OECD.

Paes de Barros, R. P., and C. H. Corseuil. 2004. "The Impact of Regulations on Brazilian Labor Market Performance." In *Law and Employment: Lessons from Latin America and the Caribbean*, pp. 273–350. (eds.) J. Heckman and C. Páges. Chicago: University of Chicago Press.

Paes de Barros, R., M. Carvalho, and S. Franco. 2006. "A Efetividade do Salário Mínimo Como Um Instrumento Para Reduzir a Pobreza no Brasil." IPEA Boletim de Conjuntura (74). Retrieved from: http://www.sbdp.org.br/arquivos/material/137_Salario%20minimo%20 e%20pobreza%20-%20nota%20tecnica%20IPEA.pdf.

Papps, K. L. 2012. "The Effects of Social Security Taxes and Minimum Wages on Employment: Evidence from Turkey." *Industrial & Labor Relations Review* 65 (3): 686–707.

Pelek, S. 2015. "The Employment Effect of the Minimum Wage: An Empirical Analysis From Turkey." *Ekonomi-TEK (Journal of Turkish Economic Association)* 4(1): 49–68.

Pierre, G. and S. Scarpetta. 2007. "How Labor Market Policies can Combine Workers' Protection with Job Creation: A Partial Review of Some Key Issues and Policy Options." SP Discussion Paper 0716. Retrieved from: http://siteresources.worldbank.org/SOCIALPROTECTION /Resources/SP-Discussion-papers/Labor-Market-DP/0716.pdf.

Pissarides, C. A. 2000. *Equilibrium Unemployment Theory*. 2nd edn. Cambridge, MA: MIT Press.

Portugal, P. and A.R. Cardoso. 2006. "Disentangling the Minimum Wage Puzzle: An Analysis of Worker Accessions and Separations." *Journal of the European Economic Association* 4(5): 988–1013.

Premand, P., S. Brodmann, R. Almeida, R. Grun, and M. Barouni. 2012. "Entrepreneurship Training and Self-Employment among University Graduates: Evidence from a Randomized Trial in Tunisia." World Bank Policy Research Working Paper 6285.

Puhani, P.A. 1999. "Public Training and Outflows from Unemployment: An Augmented Matching Function Approach on Polish Regional Data." CEPR Discussion Papers 2244. Center for Economic Policy Research.

Puhani, P. A., and K. Sonderhof. 2011. "The Effects of Parental Leave Extension on Training for Young Women." *Journal of Population Economics* 24 (2): 731–60.

Puhani, P. A. 2012. *Evaluating Active Labour Market Policies: Empirical Evidence for Poland During Transition*. Vol. 5. Springer Science & Business Media.

Reich, M., A. Allegretto, and A. Godoey. 2017. Seattle's Minimum Wage Experience 2015–16". CWED Policy Brief, Center on Wage and Employment Dynamics. Berkeley, CA: University of California.

Rios-Avila, F. and B.T. Hirsch. 2013. "Unions, Wage Gaps and Wage Dispersion: New Evidence from the Americas." *Industrial Relations* 53: 1–27.

Robalino, D., D. Margolis, F. Rother, D. Newhouse, and M. Lundberg. 2013. "Youth Employment: A Human Development Agenda for the Next Decade." Social Protection and Labor Discussion Paper 1308, World Bank. Washington DC: World Bank.

Rodriguez-Planas, N. 2007. "What Works Best for Getting the Unemployed Back to Work: Employment Services or Small-Business Assistance Programmes? Evidence from Romania." IZA Discussion Papers 3051, Bonn: Institute for the Study of Labor.

Rodríguez-Planas, N., and B. Jacob. 2010. "Evaluating Active Labor Market Programs in Romania." *Empirical Economics* 38 (1): 65–84.

Rothstein, J. 2011. "Unemployment Insurance and Job Search in the Great Recession." *Brookings Papers of Economic Activity* 43 (2): 143–210.

Saavedra, J., and M. Torero. 2004. "Labor Market Reforms and Their Impact over Formal Labor Demand and Job Market Turnover. The Case of Peru." In *Law and Employment: Lessons from Latin America and the Caribbean*, pp. 131–82. (eds.) J. Heckman and C. Páges. Chicago: University of Chicago Press.

Sabia, J. 2009. "Identifying Minimum Wage Effects: New Evidence from Monthly CPS Data." *Industrial Relations* 48(2): 311-328. https://doi.org/10.1111/j.1468-232X.2009.00559.x.

Saniter, N., and T. Siedler. 2014. "The Effects of Occupational Knowledge: Job Information Centers, Educational Choices, and Labor Market Outcomes." IZA Discussion Paper 8100, Bonn: Institute for the Study of Labor.

Scarpetta, S. 1996. "Assessing the Role of Labour Market Policies and Institutional Settings on Unemployment: A Cross-Country Study." *OECD Economic Studies* 26 (1): 43–98.

Schmillen, A. D., and T. G. Packard. 2016. "Vietnam's Labor Market Institutions, Regulations, and Interventions: Helping People Grasp Work Opportunities in a Risky World." World Bank Policy Research Working Paper 7587. Washington DC: World Bank.

Schmitt, J., M. Waller, S. Fremstad, and B. Zipperer. 2008. "Unions and Upward Mobility for Low-Wage Workers." *WorkingUSA* 11 (3): 337–48.

Schochet, P. Z., J. Burghardt, and S. Glazerman. 2001. "National Job Corps Study: The Impacts of Job Corps on Participants' Employment and Related Outcomes [and] Methodological Appendixes on the Impact Analysis." Princeton, NJ: Mathematica Policy Research, Inc.

Schultz, T. P., and G. Mwabu. 1998. "Labor Unions and the Distribution of Wages and Employment in South Africa." *Industrial & Labor Relations Review* 51 (4): 680–703.

Schwab, D. 2015. "Employment Protection and the Labor Informality of the Youth: Evidence from India". Job Market Paper, Boston University. https://sites.google.com/site /danielwschwab/home/research.

Serrano Pascual, A. and J. Waddington. 2000. "Young People: The Labour Market and Trade Unions." Research prepared for the Youth Committee of the European Trade Union Confederation. Brussels: ETUC.

Sianesi, B. 2004. "An Evaluation of the Swedish System of Active Labor Market Programs in the 1990s." *Review of Economics and Statistics* 86 (1): 133–55.

Skedinger, Per. 2011. "Employment Consequences of Employment Protection Legislation." *Nordic Economic Policy Review* 1 (1): 45–83.

SMERU. 2001. "Wage and Employment Effects of Minimum Wage Policy in the Indonesian Urban Labor Market." SMERU Research Institute, Jakarta.

Surhayadi, A., W. Widyanti, D. Perwira, and S. Sumarto. 2003. "Minimum Wage Policy and Its Impact on Employment in the Urban Formal Sector." Bulletin of Indonesian Economic Studies. *Taylor & Francis Journals* 39(1): 29–50.

Suryahadi, A., W. Widyanti, D. Perwira, and S. Sumarto. 2003. "Minimum Wage Policy and Its Impact on Employment in the Urban Formal Sector." *Bulletin of Indonesian Economic Studies* 39 (1): 29–50.

S4YE. 2015. "Toward Solutions for Youth Employment: A 2015 Baseline Report." Retrieved from http://www.ilo.org/wcmsp5/groups/public/---ed_emp/documents/publication/wcms _413826.pdf.

Thompson, J.P. 2009. "Using Local Labor Market Data to Re-Examine the Employment Effects of the Minimum Wage." *Industrial and Labor Relations Review* 62(3): 343–366.

Traxler, F. and B. Brandl. 2009. "The Economic Effects of Collective Bargaining Coverage: A Cross-National Analysis." Global Union Research Network. Geneva: ILO.

Ulyssea, G. and M. N. Foguel. 2006. "Efeitos do Salário Mínimo Sobre o Mercado de Trabalho Brasileiro." Texto para discussão 1168, Instituto de Pesquisa Econômica Aplicada (IPEA), Rio de Janeiro.

Universidad de Chile. 2012. "Evaluación de Impacto del Programa de Subsidio al Empleo Joven." Departamento de Economía. Santiago: Universidad de Chile.

Valerio, A., B. Parton, and A. Robb. 2014. *Entrepreneurship Education and Training Programs around the World: Dimensions for Success.* World Bank. Washington, D.C.: World Bank.

Van den Berg, G., and B. Van der Klaauw. 2006. "Counseling and Monitoring of Unemployed Workers: Theory and Evidence from a Controlled Social Experiment." *International Economic Review* 47: 895–936.

Van den Berg, G. J., B. Van der Klaauw, and J. C. Van Ours. 2004. "Punitive Sanctions and the Transition Rate from Welfare to Work." *Journal of Labor Economics* 22 (1): 211–41.

Van der Velden, R. K. W., and M.H.J. Wolbers. 2003. "The integration of young people into labour market: the role of training systems and labour market regulation." In Transitions from Education to Work in Europe: The Integration of Youth into EU Labour Markets", eds. Gangl, M., and W. Muller. Oxford: Oxford University Press, 186–211.

Van Reenen, J. 2003. "Active Labour Market Policies and the British New Deal for the Young Unemployed in Context." w9576, National Bureau of Economic Research. Cambridge, MA: NBER.

Vezza, E. 2014. "Policy Scan and Meta-Analysis: Youth and Employment Policies in Latin America," CEDLAS Working paper 156, Universidad Nacional de La Plata. Retrieved from: http://labor-al.org/vlaboral/downloads/Youth_and_Employment_Policies_in_Latam.pdf.

Vodopivec, M. 1999. "Does the Slovenian Public Work Program Increase Participants' Chances to Find a Job?" *Journal of Comparative Economics* 27 (1): 113–30.

——. 2013. "Introducing Unemployment Insurance to Developing Countries." *IZA Journal of Labor Policy* 2 (1): 1.

Waddington, J. and A. Kerr. 2002. "Unions fit for young workers?" *Industrial Relations Journal* 33 (4): 298–315.

Walsh, K., M. Kotzeva, E. Dolle, and R. Dorenbos. 2011. "Evaluation of the Net Impact of Active Labour Market Programmes in Bulgaria." Rotterdam. staging.ilo.org/public/libdoc /nonigo/2011/465764.pdf.

World Bank. 2015. "Can Skills Training Increase Employment for Young Women? The Case of Liberia." Washington, DC: World Bank Group.

Yannelis, C. 2014. "The Minimum Wage and Employment Dynamics: Evidence from an Age Based Reform in Greece." Royal Economic Society Annual Conference. Retrieved from: http://www.sole-jole.org/14015.pdf.

Yu, W. H. 2012. "Better Off Jobless? Scarring Effects of Contingent Employment in Japan." *Social Forces; A Scientific Medium of Social Study and Interpretation* 90 (3): 735.

Appendix B
BACKGROUND PAPERS DEVELOPED
FOR THIS REPORT

PUBLISHED WORLD BANK WORKING PAPERS

Angel-Urdinola, D., and R. Gukovas. 2018. "A Skills-Based Human Capital Framework to Understand the Phenomenon of Youth Economic Disengagement." World Bank Policy Research Paper 8348. Washington, DC: World Bank.

Machado, Ana Luiza, and Miriam Muller. 2018. "'If It's Already Tough, Imagine for Me...:' A Qualitative Perspective on Youth Out of School and Out of Work in Brazil." Policy Research Working Paper; No. 8358. Washington, DC: World Bank. https://openknowledge.worldbank.org/handle/10986/29424.

Yoong, Pui Shen. 2017. "Review/Meta-Analysis of International Quantitative Evidence on the Impact of Labor Market Institutions on Employment Outcomes of Youth." World Bank working paper and appendix A in Rita K. Almeida and Truman G. Packard, *Skills and Jobs: An Agenda for Youth*, 2018. World Bank, Washington, DC.

UNPUBLISHED PAPERS

Almeida, R., L. Caseiro, A. Maciente, and P. Nascimento. 2017. "Wages and Employability of Higher Education Graduates in Brazil: Evidence from Matched Employer-Employee Data." Unpublished presentation, World Bank, Washington, DC.

Costa, J., M. Foguel, M. França, and R. Almeida. 2017. "Brazilian Youth Choices: Categorizing and Evaluating the Time Allocation Decisions: Cohort Evidence between 1995 and 2014." Unpublished presentation, World Bank, Washington, DC.

———. 2017. "Youth School Dropout and Time Allocation: Micro Determinants 2012–2016." Unpublished presentation, World Bank, Washington, DC.

Costa, L., and M. Barbosa. 2017. "Teacher and School Quality in Brazil: Evidence for Ensino Médio." Unpublished paper and presentation, World Bank, Washington, DC.

Gukovas, R., and U. Kejsefman. 2017. "Pieces of the Disengagement Puzzle." Unpublished presentation and paper, World Bank, Washington, DC.

Gukovas, R., and V. Moreira. 2018. "'Scarring' Effects on Youth from Informal Employment and Unemployment: Analysis using PME." Unpublished paper, World Bank, Washington, DC.

Loureiro, A., and C. Szerman. 2017. "Policies to Increase Youth Engagement and Reduce School Dropout in Brazil: A Meta-Analysis & International Benchmarking." Unpublished paper, World Bank, Washington, DC.

Moreira, V., M. Morgandi, M. Weber, and T. Packard. 2017. "Estimates of Labor Market Policy/Program Reforms on Opportunities/Outcomes for Youth (Policy Reform Simulations that Appear in BER, but Applied to Youth-Only Sample, to Identify Differences in Impact)." Unpublished presentation, World Bank, Washington, DC.

Morgandi, Matteo, Rovane Battaglin Schwengber, and Truman Packard. 2017. "An Assessment of Brazil's 2017 Labor Reforms," Social Protection and Jobs Global Practice, World Bank: Washington, DC.

Rios-Neto, E. 2017. "A Framework for Youth Disengagement in Brazil." Unpublished paper, World Bank, Washington, DC.

Verhine, R., and P. Nascimento. 2017. "Mapping of Higher Education Institutions in Brazil: Access and Relevance." Unpublished presentation and paper, World Bank, Washington, DC.

www.ingramcontent.com/pod-product-compliance
Lightning Source LLC
Chambersburg PA
CBHW080421270326
41929CB00018B/3113